NIGHT FLYER /
MOSQUITO
PATHFINDER

The Stackpole Military History Series

**THE AMERICAN
CIVIL WAR**
Cavalry Raids of the Civil War
Ghost, Thunderbolt, and Wizard
Pickett's Charge
Witness to Gettysburg

WORLD WAR I
Doughboy War

WORLD WAR II
After D-Day
Airborne Combat
Armor Battles of the
    Waffen-SS, 1943–45
Armoured Guardsmen
Army of the West
Arnhem 1944
Australian Commandos
The B-24 in China
Backwater War
The Battle of Sicily
Battle of the Bulge, Vol. 1
Battle of the Bulge, Vol. 2
Beyond the Beachhead
Beyond Stalingrad
Blitzkrieg Unleashed
Blossoming Silk against the
    Rising Sun
Bodenplatte
The Brandenburger Commandos
The Brigade
Bringing the Thunder
The Canadian Army and the
    Normandy Campaign
Coast Watching in World War II
Colossal Cracks
Condor
A Dangerous Assignment
D-Day Bombers
D-Day Deception
D-Day to Berlin
Destination Normandy
Dive Bomber!
A Drop Too Many
Eagles of the Third Reich
The Early Battles of Eighth Army
Eastern Front Combat
Europe in Flames
Exit Rommel
Fist from the Sky
Flying American Combat Aircraft
    of World War II
For Europe
Forging the Thunderbolt
For the Homeland

Fortress France
The German Defeat in the East,
    1944–45
German Order of Battle, Vol. 1
German Order of Battle, Vol. 2
German Order of Battle, Vol. 3
The Germans in Normandy
Germany's Panzer Arm in
    World War II
GI Ingenuity
Goodwood
The Great Ships
Grenadiers
Hitler's Nemesis
Infantry Aces
In the Fire of the Eastern Front
Iron Arm
Iron Knights
Kampfgruppe Peiper at the Battle
    of the Bulge
The Key to the Bulge
Knight's Cross Panzers
Kursk
Luftwaffe Aces
Luftwaffe Fighter Ace
Luftwaffe Fighter-Bombers
    over Britain
Luftwaffe Fighters and Bombers
Massacre at Tobruk
Mechanized Juggernaut or
    Military Anachronism?
Messerschmitts over Sicily
Michael Wittmann, Vol. 1
Michael Wittmann, Vol. 2
Mountain Warriors
The Nazi Rocketeers
Night Flyer / Mosquito
    Pathfinder
No Holding Back
On the Canal
Operation Mercury
Packs On!
Panzer Aces
Panzer Aces II
Panzer Aces III
Panzer Commanders of the
    Western Front
Panzergrenadier Aces
Panzer Gunner
The Panzer Legions
Panzers in Normandy
Panzers in Winter
The Path to Blitzkrieg
Penalty Strike
Poland Betrayed
Red Road from Stalingrad

Red Star under the Baltic
Retreat to the Reich
Rommel's Desert Commanders
Rommel's Desert War
Rommel's Lieutenants
The Savage Sky
Ship-Busters
Siege of Küstrin, 1945
The Siegfried Line
A Soldier in the Cockpit
Soviet Blitzkrieg
Stalin's Keys to Victory
Surviving Bataan and Beyond
T-34 in Action
Tank Tactics
Tigers in the Mud
Triumphant Fox
The 12th SS, Vol. 1
The 12th SS, Vol. 2
Twilight of the Gods
Typhoon Attack
The War against Rommel's
    Supply Lines
War in the Aegean
Wolfpack Warriors
Zhukov at the Oder

**THE COLD WAR /
VIETNAM**
Cyclops in the Jungle
Expendable Warriors
Fighting in Vietnam
Flying American Combat
    Aircraft: The Cold War
Here There Are Tigers
Land with No Sun
MiGs over North Vietnam
Phantom Reflections
Street without Joy
Through the Valley

**WARS OF AFRICA AND
THE MIDDLE EAST**
Never-Ending Conflict
The Rhodesian War

**GENERAL MILITARY
HISTORY**
Carriers in Combat
Cavalry from Hoof to Track
Desert Battles
Guerrilla Warfare
Ranger Dawn
Sieges

NIGHT FLYER / MOSQUITO PATHFINDER

Night Operations in World War II

Lewis Brandon, Albert Smith,
and Ian Smith

STACKPOLE
BOOKS

Published in paperback in 2011 by
STACKPOLE BOOKS
5067 Ritter Road
Mechanicsburg, PA 17055
www.stackpolebooks.com

Cover design by Tracy Patterson

Printed in the United States of America

10 9 8 7 6 5 4 3 2 1

Library of Congress Cataloging-in-Publication Data

Brandon, Lewis.
  Night flyer ; Mosquito pathfinder : night operations in World War II / Lewis Brandon, Albert Smith, and Ian Smith.
    p. cm.
  First work originally published: ©1961; 2nd work originally published ©2003.
  Includes index.
  ISBN 978-0-8117-0869-2
  1. World War, 1939–1945—Personal narratives, British. 2. World War, 1939–1945—Aerial operations, British. 3. World War, 1939–1945—Campaigns—Germany. 4. Great Britain. Royal Air Force—Biography. 5. Fighter pilots—Great Britain—Biography. 6. Flight navigators, Military—Great Britain—Biography. 7. Brandon, Lewis. 8. Smith, Albert, 1923–2000. I. Smith, Albert, 1923–2000. II. Smith, Ian, 1954 Jan. 22– III. Smith, Albert, 1923–2003. Mosquito pathfinder. IV. Title. V. Title: Mosquito pathfinder.
  D786.B69 2011
  940.54'4941—dc22
                              2010049150

Contents

BOOK ONE

Night Flyer

CHAPTER 1

From Gestapo to RAF

I BELIEVE that I must be in a fairly good position to claim the strangest possible introduction into the Armed Forces of the Crown when I was called-up for the Royal Air Force in early January of 1941: I began my service with a week's leave and wearing the uniform of a Gestapo captain.

The explanation of this rather unlikely situation was that for some nine years before the war I had been working in British films. I had been engaged mostly in crowd work, but on occasion I had a few lines to say or a small part to play. I was in good company, for at that time Stewart Grainger, Michael Wilding, Terry Thomas and Jack Train were all likewise engaged.

I had been selected to double for Robert Donat in a scene for that delightful film *The Ghost Goes West*, which was made in 1935 by Korda's London Film Productions. I was found to resemble Donat so much that I was retained to work with the trick-camera unit on that film and later as stand-in and double on *Knight Without Armour*, in which Marlene Dietrich played opposite Donat; *The Citadel*, with Rosalind Russell as the feminine star and finally *Goodbye Mr. Chips*, with Greer Garson.

This work was most interesting, and, which was at least as important to me, it meant fairly regular work, for a stand-in was put under contract for each film. There was quite a lot to the job, for, as well as running through each scene for the benefit of the cameraman and sound department, the stand-in was often called upon to rehearse with the small-part and crowd players, so that he had to learn the dialogue and needed a fair amount of commonsense and acting ability.

I was lucky enough to become quite in demand as a stand-in for one or two of the top-line cameramen, even when I hardly resembled the star at all. I worked in this capacity with Robert Newton, Michael Redgrave, Sebastian Shaw and Rex Harrison. It was while I was working on *Busman's Honeymoon*, as stand-in for Robert Newton at Denham Studios, that I received my call-up papers for duty in the Royal Air Force.

During the pre-war years I had been one of those people who did not really believe that war would come. To me it seemed that as Herr Hitler had managed to obtain pretty well all he wanted without war, he was not likely to risk losing it all by tangling with Britain and France, two such powerful nations. When war did come, therefore, I felt very much out of it all.

I soon found that unless one had a trade, such as engineer, mechanic or carpenter, it was impossible to get into any of the Armed Forces. I had a quick bash at joining Civil Defence, but luckily the chappie who first interviewed me realised that my heart was not really in it and that I wanted something a bit more exciting. I say this without any disrespect to the men and women in Civil Defence, who did such a wonderful job, particularly during the Blitz and while the buzz-bombs were falling.

I was then in my thirtieth year. I tried vainly to volunteer for various things, including the Welsh Guards, the first regiment that I noticed were asking for non-tradesmen. All the training channels, however, were flooded with younger men who had been called-up when conscription had been introduced after Munich, a year before. I was advised to await my call-up, and eventually I was instructed to attend for a medical midway through 1940.

I was passed fit for anything and decided that the Royal Air Force appealed to me more than the other Services. Officers of the three Services were present after the medical to interview candidates and I found that I had the necessary educational qualifications for air-crew service in the Royal Air Force.

I therefore volunteered for this and had the good fortune

to be accepted. I received the information, however, that it would probably be six months or so before I could expect to be actually called-up, so I carried on with my film work in the meantime.

Early in December 1941 I was working on *Busman's Honeymoon* when my call-up papers arrived. I was to report to Royal Air Force, Cardington, in a month's time and, as the film I was engaged on finished in mid-December, I found myself faced with a 'rest' that I really could not afford. I was very glad, therefore, to receive a telephone call from the Casting Department of Denham Studios to go there for a scene in Leslie Howard's film *Pimpernel Smith*.

I was to be a British naval attaché in a scene in the British Embassy in Berlin. It was only crowd work, but I was only too pleased with the prospect of taking a few extra bob into the Royal Air Force with me. At Denham I reported to the Wardrobe Department for my uniform, then to Make-up, and finally to the set, where there was the usual organised chaos that always seemed to prevail in British films.

Everyone rushed about in a leisurely manner and nothing was done that day. We all reported on the set again at 9 o'clock next morning, and again not much was achieved. Halfway through the morning the Assistant Director called me and instructed me to dash up to the Wardrobe Department and change my costume for that of a Gestapo captain.

Francis Sullivan, that large and impressive actor, was playing the part of a Gestapo chief who was a guest at a ball in the British Embassy and it had suddenly been realised that he would not attend such an important function without his aide-de-camp. Nobody had been cast for this part, so I had been roped in.

As a precautionary measure, I pointed out to the Assistant Director that I was due to report to Cardington in ten days' time, but he assured me that the Embassy set was to be demolished in four days' time to make way for another set and that the scene had been scheduled for only three days' shooting. Therefore there should be no difficulties.

Francis Sullivan and I had to arrive as guests at the Embassy, where we had reason to believe that we would find the Pimpernel, who had been helping enemies of the State to escape. There was a scene in an ante-room, where we expected to find a vital clue in an invitation card with the Pimpernel's name on it and with a piece missing. Imagine our disgust when we found that nearly all the invitation cards had the identical piece missing.

We were then introduced to the Ambassador and made our way down a vast staircase, where we had a perfect opportunity of observing most of the assembled guests. I had to point to a bearded character standing by a large fireplace and mutter:

"What about that fellow over there with the beard?"

Sullivan snubbed me with the retort: "Don't be a fool, he is one of our men!"

It may well be thought that three days would be more than ample time for filming a sequence of this sort, but it was not so. The days went merrily by until I had only three days before reporting to Cardington. Although I am not a worrying type, I began to wonder what would happen. The film unit must finish the sequence with me or have to re-shoot the entire scene with someone else – a most expensive business.

I had a word with the assistant director, who had a chat with the director, who had a chat with the production manager, who assured everyone that all would be well: the set was to be pulled down next day and I would have a couple of days to myself before my call-up.

It was not to be. We did not finish that day, and after the next day's shooting it became obvious even to the production manager that I would be required for several more days. He therefore phoned the Adjutant at Cardington, used the magic word 'Films' and I was given a week's leave from the RAF before I had even joined it – to play a Gestapo officer too!

The scene was eventually finished and I did manage to have a couple of days to myself before reporting to

Cardington, where the Adjutant obviously thought I must be a pretty well-known actor and wanted to hear of some of my more important parts.

I spent ten days at Cardington, where I was issued with my uniform and the rest of my kit. I was to wear the uniform for the next fourteen years, although I had no suspicion of this at the time. I had various inoculations and learnt that a body of men must always march from one place to another.

Bridgnorth was my next posting for three weeks' square bashing, then, as there was a bottleneck in air-crew training, I was posted to Acklington in Northumberland, where I had to await my turn to go to an Initial Training Wing. There my idea of life in the RAF, which had been fairly comfortable at Cardington and Bridgnorth, took a distinct downward plunge.

Our billets had to be seen to be believed. We were in a barn above an inhabited cowshed, about forty of us, with one cold-water tap as the only piece of modern plumbing available for all our needs. It was February, bitterly cold, with plenty of snow around. The station had, in fact, only recently regained contact with the outside world after having been cut off by snow for several days. We of the cowshed were classified as aircraft hands/general duties, an involved way of saying that we were spare bods and could be used for any duty. These palatial billets were a couple of miles away from the camp and the journey was made in a lorry which usually stopped a hundred yards or so from the cowshed, hooted and then made off before any of us could get near enough to climb aboard.

The good fortune that I was to experience for nearly all my Service life started fairly early. Probably because of my height, nearly 6ft 2ins, I was sorted out to help in the guardroom as a Service policeman. This meant transferring to billets on the station and made life a great deal more comfortable than it had been in the cowshed.

Acklington was then a very important day-fighter station, with two Spitfire squadrons responsible for the defence of much of the north-east coast. My duties as a Service

policeman involved me in a fair amount of walking around
the airfield and the surrounding area. Whilst I was ambling
about I noticed a dozen or more wooden poles in various
places around the airfield. These poles were arranged so that
they pointed up into the air at an angle of about 45 (degrees
symbol) and were painted to look like camouflaged anti-
aircraft guns. The country was so short of light ack-ack guns
that few, if any, could be spared even for an important airfield
such as Acklington. The only weapons most of the airmen
carried were chunks of metal fencing – known as pikes. This
was quite an insight into our state of preparedness for war. I
did not see much change in these conditions in the three
months I was at Acklington, but luckily the Hun must have
been too busy elsewhere to attack us.

The next move for me was to the Aircrew Receiving Wing
at Stratford-on-Avon, where I spent an extremely pleasant
three weeks. I had never been in that part of the world before
and found it really delightful, perhaps all the more so
because there were no tourists and sightseers to spoil things.

One day I was in a canoe on the Avon when a punt
suddenly shot out from the bank and my strenuous efforts to
avoid it caused the canoe to overturn, shooting me, in full
uniform, into a very cold river. The wartime airman's
uniform was so shapeless that it looked no different from
normal when it was saturated so that I walked back to my
billets without anyone noticing.

The Air Crew Selection Board at Stratford decided that
I was too old for training as a pilot and too bulky to fit into
the small turret that air gunners used. The only job left was
that of navigator; I did not mind particularly, but I had no
choice anyhow.

I was posted to an Initial Training Wing at Scarborough
for an eight-week course. Pilots and navigators made up the
course in about equal numbers, and after five weeks the
pilots-to-be were suddenly required at an Elementary Flying
Training School. Off they went, and the navigators were put

to filling sandbags for the last three weeks of the course – a very agreeable occupation on the beach at Scarborough in early June, with the weather just about as nice as it could be.

One Sunday morning our sandbagging was interrupted by a summons to report back to our hotels immediately. Almost all the hotels had, of course, been taken over by the RAF, so that we were living in comfort.

Back at our hotel we were addressed by the Commanding Officer, who asked if any of us would like to volunteer for flying duties on night fighters. The CO could tell us very little about the job, but the main points that appealed to me were three in number: it meant a shorter course than the normal navigation course, the pay would be the same and the volunteers would have to go to the Air Ministry in London for an interview. As I was a Londoner, I did not hesitate at all but decided to try it.

The job of a straight navigator apparently called for fairly good ability at maths and that had never been a particularly good subject of mine, even when I had been at school some fifteen years before; I had been looking forward to my navigation course with a deal of trepidation. We had spent most of the first five weeks at Scarborough marching, drilling and learning elementary navigation, with a little maths revision thrown in for good measure. I had been getting rather worried about the maths, which seemed no easier after the passage of years, so that this call for night fighters came at a perfect time for me.

I was one of some two dozen who set off from our Wing for the interview in the Big City. From the very beginning everything to do with the night-fighting business was wrapped in mystery. We were instructed before our interviews began that we were not to discuss what took place during the interviews with anyone when we returned to our units. I remember being shown several diagrams and designs and having to assess relative sizes without having the slightest idea what it was all about, and I certainly could not tell from my interrogator's expression if my answers were the ones required. Anyhow, I enjoyed my 48 hours in London, and a few days after my return to Scarborough I was informed that, with half a dozen other chaps from my Wing, I had been selected for training as a night-fighter navigator.

The training was to be carried out at Prestwick, near Ayr, where Number Three Radio School was situated. I found to my delight that the course was only three weeks, compared with the three or four months of the normal navigation course. Just a small corner of the veil of mystery that always shrouded the hush-hush job of night fighting was lifted for us at Prestwick. We were to be instructed in the use of 'AI.' These letters stood for 'Airborne Interceptor', a magical piece of equipment devised by the 'Boffins' to aid night fighters in their task of seeking out the enemy in the dark. The brains that had conceived the early-warning radar system that had been such an essential factor during the Battle of Britain had now produced a radar set small enough to be carried in an aircraft and which could detect the presence of another aircraft. This information was presented to the navigator of a night-fighter crew in such a way that by the use of a little commonsense he should be able to chase and intercept an enemy aircraft in the dark. I was to be one of the very first batch of aircrew under training to be instructed in the use of this apparatus.

I was now brought up to date with developments in the air war in general and the night war in particular so that I could appreciate the situation as it was then in July 1941.

The German Air Force was known as the *Luftwaffe*, the literal translation for which is 'Air Weapon'. Its original purpose was to act as a sort of super long-range artillery for the German armies, a spearhead for the *Blitzkrieg*. It was intended to operate almost exclusively by day, and very little time, if any, had been devoted to night flying, a state of affairs that was to have severe repercussions for the Germans later.

The responsibility for the defence of Great Britain from

air attack fell upon Fighter Command, who began the war with inadequate resources, both in men and machines. Fortunately this inadequacy was offset to a large extent by a long-range warning system of radar stations, sited at strategic points round the coast and capable not only of detecting aircraft flying at medium height, say 8,000ft, 100 miles away, but also of enabling their movements to be plotted. This meant that instead of a few fighters having to maintain standing patrols all day long, they could be at readiness on the ground. When a suspect plot was seen on the radar, our fighters could be sent off to intercept the incoming raid, with their petrol tanks full and the pilots fairly well rested.

For purposes of control of our fighters the country had been split up into four areas. No. 10 Group operated south and west of Oxford; No. 11 Group from the south coast to a line running east and west through Bedford; No. 12 Group from this line to a similar line through York and 13 Group north of that.

The Groups were subdivided into Sectors, each of which contained a number of fighter stations, one of which was selected as Sector Station, with its own operations-room in which the Sector Controller could watch the movements of raids in his area and have radio control of his fighters.

The Fighter Command operations-room was used mainly for organizing reinforcement from one Group to another, if this became necessary, while the Group operations-rooms, with a broader picture than the Sectors, allocated the squadrons to counter a particular raid.

This system worked well against the daylight raids of the Battle of Britain in 1940. From the long range warning radar information came in giving the news of the approach of an enemy force, its approximate size and the route it was taking. The defending squadrons were scrambled, told the course to steer to enable them to intercept the raid as far out to sea as possible and then given any further information which might help them. Once the fighters saw their quarry, the cry of "Tally-ho" came over the radio and the battle was on.

The Sector Controller could, if necessary, bring his fighters to within about 5 miles of the enemy; in fact, however, the fighters would almost always see them before then. Bombers attacking in daylight usually had an escort of fighters to protect them and would also fly in formation so as to give each individual bomber the benefit of the protection of as many guns as possible. The job of our day fighters was to separate the enemy fighters from the bombers, shoot down as many bombers as possible and break up the bomber formations.

At night fighters were dealt with as individual aircraft and Sector had complete control over them.

As night bombers attacked under cover of darkness, they were able to dispense with fighter escort. Then, too, because of the protection afforded by darkness, they did not have to rely on the concentrated fire power of a formation for their defence. These things, added to the obvious difficulties of formation flying for long periods at night, meant that each bomber must be regarded as a separate menace by our controllers, so that a night bomber raid meant a series of individual interceptions, one fighter after one bomber.

We in this country were not subjected to mass raids, when bombers operated in hundreds all dropping their bombs within a short space of time, so that the individual interception remained the best method of dealing with the night bomber over Britain. Nevertheless, there were many difficulties to be overcome before night fighters could operate with much chance of success.

The early night fighters had lots of troubles to contend with. Their radio communication with the ground was very indistinct and had only a short range. Although they had to fly in the dark, the instruments provided for the pilot and on which he relied for blind-flying were poor. The airfields from which they flew had inadequate airfield lighting, and few airfields had decent runways. If the pilots overcame all these difficulties, even then they were not likely to achieve much more than an ineffectual chase around the night skies and then have to find the way home, without an effective homing device.

The Sector Controller could bring the night fighter to within 5 miles or so of a target, which was enough in daylight, but, even in clear conditions, at night the fighter would not see an enemy aircraft until he was about 1,200ft away, even if he knew exactly where to look. When the Sector Controller had done all that he could, the only further help was afforded by searchlights. The searchlights were being operated with sound detectors, however, so that by the time the plots were worked out and used the bomber had probably travelled quite a distance and, because of this inherent time lag, the searchlight usually trailed some way behind the bomber and was quite likely to illuminate the stalking fighter instead.

Still, the searchlights did sometimes catch a bomber in their beams and any lucky fighter who happened to be near enough could make for the cone of lights. A few German bombers were shot down by this means and anything that brought results was a help.

So far as anti-aircraft guns were concerned, a separate Anti-Aircraft Command had been formed early in 1939 and had been placed under the direction of Fighter Command. Their detection equipment, however, was similar to that used by the searchlights, and until they received better means of laying their guns they were effective only as a deterrent, forcing the bombers to fly higher and thus making accurate bombing more difficult.

The powers-that-be were only too well aware of these shortcomings and of our vulnerability to night bombers. Every effort was made during the first year of the war to put things right, with the most remarkable success, as I hope to show later. In the meantime the most desperate measures were resorted to or discussed, even if they had only the remotest possibility of success.

Such unlikely schemes were considered as that some of our aircraft should fly at right angles to the enemy's course and above them, trailing long lengths of piano wire in the hope that the wires would become entangled in the enemy's propeller's. Or, it was suggested some of our heavy aircraft should fly above and ahead of the raiders, dropping out small aerial mines on parachutes for the bombers to collide with, or magnesium flares on parachutes to illuminate the bombers and enable our fighters to dive in and shoot them down.

Most of these schemes and many more were tried out, although, with the possible exception of the last idea, the chances of success were small indeed.

The job of night fighting and day fighting in bad weather when single-seater single-engined fighters could not operate, had originally been given to Blenheim squadrons. The Bristol Blenheim was a twin-engined aircraft that had been designed as a medium bomber. It had a single machine-gun in a turret operated by an air gunner, and four machine-guns were added to the fighter version. These four guns were bolted to the fuselage of the aircraft and were under the control of the pilot, so that he had to aim his aircraft at the target in order to shoot at it. The Boulton Paul Defiant, a single-engined fighter with a similar crew of pilot and air gunner, later joined in the almost hopeless task of hunting the enemy bombers by night.

The very few successes gained by these early night fighters were, perforce, achieved in conditions of bright moonlight. It did not take the wily Hun very long to become aware of this fact and to avoid coming over in conditions of that sort.

Another difficulty that arose was that of positive identification at night. Before opening fire, the night fighter had to recognise the target as hostile. This meant getting in very close, with the attendant risk of being spotted by the bomber who would take violent evasive action before the fighter could aim his guns and would probably escape.

It was important, too, that the night fighter should have sufficient fire power to ensure that if he did get an enemy bomber in his sights he should be able to blow it out of the sky first go, or at least damage it so severely that it would be badly handicapped in taking evasive action.

No absolutely reliable and positive means of identification of friend or foe was in fact produced during the last war. On defensive night fighting visual identification always had to be made, whilst even on offensive operations over enemy territory the only exception to this rule was if an aircraft was seen taking off from or attempting to land on an enemy airfield.

Although some fairly efficient means of identification of friend or foe were produced, it will be seen that the fact that a target was not displaying 'identification friend or foe' could not be taken as positive proof that it was hostile. The target might be a friend whose IFF was not working or not switched on. In other words, IFF could give positive proof that a target was friendly, and thus save an unnecessary chase, but it could not be assumed that no IFF meant that the target was definitely hostile.

These varied and intricate problems were being tackled by the best brains available during 1939 and 1940. One by one the difficulties were overcome. A new very-high-frequency radio telephony apparatus had been developed with far greater clarity and range than the old radio. Blind flying instruments had been vastly improved and better airfield lighting with good runways had been installed at night fighter bases. AI, the airborne interception apparatus whose secrets were to be revealed to me at Prestwick, had been thought of as far back as 1936.

Seemingly endless problems had been resolved, and in 1939 and 1940 early marks of AI had been used in Blenheims, with great promise of things to come. A new night-fighter aircraft, the Bristol Beaufighter, started coming into squadron service late in 1940. This aircraft had been fitted with VHF radio, AI, reasonably reliable blind-flying instruments, and was armed with four 20mm cannons and six .303 machine-guns. This truly formidable armament was all controlled by the pilot, who had to aim the Beaufighter at the target and who fired the whole broadside by pressing a button.

The answers had been found to most of the night fighters' problems, but, unfortunately, not in time for the Blitz of 1940, when the German bombers had been so ineffectually opposed.

Fighter Command was very much a pilots' command, as one would expect, with the result that when the boffins put the magic black boxes of AI in the Blenheims little thought had been given to the chap who had to operate the set. It took Command some time to wake up to the idea that the equipment really worked and that it was temperamental. It needed a fairly intelligent member of aircrew to get the best out of it, and pilot and operator must be able to work together as a team.

It was decided, therefore, to select aircrew specifically for this job and I had been lucky enough to be awaiting training at the Initial Training Wing at Scarborough just when the very first selection had been made.

I found at Prestwick that there was a very good reason for the short three-week course. So few people had any first-hand knowledge of its operational working that all we could be shown in any detail was the theoretical use of the set and of the control knobs with which it fairly bristled. In the classroom AI sets had been arranged on benches so that we could become accustomed to the controls, the most important of which were the tuning and volume, or gain controls. An ingenious piece of apparatus, a synthetic trainer, had been devised to give us a rough idea of what we might expect to see in the air, and there were a few AI equipped Blenheims in which we could eventually see for ourselves what the whole business was about.

Our instructor explained to us that AI worked on exactly the same principle as a sound echo. If you shout into a cave, or across a valley, the sound waves from your voice hit the far side and are reflected back to you. The night fighter carrying AI transmitted a series of radio waves, and if they hit anything they would be returned to the fighter as an echo.

Just as the width of the valley could be calculated from the time the echo took to travel back, so could the range of the object hit by the transmitter's waves be estimated. On this was based the whole concept of AI.

There were three vital pieces of information that a night fighter must have in order to chase an enemy at night: how far away the target was, whether it was above or below the fighter, and where it was in relation to the fighter in the horizontal plane-port or starboard. AI could provide all this information.

The transmitter was in the nose of the aircraft and the transmitting aerial looked like a large arrowhead with two barbs. The front barb was the actual aerial whilst the second barb was a reflector which helped to concentrate maximum power forward, as the fighter was most concerned with chasing something in front of him.

To pick up the echo, there were four receiving aerials arranged in two pairs. The first pair were mounted on either wing tip for the horizontal or azimuth plane; the second pair were placed one on the upper surface of a wing and the other on the lower surface for the vertical or elevation plane. The idea behind this positioning of the aerials was that a target above and to starboard would be picked up more strongly by the aerials on the upper-wing surface and on the starboard wing tip than by the other two aerials. The extra strength in the signals received by these two aerials could be measured and would then give the information required.

The information was presented to the operator on two cathode ray tubes: the azimuth tube indicated the signals received by the wing-tip aerials, and the elevation tube showed the signals from the upper- and lower-wing surface aerials. These tubes were the business end of AI.

The synthetic trainer on which we were shown what we might expect to see in the air had two cathode ray tubes in a frame which we learnt was known as the indicator unit. It is simpler to consider these one at a time. The Azimuth tube gives range and bearing of the target from the fighter.

Running through the centre of the tube there was a luminous green line known as the time trace. Attached to the time trace and covering almost a third of the tube we saw a triangle of light that looked like a Christmas tree etched in green light. The triangular shape was formed by the ground echo or ground return; just as an aircraft would send back an echo, so did the ground, though the echo from the ground was of course very much stronger than that from an aircraft.

The lower the fighter aircraft was flying, the further down the tube the ground return would come – the Christmas-tree stem would grow short, and the foliage would spread over more of the tube – so that eventually, when the fighter was down to about 600ft in height, it would cover the entire tube and blot out any other echoes. Thus the performance of AI depended largely on the height above the ground at which the fighter could fly. This snag was overcome to a large extent in later marks of AI, but in Mark 4 AI, which was in use at this time, it was something that had to be accepted.

An aircraft echo appeared in the shape of a diamond, sitting astride the time base line – the stem of the Christmas-tree. The distance of this diamond or 'blip' from the root end of the Christmas-tree stem indicated the range of the target from the fighter. The position of the blips on the time base line showed if the target was dead ahead or to one side. The blip always remained astride the time base line, but could move over towards one side or the other as the target altered course.

The elevation tube worked on exactly the same principle, but had been turned over on its side for easier interpretation. A target that was above the fighter would produce a blip on the elevation tube with most of the diamond above the time base. By constantly watching the movements of the blips on the two tubes the operator could, after much practice, assess not only the position of the target but which way it was moving. By a series of orders to his pilot he could then intercept.

This, then, was what we were to be trained for.

I see from my flying logbook that I flew four times in the

Fighter flying at 14,000ft height. Target blip just emerging from Ground Returns. Target range about 3 miles, showing above and to starboard. (These diagrams give a simplified picture and make no allowances for the various forms of interference.)

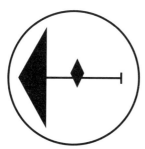 

Range of target has now decreased to just under 2 miles.
Showing about 15 degrees above and 20 degrees starboard.

Range of target is now approaching minimum range; it is about 1,000ft away, showing about 10 degrees above and 10 degrees starboard.
At this stage a visual by the pilot should be imminent.

Blenheims at Prestwick. I had absolutely no flying experience at all prior to this, so I should have been very impressed. In fact I was not. The Blenheims had been adapted for use as flying classrooms so that an instructor with a couple of pupils could huddle together in a small, blacked-out compartment and gaze at the little green etchings on the cathode ray tubes. It was most important that the clearest possible picture should be obtained and frequent adjustments had to be made to the tuning control, the gain control and various other knobs that affected the brightness and clarity of the picture. It was rather like fiddling with an early television set. Soon after the aircraft took off, the AI would be switched on and the adjustments made. This was known as 'setting up', and proved a great deal more difficult in an aeroplane than on the ground sets.

The Blenheims took off in pairs so that each could in turn provide a target for the other and enable the learner operators to see what a blip looked like in the air. Each pupil would have a go at setting up the picture and then try to interpret to the instructor what the target aircraft was doing. The instructor would then turn some of the knobs to upset the picture and the next pupil would have to set it up again and then interpret what he saw.

The Blenheims would then change over; the one that had been acting as fighter would become target and the same procedure would take place. The pupils in the target aircraft practised setting up and were also able to practice using a very important device that had been incorporated in AI.

By turning a switch the set could be used for a completely different purpose. The transmitter in the aircraft triggered off a beacon situated at the aircraft's home base. The response of the beacon could be picked up on the azimuth aerials of the aircraft and the navigator would thus be able to read off the aircraft's bearing and distance from base. This was the homing device that night fighters had needed so badly. It proved to be one of the simplest and most reliable navigation aids ever produced. The signal from the ground beacon could be coded to flash a Morse letter combination on to the AI in the aircraft, and each night fighter station had its own coded beacon.

Operators carried a map of Britain with these night stations marked on it and with the code letters of each station shown. Wherever one flew over Britain, it was always possible to pick up two or more of these beacons, so that there was no excuse for getting lost as long as the AI was working.

My total flying time at Prestwick was five and a half hours. During this time I had not had time to feel air-sick; we had been kept so busy and I had really had no opportunity of deciding whether or not I liked flying. We had clambered into the darkened interior of the Blenheims, all cluttered up with flying clobber and unable to see out at all. A door had been shut tight and we would bear the thunder of the engines starting up. A bumping motion would denote that we were taxying around the perimeter track, and an extra loud burst of sound from the engines and the cessation of the bumps would mean that we were airborne. At the end of the flight the pilot would tell us to hang on tight, as we were about to land; there would be a large bump, followed by a few smaller bounces and we would know we had landed.

CHAPTER 2

Night-fighter Squadron

I HAD thought myself extremely lucky to be on the
course at Prestwick and my luck was to hold. At nearby
Heathfield No.141 Squadron were engaged in re-equipping
with Beaufighters. They had been a Defiant squadron, with air
gunners and pilots, some of whom did not relish the change to
Beaus. It was quite understandable; air gunnery was the trade
for which these chaps had trained and many of them wished to
retain their trade. A few of the pilots preferred flying the
single-engined Defiant to the twin-engined Beau, and with the
gunners who did not wish to become AI operators they were to
be transferred to another Defiant squadron.

No. 141 Squadron therefore urgently needed some bods to
replace the gunners and obtained permission from the Air
Ministry to take half a dozen pupils from Prestwick. I was one
of the lucky ones. Instead of a further course at an Operational
Training Unit, I found myself posted to Heathfield as a
sergeant on probation. To be on an operational squadron after
only a three-week course seemed just too good to be true.

With the five other chaps who had been selected from
Prestwick I found myself a fledgling in the sergeants' mess.
For a short time we were looked upon as jumped-up young
sprogs, but soon we all fitted in well enough. It was not
unnatural that these NCOs, many of whom had been
slogging away for years to reach their rank, should be a
little envious and resentful that we had earned our
sergeant's stripes so easily.

I found that the normal set-up on a night-fighter squadron
consisted of two flights, 'A' Flight and 'B' Flight. Each of
these was commanded by a Squadron Leader, while the
Squadron Commander carried the rank of Wing Commander.
The Commanding Officer of 141 Squadron was Wing
Commander G. F. W. Heycock, who was referred to as the

CO, the 'Old Man' or simply as 'Heykers'.

I joined 141 Squadron on August 1st, 1941, and for the first few days I busied myself in learning something of the layout of Heathfield, squadron organisation and mess life. I was allocated to 'B' Flight, which had its own dispersed site.

One of the lessons that had been learned during the Battle of Britain was the necessity to disperse aircraft and their crews so that a single attack by enemy bombers could not write off the operational potential of an airfield. Aircrews had to be within easy reach of their aircraft, so huts were built at dispersed sites around the airfield. Permanent sleeping quarters and messes were also spread around as much as possible.

On night-fighter stations this entailed the building of dispersal huts complete with cooking and sleeping facilities in order to avoid the constant use of transport at all hours of the night. The night-fighter dispersal huts were rather like exclusive little clubs. They were made as comfortable as possible and crews awaiting their turn to fly amused themselves with conversation, chess and cards, or perhaps just dozed. Every ear, however, would be attuned to listen for the ring of the operations' telephone, which might ring at any moment to order off aircraft if there was any enemy activity. On most squadrons, all aircrew, officers and NCOs, shared all the facilities equally, but one or two squadrons ran things rather on a Gentlemen and Players' basis – fortunately, I was never to be on one of these squadrons.

No. 141 Squadron had been engaged in the Battle of Britain flying Defiants, an aircraft that was really a compromise between a day fighter and a night fighter. It was a single-engined two-seater aircraft whose four machine-guns were in a power-operated turret just behind the pilot and controlled by an air gunner. With its unconventional armament, the Defiant had some considerable successes at first against German day fighters and bombers, but once the enemy cottoned on to its armament the Defiant was no match for their day fighters, and was relegated to the night role.

No. 141 Squadron had been night-fighting for almost a year when they were re-equipped with Beaufighters. The re-equipment had only just begun when I joined them, so that the Bristol Beaufighter was just as new to the older members of the squadron as it was to me. There were six or seven Beaus already on the squadron, and they were in constant use as the pilots strove to obtain enough experience on them to be declared operational.

A couple of lectures were laid on to give them some idea of what AI could do, for it was something quite new to them. Nearly all the pilots had been chasing about in the dark, without much success, for a year or so. Although they hoped that this AI stuff might be of some use, I could well understand that many of them were only prepared to take it with a pinch of salt; they had seen so many of these bright ideas come to naught. Besides, most of them had desperately wanted to be on day fighters, which seemed to offer a great deal more action, so that they were rather disgusted with the night lark.

During the afternoon of August 6th I had my first trip in a Beau, flying as operator for one of the officers whose air gunner had gone to Prestwick for a quick AI course. We were up for an hour and spent nearly all the time trying out the homing device of the AI. I found that I could pick up the Heathfield beacon very easily and had no difficulty in bringing the Beau back to the airfield several times. All I had to do was to identify the beacon on my AI set, tell the pilot to turn until the blip was sitting nicely astride the time base and read off the distance as we approached. I could tell that the pilot was quite impressed; as we walked back to dispersal he said: "Well, at least part of the ruddy stuff works!"

For my part, I was most impressed with my first real flight and with my introduction to the Beau. Although I had flown in the Blenheims at Prestwick, I had not been able to see what was going on, whereas in the Beau I had a grandstand view. It struck me that I was going to like this flying business.

The Beaufighter was quite an impressive aircraft. It had a tough, bulldog look about it with its snub nose and powerful twin Hercules engines. The two main landing wheels of the undercarriage were housed in the engine nacelles when in flight, and there was a small rear wheel which did not retract. Under the nose were four canvas patches which covered the gunports for the Hispano cannons and six similar patches on the leading edge of the wings covered the nozzles of the machine-guns. The Beau certainly packed a punch.

A hatch opened downward from the belly of the Beau and the crew got in through this; it led into a small well behind the pilot's cockpit. The cockpit itself seemed filled with dials and knobs and was quite roomy. In front of the pilot was a large expanse of bullet-proof windscreen, giving pretty good all-round visibility. In the centre of the cockpit was a massive control column and on that was a button with which the pilot could fire all the guns simultaneously.

Behind the pilot's compartment were two armour-plated doors through which was the AI department. The floor consisted of a fairly wide catwalk, on either side of which were the breech blocks and mechanisms of the four cannons. On racks attached to the sides of the fuselage were racks to hold drums of cannon shells, each drum weighing about 60lb and holding 60 shells. A drum was fitted to each cannon before taking off, and had to be replaced with a fresh one if a combat took place, and reloading became necessary. The drums were rather unwieldy and difficult to fit correctly while the aircraft was in flight, but fortunately they were soon to be replaced with a belt-feed system that required no attention during flight.

There was a Perspex dome about halfway along the fuselage and under it was a swivel seat for the AI operator. The AI set was fitted behind the seat so that the way forward should not be impeded at all if the cannon needed attention. The operator was therefore facing backwards when operating his set but could swivel round in his seat if he wished to see what was going on ahead.

It was realised that night fighting with the new equipment would essentially be a matter of team work between pilot and operator so that the teaming up of a crew was of considerable importance. A couple of days after my Beau flight I was crewed with 'Lofty' Hamer, a very experienced Flight Sergeant. Straight away he told me to get into a Defiant, the only aircraft that was available, and off we went for a little local flying.

I found that I could just squeeze into the turret of the Defiant – it had not been designed for a fourteen-stone six-footer. By keeping my elbows close to my sides and crouching down in the seat I just fitted in. Once we were off the ground I gingerly moved the control that swung the turret round and found to my relief that I did not get caught up on anything.

Presumably Lofty Hamer was wondering what sort of sprog he had been crewed with. He certainly wasted no time in finding out. That Defiant began to do things that I had only dimly realised were possible in an aircraft; things I had never even seen from the ground. Now I was in an aircraft actually doing them: rolls and a loop or two; steep turns and a power dive – the lot. Then we were flying straight and level over the sea and I had come through my test. At least Lofty knew I would not be troubled with airsickness on any future flight.

I had noticed that in the Defiant I had great difficulty in understanding what was being said on the R/T, which was very indistinct indeed. In comparison, the Beau's R/T had been crystal clear, for it was fitted with the new VHF radio. There was also a separate intercom system between pilot and operator in the Beau which cut out all other sounds and was very clear indeed.

As Heathfield was near the west coast of Scotland it was by no means a highly operational station, but it was an ideal station for a squadron to re-equip. We could get to know our box of tricks with all its vagaries, while the pilots could familiarise themselves with the flying characteristics of the Beau. Although as a squadron we were occasionally called on for an operational patrol, nobody had a chase after an enemy aircraft during the five and a half months we were there.

I am convinced that it was this thorough grounding and long practice period that led to future successes. I found, too, that in these early days the quick and reliable homings that we were able to give our pilots helped tremendously in giving them confidence in the capabilities of AI.

They soon found that we could give them an immediate and reliable distance and bearing from base when we were using the beacon range. When we switched over to interception range, unless the operator was quite clueless, it was not long before the pilot was convinced that that part of the AI could work equally well. It all required lots and lots of practice on the part of both pilot and operator, however, and the spell at Heathfield gave us the opportunity for this practice.

A few days after joining 141 Squadron I reached my thirtieth birthday. I was one of the oldest members of the squadron and I found then and later that the fact that I was considerably junior in rank to men much younger than I was tended to make me feel as if I was still in my teens. Perhaps I had hit upon the secret of eternal youth!

After my initiation into real flying with Lofty Hamer I found it thrilling and absorbing. The constant challenge to master the AI soon made me realise that I had been fortunate enough to fall into what was probably one of the most interesting and exciting jobs in any of the Services.

Although we were seldom called on for operational patrols, the squadron settled down to routine. The two flights each did two nights on duty followed by two nights off. The flight starting its two days on duty would assemble at dispersal soon after breakfast; the serviceability of the aircraft would be ascertained and crews would be allotted to fly in those that were ready.

Each flight had a complement of eight aircraft plus two reserves and usually twelve complete crews so as to allow for leave or sickness. The remainder of the Beaus were not long in arriving and our re-equipment was soon completed, so that full-scale training could go on apace.

To ensure that the maximum amount of practice was obtained from every precious hour of flying, the Beaus always took off in pairs, just as the Blenheims had at Prestwick. Each would take a turn as fighter and then as target. We were flying mostly in daylight at first until the pilots gained enough experience in flying the Beaus to be able to take off and land in the dark. This meant that all the time the operator was interpreting what he could see on his AI the pilot could actually see the target aircraft visually, so that he was in a good position to judge for himself the reliability of the set and the ability of his operator.

A series of flying exercises had been worked out so that the fighter would approach the target at varying angles. At first the operator just read off to his pilot what he could see on his tubes. One exercise was entirely confined to practice on the elevation tube; that is to say, the target would be either well above or well below and the operator had to constantly tell the pilot how this height variation was changing. The operator could tell the range of the target from either the azimuth or elevation tube, and it was the range of the target from the fighter that was of most interest and importance to the pilot. The more frequently he was given the range of a target in the dark, the easier it would be for him to ensure that he was not overtaking it too fast. Then, too, knowing that on most nights he should see a target at about 1,500ft, he would be prepared for the visual sighting.

After the initial exercises had been carried out to the satisfaction of the pilot, the operator began to practice interceptions. Instead of just telling the pilot what he could see, he had to give instructions to the pilot so that the fighter aircraft turned after the target at the appropriate moment, chased it and, ideally, finished up just behind, slightly below and at about the same speed as the target.

The theory of the art of night interception was based on

facts that had been learnt the hard way by the Defiant and Blenheim crews. If a fighter was approaching a bomber on a converging course and the fighter turned after it too soon, he might well finish up in front of the bomber. Too late a turn would result in a long chase from astern, with consequent waste of time and the probability that the bomber might be given sufficient time to drop his bombs on target and scoot for home.

Careful speed control on the part of the fighter was important if the pilot was to be able to spot the bomber, identify it and then bring his guns to bear on it, if possible without being seen. On most nights, the position from which the night-fighter pilot would be best placed to get a visual on the bomber was from slightly below and almost dead astern. On an average dark night the range at which he could expect to see the bomber was between 1,000 and 1,500ft. On a very dark night, without benefit of starlight, he might have to close in to 600 or 800ft before the vital visual. He would be searching for the vague silhouette of the bomber in the darkness, but he had two important things to help him. His operator would tell him just where to look for the bomber and, if approaching from slightly below and astern, he might see the exhaust flames from the bomber's engines.

On any night there was always one section of the sky that was just a little lighter than the rest. Once the interception was well under way and the operator had told the pilot that they were on the same course as the bomber, the pilot could sort out where this light section was and tell his operator where he wanted to be for the dosing stages of the interception.

Of course there were nights when visibility was exceptionally good and one might obtain a visual at 3,000 or 4,000ft. This was usually in conditions of bright moonlight, and the Hun usually avoided raiding on such occasions.

What it boiled down to was that the operator had to pick up a contact on his AI tubes, interpret what it was doing, give the pilot instructions which would enable him to intercept the target, and at the same time give him the fullest possible indication of where he should look for the target.

The pilot, for his part, had to fly the aircraft extremely accurately on instruments in the dark and then, when he was actually trying to see the target, he must fly completely by instinct. When it is remembered that an enemy bomber would probably not fly straight and level and that there were all sorts of little things that could go wrong with various bits of equipment, it will be realised that a tremendous amount of practice was essential before a crew could work together efficiently as a team.

The flight starting a two-day tour of duty would assemble in the morning at dispersal for training, either in the form of lectures and discussions or flying practice. In the afternoon all aircraft that were to fly that night would be thoroughly tested in the air. They would take off in twos, the pilots checking their engines on the ground and during the climb; the R/T would be tested on all channels, the intercom between pilot and operator checked, oxygen switched on to see that the supply was working, and finally the two aircraft would manoeuvre in order to carry out some practice interceptions which would also check the AI.

These daylight interceptions during a night-flying test run were usually carried out at a height of about 4,000ft. It has already been seen that the range of AI Mark 4 was limited by the height above ground. The maximum range attainable, regardless of what height the aircraft flew, was about 14,000ft, so that by carrying out NFTs at that height the AI could be checked for maximum range. During daylight interceptions it was essential for the pilot to resist the temptation to cheat, even if his operator managed to get himself in the most awful tangle. When the attempted interception was finished, he could tell his operator where he had gone wrong, but if he corrected the operator's errors, either instinctively or knowingly, the crew missed the opportunity of learning from these mistakes.

When the crew was considered far enough advanced to attempt interceptions at night, there was no chance of cheating, but it was amazing how long it took some pilots to realise the importance of carrying out the daylight exercises conscientiously.

Once the NFT had been completed, crews would go off to their respective messes for a meal and then report back to dispersal half an hour before official black-out time. A night state would have been prepared by the Flight Commander which would show the names of the crews on readiness, in the order in which they would be called on to take off if required. They would, of course, fly the same aircraft they had tested in the afternoon.

Any pilots still lacking Beau flying hours would be sent off for dusk circuits and bumps. If the weather was good, and if Sector approved, two Beaus would go off for practice. The remaining crews would sit around listening to the more experienced chaps nattering about this and that. The cards would appear for bridge or poker. Books were read, letters written and a pleasant time would be had by all. I found it most interesting to listen to what the old hands had to say. I certainly picked up many useful tips.

During August I flew as often in Defiants as in Beaus, but by the end of the month all the Defiants had gone. My logbook shows that I had seventeen flights that month and flew with ten different pilots. After that, however, the crewing problems were sorted out and crews flew together whenever possible. It had been realised how important team work would be, and it became Fighter Command policy to try to keep a crew together for their entire operational career.

I had been on probation for a month and at the beginning of September I became a sergeant. I was presented with my flying brevet by the Flight Commander, and it was a very proud moment for me when I stitched the single wing brevet on my tunic. This brevet bore the letters 'R O', short for Radio Observer, but at a later stage it was decided to do away with the 'R O' and the old 'O' or Observer brevet and to replace them with 'N' for Navigator, though on night fighters we were always referred to as Navigators Radio or N/Rs. In order to avoid confusion, I will refer to myself and my fellow knob twiddlers as Navigators.

Lofty Hamer did not yet have enough flying hours on Beaus to take one up at night so that most of our September flying was carried out in daylight. We did many homings and worked our way through the set exercises that had been evolved for AI training. I found Lofty to be extremely painstaking in carrying out these exercises and very patient indeed with me. Towards the end of the month he had sufficient Beau flying time to be set off on dusk landings, and when he had made a couple of successful solo landings I was allowed to join him for our first night trip together. By the end of September I had 42 hours of day-flying and 20 hours of night in my logbook.

On the morning of October 3rd I flew with Flight Lieutenant Waddingham, the Deputy Flight Commander. He flew with each of the navigators of the flight to see how they were getting on with AI and to sort out the geese from the swans. We took off with another Beau as 'playmate', to operate under GCI control.

The aircraft plot displayed on the operations table at Sector Headquarters was made up from information received from the long-range warning radar, supplemented by Observer Corps reports and plots from new ground radar stations called Ground Control Interception Stations, or GCIS for short. They were mainly concerned with the affairs of their own Group. These GCI stations were the answer to the last of the problems that had beset the early night fighters. The best that the Sector Controller had been able to do was to bring a fighter to within 5 or 6 miles of a bomber. This was not enough even for the AI-equipped fighters. The Mark 4 AI sets had a maximum range of only 3 or 4 miles. A GCI Controller, with his new ground radar equipment, could now bring the fighter much closer to its quarry, certainly to within 1 or 2 miles, depending on the proficiency of the GCI Controller and how well his apparatus was working.

Just as the Beau crews needed intensive practice with AI, so did the GCI Controllers with their equipment; collaboration became the keynote of an association that was to be most profitable for all concerned. When they were first introduced, GCI stations were capable of controlling only one fighter at a time, but it was not long before multiple control positions were made possible.

The trip with Flight Lieutenant Waddingham went off very well on the whole. Once the GCI Controller took us over he gave us a vector; that is to say, a course on which to fly. At the same time he gave us as much information as he could about the aircraft we were chasing, its height, range and the course it was steering relative to us.

As the range closed to 4 miles, I knew that I should soon see the target on my AI, but, search as I might, I could see nothing even faintly resembling an aircraft blip.

"He's only 2 miles from you now. Crossing starboard to port about the same level. Any joy?" asked the Controller anxiously.

"I can't see a thing on the set," I told my pilot, hoping desperately that it was not my mishandling of the AI that was the reason for the target's blip not appearing.

Much to my relief he replied: "My ruddy eyeballs are just about popping out looking for the darned thing and I can't see it. Hullo! Just a moment, there's a Beau way above us, going away to port. I expect that's him. He's about a mile behind us and at least 4,000ft above. They'll have to do a darned sight better than that."

We had gone on to intercom, so my pilot switched back to R/T and told the Controller what had happened. He expressed his apologies and sent both Beaus off for another attempt. This was just as unsuccessful as the first try, but at the third attempt everything worked perfectly. The contact appeared on my AI just as the Controller's instructions and information indicated that it should. For my part, I managed to complete the interception without too many boobs.

The other Beau was then given a couple of runs which I watched, looking through my Perspex dome as it manœuvred into position behind us. It was lovely and sunny up at 15,000ft and I could see the other Beau, a tiny black dot against a few scattered white clouds, below us and about 6 or 7 miles out to starboard.

Sometimes the cloud formations were breathtakingly beautiful. Although I became a bit blasé about flying after a while, I always found night flying thrilling, while during the day the excitements were mostly confined to low flying or buzzing through the tops of clouds which formed a strange world of uncanny beauty.

We had a lot to discuss when we landed. It was obvious that the combination of GCI and AI could work but a great deal of co-operation and practice would be necessary. We had found that the main weakness of GCI was the question of sorting out the height of the target aircraft. The reason for this was that the early GCI equipment did not have its own height-finder and had to rely on the rather inaccurate heights passed through normal control. It was not long before this weakness was corrected.

I was most surprised to find that we had been airborne over two and a half hours. The time had simply flown. This was something I always found when operating AI; it was so interesting to use and the challenge it offered was so intriguing that I never became bored with it. It seemed to defy mastery – as if it were a crossword puzzle with the ability to change all its clues just as the last two or three words were being filled in.

Early in October 1941 I found myself one of four navigators who were asked if we would like to be put up for commissions. All four of us gladly accepted the offer and we were told that it was most unlikely that the recommendations would be refused by the Air Ministry. It was expected that the commissions would take about three months to come through.

One unforeseen development from this was that I learned that I would be recrewed with one of the officers in 'B' Flight who was crewed with an NCO not up for a commission. I had been getting on very well with Lofty Hamer, both on the ground and in the air. Although I felt that I would miss his quiet, matter-of-fact ways, I realised that team work was going to be so important on this night-fighter business that it was obviously right that a crew should share the same mess.

I found that Lofty agreed with this. He had twice been offered a commission but had turned the offer down. He had been a senior NCO for some time and preferred life in the sergeants' mess. Many NCOs felt the same way as he did and it was nothing to hold against him.

CHAPTER 3

New Partnership

MY new pilot was Flying Officer James Gillies Benson, an experienced flyer who had one victory to his credit already. Of the considerable amount of good luck that came my way during the war, perhaps my crewing with Ben was the luckiest thing of all. With the exception of five months in 1943, we were to remain as a crew until we came off operations in 1945. In all the three and a half years that we flew together we did not have a single row or argument in spite of frustrations, near disasters, postings, blunders and the 101 little incidents bound to occur during hours of operational flying.

The outstanding things about Ben were his personality, his power of leadership, his ability to get on with the job in hand whatever it might be, and his sense of humour. He had a deep sense of responsibility; so far as I could see, he was quite fearless, as keen as mustard and quite unflappable. Whilst I was learning my job he was patience itself, particularly in the early stages when neither of us could be sure if our failures were due to me or to the equipment. We both made mistakes, but learned never to make the same mistake twice. He was an excellent and painstaking pilot, and from our first flight together I had complete confidence in him. I knew that he would give me every bit of help possible to prove my capabilities, and, once I had done so, he reciprocated my confidence in him without either of us having to put anything into words.

When I came to write this part of the book I realised that, although I had known that Ben had considerable flying experience before I crewed up with him, I had only a vague idea of what that experience amounted to. I knew he had been on 141 Squadron for some time and that he already had one victory to his credit, but that was about all I did know.

I wrote to him, explaining the position and asking him to fill in the details of his earlier RAF career. He was kind enough to oblige. I found that his story brings out the frustrations, trials and tribulations of those early days of night fighting so well that I have left it as he told it.

*   *   *

I left the Flying Training School at Montrose in July 1940. Looking back on it, I see that I was assessed as an above-average pilot. This may have been a disadvantage as it turned out later, for it was probably thought that pilots with this classification should be given the more complicated role of night fighting rather than day fighting, which was a bit of a hit-and-miss affair.

From there I went to Aston Down, which was a Fighter Training School. The main attraction there was that it was manned by the entire remnants of No. 1 Squadron, which had just returned from France. The outstanding feature at Aston Down, apart from the regular crashes that occurred because of its smallness, was the remarkable aerobatics of No. 1 Squadron whenever there was a serviceable aircraft to fly. They included two well-known aerobatics demonstrators among their members, one of whom showed his ability by shooting down an enemy aircraft over the airfield one day with a Spitfire out of the training wing. This was regarded as a pretty good feat at the time.

I left there on July 25th and reported to 141 Squadron, where I was told that I was a replacement for one of the eleven pilots who had been shot down the previous week. The squadron had left West Malling to patrol a convoy in mid-Channel when some Messerschmitt 110s had attacked them from up sun. Only one pilot had got back to West Malling. Because the squadron had few aircraft and fewer pilots, it was retired to Grangemouth to re-equip,

The aircraft we were flying were Defiants, and in August we were put on day-fighter duties, with detachments at

Grangemouth, Dyce and Turnhouse, on the east coast of Scotland. Although we did quite a lot of flying, we never saw an enemy aircraft, and the nearest we got to an attack was when we tried to shoot down a Lockheed Hudson which had become mixed up with an enemy raid. Fortunately this did not come off!

As it had been decided that the squadron would probably go on to night fighting, we moved to the Edinburgh area to do some night-flying training, which was sadly lacking at that time. When I look back now at the meagre facilities available for night flying at that time, it seems strange to realise the fantastic difficulties put in the path of anybody trying to operate in an aircraft at night.

We were flying from grass airfields with no runways. The maximum number of lights allowed at first was six 'glim' lamps which certainly showed only a glimmer of light. These were the only lights available for both take-off and landing. There was little or no help to be had from Flying Control, and this, coupled with the fact that at that time we had very poor radios which were all too liable to pack up, made life and training in general fairly exciting.

In October 1940 I was with a detachment moved to Gatwick. Two of the pilots had some success, although the problems of flying at night in the ack-ack zone were considerable. We were still in Defiants and my gunner was a chap by the name of Blane. During October we were sent to Biggin Hill to cover night-flying operations.

The difficulties were enormous. I will always remember my first night patrol from Biggin Hill. I took off with the aid of the six glim-lamps, which were immediately extinguished as I went into the air. The airfield was being bombed at the time. I was shot at by the airfield defences as I took off, coned by searchlights soon after and then got lost in cloud, only to find that my radio had packed up!

I had been told that if I was lost I should look for a blue searchlight. Never having seen a searchlight from the air before, I found that they all looked blue as I approached them. To my horror, however, each time I tried to get a homing from one of them, I was coned or followed around.

I decided that it would be safer in cloud, despite the fact that I was completely lost. On this particular evening we had the distinguished experience of flying right through the London balloon barrage, which we fortunately did not see. Then we sighted an enemy aircraft, which we chased but lost in cloud. We were only rescued from the necessity of having to bale out by the action of a brave man at Gatwick Airport. He turned on the flashing beacon in the middle of an air raid, thereby enabling us to do a rather dicey landing there.

This sort of thing happened pretty frequently, so the squadron worked out a homing system. Immediately you found you were lost, you flew twenty minutes due south until you calculated you were over the Channel. You then went down gently until you were below cloud, flew up and down until you found the two piers at Brighton and if you headed north from halfway between the piers you would see the signal lights on a railway. You had to remember that it went through a tunnel or a deep cutting through the South Downs, but you could follow it to Gatwick. If you could not get in there, you followed the railway line to Croydon airfield. That was closed at night, but if you turned hard left and took the Purley line, you would probably see Kenley, where they might be kind enough to let you land.

One of our sergeant pilots did this one night in thick fog. He was unable to see anything at Gatwick. He carried on to Croydon, hugging the railway, then turned hard left, keeping at nought feet in order not to lose sight of it. When he thought he had just about reached Kenley, he called them up and asked them to put on their flashing beacon. It came on at once. What worried him was that it was actually flashing above him!

We had some desperate nights in December of that year, patrolling over the centre of London during the Blitz, trying to pick out German bombers against the glow of the fires. On these occasions we had to fly with the cockpit hood open without any indication as to the height of the raiders. The nearest we got to one was when we nearly had a head-on collision with a Heinkel going in the opposite direction. Unfortunately, the closing speed was so fast we could not get in a shot. We did, in fact, see a tremendous amount of London burning during the 8th and 10th of December, but there was nothing very constructive we could do about it.

It is interesting to note that on December 11th we were sent on what must have been one of the very first Intruder patrols over France. We went the whole way to Abbeville, searching around at various altitudes for returning German bombers. We did not see any but had the satisfaction of shooting at some glasshouses that were reflecting the moonlight. This was quite an adventurous trip really for a single-engined Defiant, especially as we had no navigational aids and very indifferent radio at that time.

On December 22nd we managed to get of on a reasonably early patrol. We sighted a Heinkel high above us, crossing over the Sussex coast, and eventually shot it down.

About a week later we were returning to Gravesend after a long patrol, and as we made our approach to land we were mistaken for a German bomber. To our horror the glim-lamps were extinguished just as we were coming in and we suddenly found ourselves in fog at nought feet. We hit a dispersal bay and crashed where the runway would have been – if there had been such things in those days. We were very lucky to survive really, as our wheels were taken right off by the dispersal bay. Although Blane, who was flying with me, suffered a broken nose and I had concussion and lacerations to my head, we were both keen enough to be able to be operational within three weeks. Really, I suppose, we should have been satisfactorily dead!

Be that as it may, it set us back for the rest of the month, but we returned to operational flying in February 1941, and continued through the heavy Blitzes of March, when we saw a great deal of the City burning. We were patrolling over London during one of the worst raids at the end of March and I remember seeing almost the whole of Thameshaven on fire.

Our luck was out though; it was almost impossible to see a Hun by just looking out of an aircraft unless you knew where to look.

We operated from Manston on the odd occasion and that was a very exciting place to be. It was right in the thick of it all. Without AI or reasonable radio sets, success was very hard to come by for the squadron. We did see another Heinkel over London on April 17th, but we were unable to get a shot at it. At the end of that month we went north to Ayr for re-equipping, feeling that although we had had some excitement, we really had not earned our keep.

When I look back on those months in the south it really is very hard to realise just how difficult it was to try to operate aircraft at night during that period. At that stage of the war the chief task confronting anybody who took off at night was to try and get himself and his aircraft back safely on the ground. The accident rate was extremely high. Many people got lost and had to spend most of their time in the air trying to find out where they were.

The accent at this time was, not unnaturally, on day-fighter activities. The airfields were frequently being bombed and were resolutely averse to showing any illumination at night whatsoever. If you had to take off from a day-fighter base for a night patrol they were very pleased to see you go and did not want to see you landing back there again.

There were no means for recognition of our night fighters by searchlights and ack-ack. There seemed to be no planned patrols, and wherever you went you were fired at, illuminated and coned as if you were an enemy aircraft. It was all very exciting, but it did not help you to attack enemy bombers. Nobody at this time had any night-fighting experience and very few people had much experience in flying at night in adverse weather conditions.

On the Newcastle coast, where we next appeared, there were a few targets to be chased up. In May we experienced the ignominy of being fired at by an enemy aircraft whose presence we had not even suspected. Unfortunately it disappeared and we did not have a chance of getting our own back. There was another piece of excitement that month when we had an engine failure while we were up in a Defiant. When that happens in a single-engined aircraft you just have to land without one. We did this, landing at Acklington and damaging the aircraft severely.

The squadron had a certain amount of success at this time, catching several German bombers in raids on Newcastle. I did not have the good fortune to find anything however. We continued with the good work until July and August 1941, when we started converting to Blenheims and subsequently to Beaufighters, when no doubt, your story begins.

*   *   *

The only comment I will make on Ben's story is that it underlines the point I have already made of my amazing good luck in getting on to night fighting just at the psychological time when nearly every one of the difficulties connected with flying at night had been overcome.

So far as Ben was concerned, he had a fine twin-engined Beau to fly. It was fitted with Very High Frequency R/T, which worked supremely well. Airfields used for night fighting now had good lighting and runways with an efficient Flying Control. Patrols were properly planned and there was excellent liaison between searchlights, guns and aircraft.

The only new equipment whose usefulness and reliability still had to be tested and proved was AI. It was my job to make this work, and I found that Ben was at all times patient, helpful and co-operative.

The first three months Ben and I were together were spent in practice, practice and more practice. We sorted out what seemed to us the best mixture of directions and information for me to pass on to Ben, so that I would have control of the interception whilst giving him as clear a picture as possible of what was taking place. Some pilots insisted that the navigator should just give a running commentary of what the target aircraft was doing and leave the pilot to carry out the interception. It was obvious to us both that this method did not get the fullest benefit from AI, so we stuck to our own ideas.

We found out what a pernickety, temperamental piece of equipment AI could be. After all, it was fairly fragile stuff to be installed in an aircraft and flown around the sky. The vibration of the engines, the inevitable bounces, great or small according to the pilot's skill in landing, the surges in power from the engines, all these could cause faults. Then we found that AI could squint. If one aerial was not as efficient as its opposite number, a false picture would be presented on the cathode ray tubes. We learned to watch for this on the night-flying tests, which were always carried out in daylight. I would bring Ben in behind our target so that it appeared dead ahead and level at a range of about 1,000ft and he would tell me exactly where the other aircraft was. It did not always squint, of course, but if it did we could allow for that at night. The really difficult time could arise, however, when a fault occurred in an aerial after the night-flying test had been carried out. As the aerials were rather allergic to damp, these faults were not infrequent.

No. 141 Squadron had been detailed to keep three Beaus at Drem, near Edinburgh, and crews took it in turns to spend three nights there. Ben and I went there in October and again in December, and each time we were ordered off for an operational patrol. Both times there were some Huns about but much too far south, though the time was not wasted as we practised with the local GCI.

Early in January 1942 Ben and I were sent on attachment to 29 Squadron at West Malling in Kent. They had quite a bit of operational experience and we were to pick up any hints and advice that we could. At the same time Flight Lieutenant

Braham and his navigator, 29 Squadron's most successful crew, had a similar attachment to our squadron to natter to our crews and answer questions. Interchange of information of this sort was extremely useful, and Fighter Command were to be congratulated on remembering its importance right through the war.

Unfortunately for us, the weather was so bad for the few days that we were at West Malling that no night flying was carried out at all. We would dearly have loved a crack at the Hun, but we had to contain our impatience. For me, at any rate, there was some compensation in the kick I received every time I flew at night. Even when we were off on practice interceptions there was something about clambering into the Beau in the dark that made me tingle with excitement.

In the Beau, feeling bulky with flying kit, I would strap myself in the seat under the Perspex dome and swivel myself round so as to face the front to watch the take-off. First one powerful Hercules engine, then the other, would roar into life as the ground crew plugged the starter battery in. Ben would rev up the engines and the aircraft would surge forward against the chocks. A signal from Ben and the chocks were hauled away. We would taxi around the perimeter track to the end of the runway in use – landing and take-off were always made into wind – then a final run-up of the engines against the brakes for Ben to check oil and air pressures on both engines. A final 'Okay' from Air Traffic Control and, with a roar of engines, we would gather speed as we moved along the runway with a second or two of tension as the Beau lurched off into the air. Then Ben would snatch at the lever that retracted the undercarriage and we were airborne. A wide sweep around the airfield, then we would leave its few, friendly lights as we climbed up to our operational height.

Once I became moderately competent with AI there was the thrill of the chase, even if it was only another Beau that we were after: to use the wonderful apparatus we had been given and, when everything had worked well, to hear Ben say:

"Okay. There she is now. Turn round and have a look!"

It was always exciting to see the shadowy silhouette of a Beau just in front of us and to know that if it had been a Hun we had the power to blow it out of the sky. And almost every flight gave me that thrill not just once but several times.

Most crews were beginning to think that it was about time that we began to put all this practice and theory into real operational use, and we found to our joy that 141 Squadron was to move to Acklington on January 28th. Admittedly, most of the action was to be found in south-eastern England, but Acklington was a front-line station and we might expect some action there. It was an added kick for me to return to the station where a few short months ago I had been a lowly erk.

With 141 Squadron at Acklington there was a day-fighter squadron and a Turbinlite flight; we did not see much of the day squadron as we were off duty when they were on and vice versa. We did see quite a bit of the Turbinlites, though – almost too much.

In the desperate days when every plausible idea was seized upon to combat the night bomber someone had suggested an airborne searchlight. The Douglas Havoc had been selected as the aircraft in which to mount a searchlight, complete with batteries to operate it. When all the necessary equipment was fitted into the Havoc, it was found that there was no room for guns, so out they came. Obviously a searchlight up in the sky was of no use unless guns could operate with it, so it was decided that one or two Hurricanes should take off with the Turbinlite Havoc and formate on it with the assistance of lights in the trailing edge of the Havoc's wing. It had also been found that Mark 4 AI would fit into the Havoc, so in it went.

The idea was that the Turbinlite would intercept a bomber, illuminate it with his searchlight and the Hurricanes would dive in to shoot down the blinded bomber. Unfortunately the whole operation was much too unwieldy to operate successfully. On the few occasions when an enemy bomber was illuminated, it escaped from the searchlight beam before the fighter could get close enough to fire, and once the bomber was out of the beam the fighter could do nothing. No enemy bombers were shot down by the Turbinlite fighters, and there was a rumour that a Halifax had been attacked by them on a dark night.

Once the AI equipped Beaufighter appeared on the scene it could do all that the cumbersome Turbinlite set-up could without forfeiting the element of surprise that was the night fighter's main asset. Several flights of Turbinlites had been formed and many useful trained night-fighter crews were tied up in this operation for over a year. The powers-that-be certainly persisted far too long with Turbinlites.

Ben and I were rather fed up to hear that 141 Squadron still had to maintain the detachment at Drem and we were sent there with two other crews for a week from January 30th. We gnashed our teeth at the thought that no sooner had we been moved to an operational station, than we were promptly whisked off it. We dreaded to hear of all the excitement we were missing, and the weather was so bad at Drem that we only got one night trip in the whole week. When we returned, however, we found that the weather had been even worse at Acklington and there had been no excitement apart from frantic snow clearing on the runways and wondering if Acklington was going to be isolated by the heavy snowfall.

Ben was due for ten days' leave and departed southwards as soon as we returned to Acklington. The weather remained pretty foul but I managed to do a night-flying test ran one afternoon, followed with a two-hour GCI exercise that night, both trips with Lofty Hamer as pilot. Four days later I had two similar flights with one of Ben's particular friends, Flight Lieutenant Ivor Cosby. All these flights were without any special incident, though we were all getting very keyed up.

Ben and 'Koz' had been together on the squadron for some time, and when the two of them got together in the mess things began to happen. Koz had a sense of humour much like

Ben's, so they made a good pair. I am afraid that nicknames on the squadron were rather lacking in imagination, usually being just an abbreviation of the first syllable of the surname. Thus I became 'Brandy' for the rest of my Service career.

By the time Ben returned from leave there had been one spot of excitement when two aircraft of 'A' Flight had been scrambled one night to meet a threatened raid that did not materialise. Our Flight was starting a two-day spell on duty, so that afternoon we went off for our NFT in Beaufighter No. 7577, which had been allocated to us to fly whenever it was available. It was as well if a crew could stick to the same aircraft as much as possible and get to know its idiosyncrasies.

We had been told that the latest practice of the Hun, especially when raiding coastal targets, was to drop his bombs from anything up to 20,000ft and then stick his nose down in as fast a dive for home as possible. On this particular NFT we arranged for the target to carry out these tactics, while I tried to follow him on AI. It was difficult, but it could be done; correct speed control was the main worry.

CHAPTER 4

First Blood

ON the night of February 15th we arrived at dispersal to find that we were fifth crew due to fly on the Night State list. It was a fine evening and two aircraft were sent off on a dusk patrol which would consist of GCI controlled practice interceptions a little way off the East Coast, where they would be in a good position if anything did come in from the Fatherland.

During the war the Services worked on a 24 hour clock time. That is to say, there was no 'am' and 'pm'; 1pm became thirteen hundred hours, or '13.00' and so on.

At about 18.45 hours the Flight Commander spoke to the Sector Controller on the ops telephone and suggested relieving the pair of Beaus then airborne with a fresh pair, as they had been up almost two hours. As he put the telephone down, all eyes were on him, as if we sensed that there was something doing.

"They are keeping 27 and 32 up for a while and they want two more off. There may be something doing."

The two crews next off on the Night State were out of the door almost before he had finished speaking. Ben and I, who would be next off after them were really straining at the leash. For ten minutes we were kept in suspense, then the ops telephone rang.

"Off you go. Two more. You are to go straight over to Sector Control as soon as you have made enough height to get them on R/T."

The Flight Commander was last off on the Night State. I could imagine how he was cursing his luck at being on the ground while there was something happening. I hoped we would not be too late for some action.

Meanwhile, we had grabbed our bits and pieces and were well on the way to our Beau. We clambered in and went through the usual procedure. This time it was the real thing. Soon we were taxying round the perimeter track. I had checked the cannons, then strapped myself in my seat and plugged in the lead from my helmet for the R/T and intercom. Oxygen was switched on; we used oxygen from take-off at night.

By this time we were at the end of the runway, with the other Beau just discernible behind us.

"All set?" asked Ben. "Right then. Away we go."

Away we went, down the runway, then climbing as fast as the Beau could reasonably go. Ben had an eight-channel R/T set with push-button control. As soon as we had climbed enough, he pressed the appropriate button for Sector Control.

"Hello, Homestead. Hello, Homestead. Rounder three-six. What instructions, please?"

"Hello, Rounder three-six. Vector zero four five. What are your angels?"

This meant: "Steer a course of 045 degrees. What height are you?"

"Hello, Homestead. Three-six steering zero four five, angels seven still climbing."

"Hello, three-six. Continue climbing to angels fourteen on present course."

It was a dark night, with a fair amount of low cloud, the tops of which were about 1,500ft. Up where we were, however, it was dear. We passed over the coast and saw that we were about 8 miles north of Blyth. A few minutes later we were given a southerly course to steer and were told to go over to the GCI control.

Ben pressed another button and gave our call sign to the Controller. We knew that at that time the GCI Controller could handle only one interception at a time. He already had a Beau under control on another channel and we were being kept handy until the other interception was completed.

We could see the bursting anti-aircraft shells high over Sunderland – so that was where the trouble was.

"Hello, Rounder three-six. This is Blackbird. Continue on

present course, we may have something for you. What are your angels?"

"Good show! Angels one-four. Listening out."

Apart from a few hurried peeps through my Perspex dome when Ben pointed something out to me, my eyes had been glued to the rubber visor through which I was peering hopefully at the cathode ray tubes of the AI. Suddenly I noticed a tenuous blip which just crept out of the ground returns at maximum range and then lost itself again in the grounds as the aircraft which had caused it went out of range again.

"Contact!" I yelled to Ben through the intercom. "It's gone now. I only had it for a second but I'm sure it was an aircraft."

"Which way did it go?" asked Ben plaintively.

"Didn't have time to see," I replied. "Still, I'm sure it was an aircraft."

"I'll get on to the Controller," said Ben.

"Hello, Blackbird. This is Rounder three-six. Is there anyone near me?"

"Rounder three-six. Blackbird here. Hard port on to zero eight zero. It looks like a Bandit going home. It's well below you."

Ben swung the heavy nose round and put her nose down. As he did so, he opened the throttles and she fairly hurled herself after the Bandit. The Beau was capable of about 300mph and probably 30 more in a dive. We were doing all of 330mph as we screamed down.

"Any joy yet?" Ben was asking.

But for two or three minutes there was nothing to see, though my eyes were straining to the utmost. Then, coming very slowly out of the ground returns, a blip emerged.

"Contact! Gently starboard. Keep going down."

"Ah-h-h!" breathed Ben as the aircraft responded immediately to my instructions. "Keep hold of the blighter."

"Steady now. It's dead ahead about 3 miles. What height are we and can you go any faster?"

"Height is 9,500 and we're going balls out already. Are

we catching him?"

But the sad fact was that we were not gaining on him at all.

It was only the extra speed we had gathered in the dive that had brought us closer to him. As soon as our height coincided with his and I had told Ben to level out, I had the mortification of seeing the blip slowly slide up the time base and out of range.

Ben called Blackbird Control to tell him that we had lost contact and we were informed that our target was drawing right away from us. It must have been going like a bat out of hell.

To say we were disappointed was an understatement. If only the wretched Controller had been able to tackle more than one interception at a time we might have had some joy.

The Controller brought us back almost over Acklington, then the excitement started all over again.

"Hello, Rounder three-six. Blackbird Control. We have a Bogey for you to investigate. Turn port on to zero one zero. Range 5 miles."

The term Bogey meant we had to identify with extra care as it might be a friendly aircraft. Bandit meant that it was almost certainly an enemy. In either case positive identification was essential.

"Hello, three-six. Range now 4 miles, crossing you port to starboard. Any joy yet?"

"No, nothing yet," I informed Ben.

A second or two later it was a different story. A quite firm blip showed on both tubes, over to port and slightly below.

"Contact!" I called over the intercom. "Gently port and go down. Range 3½ miles."

As Ben responded at once to my instructions he informed the Controller that we had contact.

"Do you require any further help?" asked the Controller.

"Ease the turn now. Range 3 miles. No, I don't need any more help," I told Ben.

He passed that information to the Controller and we went on to intercom. I could see that the aircraft we were chasing was still slightly over to port but the blip was slowly moving across the time base to starboard. We were flying straight now, so he was crossing us from port to starboard as the Controller had said. I could anticipate this and cut him off by turning now.

"Gently starboard. Range 2½ miles," I told Ben.

"Gently starboard. I'm still going down."

"Level out now… Keep going starboard."

Thank the Lord he had reminded me of the height; I had been watching the azimuth tube too closely and had forgotten to watch the elevation tube.

As we levelled out, Ben automatically opened the throttles slightly to keep our speed constant. We were closing in perfectly. The blip showed almost dead ahead now.

"Steady now… Range 1½… We're coming in nicely. Where do you want him?"

"Steady. Put him starboard and above. About 10 degrees starboard. What range now?"

"Just under a mile. Throttle back slightly. Can you see anything yet?"

"No, not yet. Keep giving me the range."

"About 2,000ft. Gently port now."

A moment's pause, then explosively: "Christ! There it is. It's a bloody great Dornier. Here, have a look. I can hold it now."

I needed no urging but swivelled my seat around and peered into the blackness. My eyes took a moment to become accustomed to the dark, then I saw, just above and to starboard of us, the vague silhouette of an aircraft with pinpoints of reddish lights showing from the exhausts. I could see the pencil-slim fuselage and the twin fins. It was a Dornier 217, all right. Ben, who by this time was formating immediately beneath the Dornier and was only 200 or 300ft below, decided that time for action had arrived.

The Dornier was weaving gently from side to side as it flew along. Ben throttled back very slightly and lifted the nose of the Beau. It was a little over to port now. It seemed strange that it should be completely indifferent to the presence of a

Beaufighter so close. As it drifted across in front of us, my heart was thumping so loudly it seemed impossible for the Huns not to hear it. As it passed through his gunsight, Ben turned the Beau almost imperceptibly to follow the Dornier. All hell broke loose as he pressed the gun button and four cannons and six machine-guns banged and chattered away. The Beau filled with the acrid smoke and smell of cordite.

Ben had given it a two-second burst of gunfire; but although the Dornier began to lose height, we had seen no strikes. We did not use tracer bullets at night in order to retain the element of surprise. We were now following it down in a very sharp dive and Ben gave it two more short bursts from about 300ft range. This time we saw strikes all along the fuselage and tail unit, from which there was a great red flash which illumined the whole aircraft.

Ben was having a devil of a job to keep behind it now. We kept getting into the slipstream which threw us about violently. Before Ben could get another burst in, the Dornier had entered the clouds, diving into them at a very steep angle. We were about 1,000ft behind it by then and at a height of only 2,000ft Ben pulled out of the dive. We circled the spot where we had last seen the Dornier, hoping that we might see an explosion as it hit the deck. No such luck.

We called Control to report and to ask if there was anything else for us. All was quiet now, though, and we were given a vector for Acklington. As I guided Ben home, we discussed the night's events.

"I wonder if the other chaps had any luck," I mused.

"Oh, I should think so," replied Ben. There must have been quite a few Huns around. What bloody bad luck though. I'm sure our Dornier must have gone in, but the best we will be given is a Probable, more likely we'll only get a Damaged. I should have got the damned thing with that first burst. Ah well!"

We were soon back at base, and when we taxied into our dispersal bay our jubilant ground crew were waiting to welcome us. The Flight Commander and the Intelligence Officer were also awaiting us. Although there had been several chases, we were told, ours had been the only combat.

In the crew-room we were just taking off our flying clothing when the ops telephone rang. It was the Sector Controller to congratulate us and to tell us the glad news that the Royal Observer Corps and Saint Mary's Lighthouse had independently reported a plane crashing into the sea 4 miles east of Blyth.

There had been no other combats; the guns were not claiming anything and the time and place coincided with our combat. We were told, therefore, that we could claim the Dornier as destroyed.

Soon after we had landed, the weather deteriorated. Sector decided that it was most unlikely that there would be any further activity that night, and so we were stood down except for two crews. The rest of us made our way to our respective messes and indulged in a beer or two.

Next morning I was sitting down to my bacon and egg in the sergeants' mess, feeling very bucked with the thought that we had opened the Squadron's AI score on our first really operational sortie. The radio was switched on for the news and I had the great satisfaction of hearing:

"A small force of enemy bombers attacked towns in the north of England last night. A Dornier 217 was shot down by one of our night fighters."

The bad weather remained with us for the next few days so that we managed to do only one night flight. There was no enemy activity but we carried out some useful GCI runs. Ben also had some air-firing practice, shooting at a drogue towed by another aircraft. Again we smelt that gunsmoke.

On February 21st my commission came through and I was sent off on a week's leave to London to fix myself up with an officer's uniform and kit. Luckily, I had been recommended to a first-class tailor in Sackville Street. Not only did he complete the whole business, including fittings, in five days but he did it all for the rather meagre sum allowed by Air Ministry. It all fitted perfectly and I still have the greatcoat he made for me. I had fourteen years' wear from it in the RAF and it is in very good shape even now.

Greatcoat, raincoat, best blues, two shirts, four collars, three pairs of socks, a pair of shoes and a tie had cost somewhere in the region of 24 pounds – and all the kit was absolutely first class.

I returned to Acklington on the last day of February. One of the first persons I saw was the Flight Sergeant in charge of the guard-room, where, less than a year before, I had been one of his policemen. As he whipped me up a smart salute I could hardly restrain a delighted grin; we had all moved in fear and trembling of this particular chappie.

Acklington was miles from anywhere, and probably for that reason there was always a very pleasant atmosphere in the officers' mess. We had to make our own entertainment, but we made life very enjoyable there, largely with the aid of a radiogram and some of the latest records. There was a comfortable little bar, and a civilian mess secretary saw to it that the mess was well run and the food appetising. The squadron officers were a grand bunch and the station officers helpful and friendly. In spite of its geographical position Acklington was a pretty good station to be on.

There had been a bitterly cold spell of weather at the end of February which lasted well into March. There were fairly heavy falls of snow and I well remember cycling round the perimeter track of the airfield on my way to dispersal and being very nearly blown off my bicycle by a howling gale. It was freezing cold and snowing hard. Being almost on the East Coast, it was very exposed to the east wind. As I neared dispersal I noticed airmen working on several Beaus parked in the open. It is difficult to imagine a worse job than working under these conditions on metal aircraft. Usually the engine fitters had to work with bare hands; at best they could wear mittens. In spite of all this they were always cheerful and terrifically keen.

It was easy enough for the aircrews to keep up a good squadron spirit; but in my experience, on all the squadrons with which I served the spirit of the ground crews and their willingness to work at all hours and under the most disheartening conditions really had to be seen to be believed. I do not believe that sufficient praise can ever be given to the ground crews in the RAF, particularly to those on night-fighter squadrons, for the truly magnificent job they did.

As far as possible the ground crews were assigned to their own particular aircraft-and what a pride they would take in it. Our Beau had hardly landed after our combat before the ground crew had a swastika painted on. Later, when Ben and I were on 157 Squadron, we arrived at dispersal one morning to find our Mosquito had been christened Queen of the Skies by our ground crew. They always made sure, to the best of their ability, that she lived up to her name.

It was during this extremely cold spell that I received a letter from one of the chaps who had been with me at Scarborough. He had not fancied trying for night fighters because he had always been interested in pure navigation. He had been sent to the United States for his training and had actually been on the first navigators' course to be held there. As I shivered at Acklington, I read the address on the top right-hand side of his letter:

Coral Cables, Palm Springs, Miami, Florida.

The March weather remained bad and it was not until near the end of the month that the snow began to clear. After our experience with GCI it had been decided that we must all practice 'freelance' interceptions. The GCI Controller could cope properly with only one interception at a time, although he could put the fighter he was controlling in a most advantageous position. It was obviously wrong, however, for the other patrolling fighters just to wait until the Controller could take them over.

Co-operation with searchlights would have been one

possible solution for these fighters, but most of the searchlights were way down south and there were very few left for our area. The Sector Controller was in a position to bring a fighter to within about 5 miles of a bomber, and with the aid of AI and a slice of luck a fighter might well make contact on a bomber under this sort of control. It would be far more difficult than under GCI control as the detailed information would not be available. In other words, it would be a hit-or-miss interception which the navigator would have to snap up and interpret immediately he had contact.

These practices were carried out in daylight. The pilot of the fighter would arrange as awkward an initial contact as possible for the navigator to pick up. If the navigator coped well and brought his pilot round on approximately the same course as the target, the interception would be broken off and another one set up, in order that as many initial pick-ups as possible could be achieved.

Now that crews were becoming more efficient, on all practice exercises the aircraft acting as target had instructions to take evasive action as the other aircraft made an interception. The German bombers could not be expected to fly straight and level when they were being chased so this type of practice was bound to pay dividends eventually.

Twice in March we had chases on aircraft that were possibly hostile. On the first occasion we were freelancing when I picked up a contact. We had quite a bit of trouble in getting through cloud which was pretty solid up to about 8,000ft and had been full of snow. The consequence was that ice had started to form on the Beau and the considerable extra weight had made climbing difficult. Still, we had managed to get above the cloud and now I had a contact.

To my dismay, however, I saw that I had no pictures at all on the azimuth tube, although the elevation tube was working perfectly. I literally did not know which way to turn when the blip inevitably vanished and I had the sad task of breaking the news to Ben. When we landed it was found that both azimuth aerials had fractured, probably due to the bad icing conditions.

I had no excuse when we had a second chase later in the month. We were freelancing again when I had a contact which I realised much too late was coming head-on towards us. Ben did get a momentary visual on an aircraft he had no time to identify; but although he whipped the Beau round in the tightest possible turn, I did not regain AI contact. I was furious with myself, but Ben took it very well.

The weather improved in April, but the enemy kept very quiet, at least in our area. We managed to get quite a bit of flying with the consequent practice and Ben had four sessions of air firing. By the end of the month my total flying hours were beginning to look more respectable, 146 day hours and 46 night.

On May 1st 'B' Flight was Duty flight and Ben and I were about sixth off on the programme. Two Beaus had gone off on patrol at dusk but after an hour or so the weather had deteriorated so badly that they were recalled. In spite of the weather, Sector required all crews to remain at readiness, so out came the cards and the chess sets as we settled down for a long wait. Just before midnight the Flight Commander asked Sector if there could be any relaxation in the state of readiness – in other words, if some of us could go to bed. Sector would have none of this, however; they said that some enemy activity was expected. That put us on our toes.

The weather had improved. There was bright moonlight shining through scattered low clouds as we saw when we put our heads outside for a breath of fresh air.

An hour and a half slipped away. Although we were still on our toes, the arches of our feet were aching slightly! Suddenly the ops telephone rang. The Flight Commander leapt to it. He repeated Sector's order:

"Scramble four aircraft!"

Eight chaps, bulky in flying kit, scurried around grabbing what they needed and in seconds were shooting through the door. The call had gone to the ground crews telling them which aircraft were going off. One by one we heard the roar of engines starting up – if only Sector would ask for a couple more aircraft to scramble.

The Flight Commander had been second off on the Night State, and Ben, as senior pilot left on the ground, was in charge. He picked up the ops telephone after a few minutes and we heard him ask:

"What's the form, chum?"

Sector told him that about a dozen probable Huns had been plotted heading for the Tynemouth area. Why on earth didn't they send some more Beaus off?

We waited impatiently for nearly half an hour and then a telephone rang. Our hearts leapt – then dropped through the floor when we realised that it was not the ops telephone but the ordinary station telephone. Ben answered it and we soon gathered from the tone of his voice that something out of the ordinary was going on.

The Squadron Commander, Wing Commander Heycock, was at the other end of the telephone. As was the normal practice, he had been informed that some Huns were thought to be around. He had hopped into his car, dashed from his Married Quarter down to 'A' Flight and wanted a ground crew to start his aircraft and a navigator to fly with him. At the same time he told Ben that Sector wanted two more Beaus off and he, the Wingco, would be one of the two.

Ben signalled to the next crew due off and passed the word for a ground crew to go to 'A' Flight, whilst still talking to the CO who then obviously asked him which navigators were left in 'B' Flight.

Ben looked around at us and reeled off our names. After a few moments' expostulation he put the telephone down disgustedly and told me to go over to 'A' Flight to fly with the CO.

The CO usually flew from 'A' Flight, but, instead of always taking his turn on the programme, he had arranged that he and his navigator should be told whenever there was any activity so that they could get into the air. On this occasion the message had not reached his navigator so he had ordered Ben to send me along.

It was a bit much: not only was the CO grabbing Ben's place on the Night Flying Programme, but he was grabbing his navigator as well. Still, an order was an order, so off I went.

It was always interesting to fly with a new pilot, but on an occasion like this I would have preferred to have been with Ben.

In a few minutes we were thundering down the runway. We lurched into the air and climbed as fast as the Beau could go. The Sector Controller gave us a vector to steer and we headed out over the coast, still climbing. When we had reached about 9,000ft we were told to go over to Blackbird control. They informed us that there was some 'trade' about and were soon able to give me quite a good contact. I told the Wingco that I could hold it; he informed Blackbird and we went over to intercom.

My troubles were about to begin. I had noticed that my pilot was terrifically keyed up and excited. When he had been given a new course to steer by the Controller, the Beau had just about stood on one wing as the Wingco had jerked it round, instead of the standardised controlled turn I was used to with Ben.

As soon as I took over the interception and began my instructions and patter the Beau was flung all over the sky to the accompaniment of yells, curses and imprecations from the front seat. This chap was far too keen; he did not realise that he was making my job fifty times as difficult as it need be. His violent reactions to my instructions made it almost impossible for me to assess what the aircraft in front of us was doing. Every time I mentioned the word 'turn', we whipped round in a flash and the blip would jerk from one side to the other of the azimuth time base.

There was no time to remonstrate with him. As soon as the blip showed almost dead ahead I gave no more turns for a while. In the meantime, the range was closing quite well. I gave a few more turns, pleading for gentle ones and easing him out of them almost before they had begun. He became coherent long enough to reply to my query: "Where do you want him?"

"Wherever you *blank* well like! Hurry up, man! Pull your *blank* finger out. Where is the *blank* thing?"

Luckily the *blank* thing was not far off. I managed to bring him in with the target very slightly below and to port. With the moonlight on the low cloud he got a visual at nearly 2,500ft on a Dornier 217, probably the most easy German aircraft to recognise.

The excitement at the front end of the Beau redoubled. The aircraft seemed to throw itself at the Dornier with guns blazing in a long burst. He had fired from a bit too far away, instead of stalking for a while and getting into a really good firing position. The result was no strikes, but the Dornier spotted us and became most unfriendly. It took violent evasive action, one of its gunners piping tracer bullets towards us. Tracer is always frightening at night; it seems to be coming straight at you. The trouble was that this particular tracer was actually coming straight at us. And it was hitting us.

Luckily Beau and Dornier lost sight of each other after a very short while. I still had AI contact, though, and we made another approach, rather more carefully this time, though the Wingco was screaming with frustration and excitement. Seconds later the Wingco saw the Dornier again. This time he got in closer and took better aim, for we saw strikes all along the fuselage. It went almost straight down in a dive, no guns firing now.

We followed it down and saw it go into cloud at a very steep angle. It was too low for our AI to be of use as the cloud tops were only 2,500ft, and though we watched the spot where we had last seen it we saw no flash that would denote that it had crashed.

There was nothing more doing that night, but as the clouds had gathered very low over Acklington we were diverted to Ouston, our Sector Station, where we spent the rest of the night.

When we returned to Acklington next morning I learned that Ben had eventually managed to rustle up a navigator from somewhere the night before and had been airborne. They had no joy though.

The Wingco and I were given a probable for the Dornier.

Ben and I went to Drem for a four-day detachment on May 3rd. We carried on with the usual practices there and did some useful GCI trips with our target briefed to take violent evasive action when we closed in to 4,000ft or so.

When we returned to Acklington we received the glad tidings that 141 Squadron was to re-equip with a new type of AI which needed a completely different aerial to Mark 4. This meant new Beaus as well, so the pilots were as pleased as the navigators.

I was detailed to attend a special course in the use of the new AI at the Fighter Interception Unit at Ford in Sussex. I was to report there on May 13th, so Ben and I went off on leave, he to Edinburgh and I to London.

While I was walking in Maida Vale one day during this leave I ran into Terry Thomas. I had known him from my film days when we were both doing crowd work and small parts. We were both in uniform, he in that of an Army sergeant. I remember him saying:

"Cor, what a shower! I wish I was in your mob."

CHAPTER 5

Mark 7

WHEN I got to Ford I found that the new AI was known as Mark 7. Although it worked on the same basic principle as Mark 4, the main difference was a more powerful beamed transmission which gave greater maximum range and also, to a very large extent, eliminated ground returns. The beam of the transmitter was in the shape of a cone, reaching out at 45 degrees from the nose of the fighter each way. Both transmitting and receiving aerials were in the nose of the aircraft and were concealed in a Perspex dome attached to the front.

So far as the navigator was concerned operating looked as if it would be much easier than on Mark 4. There was only one tube for him to have to worry about; on this tube, about 6in in diameter, he was shown range, azimuth and elevation in a very simple form. Taking the centre of the tube to represent his own aircraft, the blip of a target aircraft would show as a circle, or part of a circle, of light. An aircraft dead ahead and absolutely level with the fighter would show as a complete circle, the range being assessed by the distance of the circle from the centre of the tube. If the target went slightly to one side, the circle would break, and when the target had gone out to 10 degrees would show as a half-circle on that side. At 15 degrees there would be an arc which would gradually get smaller the further the target went over. At 40 degrees the arc was very small, and at 45 degrees the target would be outside the coverage of the transmitter's cone of search.

Elevation was read in exactly the same way. Briefly, remembering that the centre of the tube represented the fighter, the position of the blip showed the exact actual position of the target relative to the fighter. Thus, if one imagined the tube to be a clockface, the target's position could be read straight off the tube to the pilot. He in turn could look upon his windscreen as a clockface, and when the navigator told him a target was 2 o'clock 20 degrees he would know exactly where to look for it. This method of clockface references for interception purposes became standardised soon after the introduction of Mark 7 AI to squadron service.

The course at Ford lasted only three days, but I managed to get in five trips which averaged just over an hour each. The practice Mark 7 was installed in Beaus just as it would be when we got our own. I was delighted with it. The only difficulty that anyone could foresee was that as a target came close to the fighter the transmitter's beam became relatively narrow, so that evasive action would have to be reacted to immediately or the target aircraft would get away. To compensate for this, however, Mark 7 did give instantaneous warning of any movement of the target.

When I returned to Acklington I found that I was to assist the Navigator Leader, who had already done the Ford course, in training the rest of 141 Squadron's navigators. He took on the training of 'A' Flight while I had a go at the 'B' Flight boys. Except for one night trip on the very last day of May, all our flying was carried out by day. We fitted a black cover inside the Perspex dome of the navigator's compartment so that the rubber visor could be taken off the indicator unit of the AI. Two or three navigators could then gather round the tube whilst I explained how it worked. After two demonstrations, which included a few minutes for each navigator to operate the set, they knew enough about it to carry on by themselves.

We found it very useful and profitable to fly each of the pilots in turn as passengers, so that they could see what the navigator had to cope with during an interception. They found it all very interesting, and I am sure it was of benefit later on.

The night trip at the end of the month was of great interest.

The CHL, or Chain Home Low stations, were the low level part of the general warning system. Attempts had been made to control night fighters operating at low level, 2,000ft or less, using CHL information. The trouble had been that Mark 4 AI was unable to see so low down. Now we had AI that could operate at this level or even lower. Mine-laying or reconnaissance aircraft had been able to come in at this height almost at will. Now we had something with which to combat them and our first night patrol with CHL showed us that it would work. We were on patrol with another Beau and carried out practice interceptions just as we normally did with GCI control. We found that it all went very well but that low flying over the sea was tricky. Special altimeters were fitted to the squadron's aircraft soon after this and they proved very efficient.

The new Beau had come in fast so that by the beginning of June 141 Squadron was fully re-equipped. By dint of some pretty strenuous flying – sometimes we were up three or four times a day – the basic training of all the navigators was completed by June 3rd. There was no doubt about it, we were very pleased with our new equipment.

Early in June we heard from our pals on the Turbinlite Flight that the higher-ups had realised the futility of continuing with this cumbersome operation. Not a single success had been gained by Turbinlites. Trained crews and useful equipment were being wasted, but instead of cutting their losses and retiring the Turbinlites, gratefully and gracefully, a strange decision was made. Sector Controllers were told that the next time there was any enemy activity Turbinlites were to be given absolute priority in the use of GCI control facilities.

They did not have to wait long for their last fling. On the night of June 4th, 1942, a raid of some twenty enemy aircraft was plotted coming in to the Tynemouth area.

'B' Flight was on duty that night. Ben and I were some way down the night-flying programme. We knew that the Turbinlites had been ordered off and we waited impatiently as four Beaus, then another two, had been scrambled. We were next off. The first aircraft had gone off about half an hour after midnight. We knew that three or four Turbinlites and six Beaus were already up there. Would they want any more? We seemed to be waiting for hours; after all, this was what we had put in all those hours of training and practice for, and here we were on the ground. Fifteen long minutes had, in fact, gone by before we heard the welcome ring of the ops telephone. We were off.

We must surely have broken all records in getting off and climbing up towards the east. We could see bursts of ack-ack shells over the estuary of the Tyne as we called the Sector Controller. It looked as if the raid was well and truly on; our only chance of a chase would be on something going home.

To our surprise and disgust we were told to carry on with our easterly course, away from the raid in progress. The GCI Controllers would obviously have their hands full, but this seemed daft. We were flying at nearly 5 miles a minute, still to the east. My AI looked as if it was working beautifully, but we wanted something to chase. After about six minutes Ben suddenly said:

"Nuts to this. I bet the ruddy Controller is having a cup of tea and a bun. He's forgotten all about us. I'll give him a call…"

"Hello, Homestead. Rounder three-six. Any news? Still steering zero nine zero, angels ten!"

"Hello, three-six. Continue on zero nine zero. There should be something for you in a few minutes."

"Zero nine zero. Listening out."

"What do you make of that?" I asked Ben.

"Maybe there's another raid coming in. Let's hope so."

The Hercules engines seemed to take on a more menacing roar and I could imagine Ben settling himself down in his scat. For the twentieth time since we had been airborne I made the minutest adjustments to my already perfect picture.

"Hello, Rounder three-six. Bandits in your vicinity now. Good luck."

Mark 7 had a maximum range of about 7 miles. My eyes

were straining; I was willing something to show up on the screen.

Then it was there. Maximum range, slightly starboard and about level. Switch over to intercom.

"Contact. Range 7 miles, slightly starboard, about the same height."

"Good show."

"Range decreasing pretty fast…It looks like a head-on… Get ready for a turn port."

"Right."

The range was certainly decreasing fast. It was still a bit out to starboard – we must have been on almost parallel courses – and just a bit below us.

I knew the drill for what we would have to do. The practices were paying off. Leave it over to starboard. Wait till it was about 6,000ft away and then turn away from it through 180 degrees in a hard turn. We would have to lose a bit of height too. If we turned too soon we might finish up in front of it; too late, and we would be faced with a long stern chase. Turn towards it and we would be flying across its course and might be seen. No, our manoeuvre was to turn away from it, and if all went well we should finish up about 3,000 or 4,000ft behind, and I knew that as we nearly finished our turn I could expect to see it again on my AI coming in from port.

The range was nearly down to 6,000ft now.

"Hard port 180 degrees. Go down 1,000ft. Let me know when you're nearly round!"

"Port 180 degrees. Down 1,000ft."

It worked like a charm; we finished up just where we should have been. We closed in without any difficulty to about 2,000ft, when Ben got his visual. From a little closer in he identified it by twin fins and thin fuselage as a Dornier 217 and I was able to turn around to look for myself.

Ben wasted no time. He closed in to 400ft and gave it a two-second burst. There were strikes on the tail unit and a large white flash came from the starboard engine. A burst of inaccurate return fire came from the dorsal turret. Then the Dornier turned on to its back as the port wing went under. It dropped in an almost vertical dive, with the Beau behind, too far behind for Ben to get another shot in.

We reached 5,000ft, with the Dornier screaming away from us still going down almost vertically. It drew away from us until we lost it in thick haze. The time was 1.15am and we were about 15 miles east of the Tyne. We circled for a few minutes but did not see it go into the sea, nor could I pick it up again on AI.

We climbed again and called Homestead to inform him of our combat and to see if there was anything else doing. We could see ack-ack bursts and a few searchlight beams over the Newcastle area. Apart from the thick low haze it was clear, although there was no moon.

Homestead told us to fly at 8,000ft and put us on a north-south patrol some 20 miles out to sea. At about 01.30 we were warned that there was something near us but to investigate carefully as there were several friends around.

A minute or two later I had another contact, this time on an aircraft crossing us from starboard to port and slightly below us at a range of 5 miles. We turned quickly to port in order to cut him off, losing height as we did so. There was no difficulty in closing in on an aircraft that was weaving gently from side to side but flying level. Ben had his visual at nearly 2,000ft and I turned to watch proceedings. We had to go in to just under 1,000ft before we identified it as another Dornier 217. Our luck was certainly holding. We had really expected to see a Beau this time.

Ben gave it a two-second burst, which produced strikes all along the fuselage. It also produced some fairly accurate fire from the Dornier's turret. The tracer hosed up towards us and then swept over us. Ben gave it a second short burst, which silenced the gunner. Just as well, for in the next second Ben had to pull right up over the Dornier to avoid ramming it. The belly of the Beau would have made an excellent target for the gunner.

As Ben pulled the Beau up, the Dornier dropped away to port in a steep dive. We were a bit late in getting round and down after him. Although I could see him on AI about 3 miles away he was diving too steeply and I soon lost him as he drew away.

We were credited with a probable for the first combat and a damaged for the second. Again we had drawn first blood for the squadron with the new equipment and the Mark 7 AI had proved itself. The only weakness that had been exposed was that the navigator was at a big disadvantage when trying to follow an aircraft down in a steep dive. While his own aircraft was pointing almost straight down at the ground, his AI tube was apt to be swamped with ground returns which obscured the blip he was chasing.

There was always something to learn, even at this stage. Ben was kicking himself for not having polished off these two Dorniers properly. It was apparent that we must stalk our victim extremely carefully and try to get in a really punishing burst of fire without his suspecting our presence. Once a really determined enemy pilot knew he was being chased by a night fighter he could, and undoubtedly would, turn his aircraft almost inside out to escape. Even a mediocre bomber pilot would make himself very difficult to follow under these circumstances.

The raid had been a fairly big one for those days. Some thirty bombers, flying in two waves, had attacked the Newcastle area and had run into fairly stiff opposition from the guns. The Dorniers were obviously on their guard. Although the Turbinlites had monopolised the GCI they had had no success, and I believe that it was the very last time they operated.

During the next few days Ben managed to get in quite a lot of air-firing practice.

In the second week in June we were to have a little light relief. Flight Lieutenant Cosby was getting married and Ben was to be best man. Koz's navigator, Pete Bowman, and I were given a couple of days off to help represent the squadron at the wedding which was to be held in London.

We had worked out a very good schedule. We would board a train to Newcastle that left nearby Ashington at about 14.00 hours on the day before the wedding. We would arrive in Newcastle at about 16.00 hours and, after a cup of tea, repair to the Turkish baths for a couple of hours. Dinner was next on the list, and then by the greatest good chance No. 13 Group Fighter Command, in which we served, was holding a Headquarters Ball at Newcastle Assembly Rooms. We had all managed to get an invitation to the ball through a WAAF Officer of Ben's acquaintance. At 22.30 hours the night train left Newcastle for London. What could be better or simpler? – that was what we thought.

At about 11 o'clock on the morning of the great day a select party was assembled in the bar of the officers' mess for a drink or two before the wedding party had lunch and set off for Newcastle. Beer was the usual aircrew drink, and it would perhaps be as well at this point to state that, although aircrew personnel were not generally noted for their abstinence, I came across very few hard drinkers in the RAF. Beer usually seemed to be regarded as best. Let me also say though, that given the slightest excuse for a party, no better body of men existed anywhere to make the most of it.

Our little party was having a quiet beer or two, but, as more and more chaps came in after the morning's flying, the two or three beers became three or four or more. Nevertheless, all was under control until the Wingco arrived and insisted on putting a large rum into each beer. From that moment on the situation definitely deteriorated. Pete Bowman and I decided that we needed something solid inside us and we went in for lunch in a happy mood. Eventually the groom-to-be followed us but nothing could move Ben from the bar, where there appeared to be all the makings of a right royal party.

After lunch we went back to the bar for another noggin or two, until somebody suddenly realised that we would be hard put to it to catch our train, unless we pulled our fingers out. We were poured into various vehicles and a cavalcade of cars rushed us to Ashington station. We arrived three minutes after the train should have left, but, as the train was ten minutes late, all was well. An hilarious crowd of officers pushed us into a compartment and we were off. All was well for a few moments only, however, for we found that we were in a buffet car, not an ordinary compartment. True, the buffet car served only tea or coffee, but Ben produced a full bottle of whisky from somewhere with a conjurer's flourish and the position became somewhat more complicated. Pete Bowman and I decided that we could not face up to Scotch, so we found some seats and retired temporarily from action.

When we arrived at Newcastle, Pete and I looked for Ben and Koz. We were just in time to see Ben disappearing arm in arm with the roughest, toughest Norwegian sailor I had ever seen. We spotted Koz, who informed us that Ben had chummed up with the matelot in the buffet car and between them they had demolished the bottle of whisky, no doubt with the aid of Koz, who was now just a little worried about his best man. Koz decided that he must go forth and find him, so we agreed to meet later on at the Assembly Rooms.

Pete and I agreed that what we needed was a good long walk, so we decided to skip the Turkish bath, had a lengthy walk around the town and finished up in an excellent grill-room. We partook of a sumptuous repast, complete with wine and liqueurs. By this time it was nearly 8 o'clock. In those days of the blackout the Ball started at 7 o'clock, so we ambled gently along to the Assembly Rooms.

As we mounted the stairs we heard the soft music of a dance band and the not-so-soft sound of a voice which seemed to be demanding brandy. It was quite unmistakably Ben's voice. We tracked him to an ante-room which was in use as a coffee bar. He was being told most politely that there was no brandy there, but he seemed to think they were keeping it under the counter. His eyes were slightly glazed, but he was quite steady, so we took him off to a real bar for a drink. Koz was there, looking a little the worse for wear, though he was in palpably better shape than his best man.

Koz told us that he had been hard put to it to shake off the Norwegian sailor, whom Ben had rather wanted to take to the Ball. Koz was now a little worried about the prospect of us all getting down to London intact for the day after. I for one could see his point. He said that we should all 'stick together', but Ben was as slippery as quicksilver and had already vanished. We learned that he had caused something of a commotion earlier by storming into the Air Officer Commanding's private bar and demanding brandy. Luckily the AOC had not been there and a friendly staff officer had attended to him.

When he was not engaged in the search for liquid refreshment, Ben spent his time at the Ball looking for the WAAF officer who had kindly helped us in obtaining invitations and whom he had arranged to meet there in order to thank her. All WAAFs look pretty much alike in uniform so things were not too easy for him. He had therefore adopted the idea of tapping the shoulder of each WAAF officer that he saw, and when the face turned out to be other than the one for which he was seeking he used a formula then in current use: "Not you, Momma. Sit down!" There were several astonished females about the place.

Eventually he managed to find the right one, and I must give her full marks. She turned out to be an angel in disguise, for she assessed the situation at once and actually managed to keep Ben out of mischief, or almost. She could not stop him from sliding a few potted palms across the ballroom floor in the middle of a dance and it was through no fault of hers that Ben tripped up the AOC during a dance: that was the unfortunate sort of accident that could have happened to anyone.

By some truly remarkable chance we were all on the platform at Newcastle station some minutes before the

London train was due to leave. We found an empty compartment and settled down for a comfortable journey. Ben had different thoughts about this however. Announcing that he was going to see if he could get a drink, he had slipped through the door before anyone could move to stop him. He had long legs and used them to very good advantage, making his way along the platform, with the three of us in hot pursuit.

On his way he noticed a rather small bicycle resting unattended against some luggage. He leapt on to it and for a few magical moments he weaved among piles of luggage and waiting passengers. Soon the force of gravity was too much for him. The front wheel hit something and he dived over the handlebars, sliding along the platform for a few yards on his forehead. We dashed up and collected him. Apart from a badly grazed forehead he seemed to be all in one piece, so back to our compartment we trooped – this time keeping a very wary watch on Ben, who announced that he was chilly and put on his greatcoat, which he had placed on the luggage rack. To our astonishment he produced a full bottle of Scotch from one of its capacious pockets – 'for later on'.

The train moved off and we settled back in our seats with a good deal of relief. We were really on our way. Ben had settled in a corner and dozed off, but after about an hour the train slowed down rather jerkily and woke him up.

The train stopped, although we had thought it was non-stop to London. Ben opened a window to see what it was all about and we heard someone call out "Doncaster!"

"Anywhere I can get a drink?" yelled Ben and, quick as a flash, the door was open and he was chasing back along the platform like a hare. Out we tumbled after him; we could just see him disappearing in the darkness when a guard warned us that this was not a proper stop and put his whistle to his lips.

The three of us scrambled aboard as the train started off again. We looked out of the window, but there was no sign of Ben. Koz wanted to pull the communication cord, but Pete and I restrained him. He was very depressed about it all and we tried to make suggestions about what he should do. I believe that we finally decided that the best thing would be to ring Doncaster station as soon as we arrived in London and have Ben put on the first available train. Unfortunately we were almost certain that he would not be in time for the ceremony. It was a tricky problem.

We were pretty gloomy when, about an hour after we had drawn out of Doncaster station, we heard some raucous singing coming from down the corridor. To our great surprise and joy, Ben hove into sight, brandishing an almost empty bottle of whisky in one hand and with his other arm round the guard's neck. He had just managed to jump aboard into the guard's van and had enjoyed a little party with the occupant of the van before setting off in search of us.

We all duly arrived at the wedding. The graze on Ben's forehead gave him an air of bravado that went well with his uniform.

Squadron Leader Lewis Brandon
DSO, DFC and Bar
1942

Wing Commander James Gillies ('Ben') Benson
DSO, DFC and Bar

141 (Beaufighter) Squadron, 1942. The author is on the back row, fifth from right

The author and Wing Commander 'Ben' Benson
in front of their Mosquito *Eager Beaver*

Publicity photo of the author (on the left) with Robert Donat, 1942

1945

Date	Hour	Aircraft Type and No.	Pilot	Duty	Remarks (including results of bombing, gunnery, exercises, etc.)	Day	Night
					Time carried forward :—	697·45	432·20
						Flying Times	
					TOTAL FOR JANUARY DAY	3·55	
					TOTAL FOR JANUARY NIGHT		11·15
					GRAND TOTAL DAY	697·45	
					GRAND TOTAL NIGHT		432·2
					TOTAL OPS HOURS 337/45		
					SCORE 9 DESTROYED		
					3 PROBABLY DESTROYED		
					3 DAMAGED		
					6 FLYING BOMBS DESTROYED		
					4 TRAINS CAT B		
					1 LORRY CAT B		
5 3				Offensive Sorties.			
8 3				Defensive Sorties.			
					.... S/L OC "A" FLIGHT		
					.... Wing C.O.		
					157 SQDN.		
9.3.45	10·35	OXFORD	F/Lt DANN	TO DISHFORTH	FOR 6 GROUP LECTURE TOUR	1·15	
13.3.45	15·00	''	W/JWHITEHOUSE	RETURN TO MANNORBA		1·00	
26.3.45	14·00	''	F/O HICKMAN	TO COLERNE	WEATHER DUFF. LANDED NR SWINDON	1·45	
					TOTAL TIME ..	701·45	432·2

Facsimile of page taken from the author's log book
at the end of his 3½ year partnership with 'Ben' Benson.
January 1945

The de Havilland Mosquito Mark II in flight

157 (Mosquito) Squadron, RAF Swannington, 1944. The author is on the back row, seventh from right

CHAPTER 6

Lofty Hamer's Epic Flight

W E returned to Acklington to receive the glad tidings that the squadron was to move to Tangmere on 23rd June. Tangmere was a really plum posting, right on the South Coast near Bognor Regis. Since the beginning of the Battle of Britain it had seen lots of action. Every night flight from there had to be an operational patrol in view of the fact that the long-range warning system was not so effective against low-flying aircraft and a good deal of anti-shipping reconnaissance took place in the English Channel. A patrolling Beau would often be whizzed off to identify a plot that had suddenly popped up on the ground station's radar screen.

It was grand to be in the sunny south and 141 Squadron had the good fortune to be allotted the greater part of an exceedingly pleasant private house as a squadron mess. It was a really beautiful, large house standing in its own grounds and the owner still lived in part of it. Nearly all the original furniture had been left in the rooms, and in the lounge there was a super radiogram with stacks of excellent records. The lady of the house would bring wonderful bunches of flowers with which she would adorn the lounge. Vegetables and salads from the kitchen garden helped out the food sent to us from Tangmere which was some 4 miles away, and a hard tennis court and a squash court were available for our use. I cannot remember the name of the house now nor of the owner, but we were certainly lucky and very grateful.

As a matter of fact, for the remainder of my operational service with night-fighter squadrons the aircrew always had a large house some distance from the airfield for a mess. This was in order that the normal daily routine of a station mess should not disturb us if we had been flying until the early hours of the morning. The set-up was not always as pleasant as at Tangmere, but we lived in some really lovely houses.

With hardly any exceptions, the chaps appreciated their good fortune and respected the property.

While we were at Tangmere preparations were in hand for the Dieppe Raid, although we did not know that at the time.

I was standing outside dispersal one day when a jeep full of chaps in RAF uniform drove by. I spotted some faces I knew and waved for it to stop. They were members of the RAF Film Unit, and most of them were cameramen from Denham studios where I had known them before the war. The CO was Teddy Baird, who had been the most popular assistant director in the film business before he left to join up in 1940. They were destined to do some grand work which included superb shots of low-level bombing raids taken under operational conditions.

The stay in the south was to be short-lived for Ben and me, however, and in exactly one month we were posted as instructors to 62 Operational Training Unit at Usworth, near Sunderland. Before we left we carried out seven patrols at Tangmere, but unfortunately we hit on a quiet spell while we were there. We had one chase after a possible Bandit but did not get near enough to establish contact on AI. My hours of flying had risen to 202 by day and 82 by night.

Our move to 62 Operational Training Unit was part of a new deal for the training side of Fighter Command. An appreciation of the standard of instruction at the OTUs had been made when squadrons, particularly night-fighter squadrons, complained of the poor quality of new crews. The answer to the problem was very simple: the large majority of the instructors were sadly lacking in operational experience or in ability.

In the past, when instructors had been required from them, squadrons had used the request as an opportunity for getting rid of their least useful crews. Fighter Command had therefore decided that in future they would ask for instructors by name.

The tour as instructor would last between six and nine months and would count as a rest from operational flying.

Ben had been on Operations far longer than I had and he was certainly due for a rest. As it was realised that teamwork played such an important part in successful night fighting, crews were sent on rest together. That was why I found myself Usworth-bound although I had been on a squadron for only a year.

Very rightly, an almost clean sweep was being made of the most experienced crews on all squadrons to ensure that they did their share of instructing, which was obviously so important if well-trained crews were to come to the squadrons from the OTUs.

In the extremely sensible way in which Fighter Command usually acted, the position was explained to the crews involved. I feel it only right to say that as a member of aircrew I was always treated as an intelligent adult. I was never in the unhappy position of wondering what on earth was going on so far as my own particular relationship to the war in general was concerned. At all times we were kept up to date with developments in the main trend of the war, and through the Intelligence Section, which was an important feature of all operational RAF stations. Anyone who wished to keep in touch with current events was encouraged to do so. In my experience nothing was too much trouble for the often very hard-worked Intelligence officers, and the information available was amazing in its scope. The whole Intelligence set-up seemed to me to be worthy of the highest praise and we were to find that this applied even more later on, when we were engaged in offensive operations.

Ben and I spent three months at Usworth, where our job was the training of navigators in the basic use of AI. Mark 4 AI was used for this and we flew in Anson aircraft which had been converted into flying classrooms in which an instructor could deal with two pupils at a time. Although it was a fairly interesting job for me, it soon became very boring for Ben, who spent most of his time flying the classrooms.

In September 1942 Ben and I were informed that we had both been awarded the DFC. For some while at the beginning of the war, it had been decided that personalities should be suppressed when mention was made in the Press of any specific operation. After a while it was realised that an excellent opportunity for recruiting publicity was being missed. I do not know if a similar thing was done in the other Services, but in the RAF a form was sent to all aircrew in which they were asked to supply some details of their pre-Service life.

Presumably as a direct result of this some of the London papers mentioned my name and my connection with Robert Donat. I received a telegram of congratulations from Donat, followed by a letter in which he asked me to look him up next time I was in London. He was engaged in making a film, *The Adventures of Tartu*, at the old Gaumont British studios in Lime Grove, better known now as television studios. I had a 48-hour pass soon after and made a point of going to see him. I spent a very pleasant afternoon at the studios and a publicity still was taken, with Donat wearing the uniform of an officer in the Roumanian Iron Guard and Brandon in his Royal Air Force uniform.

A few months later Ben and I were on leave in London whilst Donat was playing in the stage show of Shaw's *The Devil's Disciple*. We saw the play and thoroughly enjoyed it before going round to his dressing-room for a chat. He was a grand actor, and it was a great pity that so much of his acting life should have been dogged by ill health.

Although I was slightly darker and a couple of inches taller than Donat, I doubled for him several times in his films as well as being his stand-in. He usually seemed to be cast to play opposite rather tall actresses – Marlene Dietrich, Rosalind Russell and Greer Garson – so that he used to build himself up more or less to my height. With a little make-up, there really was a remarkable resemblance between us.

I doubled for him in two or three scenes during the filming of *The Ghost Goes West*, for which he wore a kilt and a pencil moustache. Of course I was dressed identically to him and the make-up department had given me a moustache just like Donat's so that I was often mistaken for him. Bob was sitting just off the set one day between shots, while the final lighting adjustments for the next scene were being made with me. One of the electricians went over to him and said:

"Hello, Lew. I should think you get blooming well fed up, sitting around here all day."

Bob Donat, playing up to him, smiled: "You bet I do."

A minute or two later the assistant director called out:

"Ready for you now, Mr. Donat."

As Bob passed me he commented:

"One of your fans thinks you don't have enough to do, Lew!"

Ben's promotion to Flight Lieutenant had come through when we were posted to Usworth and I became a Flying Officer in August. Although our jobs at Usworth were important and necessary, life was awfully tame after the thrills of night fighting. We stuck at it fairly well, but in mid-September, by some ruse which I have forgotten, we managed to get ourselves down to Tangmere for four days. We wangled a few Beau flights, but the only one we did at night was one that nobody else particularly wanted to do – a dawn patrol. As this entailed being up all night in order to take off at about 4.30 in the morning, no wonder nobody else was very keen. There was no activity and we were alone for the whole patrol, so that we were not able even to carry out practice interceptions. I remember being hard put to it to keep my eyes open and I was heartily glad when it was over.

One interesting trip we did during this short stay with 141 Squadron was to Castle Camps, a new station in process of construction situated near Cambridge. Flight Lieutenant Stevens, a pilot who had been sent on rest from Tangmere at the same time as Ben, had been posted to Castle Camps for his rest. A unit had been formed there to try out high-flying Mosquitos which had been fitted with special engines and a pressurised cockpit. We had heard that there was a possibility that the Mosquito would be the night fighter of the future, so that it was an excellent opportunity of finding out something about the 'Wooden Wonder'.

We found that in spite of early teething troubles experienced on the Mosquitos the pilots were very favourably impressed with them. They certainly looked elegant and streamlined beside the snub-nosed, stocky Beaufighter.

At Tangmere we heard the sad news of the death of Lofty Hamer, the pilot with whom I had originally been crewed. He had been killed in action whilst on patrol a week before. The heroism displayed by this gallant NCO was such that we heard that he had been recommended for a VC, the only posthumous award that could be made. Unfortunately it was not granted, but that fact does not detract from his bravery.

The actual Combat Report made out by the Intelligence Officer with the aid of Flight Sergeant Walsh, Lofty's navigator, read as follows:

On September 8th, 1942, a Beaufighter, Pilot Warrant Officer Hamer, Navigator Flight Sergeant Walsh, was put on to a Bandit when airborne from Tangmere. At 1.40am, a visual was obtained on a Heinkel III, 100ft above. Beau throttled and at 300ft opened fire when about 15 miles south-cast of St. Albans Head, height 8,000ft. No strikes were seen from the first burst and a second long burst was given as the Beau closed in to 200ft. Strikes were seen all over the Heinkel, mostly on the starboard wing and the fuselage and the starboard engine burst into flame. There were several return bursts of fire, but the Beau was still below the Heinkel and was not hit. The Beau again dropped back to 300ft and a twelve-second burst of fire was given until the cannon ammunition was exhausted. There were flashes, mostly from the fuselage and tail unit, and the whole starboard wing caught fire. A large piece of the wing suddenly flew off and hit the Beau, swinging it to starboard. This enabled the Heinkel to get in a long burst of fire and the Beau's starboard engine burst into flames.

At the same time the navigator saw several red flashes around the pilot in the cockpit. He was certain the pilot was hit, but although he asked repeatedly: "Are you okay?" all the pilot said was: "You bastard." And went in again with machine-guns blazing until all the return fire had been silenced.

By this time the flames from the Heinkel's furiously blazing starboard engine were blowing back right past the Beau and its starboard wing was flapping. A few seconds later the Heinkel went down in a streaming ball of fire into the sea. The pilot said in a strange, unnatural voice: "He's ablaze now all right." Then he asked for a homing. He was told he was about 50 miles south of Tangmere. The Beau was at 6,000ft, with the starboard engine still ablaze, so the navigator suggested baling out. The pilot eventually replied in the same strange voice: "Hang on a bit. We may cope."

He throttled the starboard engine right back and the fire died down to a spluttering glow, and made for home on the port engine. From this point the pilot was obviously labouring under great strain and Walsh had to suggest to him everything that he asked the Controller. He would not let Walsh do the transmitting nor would he allow him to come forward to open the front escape hatch. That, he said, would only knock off the speed, and he told Walsh to stay where he was.

Shortly afterwards he asked the Controller for the nearest land and was told to steer 010 degrees and that searchlights would help him. Two minutes later he was told that the nearest airfield was 12 miles east. He informed the Controller: "At 2,000ft. Only a few minutes left." Next the Controller said there was an airfield alight 5 miles west [presumably Hurn]. The pilot thought he turned west but subsequent events showed that he turned east.

He then said that he could see no lights anywhere and Walsh suggested that they should both bale out and again asked if he should open the front escape hatch, but the pilot said: "No, we can't afford the speed. Hold on a sec, I think we can make it."

Then he saw the north coast of the Isle of Wight and told Walsh he should bale out, so Walsh once again asked if he should open the front hatch, but his pilot said: "No. I think I can make it."

Suddenly the port engine, which had previously cut for a few seconds, stopped altogether. The pilot, after they had wished each other good luck, held the Beau at 1,000ft while Walsh baled out and made a good drop on to the beach near Newtown, Isle of Wight. The Beau, with no engines, then lost height so rapidly that the pilot, in his presumably wounded condition, could not possibly get out and, saying to the Controller, "Afraid I'm finished. I'll have to go over now," he crashed on the mainland near Lymington, Hampshire and was killed. The Beau was a total wreck. Walsh felt that, although there was ample opportunity for them both to have taken a chance by baling out while over the sea, Hamer deliberately held on in his determination to bring the Beau back to base or over land, well knowing that by doing so he was almost certainly going to his own death.

Enemy aircraft confirmed as destroyed. Weather clear but dark. End of report.

The report speaks for itself, but I had a talk with Walsh. He told me something which throws more light on the incident. Hamer knew that Walsh was a non-swimmer. Only a few weeks before Hamer had been godfather at the christening of Walsh's child.

"Greater love hath no man than this, that a man lay down his life for his friend."

After this short session with 141 Squadron, we returned to Usworth, where we remained until the end of October. We were then posted to 54 OTU at Charterhall, in Scotland – just in time, I should imagine, to save Ben's reason. This establishment enjoyed the nickname of 'Slaughterhall' in the night-fighter world. Not undeservedly either, for the aircraft most in use there were Beaufighter 2s, with Rolls-Royce Merlin engines in place of the Bristol Hercules. The engine factory of the Bristol Aeroplane Company had received several direct hits during a raid on Bristol and had been so badly damaged that there had been a considerable hold-up in the production of Hercules engines. Beaus were in such demand that, as a temporary measure, Merlin engines were installed in a number of Beaus. The Beau I with Hercules engines was a tough and reliable aircraft, albeit rather clumsy, but with Merlins it became just a little underpowered for its extremely heavy weight. This was without doubt the cause of many accidents.

Ben had been told at our interview with the Station Commander that he would be a Flight Commander of one of the training squadrons. Charterhall was the most dispersed station I ever saw. Everything was miles from anywhere else and tons of leather must have been wasted in the interminable tramping from one place to another.

We eventually arrived at our new domain to find all the flight personnel outside the dispersal hut watching one of our Beau 2s which was coming in for a belly landing. We were told that the pilot was an instructor with a pupil crew aboard. He had been unable to get the undercarriage down. The usual drill was for the pilot to bring the aircraft down very carefully on the grass verge of the runway and it was inclined to be rather a spectacular landing. Luckily, however, the pilot in this case made an excellent job of his landing and nobody was hurt.

It was rather a shattering introduction to Charterhall and did nothing to dispel the rumours we had heard of the unreliability of the Beau 2. To be fair, though, I flew many times at Charterhall in them with Ben and with other pilots and never had a moment's anxiety. Incidentally, while we were stationed at Acklington with 141 Squadron we were at dispersal one day when word went round that one of the dreaded Beau 2s was circling the airfield. Somebody 'phoned Flying Control to ask what it was doing and received the information that it was on its way to Drem, where 264 Squadron was to re-equip from Defiant to Beau 2s. We watched as it made a perfect landing and taxied to the Flying Control tower, quite near us. The engines stopped and out stepped a trim little female figure of about 5ft nothing. She was a ferry pilot on a routine job.

We could just imagine a repetition of this at Drem, with probably the whole squadron out on the airfield waiting for their fearsome replacements to arrive!

At Charterhall the navigators who had received their basic AI training in the Ansons at Usworth would be crewed with pilots in the last stage of their flying training. Occasionally more experienced pilots who had been flying in other Commands, or perhaps on day fighters in Fighter Command, came to Charterhall to learn a bit about night fighting and to find a navigator to fly with.

The aircraft used were mainly Beau 2s, with a few old Blenheims. My job was to fly, usually in the Beaus, with a pupil crew. The routine was for the pupil crew to carry out an interception on another aircraft. I would then criticize constructively and then do an interception myself, following this with another run by the pupil navigator. I found that this period as instructor, both at Usworth and at Charterhall, helped enormously to consolidate in my mind all the lessons I had learnt during my first operational tour. I had quite a bit of lecturing to do on the ground as well and I found that on the whole the job was interesting – but it was dull compared to operational flying. The only sensible thing to do, anyhow, was to make the best of it and we were soon able to count the days towards our return to operational flying.

Two things remain in my mind from the routine of Charterhall. Flight Lieutenant Richard Hillary, the author of that fine book *The Last Enemy*, was killed there whilst flying as a pupil. He had been shot down in flames during the Battle of Britain and had been terribly burnt. I lived in the same mess as Hillary for over two months and to me, as to several other instructors there, it seemed inevitable that he would crash eventually. His physical disabilities caused by the terrible burns he had received were such that he was not really capable of flying an operational aircraft. Somewhere along the line somebody was guilty of not accepting the responsibility for telling him what he must have known in his own heart: that he must accept the fact that his operational days were over. As it was, not only was he killed but the navigator with whom he had been crewed lost his life unnecessarily.

The other memorable event at Charterhall was the screening of the film *Pimpernel Smith*, in which I appeared as a Gestapo officer. As Charterhall was in a fairly remote spot, films were shown weekly in the various messes, and it can be imagined that my appearance on the silver screen was the cause of much comment and commotion.

Almost six months to the day after we had begun our rest Fighter Command enquired if we had any special preference for the squadron we would join for our second tour. Quite understandably we had discussed this subject many times during the past few months and we had narrowed the choice down to four squadrons. Without being conceited, we knew that any squadron was always glad to receive experienced second-tour crews, so that we would most likely be posted to the squadron which we made our first choice.

There was, of course, a sentimental hankering after 141 Squadron, which had moved from Tangmere to nearby Ford. Nearly all the chaps we had known had been posted from the squadron by now, however, and they were still equipped with Beaus.

The next two squadrons we considered were 29 and 85 Squadrons. 29 Squadron were at West Malling in Kent; although still equipped with Beaus, they were high on the priority list for Mosquitos. 85 Squadron were at Hunsdon, in Hertfordshire; they had just re-equipped with Mosquitos. Both these squadrons had been very successful in the past and not unnaturally were rather favoured by Fighter Command when any new equipment came along. They always seemed to be kept on airfields well in the forefront of operations and were certainly regarded as the plum squadrons to get to.

Finally there was 157 Squadron, almost a brand-new
squadron; it had been formed in December 1941 and
declared operational by the end of April 1942. It was the first
night-fighter squadron to be equipped with Mosquitos, and
although there had been many trials and tribulations with the
Mosquitos at first, these had all been sorted out and everyone
seemed to think that the Mosquito was a really fine aircraft.
157 Squadron were at Castle Camps, near Cambridge.

We decided to ask for a posting to 157 Squadron, with 29 as
second choice. The main reason was that we thought that being
on a fairly new squadron, with its traditions yet to be made,
would give us more scope. It was a decision we never regretted.

At last the great day dawned. On February 16th, 1943, we
were posted to 157 Squadron at Castle Camps. We had
managed to escape after seven months as instructors. The
squadron was a very happy one with a grand bunch of
fellows led by a really superb Commanding Officer. Wing
Commander V. J. Wheeler had won the MC and Bar in the
First World War and had already won the DFC in this war.
Between wars he had been a commercial airline pilot and
had thousands of flying hours to his credit. Nobody knew
his age, but we referred to him affectionately as 'Pop',
though not in his hearing.

Ben had met Pop Wheeler before and had an amusing
story to tell about him. While Ben was at Gravesend with
141 Squadron they were joined by 85 Squadron. This
squadron had a fine record flying Hurricanes over Dunkirk
and they were commanded by Peter Townsend. Townsend
was furiously engaged in building up his own and the
squadron's night-flying experience. He himself had about
20 or 30 night hours under war conditions, which was
pretty good for those days.

One day in the bar at Gravesend a grey-haired gentleman
in the uniform of a Pilot Officer reported to Townsend,
saying that he had been posted to 85 Squadron and that his
name was Wheeler.

"Good show. Have you done much night flying?" asked Townsend.

"About 3,000 hours, sir," was the reply.

"No. I meant how many night-flying hours have you done?"

"That's right, sir. About 3,000 night-flying hours."

It transpired that Pop Wheeler had some 15,000 hours total flying to his credit with Imperial Airways!

A great deal has been written about those 'Wooden Wonders', the ubiquitous Mosquitos – Mozzies as they were known by those who flew in them. Originally designed as a high-level, high-speed photographic reconnaissance aircraft, it had been adapted as night fighter, light bomber, long-range day fighter and eventually it was almost doing the job of a heavy bomber. Undoubtedly the most useful and successful aircraft produced by any nation during the last war, it carried out all its roles perfectly.

In the night-fighter version the pilot and navigator sat side by side in a reasonably roomy cockpit, with the navigator to the right of the pilot and slightly behind him. This time the AI had been installed in such a manner that the navigator faced forward. This was altogether a much friendlier arrangement than in the Beau, as well as being more practical for the teamwork which was such an essential part of night fighting. The Mozzie was manœuvrable, comfortable, reliable and proved to be readily adaptable for the various modifications that became necessary as more and more demands were made upon it.

The cockpit layout was excellent, although perhaps a little cramped when both members of the crew were above average size as were Ben and I. Entry and exit were effected through a small door on the right-hand side of the cockpit, and a collapsible steel ladder was carried inside, as the door was some 8ft from the ground when the Mozzie was stationary.

The AI-equipped fighter was armed with four 20mm cannons, which were belt fed. Their muzzles were just under the nose of the aircraft. The long-range fighter, which did not carry AI, carried four machine-guns as well.

Although the Mozzie was introduced into squadron service as a night fighter as early as 1942, and in spite of the immense and rapid developments in aircraft production on both sides during the next few years, it was still the best night fighter in use anywhere when the war ended three years later. It was a truly remarkable achievement by the de Havilland Aircraft Company, who had produced the Mozzie as a private venture, and by all those who helped in fitting out the night-fighter version of this amazing aircraft.

There was one snag however. Fighter Command had perpetrated a blunder almost as bad as the Turbinlite fiasco. They had decided to install in our beautiful Mozzies, in fact in all the first batch of Mozzies to reach squadrons, a wretched new Mark of AI. This was Mark 5 AI, which had all the faults of the early Mark 4 plus many of its own. It was a retrograde step even when compared with Mark 4, but when compared with Mark 7 it was rather like going back to a divining-rod. There were times in the next few months when I thought that if I took a hazel twig, persuaded a Dachshund to lift a leg against it and then took that twig into the Mozzie with me, it would lead me to a German more readily than would Mark 5 AI.

It had been wished on to Fighter Command by the experts of the Fighter Interception Unit. While it might have been all very well for these highly skilled pilots, it was not very practical for the average squadron pilot. It had the same aerial system as Mark 4 and the main difference was that it had an extra tube, placed so that the pilot could see it and could carry out the final stages of the interception himself. All the navigator needed to do was to read out the range. At night the pilot had his hands full enough without giving him an extra tube to look at. Then, too, when he should have been searching the sky for a visual, he would have to look at this indicator tube. Apart from these points, the equipment suffered from very serious limitations that were not discovered until we had been struggling with it for several months.

I was so delighted to be back on a squadron that I tried not to let the drawbacks of Mark 5 get me down. We just had to make it work. Nevertheless it was really frustrating that, just when I had begun to think that I had acquired some glimmerings of knowledge regarding AI technique, I should begin to lose contacts that I well knew I could have held easily with Mark 7 or even Mark 4 AI. What was even worse was that in March, on two operational patrols, I was given contacts by the GCI Controllers that I failed to turn into visuals. These may or may not have been enemy planes, but it made me feel that I was letting the side down. This dislike of Mark 5 was by no means confined to navigators or even to 157 Squadron. Command were told of this dislike very forcibly by all squadrons, but unfortunately a large number of sets had been made and it took some time to get them replaced.

Consolation was just around the corner, however, for the night-fighter force had become so formidable in comparison with the greatly reduced enemy activity that it was decided to turn some of its strength to offensive operations. At this stage of the war there were some twenty or more British night-fighter squadrons, each with twenty-four or more crews straining at the leash. To initiate this new spirit of offence, half a dozen crews were selected from each of eight squadrons for training, Ben and I being among those selected from 157 Squadron. An experienced crew from one of Fighter Command's Intruder squadrons was attached to us for this training which consisted of a few lectures and a short programme of cross-country navigation exercises for us to carry out.

CHAPTER 7

The Offensive

A S far back as the summer of 1940 a few British fighters had been allowed to prowl about at night near enemy airfields hoping to catch bombers taking off or landing. It was realised that in order to obtain the maximum possible success against a bomber raid the bombers should be attacked for as much of their journey to and from the target as possible. What better place could there be for our fighters to start and finish than the enemy's airfields?

For a while this operation, which had become known as Intruder, had been carried out by a few selected pilots from the night-fighter squadrons, with the odd Hurricane or two operating on bright moonlight nights. These 'cat's-eye' aircraft – that is to say, aircraft operating by night but not carrying AI – had enjoyed considerable success and two or three Intruder squadrons had been formed. These squadrons flew Havocs at first, but they were replaced by Mozzies, which proved admirable aircraft for the job.

As these specialist Intruder squadrons became experienced, they operated in all conditions of darkness, not relying on bright moonlight to aid them in navigation or seeing their potential victims. They were not allowed to carry AI, however, because of the danger of an Intruder being shot down over enemy territory. The German radar experts might have been able to learn too much from our AI, if they had been able to gather the parts from a wrecked aircraft and use it against our bombers.

In spite of the fact that no AI was carried, the Intruders managed to shoot down a considerable number of German planes. If an enemy bomber raid was expected, Intruders would take off to patrol as many known German bomber bases as possible. They would try to arrive just at the time when the bombers were taking off; and, of course, if they saw a bomber taking off, they did not have to worry about identifying it. A second wave of Intruders would take off so as to be on patrol near enemy airfields when the bombers were trying to land. If visibility was good enough they would also shoot up aircraft parked on the airfield – an extremely difficult and dangerous operation this, but one in which they soon excelled.

Undoubtedly one of the reasons for their success in destroying so many enemy aircraft by night was that the Germans had poor night-flying training. They seemed to need lots of lights on the airfield and even kept their own navigation lights on for taxying and take-off. Ben and I were to see this for ourselves later.

In spite of the incredible successes of our Intruders, which must have been only too apparent to the Huns, they hardly reciprocated at all. Herr Hermann Goering's fatuous statement that not one bomb would fall on German soil had a very fortunate sequel. When Bomber Command began dropping bombs in ever-increasing numbers on the Reich, an order went out that all the Luftwaffe's fighters were to be used, as far as possible, for the defence of the Fatherland.

As a direct result of this, except for one brief spell which was too little and too late, Bomber Command of the RAF had no trouble from German Intruders. The imagination boggles at the chaos and confusion that could have been caused by a couple of squadrons of really intrepid German Intruders when the tremendous Bomber Command raids were assembling over England. Often at a particular time hundreds of American bombers and escorting fighters would be returning from daylight raids; the skies over the North Sea and Britain would be swarming with our aircraft and ace German crews would surely have been counting their scores in dozens.

Even if Intruding had not resulted in the direct destruction of a large number of enemy aircraft, the effect on the morale of the German bomber force must have been very great. If an Intruder is thought to be in the vicinity of an airfield when bombers are taking off or landing, lights must be reduced to a minimum and the chances of a taxying or flying accidents are increased. A couple of bombs, even the small ones that Intruders carried, are not calculated to ease the nerves of the bomber crews although no material damage might be done. A bomber shot down on or near its own base, either before or after a raid, is far more of a morale-destroyer than an aircraft 'missing' after a raid. It must become very wearing to be a frequent pall-bearer at the military funerals of one's erstwhile comrades.

Ben and I were very pleased to have been selected for Intruder training although I was rather worried at first by my sad lack of navigational experience. Although I was wearing the 'N' brevet, I had not done a navigation course. I found that low-level navigation was, luckily, fairly easy if one could use a little maths and a lot of commonsense, had an accurate forecast of wind and at the same time kept a sense of proportion.

The help given by Flight Lieutenant Hodder, the navigator member of the Intruder crew attached to us, was invaluable. A short navigation course had been incorporated in Ben's pilot training, so that he knew far more than I did about the job I would have to master.

Our first practice cross-country was carried out in daylight on March 20th, 1943. My logbook says: 'Cross-country 1a OK,' but I seem to remember Ben pointing out several errors that were creeping in, just in time for me to extricate myself. On all these navigation training flights Ben's patience and help was absolutely unbounded. He certainly helped me over the jittery period of my navigation. After our first cross-country we had a spell of bad weather, and I note that at 09.30 one anything-but-fine morning, we did a bad weather patrol, without any excitement other than that of getting down again all in one piece.

In April we carried out six cross-countries by day and two by night. Five of these were moderately successful, but even in my logbook I could record the other three trips as only 'partially successful.' Fortunately, the final night trip that we tried went as smoothly as silk; honour was saved.

157 Squadron was moved to Bradwell Bay in Essex in early April and so part of our training was carried out from there. Bradwell was right on the coast not far from Southend-on-Sea. It was a wonderful station from the operational point of view, with every facility one could wish for. The officers' mess had been the residence of the local MP, Mr. Tom Driberg, and very pleasant it was too.

In the very early hours of April 15th we were scrambled with several other Mozzies to intercept a raid heading for London. The Combat Report made out by the Intelligence Officer read:

> Flight Lieutenant Benson reports: We took off from Bradwell at 00.15 hours on 15th April 1943, and under Debden Sector control we got AI contact at range of 9,000ft, our height 10,000ft, on an aircraft coming head-on towards us, and had a visual immediately afterwards. It was above us and I identified it as a Dornier from its plan view.
>
> We did a hard turn port and saw it again, flying in and out of cloud. E/A [enemy aircraft] started fairly violent weaves and changes in height as we were closing in fast at about 270 knots indicated air speed. We overshot and last saw E/A below and to port. AI contact was also lost. E/A's course was west when we picked him up over the coast south of Bradwell and he was going east when we lost him.
>
> We were vectored back on to course 100 degrees and handed over to GCI Trimley Heath, Controller Squadron Leader Kidd, who told us to stay on this vector. Contact was obtained immediately at range of 10,000ft on an aircraft dead ahead and crossing from starboard to port. We did a hard turn and dived, as the aircraft was 1,000ft below. A visual was obtained at a range of 2,000ft, and as we came in E/A was a little above, weaving gently and changing height. We closed in rapidly and identified

aircraft as a Dornier 217.

At 200 yards I gave him a three-second burst with four cannons from astern and above, but saw no results. I fired a seven-second burst and saw strikes, first on the port engine and mainplane which immediately burst into flames. These spread down the port side of the fuselage until the whole aircraft, including the tail, was ablaze. There was no return fire. E/A went down in a shallow dive, turning to port, and finally hit the ground at 00.45 hours.

The R/T and intercom packed up when I fired and I was therefore unable to continue the patrol.

Immediately after the combat, my navigator, while changing fuses, saw another Dornier crossing behind us from port to starboard, but was unable to inform me about it in time to do anything. It was subsequently found that the ten-pin plug on the intercom amplifier had vibrated slightly out or its socket and was not making proper contact. Camera gun not used.

The wreckage of a Dornier 217 [believed to be Mk JI.] was subsequently inspected at Layer Breton Heath, Essex, and numerous 20mm cannon strikes were found in and around the port engine and propeller. Three of the crew baled out and were captured and the body of the Wireless Operator was found in the wreckage.

End of Report.

We had actually managed to destroy a Hun using the dreaded Mark 5 AI, but by the same token, we had lost one that we should have destroyed. Then came the misfortune with R/T and intercom, which meant that we could not speak to the ground or to each other.

As soon as our earphones went dead I assumed that a fuse had blown. I manœuvred round in my seat to change fuses – no easy feat in a Mozzie for someone of my bulk. The Dornier was still on its way down, flaming like a rocket. I was keeping half an eye on it as Ben banked our Mozzie to watch the inevitable crash. Between looking at the Dornier and the fusebox I suddenly caught sight of the third Dornier crossing behind us only about 1,500ft away and slightly above us. Just at that moment the crash came below us. For a second or two Ben must have thought I was banging him on the back in congratulation at our success. By the time I could make him realise, by dint of much shouting over the noise of the engines, that there was another Dornier around, it was too late to do anything about it. We had no method of communication to each other, although I was able to steer him home by sign language.

The loss of our R/T caused another incident. Our combat had taken place just north of Bradwell and had been watched by many of the station personnel. They had heard the roaring engines and the cannon fire followed by an aircraft going down in flames. The Sector Controller had told them by telephone that we were after a Hun near the airfield and so, of course, they went out to watch. Later, when the GCI Controller reported that he had put us in contact with a Bandit but could no longer get any reply from us to his repeated calls on R/T, they could only assume that we had gone down in flames. Not long afterwards Ben and I landed and two very substantial ghosts walked into the crew room.

Next day we were able to drive over to see the wreckage. The Dornier had crashed quite near to a farmhouse, the only building within miles. We had noticed that it had gone into a shallow dive, and after hitting the ground had slithered along, shedding pieces all the way, and finally had come to rest some 50 yards short of the house. One wheel, all ablaze, had actually bounced over the house and had finished up in the fork of a large tree. The farmer did not seem to realise how lucky he had been that the bomber had not crashed right on his house. He was most irate because some saplings in an orchard had been badly bent!

We heard that the ack-ack guns had also claimed to have shot down our Dornier, but the cannon shells in the wreckage disproved their claim. Incidentally, we had seen no gunfire other than our own.

The next day, we carried out our final cross-country trip. It was by daylight and included making a landfall on the Isle of Man. According to my navigation, the Isle of Man was still in the right place.

It had been decided by Fighter Command that we should operate only on bright moonlight nights until we became more experienced in our new role. An operation called Ranger had been devised which entailed flights over pre-planned routes into enemy territory. The targets were trains, lorries, barges and anything else that moved at night. In view of the curfew imposed by the Germans on occupied countries, these could be safely assumed to be enemy targets. If by chance we did see an enemy aircraft we were at liberty to attack.

With the willing aid of the Intelligence section Ben and I had worked out half a dozen sorties. These had been registered with Fighter Command so that on the first suitable night we would be able to select the most likely-looking one. Intelligence would pass on our actual times of crossing out and returning so that we would not be mistaken for enemy raiders.

We did not have to wait very long, for three days later conditions were just right for our first trip over enemy territory. Our plan was to cross out at Beachy Head, enter France near Le Treport, on past Lens and Cambrai to St. Quentin, from which a very busy railway line led to Paris. We would patrol this line between St. Quentin and Creil, about 20 miles from Paris. This line was used quite a bit by Germans going to and from leave in Paris. We hoped to assist in making at least part of their leave memorable.

I do not know how Ben was feeling about this first offensive sortie, but, although I was terrifically keen to have a go, I fully expected that the moment we crossed the enemy coast we would be continuously bathed in searchlights, fired at from the ground with every sort of shot and shell and probably chased by fighters into the bargain. I really believe, however, that I was rather more worried by my lack of navigational skill than by anything else, such was my faith in Ben, the Mozzie and my good luck.

We tested our Mozzie that afternoon. We were to fly a long-range day-fighter version in view of the fact that we could not take AI over enemy territory. All went well and we then had a long wait, as the right conditions of moonlight would not occur until almost midnight; we were due off an hour before midnight. There was a final Intelligence check-up and Met. forecast, then we were on our way to the aircraft.

Ben taxied to the end of the runway, and as he opened up the engines for take off said exultantly:

"Well, chaps, here we go!"

We climbed on course for Beachy Head, and after a few minutes, when we were crossing the Thames Estuary near Tilbury, some bright spark began firing at us from the ground. He was way behind us with his aim, but I hurriedly flashed a recognition signal and the firing ceased. Everyone should have been briefed about our trip, so someone had blundered.

It was a glorious night and we could see the moon coming up as we passed over Beachy Head. At the same time, I took a quick look around the cockpit to see that everything was in order. I noticed that the voltmeter was reading low and called Ben's attention to it.

"Hey, Ben! The voltmeter is reading 24 volts. It's usually about 27 or 28."

"Well, everything seems to be working all right."

"Yes. It's probably only the Mozzies fitted with AI where it has to be 27 volts or more for the stuff to work properly."

"Good enough. Now we've got this far on the perishing trip I don't want to turn round!"

"I quite agree. Let's press on!"

Press on we did. Low and fast over the sea, we had been told, so low and fast it was. At 500ft their radar would not get much warning of our approach. The sea crossing did not take very long – about twenty minutes. Then we were approaching the enemy coast. Climbed a bit as we neared the coast, then up to 3,000ft as we went over to give us more room in which to manœuvre if we were engaged by guns or searchlights. Meanwhile I had to look for the vital landfall which would tell me if we were on course.

Good – we had hit the coast dead on track. I gave Ben the course to steer for Lens. Nobody seemed to be taking any notice of us as we made our way to our stretch of railway, flying now at 2,000ft. My navigation was working out well. Landmarks kept showing just in the right places and the moon was shining brightly. But not a sign did we see of the wily Hun. Not a lorry, not a barge, not a train, not an aircraft, not a searchlight nor a trace of flak. It was just like a training trip.

We reached St. Quentin without incident, saw our railway and turned on to our new course along towards Creil. We were down to 1,000ft now. Within a couple of minutes we saw a train puffing merrily along in the same direction as us, its smoke looking like a blob of cotton-wool in the moonlight. Ben made a wide sweep to get into a good firing position.

As he did so I pointed out a second train about a mile from the first, coming towards it. We seemed to poise for a second as Ben came out of the turn, perfectly positioned for the attack. This was the moment we had been waiting for.

Down swooped the Mozzie, straight for the engine of the first train. It looked like a toy engine as we started our dive, but it rapidly became larger until at about 400 yards' range Ben pressed the gun button. The four cannons and four machine-guns blazed away, bringing bright flashes from the engine as the shell struck home. It was only a two-second burst though and I had expected Ben to go on blazing away until the very last moment. Then I realised that, at the very moment that the guns had stopped firing, the cockpit lighting had gone out and the R/T had a dead sound.

The aircraft was still flying well enough. We had passed over the train, climbing away from it now. The train still puffed along, perhaps not quite so merrily and with steam coming in dense clouds from places from which no steam really ought to come.

Ben switched over to intercom. To our relief we found that we could speak to one another, albeit rather faintly.

"Looks like the main fuse," I informed Ben. "I'll have a go at changing it!"

This was a major operation for a large navigator in the confined space of the Mozzie cockpit. For the next ten minutes or so I fiddled with fuses, but they all seemed to be in order. In the meantime Ben had muttered something about:

"Getting the hell out of here" – an idea that had my full support.

I had been astonished throughout the trip by the lack of hostility from the foe. I fully expected, particularly now that we had fired our guns in anger, to find every gun, searchlight and fighter within a couple of hundred miles after us.

After some time I decided that I was wasting my time with the fuses, so I turned around and left them alone. At this moment I noticed that the generator voltmeter was showing only 8 volts. This meant that the generator was not charging the batteries and was something I could do nothing about. Clot that I was – I should have remembered about that voltmeter and not wasted time changing perfectly good fuses.

Presumably Ben had had the same ideas of imminent enemy action that had flashed through my brain. He had been taking violent evasive action in all directions at some 300mph, although, as it happened, nobody seemed to be paying the slightest bit of attention to us.

Suddenly it dawned upon me that in all the excitement I had completely forgotten to keep my log up to date. The last entry was our arrival at St. Quentin which I had been writing in when the train was spotted. Consequently I had omitted to enter the time of our arrival. Although I knew where we had attacked the train, I had little idea when the attack had taken place and still less of how long we had been taking evasive action.

When I asked Ben what course he had been flying on since the encounter, I was even more worried; he told me that he had just beetled off from the scene of the attack and really had no idea. Roughly south-east perhaps and would I give him a course to steer for home.

This set me back for a moment, then I realised that the finer points of navigation must be forgotten – I must aim for England. I gave him a course of 310 degrees to steer and fondly hoped that we might arrive in the neighbourhood of the Somme Estuary, where we had originally intended to come out.

The moon was going down and a slight haze was forming. We climbed to 2,500ft hoping to see some landmark that would assure us that we were on track. We pressed on without incident and I even went so far as to give an ETA – estimated time of arrival – at the coast, which I opined we would cross in about twenty minutes.

My estimated twenty minutes joined the limbo of things lost; another ten minutes joined them. I began to feel that all was not well. A rumour was then current that the wily Hun had some sort of ray that could magnetise an area of the heavens and put the kibosh on all compasses in that area. Perhaps our compass had been affected and we had been flying south all this time – visions of a prisoner-of-war camp flashed through my mind. I passed my thoughts on to Ben, who had the presence of mind to line up our compass with the North Star. It was working very well.

Just as I was wondering if it ever would appear, we saw the coastline ahead of us. At least, we thought we did. Then we found ourselves flying slap over the middle of a large town that spread over both sides of a wide river. One of the things we had been warned against was flying near large towns. It was sheer suicide, we had been told. Nobody took the slightest notice of us and I was able at last to identify our position. We were over Le Havre, some 60 miles south-west of where I had fondly imagined we were. I gave Ben a course to steer, and as we crossed the coast, heading for Beachy

Head, two searchlights lazily flicked on to us and then flicked off again. This was the only hostile act the Hun committed against us that night.

Our worries were not quite at an end however. It was very likely that we would be plotted by our own defences as a hostile aircraft. Admittedly, we would be crossing in at Beachy Head, where we were supposed to, but we were well over half an hour late. Nor did we have any R/T with which to make contact.

We did have a Very pistol, though, with the appropriate signal cartridges, and if we had been fired on by our own side that would have been a means of identification.

No one took any notice of us, though, as we flew low over the Channel to make our landfall at Beachy Head. We flew over that very welcome landmark and made our way back to base, where we ate a not-very-well-deserved night-flying supper of bacon and eggs. On this, our first trip over enemy territory, we seemed to have made every sort of boob possible – and had got away with it. One thing was certain, though: we made none of those errors on any subsequent trip.

Three nights later we carried out a second Ranger patrol, looking for barges on a network of canals. As a navigational exercise it went perfectly, but, although the moonlight was bright, there was fairly thick haze. We saw nothing to shoot at and nobody took the slightest notice of our activities so far as we knew.

Whilst the moonlight period lasted the squadron was interspersing Ranger operations with normal defensive patrols. Ben and I did our share of both, though the defensive patrols seemed to have lost some of their thrill.

CHAPTER 8

That Was a Church Steeple

O N May 18th we took off just before midnight for an extensive tour of French and Belgian railways without having to worry about buying any tickets. We crossed the French coast near Dunkirk and flew to Amiens. From there we patrolled a long stretch of rail as far as Rheims without spotting anything, so we turned back along the same line with the intention of following it to St. Quentin, then to Mons and home via Ostend.

We were approaching the little town of Laon, when we saw the smoke of a train ahead of us. Ben manœuvred our Mozzie so as to have a shot at the engine with the moon behind it. I was not going to be caught out this time. As we were turning I scribbled away madly, keeping my log up to date. I looked up again just as we were coming into firing range. Suddenly something big and black whizzed past my side of the cockpit.

"What the devil was that?" I gasped.

"Oh," said Ben, "a church steeple. We are flying down the side of a hill."

So we were.

The train was standing in a little station. Ben gave the engine a good burst of cannons and machine-guns and we wheeled around on to our original course again. We saw several strikes and flashes from the engine and a great cloud of steam was coming from it when we left.

At Haumont, near Mons, we saw a number of trucks in a railway siding. Two attacks on them produced good results. We then went home without further incident, rather impressed with the knowledge that a single aircraft seemed to be able to roam around over enemy territory without much interference.

Two nights later we were on the night-flying programme for a defensive patrol. We had carried out the usual test run on our aircraft, which we had found perfectly serviceable, and it was late afternoon when we landed; we left our parachutes and flying helmets ready in the aircraft while we went off for tea.

There was no enemy activity that night, but after waiting round a while we were ordered off for a practice GCI with another Mozzie. We walked out to our aircraft, struggled in and settled down. Ben signalled to the ground crew, pressed a button and one engine roared into life. A moment later he signalled again, pressed the button, but the second engine could only raise a splutter.

Several more attempts to start the engine failed. A spare aircraft which had been tested was always available, so we transferred ourselves and our kit rapidly to this other Mozzie. Both engines started promptly this time and off we went, climbing up to 18,000ft for some practice runs. We acted as fighter for the first run, which went reasonably well, but towards the end of the interception I began to feel 'proper poorly'. My stomach was hurting and I could feel a headache coming on which, as I was normally very fit, was most unusual.

We became target for a while so that I had more time to feel sorry for myself. My stomach was really hurting badly now and my head aching so that my thoughts were becoming rather fuzzy. In spite of this it did occur to me that Ben was having some difficulty in understanding what the Controller was telling him. Some of the replies he was giving seemed rather puzzling although I could not put my finger on what was wrong.

A thought oozed into my fuddled mind. Oxygen! Was the oxygen switched on? Early in my flying training lectures had been given about the danger of lack of oxygen when flying high. It could produce very strange results, the most frequent being a sense of irresponsibility and even symptoms of drunkenness.

I checked the dial that indicated the oxygen pressure. That was right, I had not forgotten to switch it on, for it was reading 20,000ft. As I turned my head from looking at the dial I felt something dangling from my helmet. It was my oxygen tube. In my hurry to get in to the spare Mozzie, although I had remembered to switch the oxygen on, I had omitted to plug in my tube. We had been warned to use oxygen from take-off at night and we had been airborne over an hour. I remedied my omission at once, turned the pressure to full on for a few seconds and breathed deeply. I felt much better at once.

I glanced over at Ben; sure enough, his oxygen tube was dangling from his helmet. He plugged in and we were both okay. This lapse might well have had serious consequences.

We had another uneventful Ranger trip next night, when we were again in the St. Quentin area. Very thick haze made visibility extremely poor on this occasion, but it was a good navigational exercise. Two nights later, in our defensive role, we were scrambled after some Bogeys at 2.50 in the morning. The Bogeys turned out to be our own returning bombers.

On May 27th we were informed that we could consider ourselves fully operational for Intruder patrols and found that we were detailed forthwith for such a patrol that very night. We were to carry out a thirty-minute low-level Intruder patrol of Bergen/Alkmaar airfield. This was in northern Holland, about 5 miles inland from the North Sea, and was believed to be used by German bombers.

We took off just before midnight and made the long North Sea crossing at about 400ft, aiming to cross the Dutch coast some 8 miles north of Bergen. As we approached the coastline we made height to 2,500ft in order to get a good view of our landfall and to have a bit of height for emergencies. We found that we were almost 15 miles south of where we should have been. For once the wind forecast that I had been given was badly out. Instead of 15 knots northerly it was nearer 30 knots.

Fortunately there was a large lake just inland from where we had hit the coast, so that we were able to pinpoint our position. We had agreed on a figure-of-eight patrol about 5 miles to the north of the airfield. The idea of flying a figure of eight was that the patrolling fighter should at all times be able to see the target and be able to dart in quickly if necessary.

We flew past the airfield, keeping fairly well over to the east, and took up our patrol. As we had passed by we had seen a few lights on the ground but it did not look very active. We were staying about 5 miles north, where we would be least likely to deter any intrepid enemy aviators from taking off.

It was quite a dark night with a fair amount of haze, which thickened noticeably as we patrolled. We were at 2,000ft now and the wind tended to take us towards our target. After about twenty minutes, the lights on Bergen/Alkmaar had been obscured by the haze and we were finding it increasingly difficult to see any landmarks at all. Still, we decided to stick it out for the full half-hour.

By the time our patrol was due to finish, we had climbed to 5,000ft in the hope of seeing something through the ever-increasing murk below but without success. When we decided to call it a night, we dived for the coast on our way home. We thought we were still 8 miles or so to the north of the airfield. But no – we must have drifted right over the wretched place. Suddenly the air around us was alive with tracer shells hosing their way up towards us. Our bit of extra height stood us in good stead, as Ben stuffed the nose of the Mozzie down and we gradually left the firework display behind us. It is frightening stuff, tracer at night.

We had a very interesting change of jobs in June. Ben and I were sent, with two other crews from 157 Squadron, to Predannack in Cornwall. There we found ourselves under the orders of Coastal Command. We learned of an intriguing situation that had arisen.

The anti-U-boat warfare was mounting to a crescendo at this time. Packs of U-boats were hunting out in the Atlantic, often guided by German long-range aircraft operating from western France. To combat the U-boat packs, Coastal Command had Sunderlands, Halifaxes and Liberators operating from Cornwall, flying out over the Atlantic to spot them. They had been having a fair amount of success, so much so that the Jerries had popped a squadron or two of Junkers 88s on the Brest Peninsula to chase Coastal Command's big boys. They, in turn, had asked Fighter Command to lend them some Mozzies to harry the Junkers 88s. That was us.

The next move was for some Focke Wulf 190s to arrive at Brest and Mustangs in Cornwall to oppose them. So we had our own little war in the south-west.

Six night-fighter squadrons had each been told to supply three Mozzies complete with ground and air crews, making a composite squadron of eighteen aircraft. These were divided into two flights and Ben was put in command of one of these flights. When we arrived at Predannack almost the whole of Cornwall was covered in a sea mist which persisted for nearly a week and prevented any flying. With the aid of some of the Coastal chaps it gave us an opportunity of finding out something of our new role and working out some tactics.

Our job was to act as long-range day fighters for patrols in the Bay of Biscay and we were to be put to any use that Coastal Command needed us for. Our first patrol was in search of a U-boat that had been reported damaged and surfaced way out in the Bay. We took off at 10.30 on the morning of 11th June as one of a formation of six Mozzies. We flew straight out over the Atlantic for 400 miles.

We had been advised to fly at about 100ft for two reasons: we would be difficult for a vessel to see and any other aircraft about were likely to be higher than 100ft and would therefore be fairly easy for us to spot. Although we were to try to locate the U-boat, we had to be prepared for anything. We reached the end of our easterly leg and turned south for 100 miles. It was a lovely summer day, with not a cloud in the sky. Our six aircraft were well spread out but there was nothing to see.

We turned for home, and when we were rather more than 50 miles from the French coast we spotted a lone trawler. We had been told that the Germans were using trawlers to pass on information to their long-range aircraft or to the U-boats. There was an agreed limit of, I believe, 10 or 15 miles for trawlers fishing legitimately, but this chap was way outside those limits.

It was a very difficult decision for the leader of our formation to make. We had been told that anything of this sort was fair game but the trawler did look very defenceless. However, orders is orders, and the leader ordered an attack. We each gave it a burst as we flew over it and then pressed on, leaving it still afloat but smoking.

We had been flying for four hours and fifty minutes by the time we landed. The low flying over the sea had been very tiring for the pilots and all of us felt that our eyeballs were popping out with the constant strain of searching sea and sky. After this trip we found that special tinted glasses which were provided for us were a great help.

The next day was spent swimming and sunbathing. The day after, however, we were off at 8 o'clock in the morning. Ben and I were to lead a formation of four Mozzies on a patrol which would take us within sight of the north-west coast of Spain. As Flight Commander, Ben would naturally be called upon to lead some of these patrols. It meant, however, that with my exceedingly small amount of navigational experience I would have to accept the main responsibility for the navigation. Still, I had long ago realised that commonsense was perhaps the most valuable asset for a navigator, and so we would have to hope for the best. Luckily, Coastal Command, received very good, reliable forecasts of wind and weather which helped immensely.

On this patrol we were not detailed to look for any particular target. In order to cover as large an area of sea and sky as possible, we flew in very loose formation. Ben, as leader, had his Number Two about half a mile away, behind and to starboard. Number Three was level with us and a mile or so to starboard, while Number Four was half a mile behind and to starboard of Number Three. If anything appeared ahead or to port, Ben would lead the chase. If something came into sight over to starboard our Number Three would become leader and we would act as his Number Three.

As we were within sight of the Spanish coast, I was able to check my navigation visually and found that we were pretty well on track. We turned to fly parallel to the coast, some 20 miles from it, but by the time we had finished this leg of our flight we had seen nothing. We turned for the long sea leg home and had been flying for some ten minutes when Number Three spotted an aircraft on his starboard side. It was just a speck at first, but as we opened our throttles for the chase it got rapidly bigger. We were soon able to identify it as a Focke Wulf Kondor, the military version of the Kurier.

It was an enormous four-engined aircraft, heading out into the Atlantic, and it made no attempt to get away until it was much too late. It was a beautiful day again with just a few white clouds at about 3,000ft over towards the land.

The Mosquitos came screaming in at full speed. The Kondor's crew was keeping a poor look-out or else their aircraft recognition needed brushing up. They kept coming towards us. Probably the last thing they were expecting to meet so far down in the Bay of Biscay was us. The leading Mozzie was almost within firing range before the Kondor realised that something was amiss. It went into a very tight turn in an effort to make for safer parts – much too late, for the leading Mozzie was already pumping shells into him. Seconds later the next Mozzie was assisting.

In no time at all large chunks of Kondor were falling off. Before Ben could get near enough for a shot, down into the sea went the enemy aircraft streaming black smoke behind it. We watched it crash and part of it floated for some seconds, with a great pall of black smoke hanging over it.

Two days later we set off on what promised to be a real thriller. We were leader of the second section of four Mozzies in a formation of eight. A pack of five U-boats had been reported way down in the Bay. A strike force of Coastal Command bombers was going after them. It was thought probable that the U-boats would have a cover of Junkers 88s and we were to deal with them. As so often happens when hopes are built up, it all fizzled out. Neither the Mozzies nor the strike force saw anything at all.

Fighter Command decided that instead of maintaining the composite squadron at Predannack, it would be better to loan a night-fighter squadron. The squadron selected was 141 Squadron and we had just one more patrol before being recalled to 157 Squadron. This time, however, the weather was poor and we made an early return.

When we returned to our squadron there had been some changes. They had moved from Bradwell Bay to Hunsdon, in Hertfordshire, and at last Fighter Command had realised the futility of continuing with Mark 5 AI. They were to scrap it and we were to get Mark 4 in its place. This was very welcome news.

We flew on an Intruder patrol of St. Trond airfield, near the German border in Belgium, on June 26th. Wuppertal, to the east of the Ruhr, was being bombed, and although we saw lots of activity in that direction, St. Trond was silent as the grave.

July turned out to be quite an eventful month. To everyone's joy, the first of the Mark 4 equipped Mozzies arrived. On July 2nd we were on defensive patrol with Mark 4s. Although no Huns appeared we had two grand runs with GCI and felt full of the joys of spring.

Next night we were off on an Intruder patrol of St. Trond again. It was a low-level patrol and my navigation was spot on. We arrived at our patrol point, a few miles west of the airfield, dead on time and dead on track. We were happy to see several lights on the airfield and began our figure-of-eight patrol. Nobody seemed to be taking any notice of us, so we edged over a little closer. After a few minutes Ben said urgently:

"Hey, what's that? There's something moving down there."

"Can't see anything... Oh yes, I can. The other side of the airfield. Is that it?"

"That's it all right. That's a pair of navigation lights,

chum. I'll bet he's taxying round to take off. Let's have a look at the target map."

I spread out the special map of St. Trond airfield that we had collected from Intelligence. Ben studied it.

"There's the runway they'll be using. See, he's nearly at the end of it now. Here, take this!"

He whipped the Mozzie round into position with perfect judgment. Down we dived just as the aircraft on the ground turned on to the runway. We could see it gathering speed as its engines were opened up. The idiot still had his navigation lights on; perhaps we would be able to put them out for him.

They must have realised on the ground what was about to happen. A series of two-star red Very lights were fired in quick succession from the ground. By this time our dive had brought us just behind and below the other aircraft. It was a Dornier 217 about 300ft up.

As Ben opened fire a two-star white Very light came from the Dornier. A long burst of cannons brought strikes all along the fuselage as the Dornier went straight down. It crashed with a large explosion half a mile from the end of the runway.

Three searchlights flickered up from the airfield, searching for us. But we were no longer there. After a few minutes we were back on our figure-of-eight patrol and the searchlights went out. So did all the other lights on the airfield. We were able to maintain our position quite well, however, by the fire of the Dornier, which burned for the further half-hour we were on patrol. Occasionally the proceedings were livened up as ammunition or bombs exploded.

I was sent to Ford, in Sussex for the ten-day Navigator Leader course on July 13th. I must have done reasonably well, for soon after my return I was told that I would be posted as Navigator Leader to 488 New Zealand Squadron and would fly with their CO 488 Squadron were at Drem, in Scotland; I was to report there on August 8th.

At first I was very upset about this posting. I would become a Flight Lieutenant, but I was due for that, anyway, at the end of August. Also Ben and I were getting on so well now that it seemed silly to waste our experience. However, I had learned the wisdom of bowing to the inevitable, so that although I could not pretend to like the idea of the posting I gave up worrying about it.

Ben and I did a couple of defensive patrols which were uneventful and an Intruder patrol. This was notable only because it was the first time we had flown over Germany itself.

At the end of July Ben went off on leave. I hoped like the devil that we would somehow be able to get together on a squadron again. For the time being, though, it was goodbye.

I did flying tests with two other pilots in preparation for Intruder patrols, but the weather was bad and both trips were called off. I was particularly sorry that the second one had to be cancelled. Not only was it arranged for my last day with 157 Squadron, but I was to have flown with the Squadron Commander. He was quite a character and I would dearly have loved to have carried out an operational sortie with him.

I have mentioned earlier that Pop Wheeler had been awarded the MC and Bar in the First War and the DFC in this. Recently he had won the Bar to his DFC. He had a great hatred for the Germans. I believe that he lost a brother in the First War; certainly, when he flew over enemy territory, he never brought back any ammunition with him.

On one trip he had been over Germany he found on his way back that he still had a few rounds left. He remembered having heard that the Casino at Knocke had been taken over for the use of U-boat crews. He therefore asked his navigator to give him a course to steer for Knocke, although it was miles off their route. It appeared that the Wingco knew Knocke very well, so he proceeded to the Casino and used up the ammunition.

Whilst there was a war on he was interested only in operational flying and he just could not get enough of that. On every possible occasion he leapt into the air and always took the patrols that would take him over Germany. He was flying so often at one stage that Fighter Command had to restrain him with a series of very strongly worded signals.

Not long after I left 157 Squadron he was posted to a non-operational job, where he sulked for a short time. He then managed to pull some strings and wangled himself into an operational flying job in Bomber Command. He was posted 'missing' after a big raid on Cologne. We all found it difficult to believe somehow that such a character could be dead. He had become an almost legendary figure and I always imagined that he would turn up having organised his own private army behind the German lines.

I made my farewells to 157 Squadron and set off for Drem, where I found the most awful shambles. I met the CO with whom I was to fly, Wing Commander Burton-Gyles, DSO, DFC, an extremely pleasant and capable young man. He was, unfortunately, later killed flying from Malta.

He informed me that he would brief me a little later about my job, but at the moment he had a rather difficult interview on his hands. A clot of a sergeant pilot had, the day before, landed a Beaufighter. While he was still running along the runway, he had, for some unknown reason, pulled up his undercarriage, thereby doing no good at all to the said Beaufighter. The Wingco had torn the sergeant off a frightful strip and had ordered him to report to his office next day to receive another. The next morning, on the very day I arrived, the Wingco had been airborne in a Beau and had committed the selfsame offence as the sergeant pilot. I had put in my appearance just a few seconds before the interview was to take place.

Whatever was said, the interview was soon over and the Wingco put me in the picture. Until recently he had been a Flight Commander on an Intruder squadron and had no experience of AI. He had been called for an interview at Fighter Command, where he had been told that he was to be posted in as CO of the New Zealand night-fighter squadron, No. 488. Morale was rather low on the squadron and he was to sort it out. They would give all the help they could, and Mr. Jordan, the New Zealand High Commissioner, could probably be very useful.

He had joined 488 Squadron in June 1943, and found the reason for the low morale pretty obvious. The squadron was fed-up with doing almost nothing. They had been formed in June 1942 at Church Fenton in Yorkshire, and in September of that year had moved to Heathfield, where I had originally joined 141 Squadron. There they had remained, getting more and more fed-up with the lack of action. They were supposed to be a defensive night-fighter squadron, but had not had a single chase on an enemy aircraft since they had been formed. There was just nothing doing at Heathfield.

The only operational flying any of them had carried out had been on Ranger patrols and they felt completely out of the real war. They had achieved a fair amount of success against trains and lorries on the Ranger patrols, but the New Zealanders, anyhow, had come an awful long way to fight in this war, and they wanted really to come to grips with the enemy.

Wing Commander Burton-Gyles summed up the situation right away and got in touch with Mr. Jordan. A meeting was arranged in London and the Wingco had been given an opening straight away. The High Commissioner had asked him how the boys were and if there was anything they wanted. The Wingco told him in no uncertain terms that the boys were fed-up with flying obsolescent Beaufighters on a non-operational station and that they wanted to fly Mosquitos on a station that was operational.

Mr. Jordan thought for a moment, and then said that in a day or two he would be dining with Mr. Winston Churchill. He would see what he could do.

He was able to do quite a lot, for in July 488 Squadron found themselves right at the top of the priority list for re-equipping with the latest Mozzies.

They had moved to Drem early in August, and when I arrived the re-equipping had just begun. The Wingco had asked for an experienced navigator as leader, who would also fly with him in order that he himself should become operational with the new equipment as soon as possible. The new Mozzies were fitted with Mark 8 AI, a slightly modified version of Mark 7. I was the only navigator with experience of this type of AI, and even the Special Signals section, who dealt with the servicing of AI, had no knowledge of its workings.

The Special Signals Officer was sent off on a hurried course with a few picked men, and a 'circus', a travelling Mark 8 school, visited us at Drem for a week or two. I had to set in motion an intensive training programme and also to fly with the Wingco at every available opportunity. By dint of much hard effort all round things had started to fall into slightly better shape towards the end of the month.

On August 26th three bombshells fell upon us in quick succession. Wing Commander Burton-Gyles was posted to command 23 Squadron at Malta. Our Special Signals Officer, having just completed his Mark 8 course, was repatriated to New Zealand, and we were told that on September 3rd we would be moved to Bradwell Bay, right in the front line.

Move we did – without a CO or a Special Signals Officer and still not fully re-equipped with Mozzies. However, we were now in 11 Group of Fighter Command. They rallied round with lectures and briefings, for there was a great deal for these very keen chaps to learn. A new CO and Special Signals Officer were posted in and more new crews arrived to bring the squadron up to full strength. Some of these new crews were not trained on Mozzies or on Mark 8 AI, so that training had to go on apace.

Although 488 was a New Zealand Squadron, most of the navigators were British, as were almost all the ground crews. When I joined them, the only British pilots were, I believe, the CO and one of the Flight Commanders. The new CO was Wing Commander Peter Hamley, AFC, who was also British. He was a very experienced day pilot who had been CO of a Spitfire OTU. He had completed a short course at Cranfield, one of the night-fighter OTUs, and it had been intended that he should spend three months as a supernumerary on an operational night-fighter squadron, before being posted to one as CO. The crisis on 488 Squadron had meant that he had to be posted in to us straight from Cranfield where he had crewed up with a pupil navigator.

Just as the previous CO had done, he asked me to fly with him so that he might become operational as soon as possible. He was a very easy chap to get on with, and I explained that if possible I would very much like to recrew with Ben at some later stage. He agreed to see what could be done about this when the time arose.

Fortunately we had almost a fortnight without enemy activity and we were able to carry on with intensive training. The chaps were tremendously keen and I felt sure that there was plenty of ability too; nothing could replace experience, however, so practice, practice and more practice was the watchword.

The Wingco had decided not to put himself on the night operational programme until he had quite a bit of practice with me. In the meantime, I did three defensive patrols with Flight Lieutenant Ball, a very experienced night pilot whose navigator was on sick leave. We had some useful practice, but there were no Huns around.

On the night of September 15th I was having dinner in the mess with the Wingco when he said that he thought it would be a good idea if we spent an hour or two at dispersal with the Duty Flight. I could introduce him to anyone he did not know, and it was undoubtedly the best way for him to get acquainted with the aircrews.

After dinner we set off in the Wingco's staff car for 'B' Flight dispersal. There seemed to be lots of activity on the airfield, but we were quite unprepared for the scene that met our eyes when we arrived at 'B' Flight. There was a terrific hullabaloo. Ground and aircrews were yelling and dancing around with joy. Almost exactly a year after the squadron's formation the very first enemy aircraft had been shot down.

The excitement and enthusiasm were understandable. After a minute or two we managed to get the story. Two Mozzies had been up on patrol, practising with GCI, when some Bandits had appeared. Flight Lieutenant Jimmy Gunn, one of the most popular pilots on the squadron, had been the successful pilot. Four more Mozzies had been scrambled but all the activity was now over.

The combat had taken place just north of Bradwell. Just as when Ben and I had a similar combat in much the same place, it had been watched by the excited chaps at dispersal. They had heard the cannon fire, followed by the sight of an aircraft going down in flames. An R/T set which had been fitted up in dispersal had enabled them to listen to the Controller actually putting Jimmy on to a bomber. They had heard his triumphant "Tally ho!" when he sighted it. This had been the cause for the jubilation in which we joined.

Hardly anyone noticed when the CO was called into the Flight Office to speak on the telephone. I did, though, and I also noticed that he was trying to catch my eye as he stood in the doorway, with a serious expression on his face. He motioned me to go into the office with him.

"That was Control on the phone just then," he said. "They're a bit worried about Gunn. They haven't been able to raise him on R/T since the combat and they are afraid that he might have bought it. What do you think the form is? I certainly hate to tell the chaps unless we are sure."

Remembering my own experience when the R/T had packed up, I suggested that we might wait a little longer. We asked Control to let us have any news immediately. We checked with Bradwell Flying Control. They had not heard from Gunn. Then the ops telephone rang. Two aircraft had been reported going down together, both in flames. The CO had no option but to tell the sad news, which was only partly lightened by the fact that Jimmy had certainly got his Hun.

Most of the crews who had been airborne had now

landed. They were in the crew room, discarding flying kit and joining in the still excited buzz of conversation. I called for quiet, which was not all that easy to obtain. The CO made his announcement. A shocked air of gloom followed a brief moment of disbelief.

Into the quietened crew room came Flight Lieutenant Ron Watts and his navigator. They had been in the Mozzie on patrol with Jimmy Gunn when the raiders had appeared and had heard what had happened on their own R/T. When Jimmy had not responded to Control, they realised what had occurred.

I wandered over to them as they replaced their kit in their flying lockers. Watts and his navigator, Flying Officer Folley, were both quiet, unassuming types.

"What sort of trip did you have?" I asked. "Did you get a chase?"

"Well, er, yes. We got a Dornier 217!"

The atmosphere brightened considerably. In a moment questions were being hurled at the successful pair. I felt sure that Jimmy Gunn would have been glad that his comrades were thus given a chance to snap out of their gloom. It was confirmed later that a Heinkel 111 and a Mozzie had crashed together. We had the satisfaction of knowing that Jimmy had made his kill.

Things were pretty quiet for the next month and we persevered with training. I got quite a few hours in with the CO; my flying hours had jumped to over 500 day and 200 night. On October 23rd the Wingco and I were ordered off with another crew on an absolute stinker of a night. Something was alleged to have been plotted so off we went. It was pouring with rain and the clouds were very low indeed. We were in cloud almost as soon as our wheels left the runway. Up we went to 18,000ft, still in cloud with lightning flashing all around us and the Mozzie being thrown all over the place.

Suddenly the whole aircraft was bathed in the weirdest blue light. Little balls of blue fire were dancing over our windscreen, along our wings and making our propellers look for all the world like giant Catherine wheels. I had heard of St. Elmo's Fire; so this was what it looked like. It was most eerie. If I had been in the mood for reading I could have read the smallest print quite easily, so vivid was the light.

It stayed with us for quite a time; then after we had been patrolling for about half an hour, during which time we had never been out of cloud, we were ordered to return to base – an order which we thankfully obeyed.

Soon after I became Navigator Leader I had noticed that there was a navigator on the operational strength of the squadron by the name of Flight Lieutenant Clarke, whom I had not yet met. On enquiry I was informed that he was in hospital, having sustained a cracked skull earlier in the year.

When he eventually returned he reported to my office and I found him a very pleasant and amusing little chap. Evidently his skull had mended reasonably quickly. The main reason for his long absence had been not so much the cracked skull but the fact that the Royal Air Force medicos were highly suspicious of aircrew who had experienced hard bumps on their heads. They subjected them to many interviews with psychiatrists, about whom Clarke had several good stories.

The one that amused me most, however, did not concern the headshrinkers. He had been in a ward of an RAF hospital when the Princess Royal visited it. The ward was full of injured aircrew.

"The trouble was," he said, "she asked each chap how he was getting on and how he had received his injury."

"What was wrong with that?" I asked.

"Well," came the answer, "most of the other chaps had been wounded in combat, or jumped out of blazing aircraft or something equally heroic. I fractured my skull falling backwards off a bar stool at a New Year's Eve party in the mess."

I never did find out what he told the Princess Royal.

CHAPTER 9

Radio Counter-measures

THE squadron bagged two more Huns in November although nothing ever happened when we were up. Ben flew in to see me with the news that 157 Squadron was to move to Predannack at the end of November. They were rather dismayed at the prospect. He had lunch with us and we discussed with the Wingco the chances of a posting for Ben to our squadron. The Wingco pointed out the policy of having New Zealand pilots as far as possible.

Ben and I found that we would both be on leave in London at the end of the month so we arranged to meet. He had never been over a film studio so I laid on a visit to Denham studios. Two films were being made there; Noel Coward was working on that grand film, *In Which We Serve*, and his play *Blithe Spirit* was also being filmed.

On one of the large stages we saw an almost life-size replica of the destroyer *Kelly*, which was most impressive. It had been built on tubular scaffolding which was so arranged that the ship could rock from side to side to an angle of 45 degrees. We were allowed a good look round and found it extremely interesting. The destroyer's guns were made almost entirely of wood, yet all the moving parts worked and it was possible to insert a dummy shell. The gun would then show all the motions of a real gun being fired.

From there we went on to the set where a scene from *Blithe Spirit* was being shot. We watched Kay Hammond, in ghostly make-up, playing a couple of scenes. The ghost make-up reminded me of Bob Donat and *The Ghost Goes West*.

One of the features on a New Zealand squadron such as Bradwell was the food. We had the normal RAF food, which was pretty good on the whole, but, in addition to this, we all shared in the simply wonderful parcels these lads were sent

from home. When we were having our night-flying supper at
dispersal, there would be on the table as extras a colossal
spread of rich fruit cakes, honey, butter, jams, tinned food –
especially tinned oysters which were great favourites with
the New Zealanders – and almost everything else that it was
possible to pack and send.

In addition to all this, most airfields, and Bradwell in
particular, seemed to be first-class mushroom fields. Most
evenings in late summer and through the autumn we would
fill our caps with mushrooms on our way to dispersal. The
only injury I received throughout the war was to my
digestion. It was well worth it though.

The Wingco and I flew many hours on many patrols, but
we were not destined to have much excitement. We had
only one chase after a Hun, and that was after a long pursuit
one night in early December, when we had a visual on a
Messerschmitt 410. The wretched thing spotted us before
the Wingco could get lined up for a shot and it dived away
much too fast for us.

At the end of December the Wingco was told he would
be posted to a job that meant promotion for him. So keen
had he become on night fighting, however, that he tried
hard but unsuccessfully to have the posting put off. Before
he left he kept his promise and arranged with 11 Group that
I should be given the choice of rejoining Ben or crewing up
with the new CO who had just arrived to take over
command of 488 Squadron.

Although I was not terribly thrilled with the idea of going
to Predannack, I knew that 157 Squadron would not be there
forever. I had flown with many pilots on 488 Squadron, some
good, some bad, but I had always felt somehow that my
destiny was bound up with Ben. In the meantime I had to
remain as Navigator Leader while the situation was sorted
out at 11 Group Headquarters.

I received the following very pleasant letter from Peter
Hamley, now a Group Captain:

8th January 1944.

Dear Brandy,

As I had to nip smartly into a taxi before some Yanks got it, I did not have a chance to say goodbye, so I am writing to thank you for all the help you gave me whilst at Bradwell in becoming operational quickly, and also all the loyal support you gave me as my Navigator Leader.

I spoke at 11 Group about Benson. It appears that 29 Squadron has its full complement of squadron leaders and 11 Group are not agitating to get him back. So you will have to make up your mind whether you want to fly with Wing Commander Haine or go down to Predannack with him. As I told you, now would appear to be the time to decide, as I know Haine would be happy to fly with you.

Well, Brandy, I hope to come down to Bradwell soon to see all the chaps. Thanking you again for your cheerful help and enthusiasm.

Yours Ever.

Sure enough, next morning I had a phone call from 11 Group, asking me what I wished to do. They would have to arrange the posting and a replacement for me. They had checked with 157 Squadron, who would be glad to have me back, but I would not be posted in as Navigator Leader, as they already had one. When I said that I would like to rejoin Ben at Predannack, they told me that I might have to wait about a month so that I could hand over to my replacement when they found one.

Things worked out according to schedule. I flew with the new CO three or four times and did a couple of patrols with one of the pilots whose navigator had 'flu. Then on January 23rd, 1944 this pilot flew me to Predannack.

488 (New Zealand) Squadron were to make quite a name for themselves later, for they became part of the Allied Expeditionary Air Force and operated with great success. In

spite of the fact that they had no opportunity to fly against the enemy until their move to Bradwell in September 1943, by the time the squadron was disbanded in April 1945 they had destroyed no fewer than 67 enemy aircraft, with three probables and eleven damaged.

During this time they lost only four crews in action and eleven in flying accidents – a very creditable record indeed and I am proud to have served with them as Navigator Leader, even if only for a comparatively short time. They were a grand bunch of fellows.

The squadron mess at Predannack was the Pollurian Hotel, which was about 5 miles from the airfield and only some ten minutes' walk from beautiful Mullion Cove.

The squadron had done very well in the two months they had been there. They had been engaged in Instep patrols, as the long-range day patrols in the Bay of Biscay were now known. They had destroyed seven enemy aircraft, with one probable and four damaged. There was obviously a fair bit of action to be had, but in spite of that most of the fellows wanted to get back on to their primary job of night fighting for which they had trained so hard.

Although Ben had done a considerable amount of flying in the five months we had been separated, he had not enjoyed any success at all. This added substance to my firm convictions about splitting up successful crews.

He had quite a lot to tell me. The squadron whom 157 Squadron had relieved was 141 Squadron, on which we had done our first tour. They were commanded by Wing Commander Bob Braham, who finished the war as the second highest scoring night-fighter pilot, with no less than three DSOs and three DFCs.

There was a story about him that deserves to be true. He walked into the bar of an officers' mess one day, wearing battledress on which he was wearing only the ribbons of these two decorations, the two bars to each being denoted by little silver rosettes on the ribbons.

An American officer in the bar, observing this phenomenon, was heard to remark:

"Say, who is that guy? He's only wearing a couple of gongs, but they sure are riveted on."

Ben told me another story about Braham which I later verified. From 1942 onwards the Middle East night-fighter squadrons were being built up and the Home squadrons were asked fairly regularly for crews to volunteer for such postings. When Bob Braham took over as CO of 141 Squadron, one of the sergeant navigators rejoiced in the name of Perfect.

Sergeant Perfect did not particularly wish to go to the Middle East, but as a result of several misunderstandings he found himself scheduled to go there as navigator to a pilot who was extremely keen to go.

Sergeant Perfect whipped in an application to see the CO. This was Bob Braham, of course, and it happened that he had already asked to see Perfect and his pilot to wish them good luck.

Sergeant Perfect found himself in front of the CO and the following conversation ensued:

"Ah! Sergeant *Prefect*, so you are keen to go to the Middle East."

"*Perfect*," corrected the sergeant.

"Jolly good show! I wish you the best of luck," rejoined the CO.

Sergeant Perfect found himself outside the door bound for the Middle East and wondering how it all happened.

Ben and one of the Flight Commanders had discussed the possibility of an Intruder sortie to an airfield near Bordeaux. There was a large lake nearby and Intelligence thought that long-range German convoy spotters were based on the airfield with some flying-boats on the lake, called Lake Biscarosse. They had asked for permission to try an Intruder patrol, but for various reasons permission had been refused. They had been told, however, that an application might be made later. When Ben knew for certain that I was on my way down he put in a fresh request and had been given permission to try the patrol at the first suitable opportunity.

We flew on an Instep patrol as leader of four Mozzies on January 30th. We spent nearly four hours patrolling some 50 miles to the south-west of Ireland, where some Junkers 88s were thought to carry out an occasional patrol. We saw nothing at all.

On February 5th the weather looked just right for our Bordeaux trip and at 19.30 hours we set off on the near-600 mile sea journey to Bordeaux. We flew at 200ft, well to the west of the Brest Peninsula as we did not want to be plotted by the enemy raid-warning system; we meant our presence in the Bay to come as a complete surprise to the Hun. The flight to our target would take us two hours twenty minutes, leaving us about twenty minutes' patrol time and plenty of flying time in hand for our return journey.

Everything worked out very well from the navigational angle. We kept some 40 miles out to sea all down the west coast of France, and when we finally turned east for our target we saw that we were crossing the coast as planned, about 8 miles south of Lake Biscarosse. There was a moon, but rather too much cloud in the whole area for our liking. We climbed to 2,000ft over the coast and the lake showed up very well. Just to the north-east was the airfield of Bordeaux/Merignac, and close by was the town of Bordeaux itself, absolutely ablaze with lights. They were obviously not worried about black-out regulations there – it was the very first time I had seen a town lighted up since I had begun flying.

There were several lights on the airfield but we saw nothing moving. After a ten-minute patrol there, we had a look at the lake. Unfortunately, cloud was tending to obscure the moon and we could see nothing on the lake. We did three or four runs over it before deciding that it was useless; then we had another look at the airfield. Again we could see nothing moving and so we dived low across it to see if we could spot any parked aircraft. It was too dark. We could not see a thing.

Nobody took any notice of us – we were probably thought to be a Junkers 88 wanting to land. It seemed a pity to have brought all our ammunition all this way just to take it home again, but that was what we very regretfully did. The homeward trip was quite uneventful. We were disappointed, but felt that it had been a worthwhile effort and determined to try again if we could.

One of the Flight Commanders, Squadron Leader Tappin, and his Navigator, Flying Officer Thomas, did the same trip two nights later. As they turned in to the French coast just south of Lake Biscarosse they saw a large aircraft with navigation lights on. It was flying near the lake. As they darted in they recognised to their delight and amazement that it was a six-engined Blohm and Voss 222 flying-boat.

It was so enormous that Tappin's first burst of fire fell short simply because he could not believe that he was so far from it. He soon rectified his mistake, popped in closer and picked off the engines on one side, one by one – very satisfying.

Just after this I went off on leave to be married but that is no part of this story. Suffice to say that we took advantage of a very generous scheme initiated by Lord Nuffield, whereby aircrew and their families could stay for a holiday at any one of several of the best hotels in Britain for a nominal charge. We stayed at the Lygon Arms in the beautiful Cotswold village of Broadway.

I returned to Predannack at the end of February and we carried out half a dozen more Instep patrols, all of them fairly uneventful. On one of these we chased after three spots on the horizon, one after another, only to find a Liberator and two Sunderlands.

In the middle of March the squadron received the glad tidings that we were to move to Valley, in Anglesey. We were to re-equip with the newest Mozzies carrying the latest AI for a new and very special job. The AI was Mark 10 and we would be told details of the job at a later stage.

Mark 10 AI was an American production. Early in the war the basic principles of AI had been presented to them; we had carried on development on lines which had brought forth Mark 8 AI, whilst the Americans had developed Mark 10, which they referred to as SCR 720. We were to find that it had many advantages and only a few disadvantages compared to the British Mark 8.

On March 28th a Mark 10 'circus' arrived to enable the navigators to learn something about it. This circus was under the command of Squadron Leader Hoy, DFC, and was run very efficiently. It consisted of six Wellingtons fitted up as flying classrooms and enabled us to get down to some pretty intensive training. Mark 10 had a greater range and better coverage than anything I had previously used, but it had two tubes to watch and lots and lots of knobs to twiddle. It worked all right, but it would certainly need a great deal of practice and the ideal operator for it would be one with three arms and three eyes. No extra arms or eyes were included in the squadron's re-equipment, so we would just have to get down to some hard practice.

I managed to get rather more than my share of flying in the Wellingtons by getting myself taken on as an extra instructor after my first couple of trips. I was really delighted with Mark 10 AI; the more I tried it, the more I realised that it was exactly what we needed from the start: long-range, good coverage, reliability, an excellent beacon facility for homings, and it was difficult enough to use properly to make it a constant challenge. I could hardly wait to try it in a Mozzie, but we were not due to get them until early May.

So we did not wait. Ben had been wondering what it was all about and I kept him informed of what I thought of it. Somehow he obtained permission for us to try to fly to Ford, where 456 (Australian) Squadron had just begun to re-equip with Mozzies with Mark 10. We met several friends and acquaintances in the mess and spent a rather liquid night in the bar during which time we managed to persuade the CO of 456 Squadron to let us have a flip in one of his precious new Mozzies the day after.

We duly had our flight the next afternoon in a Mozzie with the new magic box; I hope Ben was suitably impressed. From my logbook I see that we did not return straight home from Ford but flew to Coltishall, another night-fighter station. We spent the night there – I am not sure why, but perhaps it was in the hope that we might wangle another trip in a Mark 10 equipped Mozzie, or to see if the squadron there was experiencing any snags with Mark 10.

We returned in the fullness of time to Valley, where we learned that on May 4th the Squadron would be moving to Swanington, near Norwich. We would be transferred to Bomber Command from Fighter Command and would be in 100 Group, known as the Radio Countermeasures Group. The new job on which we would be engaged was Bomber Support operations. We were certainly getting plenty of variety in this war.

The move to Swanington duly took place and we began to learn something of our new role. Wing Commander 'Sammy' Hoare had been attached to the squadron for a few weeks to initiate yet another bout of intensive training. He wore the ribbons of the DSO and DFC and was quite a character. Although he had only one eye, he managed to see better, even in the dark, than most people with two. He had experienced great success as an Intruder pilot and had commanded an Intruder squadron.

He sported a truly magnificent ginger moustache. When confronted by a moustache almost as good, he was once heard to mutter:

"Huh! Fluff, my boy. Fluff. Why, it's not a moustache at all unless both wingtips can be seen from behind!"

Our first new Mozzie arrived on May 7th. Sammy Hoare grabbed it and asked me to demonstrate this AI stuff to him. He had to make a couple of calls in the South of England; so on the way south, we did a few practice interceptions on any aircraft that came our way.

Our final call was at Tangmere, right on the South Coast. All around there, for as far as I could see, every field was packed tight with lorries, tanks, barges and all sorts of weird-looking objects. There was so much equipment down there that it seemed that this little island must tip up with all this weight at one end. What a target all this would have been for Hitler's flying bomb.

Once our first new Mozzie had arrived the others started coming in quickly and we proceeded to make the best possible use of them. Not only did we all have to brush up our navigation and master Mark 10 AI, but these new Mozzies were fitted with a navigational aid called 'Gee', which was new to us. It was fairly easy to operate and it enabled the user to obtain a fix of his position very quickly. Its coverage extended pretty well all over the British Isles and deep into enemy territory. Altogether it was a very useful piece of equipment to carry on the job for which we were training.

157 Squadron was joined at Swanington by 85 Squadron, one of the crack defensive night-fighter squadrons, and a spirit of fairly friendly rivalry sprang up between the two squadrons. We had more experience of operating over enemy territory, but 85 Squadron were in far better AI practice than we were.

We had been told that most of our patrols for our new job would be at high level, probably at about 18,000ft. The patrols would be carried out in bad as well as good weather and the timing and navigation would have to be spot on. This was all new for us, so Ben and I went off on another series of cross-country exercises, but this time they were at high level. They went off quite well, and what with these trips. Mark 10 and Gee practices, our time was pretty well taken up.

By this time we had been briefed about our new role and it would perhaps be as well to explain what it was all about and how it had come to pass. In order to do this it is necessary to anticipate the shape of things to come, as well as to look back a bit.

One of the most fascinating stories of the war is that of the constant battle that went on between British and German scientists in the field of radar and signals. In this battle there would appear to be ample evidence that our boffins were always quite a good way ahead of the enemy. There was a positive and a negative side to the battle. The positive side was the provision of control, communication and warning systems and navigational aids to one's own aircraft. The negative side was to attempt to ensure that the similar aids possessed by the enemy were hindered or jammed in some way, so that they were as little use as possible to them.

On the positive side for us were the Long Range Warning System, VHF radio, GCI control and finally AI – all of which had helped to make it possible for Fighter Command to carry out its job. Other equally valuable inventions had been produced for Bomber and Coastal Commands, but they are beyond the scope of this book. The negative side of the work of our boffins must now be considered.

The big German night bomber raids of 1940 and early 1941 had shown up the weakness of our night defences, but it had also indicated that the German navigators needed navigational aids for any but the easiest targets. Raids on the big coastal towns of the East and South Coasts, or on London with the Thames Estuary as a guide, were one thing. Finding an inland town, such as Derby or Birmingham, was quite another matter.

To assist their bomber crews, the German boffins had produced a device known as *Knickebein*. This navigational aid was based on the use of two shortwave radio beams directed on the target for the night. They would be operated from points well apart, say one from Holland and the other from France, so that the intersection of the beams was exactly over the target. The technique used was for the bomber to set course roughly for the target. He would listen for either of the two beams, which he would hear in his earphones as 'dots' or 'dashes'. Whichever he heard first he would know from his briefing which beam it was and he could then fly along it listening to the sound until the other beam started to come in. When the two sounds in his earphones became a steady combined note, he could release his bombs, for he had reached the point of intersection of the beams. Fairly accurate blindbombing through cloud was possible with this device.

The first round in the radio countermeasures battle went to our boffins when they discovered the existence of this beam system before it was actually used operationally by the German bombers at night. They experimented with the possibility of jamming it without much success. This was as well perhaps, for the enemy would have known then that the beam was being mucked about. They then decided that the best thing to do was to bend the beam so that the intersection was somewhere quite different to the place the Germans had intended to attack.

This was effected by picking up one of the beams and rebroadcasting it in a slightly different direction. This scheme worked very well on several occasions and had the advantage that there was no reason for the enemy to suspect that the beams were being tampered with. One of the outstanding successes was when aircraft attempting a raid on Liverpool were induced to drop their bombs in the Irish Sea.

As the raids on this country became fewer and the main accent shifted on to Bomber Command's offensive role, the task for our boffins became that of helping to make things as easy as possible for the crews of Bomber Command. The Germans had a fairly similar set-up for Long Range Warning and Ground Control to our own. Our boffins set to work to find out the various frequencies which were being used by the enemy and then to produce apparatus which would jam them sufficiently to make them useless.

Obtaining this information was a long and difficult job. Ground stations listened out for enemy transmissions day and night. At the same time almost every Bomber Command raid had one or more aircraft fitted up with listening apparatus and notes were made of transmissions over a very wide band. These notes were sorted out and our boffins would then decide what new types of equipment were being installed by the enemy and for what purpose they were being used. As soon as this was done, a jamming device would be evolved and very soon with every Bomber Command raid there would be a few aircraft carrying loads of the various jamming devices designed to jam every bit of radar and signals equipment used by the Germans.

The main threat to our bombers was the enemy night fighter. The whole idea of our boffins was to make everything just as difficult for them as it was humanly possible, for nearly all of Bomber Command's effort was to take place at night. Their main raids were carried out on the theory of 'saturation' bombing. That is to say, a large number of bombers would drop their bombs on a target in as short a space of time as possible.

The tactics of the German night bombers when they were operating over Britain had been based mainly on the idea of sending waves of bombers over in relatively small numbers in order to keep the Alert going in our big cities for as long as possible. Once our night defence became reasonably competent it was not called upon to deal with mass raids such as the Luftwaffe now found themselves faced with.

In their attempts to deal with the very heavy raids they experienced as the war developed, the Luftwaffe evolved two main methods of interception: route interception and target interception. Route interception was an attempt to assemble as many twin-engined fighters as possible as soon as a raid was detected and to bring them into our bomber stream, either on the inward or outward route.

This was done with the aid of instructions from the ground and a running commentary on the progress of the raid broadcast over the R/T. The instructions gave the fighters courses to steer and were usually given by reference to radio or visual beacons which had been suitably placed to cover the whole of Germany. Once the fighters were in our bomber stream they had their AI with which they could carry out interception on their own. The more skilful crews were used as leaders and equipped with the best apparatus available.

They endeavoured to get into the bomber stream at the earliest possible moment and dropped 'fighter flares' to guide the lesser brethren.

Target interception consisted of putting as many fighters as possible over the anticipated target. This method would be used in bright moonlight conditions when single-engined single-seater fighters could be used, or when insufficient early warning had been obtained to feed fighters into the bomber stream on the inward route. They would operate with the aid of flares from the leader fighters, visual signals from the ground such as searchlights pointing towards the expected target and the running commentary which consisted of a summing up of all the available information.

In order to "frustrate their knavish tricks" our boffins had to study each stage of the operation. The Long Range Warning System that the Germans had thrown all round Fortress Europe was comparatively easy to jam, either from ground stations in England or by patrols of jamming aircraft flying over the Channel and the North Sea.

Communications, ground-to-air and air-to-ground radio, were jammed in much the same way and, in addition, aircraft filled with jamming apparatus would fly with the bombers to ensure a wider coverage of the jamming.

The German equivalent of our AI was known as *Lichtenstein*, or *Li* for short, and it was just as susceptible to jamming as their other gadgets. Again this was dealt with by jamming aircraft flying with our bombers. Our boffins also produced 'Serrate', a device which actually homed on to the transmissions of the German *Li*. 141 Squadron, with whom I had done my first tour, had gone into 100 Group some months before 157 Squadron. They had been equipped with Serrate and had operated with remarkable success, homing on to German night fighters from as much as 50 miles.

Another device which helped to confuse the plotting system and the night fighters' *Li* was known as 'Window'. This consisted of strips of silvered paper which, when dropped from aircraft, produced false radar echoes. A small force of perhaps twenty bombers dropping, or rather scattering, Window would probably be plotted as two or three hundred aircraft by the enemy warning system.

The properties of Window had been known for some time by our boffins, but for security reasons it was not used by Bomber Command until the German night bombers were no longer a serious threat. The Germans did in fact use Window against Britain in early 1944, but by then Bomber Command had made extensive use of it to stimulate big raids and to create diversions which would often take large numbers of German night fighters away from our main bomber force.

With the advent of the German *Knickebein* navigation beam, a Radio Countermeasures Unit, known as 80 Wing, had been formed in 1940. From beam-bending it had concerned itself with jamming devices and such things, but it had been a ground unit. The various inventions were flown in aircraft of squadrons in all the groups in Bomber Command. It was decided later to withdraw most of the jamming aircraft from ordinary bomber squadrons and to bring them together into a new Group. This was 100 Group, the Radio Countermeasures Group, in which we were later to find ourselves with 157 Squadron. The job of 100 Group was to frustrate the German night defences, particularly their night fighters, which were by far the greatest menace to our bombers.

CHAPTER 10

Bomber Support

A BOMBER force operating over enemy territory constantly cannot stand more than a small percentage of loss to enemy action. To this loss must be added the inevitable losses due to training and flying accidents and to bad weather. The German day bombing of Britain had to be called off when losses mounted too high, and some of the early Bomber Command night raids suffered almost equally disastrous losses.

The formation of 100 Group with its jamming aircraft was only one of the steps taken to bring these losses down to sizeable proportions. The vital importance of the most careful planning of raids was realised and soon a remarkable amount of brains and ingenuity went into this planning.

Help was also obtained from Fighter Command in the shape of the actual transfer of night-fighter squadrons. Just as the German bombers had been harried from take off until landing, so too could the German night fighters be harried. That had been the role of 141 Squadron with Serrate, and now we were to join in the job of harassing, which was now given the name of Bomber Support.

There were two main reasons why bombers could not be escorted at night by fighters. One was the considerable difference in the speeds of bombers and night fighters and the consequent difficulty in maintaining station. The second and more important reason was that the main object for a Bomber Support fighter must be to destroy the enemy night fighters before they come near the bomber stream and lose themselves in it. Even with Mark 10 AI it would be impossible to pick out a German night fighter from a mass of British bombers, who would probably be dropping Window. It was therefore necessary to throw a screen of fighters around the bombers' target and, indeed, if possible, around

134

the whole bomber route over enemy territory.

This screen of fighters would operate at about the same height or slightly below the bombers' height, in order to intercept enemy night fighters climbing up on their way to attack the bombers. Patrol points for the Bomber Support fighters would be about 40 miles or eight minutes' flying time from our main bomber stream, so that once AI contact was obtained on an aircraft by a Bomber Support fighter, the interception had to be brought to a swift conclusion. In other words, less than eight minutes must pass between the original contact, the chase, the visual, the identification and the destruction of the aircraft if it were hostile. Other squadrons of Bomber Support fighters would operate as low-level Intruders at known German night-fighter bases.

A night's operations by Bomber Support fighters was worked in three phases. For the first phase a wave of low-level fighters, equipped with Mark 10 AI and carrying a couple of bombs, would take off to patrol as many as possible of the enemy night-fighter airfields likely to be involved in the night's raids. These aircraft were briefed to arrive on patrol before Bomber Command's main raid was plotted by the enemy radar. It was important that they should be sufficiently widespread to give as little indication as possible of the whereabouts of the main raid. If practicable, more than one airfield might be covered by a fighter. Once on patrol, the fighter would look for signs of activity and attempt to prevent, or at least to discourage, enemy fighters from taking off by judicious use of bombs and cannons. If any did take off, the fighter would try to shoot them down.

The second phase was a wave of fighters with Mark 10 AI but no bombs. These fighters would fly low on the first part of their journey so that they should not be plotted by the enemy until the last moment before their entry into enemy territory. They would then climb to operational height, say 15,000ft, and arrive on patrol at a pre-set time, usually at about the time when the enemy would probably obtain the first definite plots on our bombers. Their aim was to screen the bombers from any enemy fighters who had managed to become airborne.

These high-level patrols were usually continued until half an hour or so after bombing was finished, and it was most unlikely that an aircraft on a patrol of this nature would not have at least one or more chases. After a chase the fighter would return to the original patrol point until it was due to leave. There was generally a brightly burning target left by the bombers by which the fighter could position itself. Then the target area itself was usually worth investigating in order to catch any latecomers from the Luftwaffe and to screen the returning bombers. On the way back from patrol the high-level support fighters were allowed to investigate any enemy airfields they saw illuminated in order to catch enemy fighters attempting to land.

The third phase was another wave of low-level fighters, again equipped with Mark 10 and bombs. They relieved the first wave, patrolling the enemy fighter airfields at which enemy fighters were expected to land and making things difficult for them. Obviously every airfield could not be covered and quite a number of enemy fighters continued to plague our bombers, but many more were prevented from doing so.

The main idea behind all Bomber Support operations was really to worry the German night fighters. Although a very large number of enemy fighters were shot down through these operations, the chief blow was at the morale of the German night-fighter crews. Any German night-fighter crew who managed to get airborne while his airfield was being patrolled, then made his way through the high-level patrol and found the bombers, faced up to their gunners, made his way back again through the high-level patrol, then landed at an airfield patrolled by one of our low-level fighters, could certainly be said to have earned his night-flying supper and ersatz coffee. Particularly as all the jammable equipment he carried had probably been jammed most of the time. It is one thing to be a hunter; to be a hunted hunter is a very different matter.

It will be realised from this that a major raid by Bomber Command required very careful timing and planning. It was not just a matter of detailing a number of bombers to attack a German town but of ensuring that the bomber force should have the fullest protection at all times and that things should be made as difficult as possible for the German defences. While the bomber formations were assembling over England, the ground jamming stations would begin operating. At the same time the airborne jammers would be in position forming a complete jamming chain to the east, the south-east and the south. These chaps would often operate from dusk to dawn, keeping the German defences on the alert all the time.

The tactics employed by the bombers themselves provided almost endless ways of foxing the German defences. On a night when a big raid was intended on a particular target, a secondary target would probably be attacked and one or more spoof raids would be organised. These raids could be co-ordinated in time so that they would appear through the jamming on the German radar all at about the same time. They would be heading on widely diverging courses, with the smaller number of bombers on the diversionary raids dropping Window as hard as they could in order that all the raids should appear to be of equal strength. Thus, from the very beginning the enemy would have difficulty in knowing how best to deploy his fighters.

Clever variations in the timing of the diversionary raids and the main raid could produce many headaches for the German controllers. It must be remembered that even the raids on secondary targets carried quite a sting. There might well be thirty or more heavy bombers as well as the 100 Group aircraft manning the diversion, and the German controllers could not ignore these raids, even if they suspected that they were not the main attack. These diversionary raids were also supported by Bomber Support aircraft. This served a double purpose: it helped to give the impression that they were indeed major raids, and if enemy night fighters were sent there some of them would probably be destroyed by the Bomber Support fighters.

Spoof raids were laid on, often with outstanding success. The Luftwaffe suffered from shortage of aviation fuel and oils – particularly from the end of 1943 onwards. A large number of their aircraft were concerned only with the defence of the Reich, and until things became really desperate a threatened raid would provoke strong reaction from German night fighters. The more we could persuade the Luftwaffe to launch fighters into the air unnecessarily, the more of their precious oil and petrol was wasted.

There were various forms of spoof raids. The most usual was for as many training aircraft as possible to assemble over Norfolk and then set off over the North Sea, to simulate a major raid heading for Northern Germany. There might be as many as 80 aircraft involved, and all the jamming and the Bomber Support patrols would be laid on to help the simulation of a really massive raid. Just before reaching the enemy coast, but not before they had been well plotted by the German warning system, the training aircraft would turn back, having carried out a good navigational exercise.

On several occasions spoof raids of this sort brought a reaction of two or three hundred German night fighters and a considerable waste of fuel. Apart from this, some of them were shot down by Bomber Support fighters. After one or two of these spoof raids, Bomber Command would probably lay on a major raid on the very same route and catch the German controllers out.

Even when the weather was poor or when Bomber Command was having a night off, 100 Group would usually arrange some activity to keep the Luftwaffe employed. There were very few nights from the end of 1943 until the end of the War when 100 Group had no aircraft over the Reich.

There were also almost nightly Mosquito raids on Berlin to harass the enemy, and finally the tactics employed by the main bomber force could usually be relied upon to cloud the issue for him even more. One of the simplest methods of foxing the enemy was for the bombers to fly on a course which would make it appear to the Germans that the target was a town in mid-Germany, such as Mannheim. After the raid had been well and truly plotted, the main force might turn sharply north and bomb one of the Ruhr towns, while some 20 aircraft, dropping Window madly, would carry on towards Mannheim to keep up the deception.

With all the many ways they had of misleading the German controllers, Bomber Command had no need to follow any pattern in planning their raids. The Germans therefore were almost always forced to treat all plotted raids with the greatest suspicion and were hardly ever able to make the best use of their night fighters.

This, then, was the prospect before us now that we found ourselves members of 100 Group. So far as I was concerned it was a pretty pleasing prospect. I had complete faith in my pilot, in the Mozzie and in Mark 10 AI, and here I was, sitting in the front seat for the all-out offensive for which every Briton had been waiting and hoping. If I had felt fairly sure before that I was on one of the most interesting and thrilling jobs in the war, I was absolutely sure of it now. It was going to be the Battle of Germany – we would be playing away from home from now on.

We had been forbidden to fly over enemy territory or even near it with our new equipment until ordered to do so. When we received the order we knew that something special was afoot; it was on June 5th, the eve of D-Day. I had been doing some Mark 10 instructing in a Wellington in the morning. When I went to the mess for lunch I received the exciting news that we had been told to stand by for operations that night.

After lunch we did a night-flying test run in Mosquito 'E', which had been allocated to us and which was subsequently named 'Eager Beaver'. Eager Beaver became 'our' aircraft and we flew it whenever it was available for our Bomber Support patrols.

We were due to take off an hour before midnight. On this occasion we were not told much about the night's operations as an obvious security measure in case operation *Overlord*, the invasion of Europe, had to be postponed for any reason. All we knew was that Ben and I were to patrol Eindhoven airfield for forty minutes. Eindhoven was in southern Holland and was used as a German bomber base. All the patrol points for the two squadrons at Swanington that night were Intruder patrols on Luftwaffe bomber bases and all low-level patrols.

This was it.

All our experience and hours of practice was now to be put to the test. So often Ben and I had discussed our previous Intruder patrols and bewailed the fact that we had not been allowed to carry even the old types of AI with us. Now we were off on patrol with the most promising of all, Mark 10.

Anticlimax was to follow however. We reached our target without incident; and although there was rather a lot of cloud we identified it clearly with the aid of a target map with which we had been provided. We could see the airfield runways but no lights were visible, and we did not see any sign of activity at all during our patrol. Nor did we see anything else to shoot at on our way home although we looked jolly hard.

We had a similar patrol on June 8th, but this time we patrolled the neighbouring airfield of Gilze, as well as Eindhoven. We spent twenty minutes near each airfield, but, apart from arousing the curiosity of some searchlights who failed to illuminate us, we saw nothing of interest. Nor had anybody else from the two squadrons at Swanington so far.

The CO and one of the Flight Commanders of 157 Squadron had been posted just before we began operations with 100 Group. On June 9th Wing Commander Ken Davison, DFC, arrived to take over the Squadron and Ben was made acting Flight Commander of 'A' Flight.

We were not required for operations for the next three nights, but Ben and I had a useful couple of hours on the night of the 11th chasing another of our Mozzies whose pilot had been briefed to give us some really difficult evasive action. We then acted as target for him and both crews found that Mark 10 was extremely good for chases of this sort, which we might expect in our new role.

The next night we were detailed for a low-level patrol of three airfields near Rheims: Laon/Athies, Laon/Couvron and Juvincourt. We had been there on an Intruder patrol almost a year before but this time we had Mark 10 AI with us. Just before midnight we took off, climbing to 5,000ft on our way south; over the Thames Estuary, where they forgot to fire at us, then losing height on our way to Beachy Head, which we crossed at 1,000ft.

We were in Eager Beaver and she was flying perfectly as we continued losing height to cross the Channel at 200ft. As usual, just before we were due to reach the French coast we climbed to 3,000ft and made a good landfall at Criel, near Dieppe. As we set course for our patrol area, Ben remarked:

"It's a blooming dark night, chum. I reckon it would be as well to stay up here. We certainly won't see much if we go down."

"Suits me," I replied – and it did too.

We were much more likely to pick out pinpoints to help my navigation from 3,000ft than if we had gone lower. Then, even with Mark 10, I would get better results with the extra bit of height. Laon/Couvron was reached at 01.15 hours. Nothing was stirring there so we began the rounds of the three airfields.

What with watching AI, keeping my log up to date, taking an occasional Gee fix and peeping out for landmarks, I was kept fairly busy for the next twenty minutes. Then I heard Ben say:

"Hullo. Hullo. Hullo. What's going on there?"

I looked up and saw that a cone of three searchlights had appeared some 8 or 9 miles ahead of us. It seemed to be about halfway between Juvincourt and Laon/Couvron. Ben had already opened up the throttles and we were heading for it.

"This might be it," said Ben. "Keep your eyes skinned. Any joy yet?"

"Not a sausage, I'm afraid. Blimey O'Reilly! Wouldn't it be lovely if there were something there. Are the searchlights still on?"

"Yes. They're on all right. Keep your ruddy head in that box."

The seconds ticked by. Then, after about two minutes, with Eager Beaver fairly whistling along:

"Contact!" I yelled. "It's well above; range 3 miles. Turn starboard!"

"Turning starboard. How far above?"

"30 degrees. Keep turning starboard, range still 3 miles. He's way above us. Keep climbing."

"Turning starboard and climbing."

We soon found that our quarry was orbiting the cone of searchlights. By turning harder, we cut down the range and Ben got a visual of him silhouetted against the searchlight beams, just over a mile away now but still well above. Whatever it was, the aircraft was too far off for Ben to identify it. We found to our dismay that it was outclimbing us. We had got up to 9,000ft by now and the range had started to go out again.

Ben gave Eager Beaver all the urging he could, but gradually as we tried to climb up after it the range increased. Now it was nearly 5 miles away. We had been chasing it for twelve minutes. It was infuriating.

Suddenly my heart leapt. Another blip had appeared on my AI.

"Turn to port. I've got another contact. Range 4 miles, it's crossing from starboard to port, only slightly above!"

"Thank the Lord for that. Turning port. What's happened to the other one?"

"It's gone altogether now. Ease the turn… steady. Range 3 miles. It's very slightly above!"

"Steady. Leave it a bit above. How are we doing?"

"Fine. This one seems to be flying straight and level. We're coming in a bit too fast. Throttle back!"

"Throttling back. What's the range?"

"Just about 2 miles… coming in very nicely. Where will you want him?"

"Keep him above and a bit to starboard…about 10 degrees I should say. What's the range?"

"Gently port... about 4,000ft now. Still coming in nicely... steady now. He's 10 degrees starboard, slightly above... Range just under 3,000. Throttle back now."

"Throttling back... Range?"

"Just about 2,000. He's still 10 degrees starboard 5 degrees above. Any luck?"

A few seconds' pause that seemed like hours – then:

"A-a-a-ah! I think I can see him. Hang on to the contact. I'll go in a bit."

"Okay. Good show!"

A few more seconds passed. I could see the blip coming in to 800ft. Then came the words I was waiting for:

"Okay, have a look now. It's a Jerry all right. Looks like a Junkers 188."

I looked up, my night vision needing a few seconds to adjust itself. I saw a dark shape which gradually resolved itself into a Junkers 188. We were almost directly underneath it, just about 400ft below. Ben eased back the throttles gently, lifted Eager Beaver's nose slightly and at 150 yards' range fired a three-second burst at the Junkers.

There were strikes on the starboard wing roots and the starboard engine caught fire. A further two-second burst blew pieces off the port wing tip. A short third burst produced strikes on the burning starboard engine. Then the whole of the port wing outboard of the engine broke off and passed under us. A second later the Junkers hurtled straight down in flames and exploded on the ground.

I had been entering up my log and then took a Gee fix

which showed us to be over the Forest of Compiègne. It had taken just under four minutes from obtaining contact on this second aircraft to seeing it hit the ground. From the light of the burning starboard engine we had seen a swastika on the tail and dark green camouflage on the upper surface of the wing.

The time for the finish of our patrol had been up some minutes so we set course for base, which was reached without further incident. We landed just after 3am and everyone was highly delighted that the score at Swanington had been opened for 157 Squadron. For our part, it was certainly satisfying to have had an early success with Mark 10 on this new job. As for our ground crew, they had painted a swastika on Eager Beaver almost before we were out of the cockpit.

Once the ice had been broken, more successes followed quickly for the Squadron. A Junkers 88 was shot down the very next night near to where we had found our victim. The night after this, one of our crews, Flight Lieutenant Matthews and Flight Sergeant Penrose, shot down a Junkers 88 and damaged another near Dieppe.

Ben and I carried out three more low-level Intruder patrols in June, visiting airfields in Belgium, France, Holland and Germany. On the first occasion we were patrolling an airfield near Lille while our bombers were raiding Lens and Valenciennes within a few miles of us. We had a grandstand view of the bombing, which was very impressive, but we saw nothing else of interest. The two other patrols were also without incident.

CHAPTER 11

Things That Go Bump in the Night

ON June 27th Ben and I were not on the programme for that night. Patrols had been allocated to the crews who were flying, and take-off time for all of them was around midnight. Suddenly word went round that all Bomber Support operations by 157 Squadron aircraft were cancelled and all crews were to report to the briefing-room immediately for a special briefing. And a special briefing it certainly turned out to be. I know that as far as I was concerned I had the impression by the time it had finished that Jules Verne had come to life again and now held an important post at Air Ministry.

We were to be transferred, at least temporarily, to an operation with the code name of *Diver*. We were given all the available information about this new operation. Some small sort of aircraft which were to be regarded as Top Secret and which would be referred to as Divers, were expected to make attacks on the London area. It was rumoured, but not known, that these aircraft were pilotless. In the summer of 1944 this took some believing!

We were to assume as a safety precaution that they did carry a pilot. The actual size of the Diver was not known but it was believed to he slightly smaller than a single-seater aircraft. Large numbers of the Divers were expected and we were told that they would probably fly at about 2,000ft and at a speed of around 350mph. This was too fast for a Mozzie to catch under normal conditions and we were therefore to patrol at about 9,000ft in order to be able to gain speed in a dive. Perhaps this was where the code name came from.

The Divers were expected to leave the French coast in the area of the Somme Estuary. They were thought to trail fairly long exhaust flames by which we should be able to spot them from some distance. We were to patrol the French coast in the expectation that we would be able to see these flames as

145

moving lights. We were then to dive to intercept them and attempt to shoot them down into the Channel if possible.

Our patrol line was about 25 miles long. On one leg we were to fly north-east and on the return leg we were to fly south-west. Several other aircraft from ADGB, Air Defence of Great Britain, as Fighter Command had recently become, would be on patrol with us. The patrols were arranged to cover the entire night. As so many aircraft would be involved, two simple precautions were to be observed. In order to obviate the chance of head-on collisions, aircraft on the north-easterly leg were to fly at odd thousands of feet 1–9,000ft if cloud conditions permitted, but if they did not, at 7,000, 5,000 or 3,000ft. The return leg was to be flown at even thousands of feet.

The second precaution was that as soon as a fighter turned to chase a Diver it must at once switch navigation lights on. These must be left on until the chase was completed. If any enemy night fighters showed up we were expected to look after ourselves, though Control would warn us if their presence was suspected.

It all seemed too utterly improbable to be true.

A maximum effort had been asked for. The normal method of arranging the operational programme each day was for Group to enquire what would be the maximum number of fighters that were certain to be available with crews from the station for the night's patrols. Depending on the importance of the night's operations by Bomber Command, Group would ask either for a maximum effort from the station or for some part of what they knew we could produce. If twenty aircraft were asked for, obviously ten from each squadron would be involved. Group would allocate ten patrol points to each squadron and the Squadron and Flight Commanders from the two squadrons would decide which individual crews would take each patrol point.

As Group had called for a maximum effort we made sure Eager Beaver was in fighting trim. She was and at 22.55 hours

Ben and I found ourselves airborne on an anti-Diver patrol over the Somme Estuary. There was one small change to our usual set-up; the armourers had been instructed to load us with one tracer in every four of our cannon shells. Normally we did not use tracer ammunition in order to maintain the element of surprise. We were soon over the Channel making our way to our patrol point. When we reached it, we informed Control. The weather was clear but dark, so we turned on to our north-easterly leg flying at 9,000ft.

"Well, here we go," said Ben. "Some caper this is. I wonder what bright spark at Air Ministry dreamed this one up?"

"Blowed if I know! I'm certainly going to keep my AI switched on. There are dozens of aircraft around."

"Yes. The Jerries are bound to plot a gaggle of aircraft like this. If they put some fighters up there'll be some fun."

"I should say so." I took the visor off the AI indicator. "Just look at this! There're five aircraft here for a start!"

"Not to worry," he sighed. "Press on regardless!"

We pressed on regardless for some forty minutes of our hour's patrol with our remarks getting more caustic all the time. France seemed very dark and peaceful below us. It all seemed such a waste of time. Then suddenly it happened. Down there in the blackness we saw a moving light. It was followed in a matter of seconds by another and another, until within a minute there were five little lights below all heading north-east for London.

Ben was already turning after the leading light. I switched the navigation lights on and stared out at the moving lights which were all heading in the same direction but with a considerable space between each of them. They were yellow.

I looked at the one we were diving after. It was some way off still but we were fairly whistling down after it. All seemed to be well, then suddenly:

"Christ Almighty!" exploded Ben. "Just look around us. Let's get to hell out of here!"

I looked around. The sky around us was stiff with

navigation lights. Almost every fighter on patrol must have seen the lights at the same time and gone screaming down after the leader.

We weaved our way through the navigation lights. Ben wasted little time and merely transferred his attention to number three of the lights. This was about a mile behind the first one. Eager Beaver was shuddering a little as we were now diving at well over 320mph – pretty fast for an ordinary night-fighter Mozzie.

Ben had judged the interception beautifully. The Diver was now fairly close below our starboard wing, crossing slightly from starboard to port. All that could be seen was a long yellow flame. What the devil could it be?

As Ben made the final turn to bring us behind the Diver, or whatever it might be, we lost sight of it for a second. Then a huge yellow flame swooshed just over our cockpit. We had found it again – the flame looked at least 20ft long.

The Diver was whizzing along very fast indeed at a height of 2,000ft and flying straight and level. Ben had to keep the throttles full open to keep up with it although we had gathered quite a lot of speed during our dive. We were nicely behind it now.

"Here goes," said Ben, giving the thing ahead of us a two-second burst of cannons.

The tracer shells in our ammunition proved their value. But to our dismay we could see them falling well short of the wretched flame thing in front of us.

"It must be a damned sight farther away than it ruddy well looks," remarked Ben, giving it another short burst. "It seems to be about 200 yards."

The shells were still dropping short. With each burst of fire our speed had dropped slightly. Even with full throttle Eager Beaver was falling behind. Then a thought struck me. I had been sitting there feeling a bit useless on this job, but as Ben was finding difficulty in judging the range, I could give him the correct range from my AI. Sure enough I could see it clearly, only a small blip but easy to see. I told Ben:

"I've got it on AI. The range is nearly 6,000ft."

"Well I'm blowed! I would have thought it was still only about 500 yards off. Well, it's no use chasing this one any more."

As we climbed back to patrol height we discussed the strange phenomenon we had seen. It had flown straight and level even though we had been firing tracer at it. It all seemed very queer, but perhaps it might be a pilotless missile after all.

I was quite pleased that I could be of some help: using my AI as a range finder. We were over the Somme Estuary again, but we could see no more of the yellow lights. The patrol carried on for another ten minutes or so, then we saw another batch of five Divers start off on their journey. This time we had decided to ignore the leading light – which seemed far too popular. We swooped down after number three, with our navigation lights on as before. This time as I looked around I could see only one other pair of lights in pursuit of the Diver. Ben had spotted it too.

"Is he the only one around?" he asked.

"Can't see any more… No, nobody else near, anyhow."

"Right, we're in a better position than he is. Flash the nav. lights on and off a couple of times and see if that works!"

I did as Ben suggested, but the other aircraft's navigation lights were still there – a little further behind but still there. I reported this to Ben. He was now approaching the tricky part of the whole business, the final swoop.

"Okay. We'll soon fix him."

Although we were still some way from the Diver, far out of firing range, Ben let fly a short burst of cannons. We saw the tracer falling away in front of us. So did the other aircraft. He must have realised that we were better placed for an interception, so he waggled his wings and turned away. Just in time too – Ben did not want anything else to worry him now.

The Diver was down on our starboard side, coming in to

us at an angle of about 15 degrees. Ben had kept it below so that he would be able to swoop on it after the final turn that would bring us behind it. He timed it perfectly. As we turned, he put Eager Beaver's nose slightly down and I could see the blip on the AI. The only information he wanted from me was the range.

"I've got it now. Just under a mile… we're closing on it nicely… 3,000. How's it going?"

"Oh, we've still got a bit of height in hand. It looks bloody close now. What range?"

"2,000… it's still coming in quite fast… 1,500 now… 1,200."

'I'll have a go from about 200 yards. Can't see anything to shoot at but that ruddy great flame. What range?"

"Just under 1,000ft. We're still gaining pretty fast."

"Yes. This isn't going so fast as the first one was."

"Coming in to 800 now... 700, still gaining… coming in to 600."

"Okay. Here we go."

I looked up as Ben pressed the gun button. We saw the tracer go slap into the flame. Flashes came from it as the shells struck home and sent it spinning into the sea. The strange flame from its tail was still burning until it hit the water.

In the meantime, as Ben gave the fairly long burst of cannon fire, Eager Beaver bucked for a moment or two like a Wild West broncho. The cockpit was suddenly filled with cold, rushing air; there was a noise like a heavy sea breaking on a shingle beach and the wind whistled into the cockpit like a hurricane.

For the first and only time in all sorties together Ben said to me:

"You'd better put your parachute on, Brandy."

So I did.

After a few moments, however, Eager Beaver seemed to settle herself down to fly fairly smoothly. Ben decided to make for the nearest airfield in case of emergency, as there was obviously something amiss. I gave him a course to steer for Tangmere. I remember hoping that if we did have to jump for it we would at least reach dry land before the worst happened. I am a very keen swimmer, but I prefer to choose the time and place.

We reached Tangmere in due course, with Ben flying very gingerly. Eager Beaver seemed none the worse for this short trip, so we agreed to carry on to Swanington. It was always a bit of a bind to have to land away from home. Although visitors to an airfield were usually very well taken care of, we had no overnight kit with us and we did not know how long the repairs to the aircraft were likely to take.

As we approached Swanington Ben called Flying Control to let them know we were on our way. They wanted to know if we had had any luck. Ben said that we had got one and that our aircraft was damaged but he thought there would be no trouble in landing it. Nor was there any trouble. When we landed, two hours and forty minutes after take off, we were quite pleased and excited with our night's work. We were also pleased to be down in one piece, although I had not really been able to believe that Eager Beaver would let us down.

Quite a crowd was waiting to receive us and to find out what this Diver business was all about. We told all that we knew. Later we found out that only two Divers had been shot down that night and ours had been the first by about twenty minutes. I believe that we were in fact the first crew to shoot one down at night.

Next day the whole story of the Divers was released. They were the wretched things known generally as buzz-bombs to the public but as Divers or Beechcraft to the Services.

It was found that Eager Beaver's nose had almost collapsed with the excessive strain caused by our speed coupled with the vibration from the cannons. After this, the noses of Mozzies flying on this job were strengthened. We had certainly found the tracer ammunition useful, and the tip of using AI as a range finder was passed on.

We were told that we would be kept on operation *Diver* for

a while. Swift modifications were carried out to all the Mozzies. The exhaust shrouds were dispensed with, extra boost was given to the engines, we were supplied with 150 octane petrol and, of course, the noses were strengthened. With the exception of the exhaust shrouds, all these modifications were retained when we returned to our Bomber Support role.

We carried out a similar patrol two nights later but no bombs appeared while we were on our beat. The damage to Eager Beaver was not very serious, but it would take four or five days for the repairs to be completed.

July turned out to be a very eventful month. To the great joy of the whole squadron Ben was promoted to Squadron Leader and made 'A' Flight Commander. At about the same time I became Squadron Navigator Leader. This meant quite a bit of extra work and responsibility for us both, but Ben made a first-class Flight Commander, whilst for my part I liked having a say in the things that mattered.

On July 2nd we shot down another buzz-bomb while we were on a similar type of patrol as before. Again we found that four or five of them were launched together and we made straight for number three. We were the only fighter after it and we had no trouble with it. The next patrol, on July 5th, produced another buzz-bomb destroyed. On this occasion, however, the brute just would not go down until Ben gave it a really long burst of cannon fire. We were back in Eager Beaver and the vibration from the cannons put some of the instruments on Ben's blind-flying panel out of action. We landed at Ford for repairs at three in the morning and had to wait over two and a half hours before we took off again for Swanington, where we landed at 06.15 hours.

We were off again just after midnight for another anti-Diver patrol. We were lucky enough to shoot down two of the things on this trip. Again we went after the third of a group of four or five of them. We found nobody else after our first victim and only one other fighter after the second. Ben had the whole business so well taped by now, though, that he easily out-manœuvred the other chap and we were soon in much the better position to deal with the interception; the other chap saw this and cleared off.

Once the excitement of the first couple of patrols was over, it really was an unrewarding job for the navigator. He was responsible for navigating to and from the patrol line, but after that about all he had to do was to keep his eyes open for activity, let his pilot know the range when they were after a Diver and feed him with barley sugar or chewing gum from time to time. Our extensive training was being wasted.

The one weakness in the Bomber Support Mozzie in relation to its particular function was that Mark 10 AI searched only forwards. There was no warning if an enemy night fighter came up behind. Our Radar Section, under its very keen officer, Flying Officer Davies, had been working on a tail warning device which they had christened 'Monica'. On the night of July 10th it was fitted into two Mozzies. Ben and I went up in one of them with another crew in the second aircraft. Monica worked like a charm. It gave pretty reliable warning when the other aircraft came within 6000ft of us and we were full of its praises when we landed.

Permission was sought from 100 Group to fit it in all 157 Squadron aircraft; not only was this granted, but Monica became standard equipment for all 100 Group night fighters.

Next day we had the bright idea of using Monica as an extra offensive weapon. We went up with another crew whom we had briefed about our idea which was to allow the other Mozzie to stalk us while I watched its range as it came in. I could read this off my Monica tube. When the range came down to between 3,000 and 4,000ft, we whipped round in a tight turn which brought us nicely behind the stalking aircraft. It worked too.

Although I felt a slight sense of frustration at having been taken off the exhilarating job of Bomber Support to chase buzzbombs, there was a special satisfaction for me in seeing the wretched things go down into the Channel. I knew that they were intended for London, and I was born in London.

One hundred Group must have appreciated how I felt. On the 12th we were given a low-level support patrol, and two days later a high level one; both were uneventful, however. The 17th saw our last success against the buzz-bombs, making our score six in all. On this occasion we took off at the ungodly hour of 03.30 hours and found our bomb just as we were due to finish our patrol. In fact we did a few minutes' overtime.

We had found that in almost every instance Ben must have shot away part of the buzz-bomb, making it turn one way or another and plunge into the sea with its flame still alight. On one occasion only had the flame gone out and then it had just nosed straight down into the sea. We were very lucky in this respect, for it was such a small target that it was necessary to get to within two or three hundred yards to have a good shot at it.

The Divers were not always as amenable as we had found them. Flight-Lieutenant Matthews and Warrant Officer Penrose from our squadron had a rather shattering experience one night. They were on patrol and intercepted a Diver. Matthews opened fire a little too soon and had a rather long chase before he shot it down. Not long after, on the same patrol, they had a second chase. This time he was determined to go in close before he opened fire. He did. The thing exploded right in front of him. His Mozzie was thrown about like a feather in a storm for a few seconds. Then he realised that he could see nothing through his windscreen but a warm red glow was coming from behind him somewhere. His fin and rudder was ablaze but a few gentle dives blew that out. With the aid of his navigator he managed to wipe the windscreen clear of some of the soot and muck from the bomb's explosion. Very gingerly he flew the damaged Mosquito back to base, where he landed all right. He informed his ground crew that he thought there was a bit of damage at the back, which they had better look at next morning.

The whole station looked at it next morning – it really was a sight to behold. Only the framework of the fin and rudder was left, the rest had burned away. Every scrap of paint on the starboard side of the aircraft had been burnt off. The camouflage paint, the roundels and the squadron markings had completely disappeared; on the port side the paint was still there but it was blistered all over. They had certainly had a narrow escape. These two went on to become one of the highest scoring crews on 157 Squadron.

Towards the end of July it was decided to put both the Swanington squadrons on anti-Diver patrols full time. On the 21st the squadrons were transferred to West Malling in Kent, in order to be nearer the scene of operations. Although we were disappointed at being taken off our other job, there was some slight consolation in being moved to such a very pleasant part of the country in the summer. The 157 Squadron mess was at Addington House, a really lovely mansion set in delightful grounds. In these grounds were some of the most beautiful rose beds I have ever seen. They were tended by a sect known as the Seekers. Each rose tree was dedicated to the memory of some loved one who had died. I must say that the rose trees were much more pleasing to the eye than a cemetery full of tombstones.

Addington House was about 4 miles from West Malling and we used to travel past hop fields on our way to and fro.

Only Sussex and Cheshire can compete with the wonderful hostelries of Kent for dispensing the product of the hop. One of these hostelries, the Rose and Crown at Dunton Green, had been taken over just before the war by two very dear friends of mine from pre-war days, Mr. and Mrs. Byrne. We had many pleasant times with them during the next few weeks.

Nearby at Tonbridge there was a roadhouse, Hilden Manor, with an extremely nice swimming pool in which I had often swum. By dint of a little organisation we were soon carrying out dinghy-drill practice at Hilden Manor and we managed to arrange transport there on almost every fine day. It was a fine summer that year and we certainly made the most of it.

Ben and I flew on one more anti-Diver patrol from West Malling before going off on three weeks' leave. On July 23rd we took off at 03.30 hours and made for the usual patrol point near the Somme Estuary. This time there was a considerable amount of cloud down to about 3,000ft. We would obviously have seen nothing if we had flown above the cloud, so we were forced to fly below it. This proved a double handicap. Not only did it mean that we would not be able to gather speed in a dive, but our field of vision was sadly reduced. We saw three of the wretched things which we might have caught with a little more warning and a few knots more speed.

As it was, we had three maddening chases with the buzz-bomb just out of range by the time we had got behind it. Although Eager Beaver was straining every nerve we just had to sit there and watch them draw away from us – really frustrating.

When Ben and I returned to West Malling after our leave we found a complete transformation in the anti-Diver set-up. By now the interception of these things had been brought to a fine art. One lot of night fighters chased them across the Channel to within about 6 miles of the South Coast, where the guns, heavy and light, took over from them to 4 miles inland. From there more night fighters, in which included our two squadrons, operated with the aid of searchlight boxes; these fighters took up the chase as far as the barrage balloons. Very few bombs were getting through now. In the beginning, the day and night fighters had shot down the greater number of the bombs. Now, with a greater concentration of guns combined with better warning and equipment, the guns took a heavier toll. Between the 14th and 26th of August Ben and I flew on four of these new patrols without one bomb coming into our patrol section.

It must have become obvious to the enemy that, as his launching sites were being overrun by our invading armies, he would have to find some other way of launching the buzzbombs. Their answer was to fit them beneath aircraft which had begun operating from bases in southern Holland. These aircraft would fly out towards our East Coast at very low altitudes to avoid detection by our long-range warning system. They would then pop up to about 2,000ft to launch their missiles and then head back home.

On August 18th we were sent on a low-level patrol just off the Dutch Islands. The idea was to try to intercept the launching aircraft which were mostly Heinkels. If we could shoot the Heinkel down before it launched its toy, so much the better.

Almost from the moment we arrived on patrol we began a series of chases that got us nowhere. We spotted some lights on one of the islands, but they went out as we approached and we could see nothing when we got there. Then we had two long and difficult chases on aircraft, both of which turned out to be Mosquitos. We then saw what we thought must be a launching some way off. No AI contact appeared however. Again we saw a launching some distance from us but had no joy when we investigated it. Finally we returned to West Malling tired and rather dejected.

At last came the day we were all waiting for. On August 27th we were taken off Diver operations and returned to Swanington.

Divers, buzz-bombs, Vee-1s, Beechcraft or flying bombs, call them what you will, they were certainly a most ingenious weapon. I do not believe that they constituted a war-winning weapon but, properly used against the south of England when the invasion forces were being assembled, they might well have changed the course of the war. It is difficult to imagine how it would have been possible to build up the vast quantity of invasion material if it had been subjected to constant bombardment by buzz-bombs. It was originally intended to send over several hundreds a day beginning in January 1944. One can imagine the chaos that would have been caused on the South Coast.

The bombing of Peenemunde and the constant attacks on launching sites had helped to delay the initial launchings until July. Even then, Hitler regarded the 'V' weapons purely as a retaliatory measure against London. In spite of great pressure, he would not allow them to be used elsewhere until it was too late. It must be remembered that it took almost three months for the defences to finally win the battle against the buzz-bomb. Even then, it was largely due to the fact that many of the main launching sites had been overrun by the advancing Allied Armies.

I have often been asked if it was true that pilots had actually destroyed buzz-bombs by formating on them and tipping them over. This did happen – only in daylight, of course – but it was essential that the aircraft performing this dangerous feat was faster than the bomb. Tempests and the latest Mark of Spitfires came into this category and so, later, did the Meteor.

CHAPTER 12

A Beam in Your Eye

WHILE operation *Diver* had been in progress, 157 Squadron and our stable companions, 85 Squadron, had done their best to keep a strict training programme going in readiness for the return to Bomber Support. When we returned to Swanington, however, we found that we were to be given a week to get back into full swing again.

One of the first things we did was to arrange to hold an Extraordinary General Mess Meeting to discuss ways and means of providing ourselves with a decent bar for the mess. We had previously made do with a small dispensary for drinks. Now, having seen the many very pleasant drinkeries down south, we were all very discontented with our lot. Ben was elected President of a Bar Committee, and in a very short space of time a really delightful bar had been constructed entirely on a self-help basis. A large and unlikely looking cellar was transformed into an attractive and comfortable lounge bar, and the squadrons were to spend many an enjoyable evening there.

Another big improvement that we found on our return was in the Operations Briefing Room, which had been organised and was run by the Intelligence Section. It was a very important part of the station set-up and had been treated accordingly. In a spacious room were chairs and tables on which the navigators could spread out their maps to plot the night's operation. The walls of the room had been covered with some boarding in which pins could be easily inserted, and almost the whole of one wall was covered with maps which had been assembled to cover practically the whole of Europe.

Every scrap of information pertaining to our job was available to us for the asking and the scope of this information was a constant source of amazement to me. Our first briefing in the new room was on September 5th when the two

159

squadrons were first put back on to Bomber Support operations. It was most impressive and became the standard method of briefing while we remained at Swanington. The entire night's operation by Bomber Command was depicted on the huge wall map. Coloured tapes were pinned to the map showing the route to be followed by Main Force bombers; white tape denoted the route to the target and black the return route; diversionary raids – that is, secondary and spoof raids – were also shown with tapes, usually of red and blue.

Our patrol points were indicated by flat-headed pins with the numbers 85 or 157 on them. Group would allocate them to the squadrons en bloc and the Squadron and Flight Commanders would assemble before briefing to sort out each patrol separately for the individual crews. German fighter assembly beacons were shown by black-headed pins. All sorts of other relevant information was available – the disposition of searchlight and flak belts, for example – and all was presented in a manner easy to digest.

The patrols called for on September 5th were in support of a spoof raid on Hanover. The weather was pretty poor here and Main Force bombers were not operating. A combined force of 100 Group aircraft and Pathfinders from 5 Group were going off in an attempt to get German night fighters airborne and make them waste fuel. High-level support aircraft were operating with them to help simulate a major raid and to chase any Germans who might be up.

A small target-marking force of Pathfinders would make for Hanover, where they would drop their marker bombs and some incendiaries. They would be followed by some twenty heavy aircraft from 100 Group dropping Window. Meanwhile the support fighters would have taken up positions around the route and target areas.

This part of the briefing was done by the Station Commander or one of the Squadron Commanders. It was followed by a talk by the Intelligence Officer, who would pass on any extra information he had been able to ferret out.

Then Signals and Armaments Officers would have their say. Finally the Met Department reported on weather and gave us forecasts of wind strengths and directions at various heights.

Once briefing had finished, there would be a hubbub of voices as each crew sorted out the details of their own particular trip. No two would be the same, and all we were normally given as far as our own instructions were concerned were the patrol point, the time we were to arrive there and the time we were to leave the patrol area.

The spoof raid on Hanover was carried out as planned. The only thing that went wrong was that the Huns refused to cooperate. This time they remained steadfast on the ground and not one of our fighters had a chase. Probably the weather over Britain was so bad that the Jerries knew that Bomber Command would not put on a major raid. Whatever the reason, we saw nothing on our high-level patrol just to the south of Hanover.

When our patrol time was up, we decided to go down and have a look at Vechta, a German night-fighter station in the vicinity. Here, too, there was no sign of life. We then decided that, as it was very dark and hazy, there was little future in looking around much more and so we headed north, the shortest way out of enemy territory. We passed halfway between Emden and Wilhelmshaven, flying at 3,000ft, and then climbed to 4,000ft to dive over the coast at the little island of Baltrum, near Norderney.

Nobody had taken any notice of us on our hour and a half patrol. We were clear of Baltrum and still on a northerly course; I was just saying to Ben:

"We can turn for home in a minute. Course… two-six-zero degrees. I think we're far enough out now!"

Suddenly two searchlights flicked out of the darkness straight on to us. One from Baltrum, the other from the mainland.

"Well, they've left that a little late," I remarked.

"Have they indeed," said Ben, stuffing Eager Beaver's

nose down in a dive. "They're firing heavy flak along those ruddy beams."

So they were.

Luckily the flak was not as accurate as the searchlights. It was quite some distance behind us and soon gave up. The searchlights flicked out too; we were on our own again.

"Now that was an unsportsmanlike thing to do," said Ben. "You just can't trust those Jerries!"

We turned then and set off on the long sea leg back to base.

On the afternoon of September 11th we had carried out our night-flying test in Eager Beaver and had put in a good session of practice with Monica, our rearward warning device. We landed and decided to amble over to the Intelligence Section to see what was on for the night before going up to the mess for a meal.

On the way round the perimeter track Ben remarked:

"I think we'll let the other chaps have first pick of the patrols tonight. We'll take the one that's left over."

I understood the reason behind this decision. Ben was always conscious of the ill-feeling that could build up on a squadron or a flight when the Commander invariably picked the most likely looking patrol for himself; or if on a defensive night-fighter squadron, he stayed on the ground when things were quiet but leapt into the air whenever Huns were around. That might have been a good way of building up a big individual score, but it was by no means the best way of building up squadron morale.

One of Ben's jobs as Flight Commander was to allocate the various patrols to the crews in his Flight who were on operations on any particular night. He was very much aware of his responsibility in this direction. He would certainly never shirk a patrol that looked difficult, but at the same time he realised that because morale was so high on the squadron all the crews wanted a really fair chance of excitement and action.

I must say, though, that when we saw the operational plan for that particular night it looked as if we could not have picked on a worse night for such a decision. A gigantic raid had been laid on for some poor unfortunate town in southern Germany, with a secondary target in the Ruhr. With one exception, every patrol from Swanington was in support of one or other of these raids. They looked just the thing to provoke massive reaction from the German night fighters.

There was just one solitary patrol that was not in direct support of these two raids. It could not, in fact, have been much further away from the main scene of activity; it was right up on the island of Seeland, just off south-eastern Denmark, and it was off all the maps and charts we normally used, as it was so far to the north-east.

There were no other patrols of any sort anywhere near it, but a spoof raid that looked rather ineffectual had been laid on. Some training aircraft were scheduled to pop out over the North Sea and to fly towards northern Holland before turning back for home. It did not look to us as if the spoof could possibly have any real bearing on our patrol point, which was miles away.

We had realised at once that we would be left with this stooge patrol as we were taking last pick. Sure enough that was how it turned out. There was just a little consolation for us when we learned from Intelligence that there was a German fighter beacon on Seeland. This was one of the fighter assembly beacons which normally consisted of a light on the ground that could be seen from some considerable distance flashing a letter in Morse code to identify it to the German night-fighters. There was, as well, a powerful R/T transmitter which would be tied up with the reporting system and would pump out information to any German fighters who might be ordered to assemble there.

However, this beacon did not seem much consolation for what would be a round trip of over 1,000 miles, with a twenty-minute patrol thrown in. We noted that we would have to pass fairly near to the airfield of Westerland/Sylt, so we determined to have a look there on the way back if, as we were pretty sure, the Seeland patrol turned out to be a waste of time.

We had a leisurely meal in the mess, accompanied by a few sarcastic remarks about our apparent night off ops. Then we went back for final briefing and at 20.45 hours carrying what seemed to be an excessive number of maps and plotting charts, we climbed into Eager Beaver. As we taxied round the perimeter track to the end of the runway, I could not help feeling a little peeved that Ben should have chosen this night of all nights to make this gesture. Anyhow, here we were and I might as well make the best of it. We were at the end of the runway now. Ben ran up the engines in turn, with the brakes hard on, checking his instruments. I glanced round the cockpit to check that oxygen was on and everything else all right, looked at my watch and as we started off down the runway, entered the first item on my log sheet.

I felt the usual thrill of excitement as we took off into the night. There was something about it that never failed to give me a kick, even on a stooge trip such as this. We were a minute or so early, so we circled the airfield twice before I told Ben to set course. The night was dark, with no moon, but there were no clouds either, making visibility quite good. We made height to 2,000ft and crossed out over the Norfolk coast just south of Cromer. Our long sea leg of over 450 miles had begun.

Eager Beaver's twin Rolls-Royce Merlin engines were purring smoothly. I switched on the AI just to check if it appeared to work all right; it did. I switched it off as we did not want to be plotted by the enemy radar. A transmission from our AI would be picked up much further away than they would be able to see the aircraft. We had dropped to about 500ft, which also gave them less chance of picking us up.

All we could see was sea and stars. The seemingly endless sea journey soon became monotonous. We were the only moving thing except for an occasional falling star. The sea beneath us was horribly black. I took a Gee fix. We were pretty well on track; the forecast winds had been good so far. Nearly two hours had gone by before we reached our patrol point. I passed Ben some barley sugar and had some myself.

I always took a selection of things to suck on these patrols; we were issued with quite a choice – fruit drops, barley sugar, Horlicks tablets or chewing-gum. Our mouths got very dry sometimes, and it gave us something to do.

There was quite a bit of German jamming on Gee now, but I got another good fix. We could not expect to pick it up much longer at this height, anyhow. We had decided to steer fairly well clear of Sylt, our landfall would be at a little island just north of the island of Sylt. Five minutes before we were due at the island I told Ben. There was a slight change in the note of Eager Beaver's engines as we began to climb up to 4,000ft. Soon we could pick out our little island just over to starboard. We could see the northern tip of Sylt as we turned slightly to starboard for the leg to Seeland.

We had decided to carry out our patrol at 12,000ft. It seemed as good a height as any so we continued on our way, climbing steadily. We were over the mainland now, no lights below and nothing to see on my AI which I had switched on as we started climbing. Monica was on as well and nothing showed on that either. Soon we had another short sea trip to cross and, in spite of the darkness below, we could see the coastline coming up.

We crossed the strip of sea and were halfway over the next piece of land when, far ahead, we spotted a flashing light. It was flashing the letter 'Q' in Morse.

At least the beacon on Seeland was working. After flying for another ten minutes or so we passed right over the beacon, and as we did, so we saw the lights of neutral Sweden a few miles to the north-east of us. It seemed very strange to think that over there lived a nation not at war. However, we had our own little war to get on with, so we turned south-east on to our pre-determined patrol line. A four-minute leg that way, then about turn and an eight-minute leg the other way; that was the plan.

Once we had remarked on the proximity of Sweden there was nothing much to talk about. Nobody was taking any

notice of our presence so far as we knew. We reached the
south-east point of our patrol, and as Ben began the wide
sweep that would bring us back on to our new course I gave
him some chewing gum and bemoaned the fact that we had
no cards with which to while away the time.

We had hardly settled down on course when I noticed with
surprised excitement a faint blip on my AI.

"Contact," I yelled.

"Don't be funny," said Ben disgustedly.

"I'm not kidding! Range nearly 8 miles… coming in a bit
bloody fast! It's a head-on just out to port. Get ready for a
hard starboard turn. Range 6 miles."

"Okay. I wonder what the devil this can be?"

"Range 4 miles… Still out to port and slightly below."

"Do you want me to go down?"

"No. It must be on a parallel course, range 3 miles…
Ready for the turn… Now!"

I know that as the turn starts I will lose the contact as the
other aircraft goes out of our AI coverage. I also know that
I should see it again very soon, crossing us from port to
starboard. If I have judged the turn right, he should finish
up about 2,500ft in front of us. It went very well. Fifty
seconds later:

"Okay. I've got him again. Range 3,000… Gently
starboard… Go down."

"Gently starboard, going down."

"He's turning starboard… keep going starboard… harder
starboard… level out now but keep going starboard… range
coming in a bit now just over 2,000."

"We're going round the ruddy beacon. He must be
orbiting the thing. Where is he now?"

"2,000… Keep going starboard… Ease the turn a bit.
Where do you want him?"

"Starboard will do. Is he above us?"

"Just a shade… Coming in to 1,500, still going starboard.
He's about 10 degrees starboard slightly above."

"We're still going round the beacon... Ah! There he is."

"Can you hold him? What is it?"

"Can't see what it is. Yes, I've got it all right now. It's bloody dark though; I'll go in a bit. It must be a Hun. What the hell would one of our aircraft be doing here?"

By this time we, were underneath the aircraft only about 400ft away. It certainly was dark, but we could clearly see that it was a Junkers 188.

It had stopped turning starboard now and was flying straight and level. He obviously did not imagine that there was a Mosquito underneath him. Ben eased up Eager Beaver's nose as we dropped back slightly. As the Junkers drifted into his gunsight he gave it a four-second burst. The cannons rattled, the familiar smell of cordite wafted up. We saw strikes as flashes came from the starboard wing root. The Junkers gave a great lurch and lost much of its speed; Ben had to pull up over it to avoid a collision. As we went up over it, a four-star cartridge, two red and two green, was fired from it. By the light of these we saw the enemy aircraft drop very steeply away to starboard. A pinpoint of flame from its starboard engine spluttered into a large flame that we watched going earthwards.

Although I had watched all this from my grandstand seat with much excitement and gratification, my training ensured that I kept half an eye on Monica and half an eye on my AI. In the same second that the Junkers started on its way down I noticed another blip on my AI. It was about 5 miles ahead of us, slightly to port and a little below.

Ben needed no urging to believe me this time. As we turned after this second aircraft, we saw the first one crash on land just about 3 miles east of the beacon. It could be seen burning there for some time.

Meanwhile we were closing in nicely on number two. We decided that it must be an aircraft carrying out some sort of exercise with the first one. It seemed incredible to us that he had not seen all the commotion going on behind him. To our amazement, however, we had no difficulty in closing in on him quite quickly. We repeated the tactics as before and identified him from close below as another Junkers 188, flying straight and level.

What an idiot he must have been.

A four-star cartridge had been fired and an aircraft had gone down in flames – in fact it was still burning down below – and this chap had not noticed a thing.

As Ben lifted Eager Beaver's nose once more, I said:
"Make this one a real flamer."

"Okay," replied Ben, "I'll see what I can I do!"

This was not just bloodthirstiness on my part; we carried a ciné-camera which worked automatically with the cannons. At night it needed something pretty spectacular to register anything at all.

Ben proceeded to carry out instructions. He gave it a two-second burst from only 100 yards. It straightaway caught fire in the fuselage, pulled up to port, then over the vertical in an almost classic loop. It dropped flaming like a torch to hit the sea only a few miles off the coast of Sweden with a magnificent flash as it exploded.

Some fairly large chunks had come off this Junkers as the cannon shells ripped into it. We flew right through them, but apart from feeling his slipstream and getting a horrible whiff of ersatz German oil in the cockpit, we suffered no damage – at least, not as far as we could tell.

These two one-sided contests had occupied just over seven minutes, so that we had only three more minutes left of our patrol time. In view of the fact that we had flown through debris from the second aircraft, we decided to call it a day. We still had a long sea journey to negotiate and it would be silly to take any unnecessary chances.

We set course for home. As we passed over the beacon it was still busily flashing the letter 'Q'. I had a momentary thrill when I saw something on my AI, but whatever it was the blips were too blurred to be aircraft blips. We decided that it might have been Window that had been dropped earlier by the aircraft we had chased; we carried on with the return journey.

The excitement was not quite over however. We were just crossing out to the north of Sylt when I got a contact on Monica. I saw it first at about 6,000ft range, warned Ben and when it came in to just under 4,000ft we whipped round in a hard turn to see if we could turn it into an AI contact.

We did not succeed in getting AI contact, but we shook off the aircraft that had been behind us. As we were still at 10,000ft, Ben put Eager Beaver's nose down slightly so that we could gain a bit of speed on the way home. With all the night's thrills behind us the long sea journey did not seem too bad. We landed at Swanington after four and a half hours of what had turned out to be a very satisfactory stooge patrol.

The Mozzies from the other patrols had all landed by the time we arrived. Strange to say, only one of the 157 Squadron aircraft that had been on patrol that night had a chase and that resulted in one Junkers 188 damaged.

We found next day that apart from being covered in ersatz oil Eager Beaver had only a few scratches from the debris of the second Junkers. Later we were told that the film from the camera gun had shown evidence of the combats. I must admit that I was pleased about this. To return from a patrol that looked as pointless as ours had done and then claim two enemy aircraft destroyed seemed almost too much to believe.

CHAPTER 13

Teamwork

ONE of the most important jobs on a night-fighter squadron was the crewing up of pilot and navigator. It was one of my responsibilities, in conjunction with the individuals concerned and the Flight Commanders, to advise and make suggestions as to the best way of ensuring that a happy 'marriage' ensued on all occasions. In most cases the crews had been paired originally at the Operational Training Unit. Usually these pairings had been made after careful consideration and it was only rarely that changes were needed. The job we were now engaged on demanded keenness and initiative equally from the pilot and the navigator. A brilliant pilot could expect little success if he was flying with a navigator who could not get the best out of AI or whose navigation was weak. The same held true for a first-class navigator with a poor pilot.

Sometimes re-crewings became necessary through illness or the occasional posting of one crew member to a job on which he could not be accompanied by his partner. The more experienced aircrew often needed very careful handling; having gained their experience and worked out their own methods with one partner, they might dislike the idea of starting again with another.

Flight Lieutenant Doleman, known to all and sundry as 'Dolly', was a pilot on 'A' Flight who had somehow contrived to remain on operational flying practically throughout the war without being sent for a rest. He had been crewed with a series of navigators in the past, but something always seemed to happen to them and he had never settled down with one for any length of time. In spite of numerous night patrols Dolly had not enjoyed any success, yet I felt sure he was a pilot with above average ability. I had flown with him on one or two occasions and I also knew that Ben had a high regard for him.

I have never come across anyone keener on flying and the Royal Air Force than Dolly, who really seemed to live for flying. He had two other loves: an ancient Rover car named Roger and a delightful smooth-haired fox terrier named Towser. Towser was a great favourite with us all and became the squadron mascot. As for Roger, with the help of some rope to keep the doors on and plywood to keep the wind and rain out where the side windows had broken, he went on forever.

Once an even older Roger made an appearance on the station; Dolly had bought it for spares. It was obvious to everybody that the older Roger was in much better shape than the real Roger. We wondered what Dolly would do. It would have been much easier to strip the real Roger for spare parts and ride around in Roger the Second. Dolly's love was too great, however; he retained Roger the First and for weeks the ghastly skeleton of Roger the Second lay near 'A' Flight dispersal until Dolly was ordered to remove it forthwith.

Operational aircrew were given generous and fairly frequent leave, but Dolly could only rarely be persuaded to take leave at all. Even then, on more than one occasion he had to be literally ordered off the station by the Squadron Commander.

Shortly after I became Navigator Leader, Dolly's navigator had been taken off flying for some reason or other. They had not been together very long but they were getting on well and at last it had looked as if Dolly was fixed up. Losing this last partner had made Dolly extremely brassed off and he confided as much one night in the bar to Ben. Next morning in the Flight Office Ben brought the subject up.

"I'm a bit worried about Dolly," he said. "He seems to be having more than his share of bad luck with navigators. In fact he's so brassed off that he has almost given up the idea of ever getting a Hun. He was telling me last night that as he doesn't seem to be able to crew up with a navigator who is any good in the air, he may as well pick a good boozing partner! Evidently there's a chap at one of the OTUs just due to come back to a squadron. He knew him some while back and wants us to try to get him here. Dolly's a good man, it seems wrong to me. What do you think about it?"

I had already thought about it. I had asked Group for a good replacement for the navigator who had gone, but there just was nobody available then. On 'B' Flight there was Flight Lieutenant Bunch. He was an experienced navigator and had been flying with the Flight Commander, whose place had been taken by Ben. 'Bunny' Bunch had already won the DFC, and, as he was slightly senior to me, he had undoubtedly been disappointed when I was made Navigator Leader. To be fair, he did not ever show any resentment to me and always proved helpful and co-operative. He was awaiting a posting which would almost certainly have been as Navigator Leader on another squadron.

"What about Bunny Bunch?" I suggested to Ben. "I did mention it to Bunny the other day. At least he could get a bit of flying in until his posting comes through, but he's got the idea that he and Dolly wouldn't hit it off."

"It might work," said Ben. "Bunny's a bit of an old sober-sides, but I should think it's worth a try."

I buttonholed Bunny at the first opportunity. He was not going to be the difficult one to persuade, I felt. Sure enough, he agreed to give it a try – anyhow, as a temporary measure. But I must fix it with Dolly. He would not approach Dolly about it himself.

That was the first round won.

Dolly proved a bit more difficult. He gave me all the arguments he had given Ben the previous evening, but I have a knack of getting my own way. Eventually he said, grudgingly:

"All right, Brandy me boy. I'll do it for you, but I wouldn't have done it for anyone else."

On September 12th off they went on their first patrol together. It was a high-level Bomber Support patrol in the Frankfurt area and they succeeded in destroying a Messerschmitt 110. In the six months that followed they remained together as a crew, destroying six more enemy aircraft and damaging another.

Both of them were married soon after the War. I wonder if Dolly still drives around in Roger, but I do not think it likely. Roger could not really be described as a woman's car.

Although normal day-to-day servicing of our Mozzies was carried out at the Flights by the ground crews, they were given regular overhauls which might take a week or so to complete. Eager Beaver had been taken in for one of these inspections, so that we had to take another aircraft on September 13th when we went off for a high-level patrol just south of Koblenz.

We had not been in the target area for more than a few minutes when I picked up an AI contact. For the next ten minutes or so we were led a really merry chase. The aircraft we were following took continuous violent evasive action. Hard turns in either direction would be interspersed with steep dives and climbs, so that we felt rather like a yo-yo on the end of a string as we chased him. It took an age to reduce the range but we gradually closed in.

The evasive action had been so continuous that we thought we were perhaps after another Mozzie who was seeing us on Monica. If not, it might possibly be a German night fighter with a tail-warner. Eventually our quarry eased off his evasive action a little, thinking perhaps that he had thrown us off when we were, in fact, close up to him.

We sat underneath him and identified him as a Junkers 88. Ben used his normal manœuvre of easing up the nose of our Mozzie and dropping back to firing range. As he did so he exclaimed:

"Confound this bloody gunsight. I can't dim the wretched thing properly. Look, it's like a flaming neon sign."

Sure enough, when I glanced over, I saw a bright-red ring showing on his gunsight. There was a knob to turn so that the pilot could choose the exact degree of brightness he wished for. The dimmer had gone wrong, and every time Ben tried to take aim the silhouette of the Junkers disappeared in the bright-red light.

"Well, I'll have a go. If we sit here much longer he'll see us." He pressed the gun button. "Now what the hell's gone wrong? It sounds as if only one cannon is firing!"

We saw some strikes around the port engine. Instead of the usual healthy roar of the four cannons, however, there seemed to be only a measly pop-pop. It was a pity we were not in Eager Beaver!

The Junkers went down in a screaming dive and Ben lost sight of him. I could still follow him on AI though. We chased him from 15,000ft right down to 8,000ft, with some wild evasive action thrown in. Again he eased off after four or five minutes and we closed in once more. We could see sparks and flames coming from his port engine, but the propeller was still turning.

Ben gave it another burst, cursing the gunsight as he did so. The roar of the cannons was still sadly diminished, but we saw strikes along the fuselage. The Junkers then made a clever move. He seemed suddenly almost to stop dead; probably he had put down his air brakes. Ben had to pull up hard to port in order to avoid ramming him. Then down went the Junker again in a steep dive heading for a bank of clouds. Although we whipped round after him and dived for the clouds we lost sight of him and also lost AI contact.

Next day we found that two cannons only had been working. On the night of September 15th Squadron Leader Chisholm, the 'B' Flight Commander, was posted 'missing' after a high-level patrol in the Kiel area. A rubber dinghy, similar to those we carried in the Mozzie, had been reported in a position on the sea which was near to Chisholm's route. Ben and I went out next morning with a couple of other Mozzies to search for him. We would not have been able to rescue him but we could have fixed his position for a rescue launch. Unfortunately, in spite of a long search, we were unable to find the dinghy.

Two nights later we went all the way to Schleswig/Jagel

in Jutland. This was not so very far south of where we had our encounter with the two Junkers 188s. This time, however, we were not so fortunate. We patrolled for quite a while without seeing anything; then, five minutes before our patrol time was up, there was a cloud of blue smoke, a smell of burning rubber and my AI went phut. This turned out to be the beginning of quite a run of trouble with AI, although we had been very fortunate with it so far.

This particular trip, however, had provided us with one of the most unforgettable sights imaginable. As we went out over the North Sea at dusk we could see literally hundreds of aircraft in the skies around us. The heavens were absolutely full it seemed. Bomber Command had taken off in force for an early raid and we were overtaking them. At the same time, coming towards us were the Americans, who had been carrying out a big day raid. With their bombers were their fighter escorts, which made a truly impressive aerial armada.

Impressive as it was, it was becoming jolly dangerous as the twilight faded. I had switched on my AI to help avoid collisions, but the picture was so swamped with aircraft blips that it was impossible to pick a single aircraft out. I switched the AI off and switched on our navigation lights instead until things thinned out a bit.

Our next three patrols were all marred by AI troubles. On the first two occasions the failure did not occur until almost at the end of the patrols, which were uneventful. The third patrol was in an area south of Bonn on the night of September 29th. Cologne was being bombed and we had a grandstand view of the whole proceedings. The night was clear but dark, and visibility was extremely good. In the distance we could see concentrations of searchlights and the sparks which denoted flak as the bombers made their way in. At times the flak seemed to fill the sky. It seemed impossible that through all that fire some 600 of our bombers were flying serenely on their way. If ever a job called for cool courage, that of the bomber crews did, flying night after night on heavily opposed raids such as this.

Soon the target markers went down, followed shortly afterwards by incendiaries. Then with the flak building up to a crescendo, the main bombing started. As the fires spread below and we saw the flashes of the bombs, the flak and the searchlights gradually died down but the bombing continued.

We had been patrolling while all this had been going on, but I had not picked up anything on AI. About half our patrol time had gone when there was that blue smoke and dark brown smell as the AI packed up. We were useless up there without our 'eyes', so we decided to go home. We would investigate any airfields we saw lit up, just in case we saw an aircraft landing or taking off. We had been flying at 15,000ft and began descending to 10,000ft on our way home as it would be a better height under these circumstances.

We had not flown very far, however, when I noticed a contact on Monica, which was fortunately still working.

Normally we would have let him come in to 4,000 or 5,000ft before turning in an attempt to get behind him and chase him with our AI. This time, though, our AI was not working.

"Well," said Ben, "we can at least give him a run for his money."

He began to take fairly strong evasive action. I watched the Monica indicator closely. The range increased slightly but the other aircraft was hanging on quite well. I informed Ben of this.

"Right," was the response. "He'll have to get pretty close on a night like this before he sees us. Let him get in to about 3,000ft, then I'll whip round and we might just be lucky enough to get a visual."

I let the other aircraft come in as Ben suggested. We whipped round in no uncertain manner and both peered vainly into the darkness, hoping to see exhaust flames. It was no good, though, and so Ben flew straight and level for a while to give the other aircraft a chance of picking us up again. Sure enough it did. We tried exactly the same manœuvre but again without success. After this we decided that acting as a decoy duck any more would be a waste of time. Ben put down the nose of our Mozzie and we headed for home without any more excitement.

My wife was expecting our first baby early in the New Year. She was living in Bath and I had a few days' leave to arrange for the confinement. This was accomplished satisfactorily, with everybody concerned being extremely co-operative at the sight of my RAF uniform. While I was on leave I learned that Ben and I had both been awarded a Bar to our DFC.

Somebody in Public Relations must have handed out some information to the London Press. The *Evening News* ran a startling headline across the whole top of one of the centre pages:

'Mr. Chips the Second Shoots Down Six Flying Bombs' while the *Evening Standard* proclaimed:

'Double DFC for Donat's Double.'

All this was accompanied by photographs, stories and quotes from the official citation and certainly brought about a deal of leg-pulling when I returned from leave on October 10th.

We carried out half a dozen more patrols during the next fortnight without having a single chase on an enemy aircraft. That is not to say that we had no chases at all, we did in fact have several. The unfortunate thing was that everyone was on a friendly aircraft. We spent many minutes sitting right underneath Lancasters, wondering what they would say if they had known there was a night fighter underneath them. The problem of identification on a really dark night was always difficult, for we realised that if a Lancaster saw a twin-engined aircraft approach him at night over enemy territory he was perfectly entitled to shoot first and ask questions after. From our point of view, even with a Lancaster it was essential for us to get really close in order to identify it. Just for the record we were never fired upon by one of our four-engined bombers. Whether this was because of our careful approach or their remarkable night aircraft recognition is, I suppose, debatable.

During these patrols, I completed my 1,000 hours flying.

Ben and I had a very pleasant trip on October 19th. It had been decided that the Swanington Squadrons should use the airfield of Juvincourt, near Rheims, as a forward base – mainly for refuelling – for some patrols planned for us in the Munich area later in the month. Juvincourt was, of course, in Allied hands by this time, and Rheims is nicely situated in the centre of the Champagne country. When it became necessary for someone to fly there to ensure that facilities would be made available for us, that fact did not escape our notice. We found ourselves among the crew of an Oxford that flew to this centre of the champagne industry on that morning.

We concluded our business at Juvincourt and managed to arrange transport to Rheims for the early afternoon. We were shown over one of the famous champagne establishments and acquired a few cases of the sparkling beverage. One of the directors of the firm spoke very fair English and we had an interesting chat with him.

He told us that the Germans had not damaged anything there as they were very keen to keep the champagne industry going. As for the French, they had by devious means managed to hide away almost all of their really fine vintage wines from the Germans.

Unfortunately there were five of us in the Oxford and we had had to promise so much bubbly to various high-ups that we only received three bottles apiece for our troubles. Very useful, however, to put by for the wetting of the head of my expected child.

Towards the end of the month we flew on what was to be the most uncomfortable and frightening patrol we ever had. The weather over England was frightful and the main Bomber Command force was not operating. Hundred Group sent over a small spoof raid and Ben and I were detailed for a high-level patrol between the North German ports of Emden and Wilhelmshaven.

We took off at 17.55 hours – a nice early trip, we thought. Almost as soon as we were off the ground we went slap into cloud. Although we climbed hopefully on our way across the North Sea, we did not manage to find the tops of the cloud. In fact we did not emerge from cloud until we were just over Swanington three and a half hours later. We just had to assume that our navigation was going more or less correctly. We had no means of checking our position by visual means, and Gee, our navigational aid, was soon very badly jammed.

In our efforts to get above the cloud we had climbed at one time to 25,000ft without success. We decided to return to 15,000ft and arrived at what we fondly hoped was our patrol point at that height. The patrol between Emden and Wilhelmshaven took about seven minutes. As we turned somewhere near Wilhelmshaven for the return trip, the cloud in our vicinity began to light up occasionally. At first we thought it was lightning but suddenly our Mozzie gave a lurch which coincided with some very pretty light effects in the cloud. Perhaps it was flak and not lightning after all.

We felt rather like an Aunt Sally at a fairground. It was quite obvious that, with the weather so bad here, the gunners below would know very well that there would be no German aircraft flying. They would therefore be under no misapprehension about our identity. We would never know for certain if it was flak or lightning or both, but just in case Ben made things a little difficult for gunners by varying height and speed as we went not very gaily on our way.

We were down for forty minutes of this patrol and we decided to stick it out although there was no chance of seeing another aircraft in all that cloud, even if there had been one to see. All bad things come to an end and eventually we were able to call it a day and turn for home.

Eager Beaver had been out of commission for almost the whole of October, but on the 29th she was ready for us to take to Juvincourt for the patrol near Munich which was to take place as planned. We did our night-flying test in the morning and took off for Juvincourt at 15.30 hours. We had a meal and took off again after a Met briefing for our patrol. We were just circling the airfield before setting course for Munich when Ben exclaimed:

"Just look at that starboard engine."

I looked. There I saw the tell-tale signs of oil dribbling back from the engine cowling over the nacelle of the starboard engine. We had an oil leak.

A hurried conference ensued. Obviously we would be mad to attempt to go on to Munich, much as we had looked forward to doing so. The oil-pressure gauge was only slightly down on that engine, but we could see the stuff bubbling from the cowling. If we landed at Juvincourt we would not be able to carry out our patrol even if the fault was repaired almost immediately. The timing on these patrols had to be exact. If the fault took some time to repair, we might be stuck there for any length of time. The prospect of that did not appeal to us at all.

We decided to return to Swanington. If we did run into trouble with that engine, we had another one left and Mozzies had a wonderful single-engined performance. There were plenty of airfields at which we could land in emergency so we pressed on home, rather disappointed that such a likely looking trip should have petered out in such a manner.

There was another big raid on Cologne next night. Our patrol was an unusual one; we had been detailed to patrol the target area for half an hour but not to begin our patrol until ten minutes after the last bomber should have left. Visibility was quite good when we arrived although there was a fair amount of high cloud. Cologne was burning and we could see the lights of many fires showing through smoke that was drifting across the city.

We had hardly settled down on patrol when I got a contact. We closed in on a Lancaster which Ben saw silhouetted against the background formed by the smoke below. Ben had seen him quite clearly and had made the identification at nearly 4,000ft. We wondered why he was so far behind the others and decided to follow him for a while. We slid out starboard and let him draw away to 5 miles while I continued to watch him on AI. We were quite a bit faster than the Lancaster, so Ben flew a weaving course behind him.

After about five minutes, as we were turning back towards him, a contact appeared well over to our port side and some 3 miles behind the Lancaster. Aha! we thought; this is a German night fighter stalking the bomber. As we closed in and found that it was on the same course as the Lancaster we were even surer. We had to get in to 1,200ft before Ben got a visual on the exhausts of another four-engined aircraft – what a disappointment.

Still, Ben thought there was something strange about those exhausts. They were nothing like the Lancaster's in colour or shape, so we went right in for a close look from about 100ft below. To our surprise it was a Liberator. What on earth was a Liberator doing over there?

It was quite unmistakable, however, so somewhat reluctantly we let it go. We wondered if it might be a captured one that the Germans were using, but in our position we had no choice but to break away, wishing that we could borrow a searchlight for a second or two to see if the Liberator had roundels or a swastika painted on her.

On November 1st we were detailed for a low-level patrol of Fritzlar airfield, near Kassel. The weather in the area was shocking when we arrived, with low cloud for miles around the patrol beat. We stooged around for a while in cloud, then, as we were obviously not of any use there, we climbed up to nearly 12,000ft before we were clear. It was quite pleasant up there with a little moonlight. Some way to the north-west we could see a large hole in the clouds, so we went over to investigate.

There was a very big area free of cloud there, and as we dived down we could see that visibility was exceptionally good. We soon confirmed our whereabouts – Kassel was some 3 or 4 miles behind us as we continued our descent to 3,000ft. Almost at once we spotted a train, which Ben attacked with very good results. There were several strikes on the engine which emitted clouds of steam.

As we zoomed up from this attack we saw another train farther along the line. Ben dealt with this train as with the previous one. Soon after this the cloud closed in again so we climbed up once more and headed for home.

CHAPTER 14

Eager Beaver's Last Patrol

WE flew our last patrol in Eager Beaver on November 6th. She was getting rather long in the tooth for this very testing job and the squadron was getting some new Mozzies. Koblenz was the target that night. As there were several German fighter beacons in the vicinity, we expected some action. Almost as soon as we arrived on patrol we got a contact. A long chase after an aircraft which was taking the most violent evasive action ended when our AI went dead just as the other aircraft seemed to have settled down on to a steady course.

Four nights later we were on a high-level patrol in the same area. Just before we reached our patrol point I had a contact on an aircraft coming towards us. For the next twenty-five minutes we were engaged in the most amazing night dog-fight without ever managing to get close enough for Ben to see what we were chasing. I followed him on AI through the most violent evasive action I had ever known. It seemed probable that he was either a Mosquito or a German night fighter equipped with a tail warner. Twice we went in really tight complete circles, which made it appear as if he was trying to get on to our tail.

Eventually he went down in a very steep dive which we followed to 2,000ft height before we lost him. Whatever it was, the pilot was extremely skilful. Luckily he met his match in Ben, otherwise we would have become the quarry.

We climbed back on patrol, disappointed but exhilarated. Still, perhaps that one deserved to get away.

Hardly had we reached patrol height again than we had another contact. A visual took only four minutes this time.

The other aircraft was dodging around a bit but was flying rather slowly. Our airspeed was only a 190 knots. Although Ben got a quick visual, identification proved rather more difficult. We were underneath him looking directly up for quite a while before deciding that it was a Junkers 88. It was a very black night and there was a certain resemblance to a Mosquito. To make absolutely sure, Ben slid out first to one side, then to the other to see it from as many angles as possible.

Once we had assured ourselves that it was indeed a Junkers, Ben went through the usual drill of dropping back as he lifted the nose of our Mozzie and gave it a one-and-a-half-second burst – exactly a hundred rounds of ammunition we found later. The result was spectacular. There was a very bright flash from the tail of the Junkers and chunks of debris rattled over the Mozzie. Down went the enemy aircraft almost vertically. We followed rather more gently. Although we lost sight of it, for it was not on fire, I was able to see it on my AI.

As I watched the blip, I saw two smaller blips break away from the main one. I whipped the visor off the indicator unit of the AI and showed Ben this phenomenon. What we could see were probably two parachutes opening up as the crew abandoned ship. We orbited the area and a few seconds later we saw a big flash on the ground in a position just west of Mainz. This was over 120 miles south-west of where we had picked up our original contact.

At midnight on the 15th we were off to the same area once more. We had the maddening experience of chasing five separate contacts each one of which finished up with a visual on a Lancaster. These contacts were well separated in time and position and were all obtained some time after the bomber stream should have been well on the way home. The final visual was on a Lancaster with one propeller stopped. As our patrol time was up by then, we decided to give this chap an escort to the Dutch coast. We therefore dropped back from him and I watched him on my AI screen to make sure that no German night fighter approached him. Ben had to weave from side to side so that we would not overtake him.

Not one of these friends could have had the slightest suspicion we were near them. As I have said before, any of our bombers were perfectly entitled to fire at a twin-engined aircraft that approached them at night without waiting to identify it. After all, the fighter would be using AI, or rather *Lichtenstein* if it was a Hun. With this help it would come in from the darkest quarter; it would be armed with cannons; and if the bomber waited for the other chap to make the first move it would be too late. We were prepared for this, and although we intercepted over thirty of our bombers during our 100 Group patrols, we were never fired on.

The reason I am making this point is that when I came off operations in the February of 1945 I was sent on a lecture tour of stations belonging to 6 Group, a Royal Canadian Air Force bomber group and to the Group Headquarters. My instructions were to put them completely in the picture of the various operations carried out by 100 Group to help the bombers, particularly from the night-fighter aspect.

I gave a series of lectures, usually to 300 or more aircrew at a time. Invariably all the senior officers were there and the chaps made wonderful audiences, really attentive and interested in what I was saying. In the question period that followed each talk it became quite clear, however, that none of them believed that a Mozzie could approach them over enemy territory and sit below them as we had so often done. They agreed that they would fire on sight at any twin-engined aircraft under those conditions.

Perhaps it was as well that they had such faith in their warning devices. Anyhow, I soon caught on to the fact that it would be silly to press the point. I encountered the greatest disbelief of all, however, when I gave my lecture at the Group Headquarters.

During the first half of December we flew on half a dozen patrols. Bomber Command was roaming far afield over the Reich now, so our patrols moved with them. We rarely had a trip of under four and a half hours, rather a long time for two chaps to spend together in the confined space of a Mozzie cockpit, and yet another reason why it was so important for a crew to get on well together.

At about this time we heard from Intelligence that the German night fighters had a new tail warning device which they called *Naxos*. We had suspected this for some time, but the Swanington squadrons were still managing to shoot quite a few down.

Another interesting story from Intelligence demonstrated that the German radio countermeasures chaps had been a little too clever on one occasion at least. When Mozzies equipped with Mark 10 AI had at last been allowed over enemy territory, the casualties amongst the German night fighters had gone up enormously – so much so, that the German boffins could not believe that it was entirely due to the AI we were carrying.

It so happened that just at that time a new IFF, Identification Friend or Foe, had been introduced into their night fighters. Immediately they jumped to the conclusion that we had somehow learned of this IFF and were equipped with a device which homed us on to it. Orders went out to scrap the IFF – which for all I know might have been wonderful – but, of course, their night-fighter losses did not go down.

On the night of December 17th Bomber Command's targets were Munich, Ulm and Duisberg. Munich and Ulm were way down in southern Germany and Duisberg just east of the Ruhr. Our patrol was in support of the southern raid and we were to patrol between Stuttgart and Ulm. We had not chased a Hun for over a month and were hoping our luck would change.

It was a long way to go, two solid hours each way for only a twenty-minute patrol. We wasted no time and made straight for our patrol point, crossing in over the Belgian-Dutch border and plodding on over land at 15,000ft until we reached our destination. For twenty minutes we scoured the skies between Stuttgart and Ulm without anything appearing on our AI, although we saw lots of activity where the bombing was taking place. We tried flying at 10,000ft and 18,000ft, but there was just nothing doing for us.

We had plenty of petrol left so we decided to go out of our way a bit and see what we might find in the Frankfurt-

Koblenz area. This proved a happy decision. As we approached Frankfurt at about 12,000ft I got a contact on an aircraft flying south. It was well above us so we whipped around and climbed after it.

Whatever it was, it was certainly flying fast and high. Try as we could, we just could not catch it. Eventually, when we were up to nearly 20,000ft, we lost him, still well above us and going like a bat out of hell.

It seemed as if this was just not our night.

Round we turned, heading for Frankfurt again, when we spotted a cone of searchlights shining up into the sky near Wiesbaden. We made for these, and a minute later I had another contact. Our combat report read as follows:

Squadron Leader Benson reports:

> Contact obtained near a cone of five steady searchlights. Our height 16,000ft. We followed down to 6,000ft and up again to 12,000ft. Target weaving violently and making steep turns in either direction. Then followed down to 2,500ft still on AI and we found ourselves on the circuit of a fully lit airfield. Visual obtained on Junkers 88g, indicated air speed 320mph, height 2,500ft. At this time we were certainly not more than 50 yards away and below the enemy aircraft. I raised the Mosquito's nose and was about to open fire (despite the fact that I thought we were much too close) when we were illuminated by a searchlight. At this moment the Junkers 88 fired a four-star cartridge – two reds, two whites. These completely blinded me. As I knew we were dead behind him, I opened fire but saw no strikes. Then I saw the enemy aircraft, illuminated by the falling cartridge, below and peeling off to port. I jammed the nose down and had a quick shot which produced several strikes outboard the starboard engine. He continued steeply down to port and we followed him round to the other side of the airfield, going very fast.
>
> We were again illuminated, this time by two searchlights. The enemy aircraft fired another cartridge

which illuminated it and it was seen above us and slightly behind. Our height was then only 800ft. We could not get into firing position and contact was lost. Several white cartridges were fired from the airfield, which we continued to patrol for some time afterwards without obtaining contact again. Excellent work by Flight Lieutenant Brandon, who kept contact despite violent and continuous evasive action of every sort, especially when below 2,500ft. The dog-fight on AI before the visual lasted for nearly forty minutes.

Claim: One Junkers 88g damaged.

By this time Ben was truly a master of his craft. His instinctive reactions under extremely difficult conditions enabled him to get a good shot at the enemy aircraft when most pilots would have been completely put off by the searchlight at so low a height.

It was very bad luck that after we had such a long chase, the searchlight and the four-star cartridge should almost have blinded Ben at the very moment he was about to fire. It takes quite a time to regain one's night vision under such circumstances, yet he handled the Mozzie perfectly.

On December 23rd there was a spoof raid on Limburg, just north-west of our happy hunting ground of Frankfurt. We were airborne at the nice early hour of 16.45 for a patrol near Frankfurt. Soon after reaching our patrol point we had a chase which resulted in a visual on a Lancaster. Disappointed, we flew towards Wiesbaden where we found another contact almost at once.

We were at 14,000ft. Our target was flying in a southerly direction and climbing, but at an incredibly low speed. Ben had to weave from side to side in order not to overshoot although we were climbing after it and the Mozzie was not too fast a climber. We followed the aircraft over the target indicators that had been dropped on Limburg. It then turned right about on a course that took it, and us, first over Wiesbaden and then south-west towards Neunkirchen. A chase of about half an hour.

During this time it alternated between the very slow climb up to 18,000ft, level flight with violent weaves for a few minutes, then a rapid dive down to 6,000ft and the fantastically slow climb again.

Eventually Ben managed to get a visual and immediate identification on a Junkers 88. It was down at 6,000ft at this time and was flying level but weaving violently. Ben followed it through a couple of weaves and then gave it a short burst from 200 yards. We saw no strikes. Although it was very dark we could still see the Junkers weaving from side to side. Ben followed it through three or four more weaves and then had a shot at it when it turned in towards us from starboard.

There was a large flash from the starboard engine. The Junkers dived steeply to starboard and we followed it down to 1,000ft before losing the contact.

We climbed to 5,000ft and circled the position for a while. Some three minutes or so later we saw a red flash below us to the south. This was followed by a glow which we could see through thin cloud. However, we could not be sure if this was from the aircraft we had attacked. When we landed back at Swanington we claimed a Junkers 88 Damaged but next day Group raised the claim to a Probable as no other combat had been reported in that area around that time.

The next night was Christmas Eve. Bomber Command was to drop some presents on Cologne and Bonn. In the mess at Swanington it had been decided some time before to have our Christmas dinner on Christmas Eve. As a maximum effort had been asked for from the station for the night's operations, we were very pleased that we all had an early time for take-off. It was arranged that dinner would be held back until we returned, giving us something to look forward to.

We left Swanington at 16.30 hours on our way to Limburg. We had put in quite a lot of flying time in that area during the past few weeks and considered ourselves rather as specialists around Frankfurt – a couple of Frankfurters almost.

We had been on patrol at 14,000ft for about half an hour when we obtained a contact. We were just north of Limburg and the aircraft was well below us. Down we went pretty smartly to 8,000ft after a target that was flying level at that height but weaving quite violently. As we closed in, Ben had fleeting visuals two or three times. Each time, however, he could not hold on to them nor could he identify the aircraft.

We continued to follow him on AI, and he turned through two complete orbits before settling down on a north-westerly course. Shortly afterwards we saw some target indicators go down ahead of us. We had closed in on the aircraft and Ben got a visual on a Messerschmitt 110 at a range of 2,000ft, silhouetted against the light of the target indicators.

"Okay. I can see him all right now," said Ben. "Just look at that. No wonder we've taken such a while to close in."

As I looked up, I saw the Messerschmitt go across us from starboard to port. It went a fair way out to port, then went right up on one wing and came back in front of us, crossing the other way in this violent weave. Ben followed it through several of these weaves, fairly well throttled back and far more gently than the Messerschmitt. Then, from about 150 yards he gave it two short sharp bursts, firing at the exhaust flames.

The second burst set the port engine and the whole of the port side of the fuselage alight. We dived under some large pieces of debris that came flying back and heard them swoosh above the cockpit. The Messerschmitt was well alight now and going down over to our starboard. We saw it hit the ground and explode near a small town by the name of Dottesfeld, where we could see it burning brightly.

"About bloody time we shot one down again," remarked Ben. "Look at it burning. I wonder if the camera gun would pick that up?"

"Why not have a go?" I suggested.

So we did.

We had a good look around to see that there was no high ground and Ben did two runs right down to within a few hundred feet of the burning aircraft. All in vain though, nothing appeared on the film when it was developed.

We landed back at Swanington at five minutes to nine. Dinner had been laid on for half-past so after a pretty rapid de-briefing we set off for the mess. We were fortified with the news that, in addition to our Messerschmitt, Jimmy Matthews and Penrose had destroyed a Junkers 88 and Dolly Doleman had destroyed two more Messerschmitts.

As can be imagined, this gave the squadron something to celebrate. Four enemy aircraft destroyed in one night was by no means a record, but this had been accomplished on Christmas Eve, just before a party.

A single crew from 85 Squadron had, in fact, destroyed four enemy aircraft in one incredible patrol over Germany on November 4th, 1944. 85 Squadron were our stable companions at Swanington and the successful crew was Squadron Leader Burbridge, one of the Flight Commanders, and Flight Lieutenant Skelton, the Navigator Leader. This crew became easily the top-scoring pair on the Bomber Support job.

At about this time there was an incident on 157 Squadron that might have had most unfortunate results. One of our rather inexperienced crews returned from a patrol one night and claimed to have destroyed a Junkers 88. They had shot it down somewhere near the Battle Area, which was then in Holland. We were all extremely pleased with this success, for of course there was no better way of gaining experience than by shooting down an enemy aircraft in combat. Our pleasure at this success was rather dimmed by the fact that on that night we lost one of our crews, their Mozzie having failed to return.

A couple of days later, however, we were overjoyed to receive a signal from Holland to the effect that both pilot and navigator were safe and would be back with us shortly. When they did arrive back it was revealed that, without a shadow of a doubt, our inexperienced crew had been the cause of their worries. It was not a Junkers 88 that the new boys had shot down, but one of our own Mosquitos.

The crew who had returned from Holland reported that they had been returning from a high-level patrol, during which their AI and Monica had both packed up. They were just approaching the battle line and the pilot was pointing out to the navigator the flashes on the ground ahead of them. Suddenly they heard a terrific bang. Immediately their starboard engine burst into flames. The pilot realised that they were being attacked by a night fighter, but he could do nothing about it, for the Mozzie was at once almost out of control. The port wing kept dipping down and he was finding that it was all he could do to hold the aircraft level.

He warned the navigator that they would have to jump for it, then told him to jump. When he attempted to get out himself, however, he found it extremely difficult. The small door through which he had to escape was on the starboard side. Each time he let go of the control column, the Mozzie dropped its port wing and he just could not get out of the door. Eventually, after a superhuman effort, he managed to heave his way out and parachuted down to safety.

I say parachuted down to safety, but in fact, as he and his navigator floated down, the same thought was running through their heads. Which side of the battle line would they land on?

They both recalled having seen the line ahead, but had they passed over it before they were attacked?

Because the pilot had baled out some several seconds after his navigator, they had lost touch with each other. However, they decided independently to avoid capture if they were on the enemy side of the line. They remembered their escape drill, hid their parachutes and then holed up. After several hours they were both relieved to hear British voices and came out of hiding.

All their information tied up only too well with the combat report made out by the Mozzie crew who thought they had destroyed the Junkers 88. Time, place, height and method of attack all corresponded exactly. There was no doubt about it and Group had to be informed that the claim of one Junkers 88 should be erased from the record.

I believe that no action was taken against the offending crew apart from an interview with the Squadron Commander and having to stand their victims a few pints of beer at the bar. There was little need for further action – they were far too horrified by their mistake.

This problem of night identification was always a tricky one. A fairly successful device, involving the use of infra-red lights, was evolved by our boffins late in the war. Nevertheless, if an aircraft being chased did not show that identification, it still was not proof positive that it was a hostile aircraft. If the aircraft did show this identification, however, it would often save the fighter a long and unnecessary chase.

München-Gladbach and Bonn were the targets for Bomber Command on the night of December 28th. We went off again on a high-level patrol south-east of the Ruhr. We were airborne for over four and a half hours, but my logbook says: *Uneventful patrol.*

Uneventful patrol: I suppose that is quite correct so far as the log book is concerned. In actual fact, every patrol was prospectively a thrilling adventure. We were pitting our wits and our skill against enemy night fighters who were similarly equipped to us. Furthermore, they were operating over their own territory and with the aid of ground control – although the fact that our Mosquitos and AI were both superior to anything the Germans produced made up for that advantage.

The morale of the German night fighter crews was very high when the fighters of 100 Group came into the picture. They had chalked up enormous numbers of successes against our bombers and had suffered very little losses in so doing. The almost immediate and considerable jump in the number of casualties to the German night fighters came as a severe jolt to them. Soon their mounting losses and the harassing tactics of the Intruder squadrons of 100 Group began to seriously affect their morale. To the 100 Group activities must be added the probability that most of the German night-fighter crews must have suspected by then that Germany was losing the war.

On comparing notes with other crews both on 85 and 157 Squadrons we found ample evidence that many German night fighters were being shot down after chases that seemed to prove that they were making little or no effort to approach the target area, or to get anywhere near our bombers. Certainly in November and December of 1944 there had been over a dozen combats with enemy night fighters who were flying aimlessly about when intercepted. They would often be weaving violently around but keeping well away from any obvious activity such as a burning German town.

For some while almost all German aircraft production had been devoted to the manufacture of fighter aircraft and a large proportion of these were night fighters. There was quite a large force of enemy night fighters opposed to us at first. We had started with only four fighter squadrons in 100 Group, two for low-level patrols and two for high-level. In early November 1944 two more squadrons entered the Group. For the first few months after D-Day, therefore, a maximum effort from 100 Group could produce only about sixty fighters at a time when the Germans could probably muster two or three hundred.

From November onwards it was obvious that a number of German planes took off at night only because they were ordered to and were then worried only by the thought of getting down all in one piece again after a suitable interval. As they were not under close ground control, they could toddle off to some safe-looking area well away from all activity; fly around for a while, shoot off a few rounds of ammunition and land back for their night-flying suppers with a grand story of their adventures against the British bombers. It was unlucky for some of them that our fighters were so spread around that the safe area did not always turn out to be safe at all.

Late in December Ben and I were told that we would be coming off operations in the near future. Bomber Command was shortly to open its own school for Bomber Support training. Ben was to be the first Unit Commander and I was to be Chief Ground Instructor. No actual date was yet known but it would probably be early in the New Year. In the meantime we decided to get in a few more trips if possible.

On New Year's Day we went off on a high-level patrol near Bonn. The target for the main force was to be three Ruhr towns. Knowing that our tour of duty was coming to an end, we were perhaps even more anxious than usual for some activity so that we might end on a good note. We had three chases on friends, one of which led us far to the south. By the time we returned to Bonn the bombing was all over and our patrol time finished.

It was a beautiful night, so we decided to go down for a Ranger trip on our way home. There was a fair amount of moonlight so we had a good chance of seeing something to shoot at. Sure enough, about 30 miles north-west of Bonn we spotted a convoy of lorries moving along a road. Ben gave the leading lorry a long and very accurate burst of cannons. We saw several strikes and the lorry went right off the road into a ditch. As we pulled away we saw that two or three others had finished up in the ditch. We were already about half an hour late, so we did not go round again for another crack at them.

When we arrived at Swanington we had been up for nearly five and a half hours. We were the last Mozzie on the station to land. When we taxied round to our dispersal hut and clambered out of the cockpit there seemed to be rather more than the usual crowd to meet us. In the forefront of the crowd was the Squadron Intelligence Officer. He came dashing up to me and said:

"Well, Brandy, you've got one Confirmed today at least!"

It seemed a strange greeting. I wondered what on earth he was talking about. Then it struck me that possibly one of the aircraft we had recently claimed as Damaged or Probably Destroyed had been upgraded by Group to a Destroyed. Still, it seemed a funny time to tell me that.

I suppose I looked rather blank, for the IO took pity on me.

"Not to worry, lad," he said. "There was a telephone call for you which came through just after you had taken off. I took it for you. It was from Bath. You are the father of a daughter."

This certainly was a complete surprise for me. I had telephoned my wife only the night before. She had said I was not to telephone again for at least a week as the baby was not due for another fortnight and she herself thought it would be longer. However, Susan Jane had decided to come into the world on New Year's Day and was not to be denied.

I managed to wangle a flight to Colerne, an airfield near Bath, and arranged to be picked up from there a couple of days later, when I had reassured myself that all was well.

Mother and baby were doing fine.

On January 5th, 1945, the main target was Hanover. Our patrol point was near Osnabruck, some miles to the west. Nothing much happened for a while, then we got a contact which we chased towards the target area. I could see that the aircraft we were after was dropping Window. It showed up quite clearly on my AI screen so that it was most probably a friendly aircraft. Anyway, it was miles off the bomber route, and as we had nothing better to do we decided to investigate.

We had just identified it as a Lancaster when I got another AI contact. We chased this to the south of Hanover, where the bombing was in full blast. About 10 miles south of the city the aircraft we were after began to spiral down very quickly. Although we followed it, diving steeply after it, we lost the contact below us. We circled down at 2,000ft for a short time, but as we did not regain contact we climbed up towards Osnabruck again. We had reached Minden, halfway between Osnabruck and Hanover, when I obtained another contact coming towards us.

We were at a height of 7,000ft by now and the target was above us. We whipped round at the appropriate moment and found that the aircraft was flying almost due east. He was going very fast and climbing on a straight course as he went up. Ben had our Mozzie absolutely flat out for most of the while and gradually we began to close the range.

The aircraft led us over the southern tip of the Hanover fires and we were pounding along, still climbing after him. At long last we reached his level and at once Ben had a visual on two pairs of brilliant yellow exhausts. The other aircraft was 2,500ft away and absolutely level with us, dead in front. Ben found that as soon as he went down slightly he lost sight of the exhausts. This brilliant yellow was something quite new to us and we felt sure it was a Hun.

We kept slowly drawing in. At a range of 800ft Ben identified it as a Heinkel 219 by its twin fins and the dihedral of the tailplanes. I saw by our altimeter that we were at 19,000ft. No wonder it had taken so long to catch the brute – the Mozzie was not a particularly fast climber.

At a range of 200 yards Ben gave two fairly long bursts from dead astern. We saw strikes from both bursts along the fuselage and from the port engine. Some large pieces came back from the engine and we dived to avoid them. The Heinkel went down in a steep dive to starboard. We were able to follow it visually at first, for a great sheet of flame came from the port engine and some more pieces flew off.

After a few seconds the speed of the dive blew the flames out so we continued to follow it on AI right down to 6,000ft. Still turning in a wide orbit to starboard, we followed it up again to 12,000ft. Then it went down again in a very steep dive that we were unable to follow. We remained in the area and about a minute later we saw it crash and explode. It remained burning with occasional explosions of ammunition until we left the position. That proved to be our ration of excitement for the night and we made our way home soon afterwards.

Next day our posting came through. We were to report to Great Massingham, about 12 miles from King's Lynn on January 21st. We were ordered to take a fortnight's leave before reporting so that we could do only one more patrol.

We took off for a patrol in our favourite area of Frankfurt. We had been flying for about twenty-five minutes when I noticed that the generator voltmeter was reading low, just as it had on our very first trip over enemy territory. We had to turn back. It seemed an awful anti-climax. It was only the second time we had ever had to make an early return and it had to be on our final patrol.

Strangely enough, the only time I ever felt rather jittery during all my operational flying was just before this very last trip. That night as I went to bed I remember well a profound, feeling of relief that it was all over. Although I had found operational flying exhilarating rather than worrying, I must have been under quite severe nervous strain all the same. It was not until I actually knew for certain that I was being taken off operations that the reactions set in and it lasted for three or four days.

I had flown on 82 defensive and 53 offensive sorties since the summer of 1941.

The superiority of the 100 Group Mosquitos and their crews is borne out by figures. Although we were operating against radar-equipped German night fighters operating over their own territory, during the ten months 157 Squadron was in 100 Group they destroyed 36 enemy aircraft, with 5 probables and 13 damaged. They were also responsible for the destruction of 38 buzz-bombs. The squadron's losses were only 7 aircraft and 6 crews.

Our friendly rivals at Swanington, 85 Squadron, had even better results. I am not sure of their final totals but over 90 aircraft were destroyed altogether by the two Swanington squadrons.

It is interesting to hear the story from the enemy point of view. Wilhelm Johnen, a German night-fighter ace who finished the war as Commanding Officer of a night-fighter wing, comments on the 100 Group Mosquitos in his book *Duel Under the Stars*. One of his chapters is entitled 'Achtung I Mosquito!' and in it he writes:

Fast Mosquitos from the mainland were despatched to join the bomber stream and take over the task of air cover. The Mosquitos lived up to their name. They were the night fighter's greatest plague and wreaked havoc among the German crews. The radar equipment of this wooden aircraft surpassed anything that had previously been seen. It was technically so perfect that at a distance of 5 miles they could pick the German night fighters out of the bomber stream like currants out of a cake... It was incredibly difficult to get a bomber in our sights for the Mosquitos sought us out and led like rockets to the aid of the bomber. Not only had we the enemy in front of us but also in our backs. All this was a great strain on the German crews. The losses rose appallingly... The Mosquitos not only pursued us in the bomber stream but, as a result of their enormous fuel capacity and endurance, waited for us as we took off from our airfields. They attacked us throughout the whole operation and interfered with our landing. It was almost a daily occurrence that shortly before divisional ops several Mosquitos would fly over the airfields and shoot down the Messerschmitts as they took off.

My heart goes out to those poor harassed German night fighters.

Ben and I duly reported to Great Massingham. We had both been promoted; he was now a Wing Commander and I was Squadron Leader. We had a very interesting time forming our new command, 1692 Bomber Support Training Unit. As soon as we had it running reasonably well, I was detailed for a lecture tour of Number 6 (RCAF) Bomber Group, as I have said previously. On the day I returned from this tour we heard that we had both been awarded the DSO.

We called in at the Station Equipment section to enquire if they had any DSO ribbon. No, they were sorry but they had none in stock. Should they order some for us?

We thought that might take quite a while and, as we had decided to go into King's Lynn that afternoon, it seemed more sensible to get the ribbon there.

In King's Lynn we found an establishment that proclaimed itself to be a Military Tailor. We entered and a young lady came to serve us.

"Do you stock medal ribbons, please?" I asked.

"Certainly, sir," replied the young lady, reaching for a fair-sized box which she opened for our inspection.

There was quite a pretty selection of medal ribbons in the box but no DSO ribbon.

We explained that there was no DSO ribbon in the box and tried to describe what it was like.

"A broad pinky-red band with a thinner blue border on either side."

"Just a moment, sir. I'll go and ask!"

She returned after a short while.

"No, I'm afraid we haven't anything like that," she said, then, pointing to the box:

"Wouldn't one of those do, sir?" she suggested.

Epilogue

LOOKING back, I am very proud to have served in the Royal Air Force. I find it hard to believe that anywhere, in any war, has there ever been anything to compare with the spirit, morale and comradeship that existed on an operational Royal Air Force squadron during the last war, from the Commanding Officer down to the lowliest airman on the squadron.

As regards the job I found myself doing, I would not have changed it for any other. It was just right. It required initiative, intelligence and level-headedness. It provided excitement and interest on every trip. We were treated as intelligent adults. All this, against the wonderful background of squadron life, made my wartime service extremely happy.

In all probability it was the last occasion when men could sally forth to do battle with the enemy's champions like the knights of old.

Around the time of Dunkirk, the war looked pretty hopeless for us. History tells us that we were saved by the 'few', during the Battle of Britain. A large part of the credit for that victory must go, however, to the boffins who produced the radar which gave the early warning and the control that ensured the best and most economical use to be made of the few pilots and aircraft then available.

Although the word 'Radar' is of American origin, being derived from Radio Detection and Ranging, it should be pointed out that we British were far ahead of the Americans in its development. From Sir Robert Watson-Watt's very fine book *Three Steps to Victory* I should like to quote the following:

Nowhere in the world did there exist in 1940 any airborne radar: when Bowen went to America as a member of the Tizard Mission he found early ground radar, but no airborne radar. The first airborne radar to be installed in an American aircraft was a British Mark 4 AI and it was installed in the USA by British personnel.

From the official history of the US Army Air Forces in the Second World War again I quote:

> All radar equipment and most of the radio equipment used by the Eighth Force during 1942 and well into 1943 was of British design and manufacture.

Surely a feather in the cap for our boffins!

So far as the air war was concerned, once the problem of day bombing against this country had been solved by the Battle of Britain, the night bombing by the Germans assumed greater importance. Once again radar came to our rescue in the forms of long-range warning, the Ground Control Interception stations and the little black boxes of AI that went into the night fighters.

Incidentally, AI was perhaps one of the best-kept secrets of the war. When one considers the great number of people involved in its manufacture, servicing and actual use, it is amazing how few outsiders knew anything at all about it.

The next big step in the air war was from defence to offence. Once the Americans mastered the art of daylight bombing and, in conjunction with the RAF began round-the-clock bombing of Germany, the war was won. In the meantime, however, the Royal Navy had to keep the sea lanes open and the Army had to go in and consolidate, both vitally important jobs in the last war, although it is highly unlikely that either would be necessary in the event of another war.

I am convinced that the one German decision that had far reaching effects which have perhaps not been realised was the decision that all fighters would be retained for the direct defence of the Reich. This resulted in the failure of the Luftwaffe to use squadrons of Intruders over here when the bomber offensive was building up, and even more so when it was reaching its height in mid-1944. If your cities are being attacked by bombers, the bombers must be harassed on every inch of their journey – and at take-off and landing too. An aircraft is at its most vulnerable when taking off or landing and an aircraft shot down in sight of its home base is a great morale destroyer.

In spite of this, the Luftwaffe did not use Intruders from the early part of 1941 until a last-minute flurry in late 1944.

A second let-off was the failure to use buzz-bombs against southern England when the invasion forces were being assembled.

Radar and the 'few' saved us from losing the war; to whom should go the credit of final victory?

There is really only one possible answer. It was entirely a matter of teamwork, and in that team, not necessarily in the order of their importance, were the three Services, our Allies, the Boffins, the Commonwealth, the British public and the incredible stupidity shown at times by Herr Hitler and his advisers.

This formidable team was so very ably led by the only individual that I firmly believe was irreplaceable, Sir Winston Churchill. In the darkest days he provided the inspiration that welded the country into the unified force that was essential for the winning of a modern war.

The other leaders, the admirals, the generals and the air marshals, who emerged from the war with great reputations, just happened to be in the right place at the right time. I believe that there were always men who could have replaced them and have done just as well given equal opportunities. There was only one Churchill.

Finally, from my personal point of view, I must mention again the extreme good fortune which followed me throughout my operational service in the RAF. I must also congratulate myself on my service, my comrades and my job, none of which could have been bettered.

BOOK TWO

Mosquito Pathfinder

Prologue

The 4th of December 1944 – 1900 hours – target: Karlsruhe. On the left, slightly higher than my head and facing forward, the pilot peers into the black night. I flick the switch on the nozzle of my oxygen mask, and he turns his head in my direction.

A nasal, humid sound: "Alter course to one-six-four degrees. We'll be over Aachen in two minutes."

The intercom crackles back: "OK."

Navigation charts are laid out on the plotting board lying on my knees. And in front, racked up against the fuselage, the green display on the instrument panel flickers in the dim light from a shaded bulb. On my left is the selector panel. I lean across to select the target indicator flare switches, and they click into place. My feet rest on the floor of the Mosquito – 'O Oboe' – and my knees dig uncomfortably against the board as I lean forward to work on the charts.

The borders of Germany, Holland and Belgium meet at Aachen. The charts show that enemy flak batteries are stationed just beyond Aachen and we will be flying over them in about a minute. But they probably won't bother the eight Mosquitoes flying fast at 30,000 feet above them. They'll keep their shells for the heavy Lancasters labouring below at 15,000 feet.

Feeling stiff, I lift my head and straighten my back. I imagine the taste of the beer that I will be drinking in the Mess in, maybe, three hours time. This is my ninetieth 'op' – operation over enemy territory – and somebody might buy me a pint for that. Though perhaps not – it wasn't much of a landmark in 109 Squadron.

The noise of the aeroplane is a stuffy drone that bores into my mind. My head aches a bit.

Suddenly there is a jolt, and I glance sharply to the left. Out

207

of the window beyond Johnny's head I see, for an instant, the grotesque black belly of an aircraft sliding by. Nothing happens for a moment, the drone persists – the course holds. Then with a sickening lurch, the plane cartwheels through the sky.

"Johnny!" I scream, as I am flung furiously against the instrument panel, then twisted through the air and thumped to the floor. But the floor itself is twisting. I grab the metal struts at the base of Johnny's seat, pulling my face hard against them as my legs spiral above me. Urine flows uncontrollably, and my chest feels tight and painful.

Sliding my head round, I see Johnny wrestling with the joystick, but we are spinning viciously and out of control. He snatches his arm up and turns the handle of the escape hatch. It rips away, sucking the warm air of the cockpit with it. He reaches down to me, then starts pulling at the buckle of his seat harness. He twists awkwardly out of his seat – his parachute on his back – and grabs at the joystick. Clutching it, he begins to rotate with the spin of the aircraft. Again he tries to reach down to help me. I stretch my hand up to his. But he seems to lift like a balloon, hover for a second, then shoots out of the black, gaping hole above him.

I pull my head further round, and see, in the dim light, my parachute strapped to the side of the aircraft. It is within reach, but if I let go of the struts then the violent spin of the aircraft will fling me out of the open canopy above. There is nothing I can do.

I pull my face hard against the struts. I tilt my head round a bit, so that the top of my head is facing towards the nose of the aircraft. I grip tighter, because I want to die wrapped in the warmth of the aircraft's body. A dread of falling through space, formlessly, makes me shudder and I hug the struts closer. I tilt my head so that it will hit the ground at the same instant as the aircraft, and I will feel nothing.

I'm calm. I'm going to die. But I can't do anything about it. It'll be quick. And it won't hurt. I feel so calm.

There's a yellow-red glow in the aircraft. The engines must be on fire! Please God I don't feel the pain of burning before I die. I begin to hum – just a constant, quiet, surprising hum.

Then my legs slam to the floor, and the aircraft is no longer spinning – diving steeply but no longer spinning. I might live. My body quivers, and I feel the most intense fear.

I'm feeling unsteady, but I'm sitting. I claw at my parachute, still strapped to the side. Tearing off the straps, I fumble with it, and pull it and clip it onto my harness.

Surely I'll hit the ground at any minute, we've been falling for so long. I pull myself towards the blackness but something jerks my head back. I pull again, and my neck is torn violently back. I tug my neck frantically, but still my head won't move. The ground must be near now – I'm frantic with fear. I nearly made it, for God's sake, I must make it.

My helmet! It's still connected to the intercom cable. I wrench it off – my head feels light. I'm shaking as I scramble to the escape hatch. As I get close, a freezing wind stings my face. I feel like I am in water – nothing I push on stays firm. Push, for Christ's sake, push. My legs are dangling inside the aircraft, my top half is out. I push one more time and thrust myself up, and I'm floating free.

Tumbling, tumbling – floating free. A smooth, unremarkable hissing sound fills me. I pull the rip-cord.

CHAPTER 1

Volunteering

Mum, Dad and I crowded round the wireless as Neville Chamberlain said "…this country is at war with Germany." I walked to one of the comfortable chairs, and flopped in it. So, it's war. How exciting!

But Mother was crying and Dad looked grim. Twenty-five years ago he had been as elated as I at the prospect of going to war. Now he was sombre. "There's no glory in it, son. Just blood and mud." He was in the trenches in Flanders before he was eighteen years old and still carried pieces of shrapnel around in his back. "Anyway, it'll all be over by the time you are old enough to fight." I was sixteen years and five months old on that 3rd of September 1939.

I prayed that night that the war would not end until I had a chance to fight. But I didn't fancy the Army that much. Dad was right; it must be wet and cold a lot of the time. And those bayonets! Ten inches of cold steel ripping into my belly. No, not the Army. And not the Navy either. It had taken me a long time to learn to swim, and I still didn't feel too safe. Those oceans are deep too – thousands of feet – no, not the Navy either. So, it's the Royal Air Force then. That Roy Evans from Simpson Street looked good in his blue uniform. And all the girls fancied him. Yes, a pilot in the Royal Air Force, that's the job.

The next year and three months passed so slowly. Salford seemed to become even more dreary. All windows were blacked out in case of air attack and the terraced streets seemed lonely and unfriendly. It was always good to arrive home at night. Mother would be washing up, putting the plates on the wooden draining board. Dad would be reading the newspaper in front of the blazing coal fire.

But even in the house things were beginning to change.

Rationing was biting harder and harder. Less meat than usual and only one egg a week. I noticed that. Some weeks we would run out of our coal ration and we'd sit huddled in our overcoats in the kitchen. And then sometimes the lights would go – we never seemed to remember where we had last put the candles. I remember feeling hungry sometimes.

I had left school last summer, and got a good job as a clerk in the Cost Office at Mandlebergs. They made barrage balloons and it was a real privilege to be working for them – in an office as well. My mother was proud, and sometimes boastful, that I had got an office job rather than a manual job in the textile factories. She was always moaning at Dad that he had never done better than be a lorry driver.

But it seemed dreary against the background of war. I worked in a big office, with twenty or thirty other people. Everything was brown – the desks, the walls, the linoleum on the floor. Time hung endlessly, especially towards the end of the day. I had to fight to keep my eyes open, and the lines in the ledger would merge with each other.

The war news was depressing. France gave up, almost without a fight. We were lucky to get our Army out at Dunkirk. Dad joined the Home Guard and Mother worried. Nobody openly talked of defeat, although I heard that Jim Pritchett had got drunk at the 'Grosvenor' and said that we were going to lose the war. People were angry with him, but nobody disagreed too strongly.

Churchill changed all that. Even in a cold house, as we sat in our overcoats, Churchill convinced us that it would all turn out all right. His speeches gave us marvellous feelings. "I have nothing to offer but blood, toil, tears and sweat. You ask, what is our policy? I will say – it is to wage war, by sea, land and air, with all our might, and with all the strength that God can give us. You ask – what is our aim? I can answer in one word: victory. Victory at all costs. Victory in spite of all terror. Victory, however long and hard the road may be."

And things did seem to get a bit better. The Royal Navy

sank the *Bismarck*, and the RAF were shooting down German planes by the hundreds. Our Spitfires looked magnificent in the Pathé newsreels, and I would think to myself, "I'm going to fly one of those soon."

There were tremendous air battles in the south. At the end of the summer, the Germans gave up their daylight raids on the airfields, and started bombing cities by night. Every couple of nights, we would hear the harsh wail of the air-raid sirens. It always made my stomach drop. Then we would grab anything we could carry and dash to the Anderson shelter in the back garden. It had taken Dad and me a whole weekend to dig the hole and erect the shelter. It took up nearly the entire garden and we could get maybe six people in with a squeeze.

A couple of minutes after we lighted the candles and got settled down, we would hear the enemy aircraft overhead, and the muffled explosions as the ack-ack gunners fired at them. But there were never any bombs; they just flew over us and dropped their bombs on Liverpool. That changed just a few days before Christmas in 1940 when they came for Manchester and Salford.

The sirens sounded at about six o'clock as usual, but this time the sound of gunfire came immediately. I stepped outside the back door before entering the Anderson shelter. As I looked up into the black sky, suddenly it was daylight. Dozens of flares were being dropped by the bombers, and I hurried down the steps. The raid lasted about twelve hours. The bombs thumped all around us and none of us dared go outside. The ground shook and every now and then the shelter would shudder, and dust and plaster would fall from the roof.

In the early morning it stopped and we shuffled out, stiff and tired. We walked around the neighbourhood, expecting to see a wasteland, but there was surprisingly little damage. The events of the evening quickly spread through this tightly knit, working-class community. The raid had been concentrated on the city centre and Trafford Park, an area of factories, huge warehouses and railway tracks. United's ground lies in Trafford Park and it had been hit several times. We heard that the offices on Bury New Road, where Dorothy from next door was on fire-watch, had received a direct hit. She was dead when they brought her out.

I walked up to Market Street, which was devastated. I picked my way through the rubble that lay strewn along the street. Now and then a wall nearby would come crashing down, and in many places firemen stood on top of their turntables and hosed down the embers that were kindling in the debris. Smoke swirled about. In spite of all the activity and the people moving about, it all seemed rather unreal in the cold, crisp air of the morning.

I carried on up to Piccadilly, heading for the RAF recruiting office. This was as good a time as any to join up. A sergeant was inside sweeping up broken glass. "I want to fly with the RAF," I said.

He looked up and smiled kindly. "Jolly good, lad – sit down and fill in this form." He was still tidying up the office by the time I had finished. "OK, son," he said, "we'll be in touch."

I walked home quickly. Swinging open the door, I said excitedly, "I've volunteered for the RAF." Dad was very proud of me, but Mother cried.

A few months later I turned eighteen, but still I had heard nothing from the RAF. The Forces usually notified recruits of their call-up before their eighteenth birthday, but still I had heard nothing. Rumours that I had wangled a 'reserve occupation' began circulating in the street. "After all, Albert is still in civvies, and Mandleberg's is making barrage balloons."

Then it arrived – an official letter with the RAF eagle on it. REPORT TO RAF CARDINGTON FOR CLASSIFICATION. That's official, and I showed it to everyone in the street. There was great discussion about where Cardington might be. Bill Riley in the Post Office told me where it was and how I could get there. It was down south, in Bedfordshire, and I was to stay a night there. I hadn't been out of Manchester much. There was the annual holiday in Abergele – it took ages to get there on a chugging steam train. And I also went to school camp once in Harlech. My only other excursion was to Hanley in the Potteries to watch United play Port Vale in a cup tie. Bedfordshire! This was a very serious thing, joining the RAF.

On 13 June 1941 about forty of us stood around, self-consciously, in a large room at Cardington. Some of us were my own age, and some were older, already wearing Air Force blue. An officer told us what was going to happen over the next two days, and we were assigned our beds. The medical checks took up most of the first day, and at the end of it we would be told if we could continue on to the next day. I made a nervous friendship with two other boys my age, and we were shunted round to so many rooms and buildings. I felt uncomfortable naked, weighing in at 8 stone 10 pounds. And the doctors poked and prodded me everywhere. It was unpleasant. The prick of the needle hurt when they took my blood sample. I nearly fell off the treadmill as they ran it faster and faster to test my stamina and heart beat. The eye tests alone took an hour. I failed the mercury test twice – blowing mercury up a glass tube and keeping it level for sixty seconds. The orderly was patient, and he told me to concentrate on puffing. As I did it the third time, I felt I was getting the hang of it. He coached me along, and I managed to do it.

As the end of the day got closer, people became tense. Each of us went in front of the Medical Board in turn – shuffling uncertainly into the room in front of a panel of old people.

"Smith, A?"

"Er," head nodding, "yes."

"Passed."

Others were not so lucky and they were issued with railway warrants and left immediately. The rest of us were told to report the next morning for aptitude tests. We searched out the buildings where our beds were. It was beginning to get dark. It was very strange lying in a bed looking across at someone else a yard away. I felt vulnerable and pulled myself into a tight ball. But I went to sleep quickly.

The next morning we sat at individual tables in the big hall and did written tests. I finished half an hour early at twelve o'clock. Outside it was a hot and sunny day. I sat with my new friends on the grass and we chatted – about our home towns, about football. The grass smelled sweet and I think I felt a bit dizzy from the unfamiliar openness of the countryside.

After two hours we were back in the big hall, empty now of the desks that we had used. Each of us waited our turn. Finally it was mine and I walked into the room. It was the same room that the Medical Panel used, but this time, although there were only five people on the panel, the room seemed bigger.

"Sit down," a voice said. So I sat in the chair in front of the panel. They whispered – at least I could not hear what they were saying – amongst themselves. There were five of them. They looked very old and distinguished in their RAF uniforms. And every one of them had medals. They nodded at each other, or shook heads. Some leaned back and yawned. Finally, one said, when I was not expecting it, "You are accepted for training as navigator in the Royal Air Force Volunteer Reserve."

"No, I want to be a pilot. I mean, I'm sorry. I mean I..."

"Navigator." I was startled by the deep booming voice. "Navigator is the Board's decision." Five pairs of eyes stared at me for an age. Then one of the faces smiled. "Smith, your record in mathematics is excellent and you even got the time/speed/distance question right."

Back in the big hall I recovered my spirits as the excitement of the group built. We were all beaming as we went through the swearing-in ceremony. On the train home I reassured myself by thinking that pilots are only drivers anyway. Then it struck me: "There are no navigators in Spitfires." I was near to tears.

But back in Salford, everyone was impressed. "Bert Smith's going to be a navigator."

"Is he? What's that then?"

"You know, he tells the pilot where to go."

"Oh fancy! How'll he find his way in the dark?"

"Well, they have special goggles for that and they wear them at night."

"He'll drop the bombs too – on the Germans."

"Oh fancy! Tell him to drop one on the buggers for me."

A few weeks later, I received my orders: "Report to the Aircrew Receiving Centre at Lord's Cricket Ground, St John's Wood, London on 3 September 1941 at 1400 hours." London! Of all places! The Tower, Traitor's Gate, the Strand, Fleet Street, St Paul's, The Windmill and Lord's Cricket Ground. That's where the Ashes are. I might even get to see them.

Mother was too upset to see me off at London Road Station so Dad came with me on the tram – two trams in fact. One to Victoria and the other through the city centre to London Road. He seemed as if he wanted to say something but he remained silent, smoked his Woodbines and fidgeted uncharacteristically. I was apprehensive, yet excited – about it all, now the moment had arrived. Going to London – getting my blue uniform – and flying in aeroplanes.

We were far too early for the train, but it finally arrived at the platform, black smoke belching from the chimney. I felt grown up, standing at the window of the eight-seat compartment. It quickly filled up and I was glad that Dad had sent me to the urinal before getting on the train – I wouldn't have another chance until the first stop at Crewe. Dad stood on the platform looking up at me strangely, and as the guard's whistle blew and the train began to move he followed it along. There were tears in his eyes – I'd never seen him cry before – and at last he was able to say the words that had been troubling him so much. "And watch out for loose women, son!" he shouted, before coming to a dejected halt as the train outpaced him. I felt embarrassed by his distress as he waved goodbye, but also I had never felt so close to him.

I sat back in the seat. I didn't know much about girls, practically nothing in fact. But I knew that I liked them and I resolved to look into the matter of 'loose' women at the earliest opportunity.

My mind kept wandering from the *Daily Herald* that Dad had bought me, so I looked out of the window as grey Manchester receded, to be replaced by unfamiliar green fields. I tried to imagine what it must be like to live in the country – but I couldn't. The first stop was at Crewe – all north-south trains stopped at Crewe during the war. The platforms swarmed with men and women in uniform, and in transit; some going on leave, others returning from leave or joining new units.

Over there two soldiers were under arrest, and in the custody of Military Policemen. So many people on the platforms – standing, sitting, walking, running, alone, in groups, drinking tea from the WVS canteen. Kit bags and equipment everywhere, so many people mingling with the sounds of the station – the tannoy, shouts, clatter, steam, whistles, slamming doors. I was fascinated by it all.

Rugby was the next stop. There's a famous public school there – Tom Merry, Harry Wharton and all that. Then a place called Bletchley. Then there in the distance the twin towers of Wembley Stadium. I recognised them immediately from pictures I'd seen. And shortly I was in the crowds in Euston Station. In London for the first time!

I knew that I had to get an underground train to St John's Wood, the station nearest to Lord's. I spotted the Underground sign – I'd seen them in pictures too – followed the grain of the crowd, went through a ticket barrier and arrived at the platform clutching a ticket and with ninety minutes to get there. Seventy minutes later, I was still on the underground train and arriving at Charing Cross for the third time.

Terrified at the prospect of a court-martial for late arrival,

I rushed through the exit signs up to the Strand. I got into a London taxi – big and black and easy to recognise – and arrived at Lord's at ten to two with ten minutes to spare. It cost me four bob, leaving me with two pounds sixteen shillings to see me through to my first pay parade in a fortnight's time.

"I am reporting for duty, Sir," I said properly to the RAF Service Policeman at the main gate – my first sight of an SP.

"Name?"

"Smith, Sir."

"First name?"

"Albert, Sir."

"D Stand, and wait to be called."

The accent was unfamiliar, but I thought it must be Cockney.

There was a game being played on the famous ground as I took my seat in D Stand. "Arrer 'n' Eton" I was told by a knowledgeable youth in the next row. I smiled my thanks as the tannoy rang out authoritatively "Arbuthnot" and I looked round to see a person walk out to the offices behind the Members' Stand. Two hours later the Rs were being called, and shortly after, the first of the Smiths – me, just as the last wicket fell to a catch behind.

I reported to the office, had a quick medical, signed a few forms, then joined the others in the famous Long Room. "Wally Hammond's walked through here," I thought. We were called and assigned to our flights. Mine was B Flight, which was told to "fall in in threes" by a burly corporal. That didn't mean much to us, but the big corporal soon had us how he wanted us and shortly afterwards we were quick marching through St John's Wood.

It took some concentration to avoid stepping on the heels of the lad in front of me, and the bloke behind me wasn't concentrating at all. We marched to Regents Park Zoo where the cafeteria had been converted into an RAF Mess. We were all very hungry and the RAF sausage and chips tasted great.

Our billet was at Stockleigh Hall, a block of luxury flats, stripped of all their luxury, down to the bare floorboards. This was just five minutes away from the zoo and we were marched there and back three times a day during our two weeks at ACRC – 'Arcytarcy'. The rooms were empty except for blankets and 'biscuits'. Biscuits were mattresses two and a half feet square and three of them made up a bed. They always moved apart during the night, so we woke up each morning stiff and sore.

On that first evening our big corporal told us that we were free until reveille at 0630 hours. The Cockneys quickly dispersed into their city and a group of about ten of us made our way along Baker Street to find Sherlock Holmes's flat.

We were awakened at half-past six with shouts of "Wakey, wakey!" By half-past seven our squad was called to a halt outside the zoo and we waited our turn for breakfast. It was Finnan haddock – yellowish green, in a scummy sauce. It was the first time I had ever had fish for breakfast.

After breakfast, we were 'fell in' by our big corporal and marched to the store somewhere near Baker Street to be kitted out. First two kitbags – 'Airmen, for the use of'. Then our uniforms (small, medium or large). Underwear, thick and two of each. Boots, ground sheet (which also served as a cape), haversack, webbing, tin hat, water bottle, gas mask, mug and plates, irons (knife, fork and spoon), overcoat, gloves, brushes, and a 'housewife' (a canvas hold-all containing cotton, wool, needles, pins, elastic, buttons and a thimble).

By the time we had finished, our two kit bags were packed full. "Right, lads," said our corporal. "Pick up your kit bags and get fell in." With one on each shoulder we staggered back to Stockleigh Hall, where we collapsed onto our biscuits. But within minutes we were 'fell in' again and marched off to Abbey Close.

I learned to hate Abbey Close. It was just around the corner from Stockleigh Hall and housed the medical section. Here we received our jabs, and once more the name Smith, far down the alphabet, was a liability. The same needle was used for each injection. It was sharp for the Arbuthnots, but not by the time it reached the Smiths. We each had three jabs and one inoculation – two jabs and the inoculation in the arm, and one jab in the chest. Two or three potential war heroes passed out at the first jab, and were slid unconscious along the polished floor to receive the remainder. The changing room afterwards resembled a casualty clearing station as we rubbed our arms and struggled to calm down. But that wasn't the end. Next was the dentist – and I dread the dentist. "Good God!" he said as I opened my mouth at my turn in the chair. "You've still got a baby tooth." It hurt sharply as he pulled it out.

We were given the next day off and began to make our transition from civilians to airmen. We parcelled up our civilian clothes and sent them home. After many swaps, adjustments and re-issues, we became Aircraftmen Second Class – AC2s – in His Majesty's Royal Air Force.

The next morning we paraded outside Stockleigh Hall in Air Force blue for the first time. For the next two weeks we square-bashed in the streets behind Abbey Close. After our first dislike of drill, we began to take some pride in our ability to all stamp our feet at the same time. And after the blisters had healed, the big boots began to feel as comfortable as pumps.

We vied with other squads outside the zoo to look the smartest, and often we were – but then the competition wasn't very strong, the other two squads being u/t (under training) pilots and therefore, we thought, quite inferior to us.

Most evenings at Arcytarcy I walked into the City or the West End. I would stand and stare at all the places I had heard and read about, returning to my biscuits to fall asleep immediately, until "Wakey, wakey!" And at the end of two weeks, I had not met one single 'loose' woman.

We were posted to Paignton ITW – Initial Training Wing – in Devon. We marched off to St John's Wood station carrying our kit bags and travel rations – corned beef sandwiches and individual, sickly sweet fruit pies. We said goodbye to our corporal and left London. A few hours later we were in Paignton. The leaves on the trees were golden brown and they shimmered in the crisp sunshine. Our billets were commandeered guest houses around the Tembani Hotel, which served as the Mess and Squadron Headquarters.

At ITW we were drilled, exercised and marched up daily to the Country Club for elementary navigation training. I wrote home regularly, and felt homesick. Mother sent me food parcels and, once, since I had written that I was cold in bed, a hot water bottle. I was unable to hide it when I opened the parcel. I took a lot of stick over that.

The closest we got to battle was guard duty, but our Flight Officer told us it was important. He was about the same age as us, resplendent in his brand new officer's uniform and similar to us in some ways, but not in others. He was non-aircrew, and had been to public school. He told us pompously, with a strange accent that seemed to come from the back of his head, "The Hun is looking at us from the other side of the Channel," pointing dramatically in the direction of the coast, "waiting to invade our shores. Be on your guard, men, and be intensely alert." We tried hard not to laugh.

But for those of us not from the warrior caste, guard duty on the 2000 hours to midnight rota was the most unpleasant. Sudden sounds of movement nearby would make me alert and fearful. I would drop my unloaded rifle to the horizontal position and ask breathlessly, "Who goes there?"

"Piss off, Smith," was the usual reply. My comrades would stagger drunkenly past me, complaining about their lack of success with the Paignton girls. I would spend hours thinking where all these 'loose' women might be, standing miserably on guard duty outside the billet with the rain pouring off my tin hat.

But Paignton was important and special for me. I had been drunk for the first time in my life – on two pints of draft cider at tuppence a pint. I felt as if I was dying, and my friends put me to bed. The next morning I vowed never to get drunk again. But I did, next pay day. It was on beer the next time and I vomited before I went to bed, so I felt better next morning.

This was our life through October and November 1941. In December we heard about Pearl Harbor. Hitler declared war on America, and that seemed important to us somehow. As Christmas approached, coinciding with the end of our course and our first leave, there was constant speculation over our individual postings to navigation school. It would be to Canada, Rhodesia or, if you were one of the really lucky ones, to Miami. I was fitter than I had ever been and could drill with precision. I was protected from tetanus and typhoid, had no decayed teeth and could plot a course from A to B on a Mercator chart. But I still hadn't been up in an aeroplane, and had made no progress at all in the matter of girls. But perhaps that would all change soon, for I was one of the lucky ones. Christmas leave in Salford, then to navigation school in Miami. Miami, America.

Christmas 1941 was austere. There were no turkeys, not even any chickens. But I was on leave and felt good. I enjoyed people seeing me in my uniform, and explaining to people the white flash in my forage cap that denoted that I was aircrew 'under training'. There was a bonus at the end of my leave. Our transit camp was at Heaton Park, a tuppenny tram ride from home. Now the Cockneys were in our city, and we left them to their cold billets as we drank in our local pubs and slept at home. We reported to Heaton Park at 0900 hours every morning, and stood on parade for two hours, only to receive the order "Dismiss and report back tomorrow at 0900 hours".

Standing on parade was cold and boring, so we sang to pass the time. "Why did we join, why did we join, why did we join the bloomin' Air Force, ten bob a week, bugger all to eat, bloody great boots makin' blisters on yer feet. Why did we join, why did we join, why did we join this bloomin' Air Force, sittin' on the grass, polishin' yer brass, bloody great spiders crawlin' up yer ass."

Finally, after two weeks we received the order "Dismiss

and report back at 1530 hours with full kit to proceed for embarkation".

It was difficult to say goodbye to Mum and Dad again. But imagine – I was going to America.

CHAPTER 2

America

A cold dusk was falling as we fell in in the familiar threes, and moved off with instructions not to lose the man in front. Through blacked-out streets and over rough ground we marched for more than an hour.

"Halt!" The squad stumbled and compressed to a standstill. The outline of a small railway station was dimly visible, and we were ordered to board the dark, cold carriages of the waiting train. None of us knew where we were, or where we were going, as the train jerked out of the station. Tired, we dozed fitfully. The journey was long and tedious, and there were several juddering stops. With no corridors we urinated out of the windows of the carriage doors. And finally at another stop a voice bellowed, "Gerrout, and fall in in threes!"

We were on a quayside, and a rusty ship stood before us in the dawn light. In single file we climbed the steep gangplank, and followed each other down many flights of wooden stairs into the bowels of the ship. Our living quarters were like the inside of a tin can, bare except for a latticework of pipes. Wooden tables and bench seats were bolted to the floor. Each of us was issued with a hammock, two dirty, stained grey blankets, and a sausage pillow. We stored our kit and explored our surroundings. Few of us had been aboard a ship before. Information filtered down from above. We were at Avonmouth in the Bristol Channel. The ship was the *Vollendam*, a Dutch passenger ship. She had been torpedoed twice, and survived. The thought of the Atlantic crossing made us apprehensive.

For two days she stayed moored at the quayside as more servicemen were packed aboard. There were u/t aircrew like us, Canadian soldiers going home, and Royal Navy sailors who would bring American destroyers back to England.

On the third morning the ship's crew was active, and the judder that rattled through the ship as its engines revolved sent everyone running onto deck to see the quayside drift away. By early afternoon we could see the southern coast of Ireland, and the ships that had been joining the *Vollendam* in ones and twos had swollen to a convoy of over thirty. Down below, the tin can was stuffy, and the steady drone of the engines made the air thicker. By early the next morning the ship was rolling rhythmically. My head was dizzy, my mouth kept filling with water, and my stomach felt loose and fluid. I rolled out of my hammock and walked on weak legs to a wooden bench. Nausea gripped me and vomit suddenly streamed onto the floor. I sat motionless, gazing at the pool of sick, retching occasionally as the smell of porridge and greasy bacon wafted about me. The heat seemed to encase me.

I followed others, climbing unsteadily to the deck. The fresh sea air made it less uncomfortable retching over the rails of the ship. Twice, as the nausea lessened, I tried to return to the tin can, but couldn't make it past the second flight of stairs before the nausea returned, and I scurried back to the rails.

For two days I sheltered from the wind behind a door on deck, frequently shuffling the few feet to the ship's rail to vomit again, dressed in two pairs of underwear, uniform, scarf, cap, greatcoat – and wrapped in two stinking blankets I still felt cold and weak.

On the third night the weather deteriorated, and by morning the little destroyers on the edge of the convoy were plunging steeply into the mountainous waves, reappearing again almost vertical. I watched them all day, cold and miserable, taking in the occasional sip of water from a canteen. In the evening the weather got even worse. A dizzying pattern developed – a harsh lurch – then a crash down again into the boiling sea.

I thought it was going to sink – but by then I didn't care if it did.

The gale went on and on. In the grey light of the fifth morning there were no other ships to be seen. The convoy had broken up, and the *Vollendam* was a sitting target for German U-boats. But I didn't care about that either.

On the fifth night watery spots appeared all over my body. They itched, and as I scratched them, they smarted, and itched all the more. By now I reeked of stale sick, sweat and salt, and I looked like a leper. Occasionally someone would stop and peer down at me before hurrying away.

On the sixth morning I staggered to the sick parade and joined the queue. When the ship's medical officer examined me two hours later, he admitted me into sick bay with severe sea-sickness and dermatitis. Stripped naked, and covered in camomile lotion, I was led to a bunk, and fell into an exhausted sleep.

Slowly – ever so slowly – the weather improved, and my spots began to dry up under a daily coating of parched camomile lotion. I was able to get up and walk around the sick bay, and on our twelfth day at sea I was discharged and returned to the tin can. The next day I stood on deck searching for land in the distance. Finally the dark strip above the waves that I had imagined so many times became firmer. At last I was sure it was land – Halifax, Nova Scotia, a passing sailor told me. The place looked desolate, covered in a white uneven blanket of snow. But it was land, and I felt a great relief walking down the gangplank. I frowned at the thought of the poor sailors who would spend most of the war at sea.

I felt strangely elated, sitting on the train as it puffed through the snow-covered forests of Nova Scotia. By night-time we were sitting in a long warm hut in Moncton, New Brunswick – the Royal Canadian Air Force transit camp. In Britain we were accustomed to the shortages of war, but here there were bowls with butter and sugar on the tables, and you could take as much as you liked. And there was real white bread – the first I'd seen in more than two years – and urns of fresh milk from which you could help yourself.

The three days at Moncton were pleasant and easy. We were allowed to do as we pleased while awaiting the train for Miami. We all visited the little town of Moncton, and were warned not to touch anything metallic with ungloved hands, otherwise your skin would stick fast. The barracks were cleaned daily by the permanent staff – I had never had someone tidy up for me before – and were warm and comfortable. We lazed around, lying on our beds much of the time and listening to the drone of Harvard aircraft in the skies above.

A posse of Mounties escorted us to Moncton railway station. They were big, rugged men. Their red uniforms, high black boots and yellow stripes down their trousers – and, of course, their hats – fascinated us. They were friendly and seemed to like the British. We felt close to them by the time they left us at St John on the border.

The train was much bigger than those at home – more colourful and wrapped in shiny metal. The stations had no raised platforms like those at home, and the stairs on the train reached right down to the ground. Each coach had a middle passageway, and tables to eat from. It felt much less confined than the single separate compartments in England. And they were all heated, with double-glazed windows!

We stopped briefly at St John, then travelled along the eastern seaboard of the United States. Miles and miles of land, of wilderness. The United States – I am in the United States! I felt light-headed with the thought of it all. We were all glowing with excitement, and the noise in the carriage was loud, but it was a good-natured noise, and didn't seem out of place.

We stopped in Boston first, and it looked wealthy. By mid-afternoon we were pulling into Grand Central Station in New York, and were stacked up on top of each other hanging out of the windows. The platform was even busier than wartime Crewe. Women in hats and expensive-looking coats. Men in double-breasted suits and trilby hats, looking like Jimmy Cagney and Pat O'Brien.

We couldn't get out of the train, but we stared out of the windows as we pulled off. Elbowing for more room, the angle of vision got narrower and narrower, until a sliver of skyscrapers disappeared into the failing dusk.

At Washington DC we were let off the train for six hours. The White House was floodlit, and I imagined FDR – Franklin D. Roosevelt – eating dinner from his wheelchair.

After that the landscape changed. Endless miles of countryside. In Georgia and Tennessee we stared at the black shanty towns in silence, and wondered at the poverty and despair in a country as wealthy as America.

The group of recruits who stepped from the train at Miami were conspicuous. Dressed in baggy, crumpled khaki trousers, ill-fitting khaki shirts and blue forage caps, we felt pale and incongruous. Stretching out in the two luxurious coaches that came to collect us, we stared like school-children at the huge American cars, the wide streets, and the palm trees.

Our billets were palatial – student quarters of Miami University near Coral Gables. The rooms were fit for officers. Spring-interior mattresses, carpets, and domestic staff to make the beds and clean the rooms. We queued up to taste our first ever Coca-Cola, a nickel each from a dispensing machine – something we had never seen before either.

I shared a three-bedded room with two trainees whom I had not met before. James Kevin Barry Veale, Paddy to everyone, was a strikingly good-looking Irish Scot from Dundee, with a quiet confiding voice and manner. Bernard Culpin was a Yorkshireman from Mexborough, an agreeable bloke with a quick sense of humour. We quickly felt comfortable and relaxed with each other.

There were two training flights there already when we arrived – one was British and one American. Another American flight was joining the course with us. They wore smart cotton khaki, were sun-tanned and stronger than us. There wasn't much mixing. We viewed each other with curiosity, and were friendly to each other. They were a

confident lot, but seemed flattered when we started wearing
our ties tucked into our shirts like they did.

Every morning the four flights formed up to march the
short way to the University for instruction. A barking,
clipped English voice sounded: "Fall in, A Flight." Then a
lolling American drawl: "Let's go, B Flight."

Our instructors were civilian Pan American Airways
navigators. I loved learning about 'dead reckoning' and
'astro navigation', and usually finished top in the progress
tests. But Paddy wasn't comfortable with it, and I gave him
extra lessons in the evening. It wasn't enough, so we
arranged to sit next to each other during the tests. As I
finished an answer I would push it to the top of the table for
Paddy to copy. We should have realised that we would not
be sitting next to each other over Germany, but at the time it
seemed the friendly thing to do. And Paddy had become a
great friend.

We shared the University with the regular students, who
all seemed superbly wealthy. They were bigger than we
were, and looked healthier. Their expensive cars filled the
car park to the brim. We could not imagine how people so
young could have such wealth. I used to wander through
the car park – sometimes with my friends, sometimes alone
– admiring the cars. One day I was inspecting a car, leaning
on it and peering in through the window when I heard a
voice say politely, "Excuse me." I turned to see an
attractive dark-haired girl. I was embarrassed and felt
awkward, and mumbled some apologies. She said, "Are
you English?" Then we chatted for a while and I felt less
uncomfortable. She said she liked my accent. As we
became more familiar a thought kept running through my
mind: "Would she come out with me? Ask her! Ask her!" I
had never asked a girl out before, but finally I said it – and
very strange it sounded. "Will you come out with me on
Saturday?"

"Yes," she said.

So we met on Saturday. She brought some friends for
Paddy and Bernard. We went dancing and I kissed her

goodnight. She was the first girl I had ever kissed; her name was Pearl, and I felt a strange lightness in my groin.

I was in love. We met once or twice a week, and I felt flattered that she wanted to see me rather than other boys.

The Americans were always good to us. Well, I can remember once or twice when I was called a 'goddamn limey'. But I did not understand what it meant. Then once I bumped into someone at the bar and he called me a 'Limey son of a bitch'.

Pearl said to him, "How dare you!" And the American walked away.

As part of the American hospitality programme each of us was adopted by an American family, and mine was Mrs Dougherty. She was from New York but lived in Florida during the winter. It seemed incredible to me that someone could have two homes. But she was very kind. Every Sunday her black chauffeur, James, would arrive at the billet to collect me in her limousine, and we would drive to her house outside Coral Gables. There were always two or three other Americans there of my age group. We swam and played tennis together. They always seemed more powerful and they always won. But there was no great rivalry. Everyone was friendly and at the end of the day James would drive me back to the billet. I tried to talk to James but although we were always very polite to each other, we never seemed to keep a conversation going for more than a couple of sentences.

The food in Florida was marvellous, absolutely outstanding. We ate in the University refectory every day. For breakfast there were huge platters of fried egg and bacon, as much as you could eat. Enormous T-bone steaks that lapped over the plate for dinner, with huge portions of chips and as much vinegar and salt as you liked, followed by large bowls of fresh fruit salad with lashings of cream, then delicious American coffee that tasted nothing like the Camp coffee we had at home. I thought of the people back home – if only they could see how much food I was eating, how sunny it was, how much colour there was, how happy I was!

On 13 March 1942 at 1840 hours I was airborne for the first time in my life. The aircraft was a Commodore, a flying-boat, moored in the PanAm base on the coast, south of Miami Beach. I felt sick as soon as I climbed aboard – the air inside the aircraft was stiflingly hot, smelling of hot oil and glycol. I vomited shortly after we took off and all around me the other 'rookies', as the Americans called us, were being sick too. The smell of the boat on the Atlantic crossing came back to me. We were on a two-hour familiarisation flight taking drifts on white caps. But few of us were fit to take our turn lying down in the nose of the aircraft to line up the bomb sight wires on the waves five thousand feet below us.

Before the nausea came there was a marvellous feeling as the aircraft accelerated to take-off – speed, real excitement. Then, as the plane left the ground, I felt a slight jolt, as if someone had pulled apart two things lightly glued together, and I felt disbelief that we could be flying. As I leaned to look out of the window my heart sank, and I pulled myself back. Nothing around me but the skin of the aircraft. Then I started to feel sick. The two pilots and our navigation instructor chatted to each other and smoked cigarettes.

My next flight, five days later, was much happier. I didn't feel sick at all and the view of the Florida coast was breathtaking. More flights followed and on the seventh it was my turn to be navigator. It was a cloudless night and I shot three stars with my sextant to obtain three lines of position on the Mercator chart. They should all have crossed at a point, but when I plotted them on the chart I had a triangle covering an area of over 300 square miles. I was in a state of panic. All I could do was take the mid-point on the triangle and pray to God that I was right. I started sweating. Tentatively, I squeezed my way up to Captain Dwyer, the pilot: "Change course to 281 degrees."

Captain Dwyer was smoking a massive fat cigar. He blew out a huge quantity of smoke that made me splutter and said, "OK, son."

I returned to my plotting table, sat down and buried my face in my sweaty palms. Raising my head, I looked at my navigator's compass. It was reading 264 degrees. Horrified at this pilot error and the prospect of dying, I rushed to the front of the aircraft.

I plunged against Captain Dwyer's shoulder. He looked up with concern.

"Please, Sir, I think we should be steering 281 degrees."

He smiled slowly and replied kindly, "Well, son, I reckon 264 degrees is just about right from here."

Confused, I rushed back to my plotting table and hurriedly calculated that we were 72 nautical miles southeast of Miami and heading for a place called Cuba. I took another three shots and was plotting them on the chart when I was startled by a sound in my earphones. It was Captain Dwyer.

"Come to the front, son." I scrambled quickly to the front and tapped him on the shoulder. "We'll be landing in ten minutes, son. You did well tonight, you were pretty close."

"But, er, why did you steer 264? I'm sure 281 is right."

"Well, son," such a long and friendly American drawl, "I've bin in towch with bayse owl nayt aynd thay gayve may au cowrse whayn ay aysked thaym." In any case, he said, the lights of Miami have been in sight for the whole of the flight.

But such disappointment was set against the dazzling and glamorous background of America. We spent many afternoons sitting by the pool of the Biltmore Hotel close by the University. Painful sunburn, then the wholesome and healthy feeling of my first real suntan. In the land of the film stars, I had the incredible fortune to meet two of them. Esther Williams brought her swimming extravaganza to the Biltmore for a week, and we saw her every day. Better still, I was one of the six lucky ones out of the hat to be entertained by Betty Grable on the private beach of her Miami Beach Hotel. The most beautiful woman I have ever seen, we gazed adoringly at her as she expressed concern at the dangers we would shortly face in Europe – a place very far from our thoughts as we admired the most famous pair of legs in the world.

Most Friday nights we travelled along the Causeway to Miami Beach to spend the evening in one of the dance halls, drinking Cuba Libres – rum and coke – and dancing with the hostesses at twenty-five cents a dance. Occasionally we went to the sleazy night-club outside town where the showgirls danced topless. That was very exciting and I would stare foolishly at the girls' breasts, an image of the dour, prim streets of Salford sometimes flashing in my mind. Some of our more adventurous friends visited the brothel and mesmerised us with their stories. Paddy and I went one evening and stood nervously outside, looking up the dimly lit stairs to the salon. But then we funked it and went to the dance hall instead.

Saturday nights I met Pearl, and we would go dancing or to the pictures. Or else we would drink and talk in the drug stores, and sometimes we went to a house party. I looked forward to seeing her all week. She was loving and protective, co-operative up to a point – but so far and no further. Just once, late at night on her veranda, she became utterly defenceless and mine for the taking. But then I got too excited and that was the end of that – damn, damn, damn!

And on Sundays there was the luxury of Mrs Dougherty's palatial winter home – the hospitality she extended to me was very touching, as were the efforts that the charming young Americans made to make my day off relaxing and pleasurable. Today, many years on, I still remember the Americans with affection from those sunny afternoons.

Our course ended on 12 May 1942 with the inevitable two days of examinations. Everybody achieved the pass mark and I was top of the course with 91.4%. At the passing-out parade the UK cadets were issued with a cloth navigator's brevet and Sergeant's stripes – our American friends with silver wings and a commission. Three days leave followed and we toured Florida in a hire car. So as to keep the adventure cheap, two other cadets joined Paddy and me in hiring a car. Trouble was, none of us could drive, and we argued for a long time over who should be selected. Back home I had watched my father drive the van where he worked, and on Sundays I used to study how James, Mrs Dougherty's driver, did it. I knew that you pressed on the left foot pedal when changing gear, and that the right pedal was the brake. This was more than any of the others knew, so I was the reluctant choice by a three-to-one majority.

There was no trouble at the garage.

"Driven before?"

"Er – no." (Better be honest about it.)

"No licence then?"

"Er – no." (Shit, that's it then.)

"Twenty bucks a day and you pay for any damage. Sign here."

They started the engine for me – three times they did it as I stalled it twice. They had turned away by the time we were jerking and juddering down the road. The wide roads were attractive – and necessary, given my lack of proficiency.

Entering narrow spaces was a major challenge at first as I couldn't co-ordinate clutch and accelerator. So I would stop the car, get out, check alignment, wrestle the wheel a little bit, get out to check alignment again, get back in and then, keeping the steering wheel straight, I would let the clutch out. It worked every time and three days later as I drove back to the garage, I imagined myself looking like Errol Flynn – driver's window down, my elbow resting nonchalantly, if uncomfortably, on the sill, and a lighted cigarette drooping from my lips.

Too soon we were boarding the Chattanooga Choo Choo for Moncton, and saying goodbye to our American friends. Everybody exchanged addresses and promised to keep in touch. Pearl and I wrote to each other for quite a long time, but the space between letters got longer and longer. And anyway, back in grey Europe, America and Pearl seemed more and more like a dream.

We had been told that we could leave the train at New York for five hours and Mrs Dougherty had arranged for her son, Chuck, to meet me there. He gave me a whirlwind tour of the city – Fifth Avenue, Madison Square Gardens, Central Park – all magical names. Lunch at Tiffany's – such sumptuous food. The Empire State Building – the tallest building in the world – and we went all the way to the top – gun-toting cops, yellow taxi cabs, Bronx tenements, Manhattan skyscrapers, and lights – so many lights. Finally, another expensive meal, and back to Grand Central Station. Elated, I tried to express my thanks to this stranger who had shown me the greatest city in the world.

Three of the lads didn't arrive back to catch the train, and we never saw them again. The rest of us settled down to enjoy the journey and talk about our stay in America. We were all loaded with presents, and things that were not available in wartime Britain. For Mother, nylon stockings, hair clips, cosmetics, toilet soap, hair shampoo, and a cameo brooch. For Dad, 200 Lucky Strike cigarettes, 'toasted' like the ones Jimmy Cagney smoked. For Granddad, a bottle of rye whisky, and for Nan, a silk kimono, which she never wore.

I was dreading the journey home and felt sick at the thought of the mountainous seas. We were on the *Empress of Canada*, a large luxury liner and fast enough to cross the Atlantic alone. In only six days we reached the Firth of Clyde, and the Atlantic had been like a millpond.

It was June when we arrived back in Britain, but the evening was cold and damp as we boarded the lighters in Greenock Harbour. After America, the blacked-out coast looked secretive and sinister, and the bulbous dark clouds, tinged with dirty white, that rolled over us felt oppressive. We headed towards the dim grey warehouses that made jagged shapes against the withering dusk. Debris and scum bubbled against the wharf as we berthed by the steps leading up to the quayside, where we fell in in threes, and were marched to the waiting train, its compartments cold, unlit, dirty and dank. There was little conversation as we took our seats, dejected at the first sight of the forgotten shabbiness of wartime Britain.

CHAPTER 3

Final Preparations

The PanAm training in America was only good for daytime operations, not the night bombing that we would shortly be doing. So we all met up again at Advanced Flying Unit – AFU – at Bobbington near Stourbridge in the Midlands. It was one of the hundreds of RAF bases hastily cut out of flat countryside – three runways with a perimeter track and dispersal points for the aircraft. Monotonous ranks of huts, indistinguishable from one another, served as living quarters, admin headquarters, messes and training rooms. I reported to the guardroom where the duty corporal stood officiously by the counter.

"Yuh?" he said in an impatient Cockney accent – obviously unimpressed by my three new stripes.

"I've come to report on course 253."

"Name?"

"Smith – 1438275." It was RAF practice for Smiths to add their number when giving their name.

Scanning his clipboard he announced, "Hut 17." He then dismissed me from his responsibility with a tick from his RAF issue pencil against my name.

"Er," I began, hesitating at the inhospitable jerk of his head in my direction. "Er – could you direct me to hut 17 please?"

"First left, follow yer nose an' use yer tongue."

It was much friendlier in hut 17, already nearly full of familiar faces all trying to tell everyone else what they had done on leave over the last two weeks. The contents of the hut were standard RAF issue – twenty-four two-foot-by-six-inch wire mesh beds, twelve of them each side, twenty-four unpainted bedside cabinets, brown lino on the floor, and two black stoves, one at each end of the room, their chimneys disappearing into the roof. Finally, two trestle tables and eight wooden collapsible chairs – already in use by the letter writers and card players. As I looked around, the last of the day's light was being obscured as the heavy black curtains were drawn across the window panes, which were reinforced with criss-cross white gummed paper strips. The glare of the naked white bulbs became brighter.

At AFU we practised navigation in Avro Ansons flown by experienced pilots, most of them ex-operational. Time after time we covered the prescribed routes: Base – Ludlow – Worcester – Harwich – Upper Heyford – Pershore – Base. Base – Rhyl – Douglas – Colwyn Bay – Base. And so on, criss-crossing the British Isles by night and by day. On a daylight flight towards the end of the course one of our engines failed, and as the Anson couldn't fly on one, we landed wheels up in a field near the Wrekin, slithering to a halt with only yards to spare before the hedge and ditch.

Otherwise our time at AFU was tedious and boring, and there was little activity in the town of Stourbridge. All of us looked forward to the end-of-course leave, but we had learned important skills. My final assessment, which I would take with me to Operational Training Unit, read 'Reliable navigator – good knowledge in all subjects'. We were posted individually to several different OTUs, and I parted company from my special friends, Paddy and Bernard, on Stourbridge railway station. We had become firm friends. Apart from relations in Salford, these were the best friends I had ever made, and I would never see them again.

My OTU, RAF Chipping Warden, was much like RAF Bobbington at first sight, but this posting would be different from the previous ones. At the end of it I would be fully trained and ready for operations, and here I would meet up with four other aircrew who would fly with me over Germany.

Seventy-five of us reported to the crew room on the day after our arrival – fifteen each of pilots, navigators, bomb-aimers, wireless operators and rear-gunners – all glancing nervously at each other. After a welcoming speech by the Station Commander, a Group Captain, we were told to 'crew up'. There was no system and we just mingled around nervously. Most of us were Sergeants, with a few sprog Pilot Officers who had been given commissions at the end of their training. The only exception was a Flight Lieutenant among the pilots, who must have been a regular. He was a lot older than the rest of us, maybe 27 or 28 years old. He made his way over to the group of navigators.

"Which of you is Sergeant Smith?" he enquired purposefully. I froze. Did he mean me?

"Er – me?" I croaked, wishing he would go away.

"Would you like to be my navigator?"

I felt mute. How did I say no, as I wanted to? "Er, I suppose so," I mumbled, lacking the courage to refuse.

"Right then," he said, as two Pilot Officers, one a bomb-aimer and the other a rear-gunner, joined us. "We crewed up in the bar last night – this is Jim Eckton, our bomb-aimer, and this is Roger Smith, our Canadian rear-gunner. I'm Paul Peters. Let's find ourselves a wireless operator before they all go. Go on, Smithy, pick one."

They were going fast so I grabbed the first one I saw. "You crewed up yet?" I asked him – a Sergeant about my own age.

"No," he said. "Are you?"

"Yes, with those three officers over there."

"Don't fancy that Flight Looey," he grumbled.

"He seems all right and he must have been flying for years at his age," I coaxed. "Come on, you'll get a sprog pilot if you don't," I added as a pink-faced, boyish-looking pilot approached us.

"Are you…"

"Yes," I interrupted, taking my prize by the arm and steering him triumphantly to join the waiting team. Tony Wray from Sheffield completed the crew.

Tony and I roomed together in the Sergeants' quarters and saw little of the other three for the first few days, living as they did in the Officers' quarters and eating in different messes. For a week we reported to our own sections while the pilots were converted to flying the Wellington. We first took off as a crew in Wellington 'T Tommy' on 20 October 1942 at 1435 hours. It was a sunny day and the ground was visible for the duration of the four-hour flight: Base – Reading – Goole – Reading – Base. The wind speed was a constant 15 knots at 285 degrees, and I navigated the aircraft back to base exactly on ETA. Pretty good, I thought, back in the crew room as we stowed our flight gear.

Not so Pete, as Paul Peters was known. "Let's have a look at your chart, Smith," he said, as the others dispersed to the Mess. "It took you forty minutes to correct the forecast wind," he mused as he studied my log meticulously. I was astonished at his pilot's knowledge of navigation – normally they didn't have a clue.

"I didn't know you could navigate, Pete," I said.

"Didn't I tell you?" he replied. "I did a specialist navigation course before the war. I taught navigation for two years in Australia before I got a posting back to the UK to go on ops."

"Oh, God," I thought, "he knows more about navigation than I do."

"We strayed off course twice then, Smithy?" he asked. Was he asking me or did he know? He knew.

"Well, yes, but my change of course took us to the turning points."

Pete pursed his mouth slightly. "True, but if we stray out of the stream on ops, then we'll get picked off by flak or fighters. It's easy enough to find Goole and Reading on a clear English afternoon, but imagine flying on ops at night in 10/10ths cloud, and returning to a tiny airfield in England after five hours flying." I was surprised how reasonable he seemed, as I stared at my shoes and nodded my head ever so slightly but very fast. In the silence that followed I felt a slight hostility replacing the reasonableness. I tried to think of an excuse, but I couldn't. With the new Gee box – a radar aid by which you could fix the aircraft's exact position in a matter of minutes – I should have made a course change long before I did.

"Sorry, Sir, er, Pete." I felt as if I was back at the school I had departed only months before.

I walked slowly back to the Sergeants' Mess. Of course he was right. With Gee, staying on course should be a piece of cake. A sentence in the Group Captain's welcoming speech came back to me: "Barring accidents and bad luck, the better the crew, the better the chances of survival." I began to think about what lay ahead. It began to seem a bit more real, and gave me slight butterflies in my stomach. It was a feeling – not strong, but not avoidable either. I resolved then that whatever happened, my navigation would not be the cause of our deaths.

Pete was obsessive. Even if I had not resolved to get it right, he would have made sure – he pushed all of us. Time after time we practiced the routines. We rarely sat around in the crew room with the others, smoking, chatting, reading newspapers and talking about girls. Instead Pete would take us out to a Wellington, always saying, although the words always made their impression anew, "We're either going to die in one, or climb out of one." We would practice the emergency drills until we were sick of them. "Pilot to crew – dinghy, dinghy, dinghy, prepare for ditching."

"Navigator, OK."

"Bomb-aimer, OK."

"Wireless op, OK."

"Rear-gunner, OK."

A short interval.

"Pilot to crew – abandon aircraft."

We would all scramble up to the front, climb out of the top escape hatch and assemble on the port wing.

"Did you remember to pull the dinghy release, Smithy?"

"Yes, Skip."

By halfway through the course we could clear the aircraft in less than three minutes in full flying gear. We practised bailing out – dropping through the bottom escape hatch onto the tarmac. We took turns rotating the rear turret and dragging the rear-gunner out. We could all release the astro-dome from its housing, giving us an additional exit from the aircraft. We could find every fire extinguisher, axe, oxygen and intercom point with our eyes closed. We even practised rudimentary operation of the aircraft controls in case Pete got the chop. We could all fire the guns, and Jim showed us how to aim the bombs, and to jettison them. I showed Jim how to use the Gee box and plot the fix on the chart.

We were up in Wellington 'T Tommy' two or three nights a week on ops exercises. They were four or five hour flights simulating operational conditions – fully laden with petrol and sand-filled bombs, briefed before take-off, and interrogated after we landed. Tony practised taking loop bearings on radio beacons and I tried to navigate without the aid of the Gee box in case it blew up. Pete practised flying on one engine, and standard beam approaches to the runway – even he seemed satisfied with our progress.

Jim Eckton and I had become instant friends, and shortly after he had crewed up the two of us cycled the seven miles to Banbury for a booze-up. The first pub was dingy – a few locals standing at the bar, two playing dominoes. They looked at us with a touch of hostility as we walked up to the bar and greeted our smiles with a slightly lingering gaze before they looked away. But the biggest problem was the total absence of girls. We had a pint of mild then left for the pub opposite. There weren't any girls there either, so after another pint we moved on to a pub that was selling bitter, deciding to stay there for the last orders at about 9.30pm – the beer was running out, as it often did during the war.

"You don't look too good, Smithy," Jim said as we started our last pint. Later I remembered trying to focus on the barman by closing one eye and gripping the bar rail tightly. Jim prized my hands away and I felt unsteady. He put my arm over his shoulder and I giggled and mumbled incoherently. The air changed suddenly from warm to cold, and I could feel a damp sweat on my forehead. I remember a big liquid hiccough and the smell of sick, then everything was spinning and I seemed to be lying on the pavement.

I woke to find myself sitting on the floor and propped up

against the wall in a corner of a big, dark, cold room. There was the acrid smell of vomit from the front of my tunic. As I retched again, a shape lying on a bench beside me moved.

"You all right, Smithy?" It was Jim.

"Where the hell are we?"

"Banbury Station. You passed out and some of the locals helped me carry you here."

"What time is it?"

He peered at his watch. "Four o'clock. Do you think you can ride your bike?"

It took an hour and a half to return to base, as I kept falling off. Dawn was breaking as we parted company in camp to go to our separate huts.

"Thanks, Jim," I muttered sheepishly.

"Pleasure."

Our routine continued – constant flying, constant drills. Towards the end of the course, on a foul dark night, the Gee box started smouldering and packed up. After an hour or so I was totally lost. Tony got me some loop bearings, which put us somewhere near Sheffield. We came down to two thousand feet to try to get below the cloud in the hope of spotting a flashing beacon. Mindful of the balloon barrage surrounding every town at night, I warned Pete, and Tony switched over to the balloon barrage warning frequency. Instantly the banshee wailing of the warning curled the hair at the back of my neck, and we sat wide-eyed until the awesome sound started to fade.

Two weeks later we did our final exercise over the North Sea toward Europe, turning back a few miles from the Dutch coast. Most of the crews were posted to the conversion unit for training on four-engined aircraft – the final step before joining a squadron. But two crews would go instead straight onto ops with one of the few remaining Wellington squadrons. We were one of them. Our posting was to Croft, the satellite of Middleton St George, to join 427 Canadian Squadron.

Jim and I went to London for the first two days of our pre-ops leave. We stayed at the Strand Palace, went to the Windmill – twice – drank innumerable pints and went home almost penniless for the rest of the leave on 22 December 1942.

Christmas leave in Salford, like the last, was dreary and uninspiring. Most of the young men and women my age were away in one or other of the services, and the school children had been evacuated. The civilians were working in the factories from eight in the morning until seven at night, so the streets were empty. War had taken the colour out of the town. Dun sand-bags were everywhere and burned-out buildings stood out, sombre and deserted. Civilian rations had been cut to the bone, and only the black market offered any variety. But few people in Salford could afford the price of a black market egg or a quarter of tea.

My leave in Salford petered out in a cold, grey, draughty train.

CHAPTER 4

427 Squadron

The crew met up again at Darlington Station on 27 December 1942. We knew surprisingly little about what lay in store for us in an operational squadron. We knew that a tour was thirty ops, at the end of which – if you hadn't got the chop – you were screened for at least six months before doing a second tour. Most of our instructors at OTU had done a tour, but they seemed reluctant to tell us of their experiences.

A truck collected us from the station, and took us to RAF Croft. The squadron was newly formed and only just operational – just two mine-laying trips off the Dutch coast. The aerodrome was muddy and unlived-in, its walkways still under construction. But there were sheets on the beds in the hut that Tony and I shared – a special perk for aircrew.

In our first two weeks at Croft there was no flying due to the atrocious weather conditions. So we took the opportunity to make an early exploration of Darlington. Usually it was Jim, Tony and I who spent the evenings in the Golden Fleece pub. Pete rarely joined us, preferring to spend his free time with Flight Lieutenant Shead who had joined the squadron with his crew before us. Roger never came to the pub with us, and seemed cold and solitary.

The Golden Fleece was warm and friendly, and always crowded with aircrew from Croft and Middleton St George. Two of the Canadians had guitars and frequently gave impromptu performances. And towards the end of the evening everyone joined in the popular epilogue:

"Oh please don't burn our shithouse down
Mother has promised to pay
Father's away on the ocean wave
And sister's in the family way

Brother dear has gonorrhoea
Times are bloomin' hard
So please don't burn our shithouse down
Or we'll all have to shit in the yard."

Everyone sang loudly, and the civilian blokes clearly loved it, and cheered and clapped as time was called and the pub emptied. And we enjoyed it too. We enjoyed the end of another day when the weather showed no sign of relenting, putting off for another night our first confrontation with the hated Germans. But as we dozed on the bus back to camp, at the back of our minds was the thought that we could not put it off for ever, and that soon we would be in battle. It might even be tomorrow night, and one night it certainly would be.

We were apprehensive about any improvement in the weather. The cloud base on 9 January 1943 didn't seem to have lifted any, but we clustered around the notice board at 'flights' and read painfully that seven crews were ordered for an 1100 hours briefing and that we were one of them.

My stomach knotted and I felt sick. I went to the toilet in case I vomited, but managed not to. Volunteering for ops was one thing, but actually going on one was quite another. Thoughts of being labelled LMF – Lack of Moral Fibre – with its dreadful stigma, forced me back to the crew room where Pete, excited as I had never known him before, lifted our spirits a bit. "It'll probably be a mine-laying trip to break us in." He probably already knew that it was – he spent a lot of time in the Flight Commander's office.

At 1055 hours we trooped into the briefing room past the two Service Policemen at the door. The air was already thick with cigarette smoke, and the babble of voices sounded unusually shrill. We sat down near the front and stared at the curtained wall chart on the stage. Some people attempted jokes – forced and childish.

"Probably be the Ruhr – an easy one to start us off."

"Can I have your egg if you don't come back."

"Don't forget to eat the flimsy before you bail out." Our smiles were artificial.

"Attention!" My legs felt weak as I stood up. Senior officers filed onto the stage and the doors closed behind them. The Wing Commander pulled back the curtain, revealing an outsize map of Europe, with red ribbons tracing our outward and homeward routes. Pete had been right. It was a mine-laying trip to Terschelling – one of the Frisian Islands. Tony lit my cigarette and I began to feel less weak.

The drop location in the North Sea was pin-pointed on the map. From a few miles into Holland we were briefed to fly over Terschelling at 500 feet, releasing two 1500lb mines exactly forty seconds after crossing the island. There would be moderate flak from the island "which shouldn't worry you too much," said the Wingco, used as he was to the intense heavy flak he used to meet in his first tour over Germany.

"It might be moderate," whispered Jim, "but what if it's accurate?"

Pete leaned across. "Don't think about it – and shut up," he hissed as the briefing continued. The 'met' man promised that the weather would improve for take-off and that it would be even better for our return.

We stood to attention again as the briefing officers marched out of the room at the end of an hour-long briefing. There hadn't been very much to brief us about, but for all seven crews this was the biggest one to date – our first.

As the others of the crews dispersed, the navigators stayed behind to plot the courses using the forecast winds. Pencils were sharpened and equipment checked before being packed away with log sheet and charts in our green navigation bags, to be left guarded by the Duty Officer.

Take-off was 1645 hours. Operational meals would be served in the Mess at 1415 hours – fried egg, bacon and fried bread – very special food indeed, and it helped to overcome the nervousness. The WAAF staff seemed friendlier than usual, and even managed a smile as they handed us our plates.

We sat around in the Mess after the meal, some trying to doze, others chatting quietly, the pre-op atmosphere descending over the Mess ante-room. I couldn't chat, or go to sleep. Couldn't read the newspaper either. I sat staring at the ceiling and glancing at the clock. It seemed to gather pace as the time neared to make a move.

As if at a signal, people made their way out of the Mess for the short walk to 'flights'. Locker doors in the crew room creaked open, and flying gear was taken out. Only the rear-gunners wore full flying clothing as protection against the cold. There were hot air pipes in the Wellington, so the rest of us made do with flying boots, our white submariner's pullover under our battledress blouse and the fur-lined Irvin jacket.

Parachutes were drawn and signed for at the parachute section, and flying rations and thermos flasks collected from the duty corporal at the table in the corner of the crew room. Mae Wests were donned and tied up, helmets and oxygen masks hung round the neck, trailing the intercom cord.

The navigators trundled one by one to the nearby briefing room to collect their green bags and the rice-paper flimsies containing the night's secret information – frequencies, beacons, codes, colours of the day, call signs.

Crews gathered together before climbing into the camouflaged bus that took us out to dispersal. And shortly after, we were climbing out again as the driver called out "C Charlie". Lit only by the torch lights of the ground crew, the Wellington stood silent and sinister, bombed-up, armoured and fuelled. We climbed aboard, checked the circuits, and declared everything in order, before climbing out again to formally accept the aircraft from the groundcrew. Pete signed the form 700, acknowledging 'C Charlie' free from defects.

The groundcrew moved away, wishing us "Good luck" and asking us not to "bend anything". We sat around outside the aircraft, smoking cigarettes, except Pete who didn't smoke. One by one we observed the pre-op tradition of urinating on the tail wheel, until with thirty minutes to take off, we took our turn to climb the ladder at the front of the aircraft. First the rear-gunner in his electrically heated 'inner' and Irvin jacket and trousers, to make his cumbersome way along the cold, damp fuselage – over the main spar that straddled the interior halfway down – finally squeezing feet first into his turret, closing the sliding doors behind him. Tony followed him up the ladder, then me, then Pete, and finally Jim.

In the Wellington the bomb-aimer, when not lying in the bomb-aimer's position in the nose to aim the bombs, take a drift, map read, or get a pinpoint, sat next to the pilot on a 'drop down – lift up' strut. An armour plate behind the pilot separated the captain of the aircraft from the wireless operator's cubicle. That's where Tony sat, his radio equipment stacked in front of his Morse key on its tiny table. And behind Tony, my curtained 'office', containing a plotting table, fixed chair (padded and comfortable), compass, air speed indicator, altimeter (to check on the pilot) and, on the left, in pride of place, the Gee box. Tonight it would be effective just about all the way to the target on the enemy coast, beyond which the pulse would be lost in the noise of the German jamming.

I emptied the contents of my green bag onto the table, laid out my chart and stowed my instruments The bottom hatch banged to, and I heard the inside lock clamp shut. The engines whined as the starter 'acc' on the runway coaxed each cold engine into motion.

A click as Pete flicked the switch on his microphone. "All OK?"

"Navigator OK."

"Bomb-aimer OK."

"Wireless operator OK."

"Rear-gunner OK."

The brakes hissed and the aircraft began to taxi around the perimeter track to take its place in the queue at the end of the runway. Our turn to line up – a green from the caravan – a roar of engines and we were trundling down the runway gathering speed as the propellers dragged the air back over the wings.

I started writing in my first operation log:

1645 hrs Airborne – Gee on – IFF on – climbing.
1700 hrs Filey – 5000 feet – set course 53 degrees 10 minutes N – 05 degrees 20 minutes E – course 110 degrees compass.
1710 hrs IFF off.
1720 hrs Guns tested – bombs selected.

I took a Gee fix and plotted it – 53 degrees 56 minutes N – 00 degrees 28 minutes E. We were drifting off track.

"Hello Skip." It was always 'Skip' in the aircraft. "Change course 115 degrees."

After a few seconds, "On course 115 degrees." I wrote it up in my log:

1722 hrs Gee fix – 53 degrees 56 minutes N – 00 deg 28 minutes E. Wind 238/240 knots.
1725 hrs Alter course 115 degrees – ETA end of leg 1842.

For the next hour, as we traversed the North Sea, I took Gee fixes – all dead on track – and checked my ETA – still 1842. I had the wind speed and direction spot on.

Pete on the intercom: "Enemy coast in sight."

Tony turned round and looked at me through a chink in my curtain. We exchanged mock grimaces as he turned to make his way to the front turret to have a go at the searchlights, if there were any. Jim went into the nose to release the mines and set his forty-second interval on the bomb release, then peered down through the Perspex to pick up his pinpoint. I went up front to stand by Pete's seat – redundant for the moment.

We came down to 1000 feet, flew between the islands of

Texel and Vlieland, then changed course to take us back out to sea over the island of Terschelling. Jim picked up the pinpoint and we dropped to 500 feet to cross the island. Everyone was motionless and utterly quiet. From the darkness below a red spot appeared. Quickly it grew larger, and was followed by another, and another, and another. Ugly red dots were snaking right for us – and now only seconds away. Instinctively I drew back as dazzling red lines tore across my sight – to right and left. Surely they must hit us…

And then we were past it, and on our timed run. Jim was counting numbers on the intercom: "20 – 10 – 5 – 4 – 3 – 2 – 1". The aircraft lurched upwards as the mines were released, then steadied itself, and started to climb back over the sea, banking onto course, homeward bound. Tension gone, I returned to my seat and took up my navigation:

1902 hrs Mines gone – set course Filey 285 degrees. ETA 2007.
2002 hrs Coast sighted – IFF on.
2008 hrs Filey – set course base 320 degrees ETA 2042.

We joined the other aircraft over Croft on ETA and landed at 2100, our first operation completed.

A truck collected us and took us up to the interrogation room, which was filling up with noisy crews. Everyone wore a swaggering half smile and chatted with animation as we awaited our turn to be interrogated by an intelligence officer at the trestle tables. I was smiling comfortably. I felt relaxed, and elated as I drank the tea, heavily laced with rum.

The post-op bacon and egg was delicious and there was even time for a pint at the bar before it closed. I walked back to the hut with Tony, anti-climax setting in and bringing with it a drowsiness borne of nervous tension – imprisoned and then released – and helped by alcohol. This would be the pattern for the foreseeable future – civilian routines and occupation now long forgotten. The events of the evening kept coming back to me – the briefing, the hatch closing, the testing of the guns. And the flak. Only the light stuff, and for only a few seconds, but fired by German soldiers on the ground, trying to kill us.

"You know, Tony, thing's seem different somehow."

"Yeah, I know what you mean. We're at war."

Tired as I was, I recorded my first operation in my log book in the regulation red ink for a night op:

Date: 9.1.43
Hour: 1645
Aircraft: Wellington III 'C'
Pilot: F/L P Peters
Duty: Navigator
Details: Operations (1) Mine-laying Terschelling –
               2 x 1500lb mines
Flying Time: Night 4 hours 15 mins.

[Official Record of Bomber Command: 9/10 January 1943. Mine-laying. 121 aircraft – 78 Halifaxes, 41 Wellingtons, 2 Stirlings – on a large mine-laying operation in the Frisians, the German Bight and the Kattegat. 97 aircraft reported laying mines in the designated areas. 4 Halifaxes lost]

The weather deteriorated again over the next couple of days, but we couldn't go to the Fleece as we were broke and it was still four days to pay day. We had just about enough money – sixpence each – for the Saturday night dance in the church hall in Croft village. There were lots of girls there – mostly Land Army and WAAFs from the squadron. As operational aircrew, we were their preferred dancing partners, and they were quick off their mark at the announcement of a 'Ladies Request', of which there were several at wartime dances. But I still felt uneasy and awkward with a girl until I got to know her. And, perhaps, sensing my embarrassment, they always tended to drift away. Since America I had got nowhere near to the physical act of making love. Even if I had, I wouldn't have known what to do. I worried that I might die innocent and uninitiated.

The clouds lifted again, and an ops list was pinned up on the crew room notice board on the morning of 14 January. The seven crews listed were those that hadn't been on the mine-laying trip. I was relieved. I wouldn't be going on ops until tomorrow night at the earliest, and that was a long way away.

The operation was scrubbed at the last minute as the weather clamped down again. The seven aircraft had been taxiing round the perimeter track towards the runway as the wireless ops heard the message to return to dispersal.

On the following morning Jim and I were in the crowd around the notice board when the day's battle order was posted. The same seven crews were listed – briefing 1400 hours.

We hung about in the crew room for a while, smoking cigarettes and lolling around before making our way back to the Mess – Jim, Tony and I. We had been paid the previous morning and the money was burning holes in our pockets – two pounds sixteen shillings.

"The Fleece tonight?" Unanimous agreement.

"How are you doing with that barmaid, Smithy?" asked Jim.

"Not bad – got my hand down her blouse after the dance last week." I hadn't, but I had to pretend I was making progress. The tannoy interrupted us.

"Pilot Officer Eckton and Sergeant Smith report to the crew room immediately." And it repeated the message four times. Jim scrunched up his face.

"That sounds ominous," he said. "Perhaps we're on ops." He shook his head slightly. "No, that can't be; they'd have called for Tony too." Whatever it was, Tony didn't want to be included, and declined our invitation to go with us to 'flights'.

The Squadron Commander, Wing Commander Burnside, was in the crew room with Squadron Leader Williams, the A Flight Commander. We stood at the door and saluted.

"Ah – Smith," said the Wing Commander. "You're flying with me tonight, and Eckton, you're flying with Squadron Leader Williams. Night flying tests 1230 hours – briefing 1400." He resumed his conversation with his Flight Commander as we mumbled our "Yes, Sirs". Then, seeing our dismay, he added less formally, "My navigator's gone sick, and so has Squadron Leader Williams's bomb-aimer. Take it as a compliment – off you go."

Grim-faced, we hurried back to the Mess with little time left before NFT.

"Some bloody compliment," I murmured to myself.

"We have to do them some time, Smithy," said Jim with a smile.

"Yes, but hell – with a strange crew?"

Jim's smile faded as he nodded in agreement.

At the briefing we separated to join our makeshift crews. Wing Commander Burnside, my pilot for the night, was in charge of the briefing. His pedigree was well known – he had a DFC and this was his fortieth operation. I calculated his seniority to me in my head – seven ranks and thirty-eight ops.

He pulled the curtain from the wall chart, and all eyes followed the red ribbon. It didn't go east as we expected, but due south to Lorient in north-west France. This, with St Nazaire, was the haven for German U-boats, sheltered there in huge concrete pens.

I looked across at Jim. "Cookies!" he mouthed, and I nodded. But instead of a 'cookie' – a 4000lb bomb – our bomb load consisted of 810 four-pound incendiaries. It wasn't an attack on the U-boats, but on their supply ships in the open docks. This was a main force attack, led by the newly formed Pathfinder Force, who would drop flares over the target. Gee was expected to be effective to within sixty miles of Lorient, and with only light cloud it was going to be an easy target to find.

Heavy flak, the high-altitude stuff, at Lorient was classed as moderate, and fighter opposition from the Luftwaffe relatively scant. This news was reassuring and I felt less frightened.

As normal, the navigators stayed behind to plot the course, which took us south-south-west to Lyme Regis on the South Coast, then across the English Channel, over Brittany and on to Lorient. The flight plan would take us there and back in six hours fifty minutes, by far my longest flight to date.

"Good luck, Jim," I offered as, later, we separated to join our respective crews in the crew room.

"Same to you, Smithy – Fleece tomorrow?"

"You bet."

I felt uneasy flying with a strange crew, especially with the high-ranking Wing Commander Burnside as skipper. I stuck rigidly to RAF procedures.

"Navigator to pilot – set course 185 degrees magnetic – ETA south coast 1832 hours."

The intercom was quiet for most of the next ninety minutes until the bomb-aimer confirmed by visual fix our arrival over Lyme Regis and subsequently our landfall on the Brittany coast where the Gee signals began to fade. There was no flak at all over occupied France as I gave the pilot the final course to the target.

Normal procedure didn't allow the navigator to go up front as Pete had invited me to do on the previous operation, so now I had little to do but listen to the voices of the pilot and bomb-aimer on the intercom.

"Flares ahead," from the bomb-aimer.

"OK bomb-aimer," answered the Wingco. "Take over."

"Five degrees to port," and a few minutes later. "Hold course – five minutes to aiming point – open bomb doors."

"Bomb doors open." An involuntary "Christ!" screeched from the bomb-aimer as a loud explosion flung the aircraft onto its side. The temperature fell rapidly as shrapnel tore a hole in the canvas, letting in the cold air. Wide-eyed and breathless, I grabbed for my parachute, but quickly the aircraft was straight and level again, and the pilot was on the intercom.

"OK everyone – resume bombing run."

"Left, left – steady – steady – right – steady – steady – steady." Two muffled bangs as flak exploded nearby. "Steady – steady – bombs going." The now familiar lurch as the aircraft was relieved of its load. "Bombs gone." We held course for the photograph, waiting for the camera light to go out on the instrument panel. "Bomb doors closed," as we cleared the coast and flew out into the Bay of Biscay, then back to starboard to take us round the flak and on to the Brittany coast.

"Aircraft going down in flames to starboard, navigator," from the pilot. I noted it down in my log.

"Everyone all right?" asked the pilot, and we all replied in turn. We had a sizeable hole in the fuselage near the flare chute on the starboard side, and several shrapnel holes down the same side, but no damage to the controls. We settled down in our positions, and nearing the coast of Brittany the pulses began to push their way through the grass on the Gee box screen.

"Wireless operator to pilot. All 427 squadron aircraft directed to divert to Tangmere. Weather at base unfit for landing."

"OK wireless operator. Navigator, give me a course to Tangmere." I made the alteration in my plot, and shortly we turned onto the new heading. Within the hour we were joining the circuit on the famous Battle of Britain fighter base on the South Coast, and the screech of the tyres on the runway signified my second successful mission.

[Official Record of Bomber Command: 15/16 January 1943. Lorient. 153 aircraft – 65 Wellingtons, 48 Halifaxes, 40 Stirlings, 4 Lancasters. 1 Stirling and 1 Wellington lost. Bombing was more accurate than on the previous night. At least 800 buildings were destroyed and 12 civilians killed. Most of the inhabitants had fled the town the previous day.]

The interrogation room was already filling up with crews from 427 squadron and another Wellington squadron from North Yorkshire when we arrived there – but no sign of Jim and his crew. The room grew noisier and smokier as more crews arrived and the post-op interrogation began. Still no sign of Jim. After we'd been interrogated, the rest of the crew made their way to the Mess, but I stayed on to wait for him. The Wingco stayed too, sitting with the intelligence officers, discussing the results of the operation and, from time to time, talking on the telephone.

Gradually the room emptied. I sat alone at a table, smoking and drinking tea. Again, the Wingco talked on the telephone, then made his way over to my table.

"You waiting for Eckton, Smith?" he asked.

"Yes, Sir."

He breathed in through his nose and put his hand on my shoulder. "Squadron Leader Williams and his crew are officially posted missing. Go and get your meal."

An airman showed me the way to the Sergeants' Mess. I ate mechanically, and the food made no difference to a light feeling in my stomach. Later, I lay awake in a hastily made bed with damp blankets, and felt dizzy. The same words kept going through my mind – Jim's got the chop – his second time out – poor old fucking Jim. And then my thoughts went back over the evening. "Ah, Smith – you're flying with me tonight, and Eckton, you're flying with Squadron Leader Williams." Bloody hell, what luck. Could have been the other way round – me getting the chop and Jim lying here awake thinking of me. Better as it was – Jim, not me. No – that's not better. God knows.

Tangmere was busy the next morning. Shortly after 0900 hours the Wellingtons left their dispersals to taxi round the perimeter track towards the runway. One by one they lifted off, wheels retracting, before banking in a climbing turn to port and on to the northerly course that would take them belatedly back to bases in North Yorkshire. We watched them go from the watch office, the rest of the Wingco's crew and me. Our aircraft, 'E Edward', had been damaged enough to be declared unserviceable and we had to stay behind and wait for the riggers to repair her. Later that day the Wingco took off with another crew, leaving its pilot, Sergeant Taylor, behind to fly us back once 'E Edward' was repaired.

We expected to be away the next morning, but it was five more days before we took off and set course for base. It was boring hanging about at Tangmere where there seemed to be little activity. We swapped stories with the Sergeant fighter pilots, but they didn't spend much time in the Mess after the evening meal. But there were French WAAFs on the station and they interested us. The rear-gunner and I picked up two of them in a pub in nearby Chichester, and they were decidedly friendly. They'd heard all the fighter stories and were eager to hear us talk about bombing ops. We all went back to camp together, and we smuggled them aboard 'E Edward', impressing them with the inside of a Wellington.

We were surprised by a Service Policeman, who called out to us from the tarmac, but he was reassured when he recognised us. He left when we told him we were just checking the equipment. We hoped that the French WAAFs would show their thanks for the tour, especially as we had heard that all French females were promiscuous. And it looked promising – I'd never been kissed like that before. But that – and a willingness to have her shirt buttons undone to reveal her bare breasts – was all I got. She declined, apologetically, to go any further, and after a short while she detached herself from me and returned to the WAAFery – out of bounds to male personnel. I climbed into bed aching and frustrated. Still, it had been pretty good, and I probably wouldn't have made it anyway. Must try to do something about that.

We landed back at Croft at 1445 hours on 21 January – six days after we had taken off. Tony was in the crew room waiting for me, and as we sat talking, Pete joined us.

"Any news of Jim, Pete?"

"No, none. Two aircraft were seen to go down in flames. Not much chance of getting out of a diving Wellington. So, we're short of a bomb-aimer." A wave of deep sadness filled me, and my frown squeezed the tears back into my eyes.

After a pause, Pete continued, "And we're short of a rear-gunner."

"Rear gunner? Why?"

"He went sick. They took him off to hospital. All his kit's gone too. Supposed to have stomach ulcers. Never mentioned it before our first op."

"LMF?"

"Don't think so. Whatever it is, he's off strength and we need a replacement."

From five, we were down to three after only two ops – in fact, only one op for Tony and Pete.

"By the way," Pete continued, "I'm acting commander of 'A' Flight."

The squadron was on ops that night, mine-laying off the Frisian Islands. Tony wanted to go to the Fleece, but I didn't feel like it and he went off with two of his wireless mates. I had a night in the Mess after wishing good luck to the ops crew, and had an early night.

We were up at 'flights' by 0900 hours on the following morning. We walked along the corridor to the crew room, passing the open door of the A Flight commander's officer on the way. Pete was sitting behind the desk – unsmiling and uncommunicative. We soon found out why. He'd lost his mate too – Flight Lieutenant Shead and his crew hadn't returned from the previous night's mine-laying op. But he would soon get over it – as I would over Jim.

The January weather deteriorated again and there was no flying for a week. The cloud base lifted on 29 January and immediately an ops list was posted. Later that day, with a borrowed bomb-aimer and rear-gunner, we took off in 'L London' for Lorient with the same incendiary bomb load. The weather had improved at base but not over the English Channel and northern France. We were in constant 10/10ths cloud, and with severe icing on the leading edges we couldn't get past 14,000 feet. With half an hour to go to the target and with the Gee pulses just about gone, Tony – listening out – received a message from base to "bomb on Gee". We were still in 10/10ths cloud when we bombed on ETA. On the way back Pete came down to 5000 feet before the ice started to break off. We landed back at base fed up after a long, muscle-aching, seven-hour flight. With no flak and impossible conditions for night fighters, all six aircraft returned safely.

[29/30 January 1943. Lorient. 75 Wellingtons and 41 Halifaxes of 1, 4 and 6 Groups. 2 Halifaxes and 2 Wellingtons lost. Crews encountered thick cloud and icing and, with no Pathfinder marking, the bombing was well scattered.]

It was Lorient again seven nights later, but this time we carried a 'cookie'. It didn't look like a bomb, with no sharp end or tail fin – just a huge bloated black cylinder with a thin case for maximum blast. It was a two-wave raid without the Pathfinders on a clear night with the target easily identified by the light of the moon.

The first wave dropped incendiaries and the second wave aimed their 'cookies' at the clearly visible U-boat pens. The flak appeared to be aimed at the Halifaxes and Lancasters above our 15,000 feet. Still it was a relief to feel the aircraft leap upwards as two tons of explosives fell away. The 'cookie' explosives were distinctive – a white flash that shimmered outwards in waves. There were a lot of 'cookies' that night.

[14/15 February 1943. Lorient. 128 aircraft – 103 Wellingtons, 16 Halifaxes, 9 Lancasters. 1 Wellington lost. This was an all-incendiary attack without the Pathfinders. Bombing was concentrated and large areas of fire were started.]

The flight back to base – on a beautiful clear night – was almost enjoyable. I stood under the astro-dome for a while and took some star shots – there were dozens to pick from, with every single star in the northern hemisphere available. The triangle on the chart was pretty good too – the centre of it less than ten miles from our true position after I checked with a Gee fix.

It was a relaxed, jovial atmosphere in the interrogation room, and also afterwards in the Mess, until the news came through that one aircraft hadn't returned – Pilot Officer Parsons and his crew. They'd taken off six minutes after us.

The intervals between our ops had been six, fourteen and six days, but the weather was improving and it was no surprise to be on ops three nights later – especially with Pete as acting Flight Commander and able to put us on the list at will. The target was, once again, Lorient, and once again a two-wave attack. We were in the incendiary wave this time – our bomb-aimer, a borrowed Sergeant Ferguson, landing them in a straddle across the Pathfinder markers from 16,000 feet.

[7/8 February 1943. Lorient. 323 aircraft – 100 Wellingtons, 81 Halifaxes, 80 Lancasters, 62 Stirlings. 7 aircraft – 3 Lancasters, 2 Halifaxes, 2 Wellingtons – lost. The Pathfinder marking plan worked well and the two Main Force waves produced a devastating attack.]

We were on the battle order again only two nights later, 9 February, but there was driving rain and the op was scrubbed. It was on again the following night, but again was scrubbed before briefing. Finally, two nights later the twice-scrubbed op was on at last. Lorient – where else? – this time with eight 500lb bombs.

[13/14 February 1943. Lorient. 466 aircraft – 164 Lancasters, 140 Wellingtons, 96 Halifaxes, 66 Stirlings – carried out Bomber Command's heaviest attack on Lorient

during the war. The ordinary squadrons of Bomber Command reinforced for a 1000-bomber-type raid, dropped more than 1000 tons of bombs on a target for the first time. The raid was carried out in clear visibility and considerable further damage was caused to the already battered town of Lorient. 7 aircraft – 3 Wellingtons, 2 Lancasters, 1 Halifax, 1 Stirling – were lost, 1.5% of the force.]

The trip was uneventful until we arrived back over England to find it covered in dense fog. We were ordered to divert to Harwell near Oxford. There were fifteen other aircraft on the circuit and we landed at 0100 hours. There were no beds left, so we slept on chairs in the Sergeants' Mess, returning to Croft the following day.

We lost another aircraft three nights later. It strayed from its course on the way back from Lorient and landed in Southern Ireland. And yet again, in that terrible winter of January and February 1943, it was another nine days before ops were possible. Bomber Command – obsessed with Lorient for a month – just as abruptly lost its obsession and turned back to Germany.

CHAPTER 5

The Ruhr

At the briefing on 26 February, the ribbon on the wall chart snaked its way eastward. To a man, we leaned forward and squinted to see where the ribbon led. As my eye followed the ribbon eastwards, I felt a mounting panic. Somebody whispered "Cologne" very quietly, and the name was repeated until everyone seemed to be saying it. "Yes, Cologne," said the AOC, and a silence followed. A major German city – with major German defences – but at least not the hated Ruhr Valley. I felt a little better, but not by that much; we still had to face the barrage of exploding shells that protected all German cities. For some reason, I feared the night fighters hardly at all – but the flak, it terrified me!

On this op, however, a small distraction arrived in the form of our newly acquired permanent rear-gunner – another Canadian and another Smith: Sergeant Melvyn C. Smith. Mel was big and brash, boastful and fearless (or so he said), and he raised our spirits. He alleged that he had joined the RCAF because he was on the run from the police in Canada, and that he'd had more women than hot dinners. I felt that I could learn something from him. He took off the metal tops of bottles with his teeth – I winced every time he did it. Strangely, though, he made me less scared.

It was a big raid with more than 400 aircraft involved: Lancasters, Halifaxes, Wellingtons and Stirlings. There weren't any Pathfinders. Instead, the leading aircraft dropped flares on ETA. Several fires were burning ahead of us but the bomb-aimer couldn't pick up the aiming point, so we dropped our 'cookie' on one of the fires. I didn't go up front, and since I had only heard a few faint explosions I was unaware of the flak barrage, and I felt easier for it. Resuming my plot after leaving the target area, I was unperturbed by the click of a microphone switch in my headphones.

"Dive port; go, go, go!" Mel's voice sounded demonic.

My seat fell away from under me as the aircraft plunged into a steep dive to port – my gear tumbled to the floor from the plotting table. The guttural rattle of Mel's guns made my chest tighten. The fighter overshot us – its tracer slanting above and to starboard. We straightened out. The bomb-aimer (already in the front turret) and Tony quickly went into the astro-dome where Pete and Mel were already scanning the sky for the night fighter that had attacked us. We must have lost him when he flashed over the top of us, for we didn't see him again and we arrived back at Flamborough Head without further incident, soon to be taking our turn at the interrogation table. Again, the chatter over the post-op meal was silenced by word of the loss of two of our aircraft. Sergeant Taylor, who had flown us back from Tangmere, had tried to land at Woolfax, the satellite of North Luffenham, but didn't make the runway and crashed. There were no survivors. Another aircraft, piloted by Sergeant Harwood, failed to return. Our losses were mounting, but our brief encounter with the night fighter reaffirmed my scant, if utterly myopic, regard for the threat they posed to my safety. And our new rear-gunner had saved us all, sighting the night fighter before it could get in a burst. "Well done, Mel," we acknowledged. "No fucking fighter's going to get us!" he said bravely.

[26/27 February 1943. Cologne. 427 aircraft – 145 Lancasters, 126 Wellingtons, 106 Halifaxes, 46 Stirlings, 4 Mosquitoes. 10 aircraft – 4 Wellingtons, 3 Lancasters, 2 Halifaxes, 1 Stirling – lost, 2.3% of the force. Most of the bombs from this large raid fell to the south-west of Cologne. Figures from Cologne itself suggest that only a quarter of the force hit the city. An increasingly familiar list of destroyed and damaged buildings was provided – much housing, minor industry, churches, historic buildings, public utilities and offices. The worst incident was when 40 to 50 people were

trapped in several blocks of flats hit by a 4000lb bomb in the Einhardstrasse. The wreckage began to burn before the rescue workers could free the trapped people and most of them died. The total casualty list in Cologne was 109 people dead, more than 150 injured and 6,322 bombed out.]

On 1 March Pete, Mel and I went to Topcliffe in a Mark III Wellington to swap it for a Mark X. It was a clear day and, with Topcliffe only twenty minutes away, Mel went into the nose to map read while I went into his turret. As the runway started gathering speed, I regretted my foolishness, with just a piece of Perspex between me and the outside. The runway fell away below me and I leaned back heavily against the turret doors, fearful of falling out through the Perspex. But I quickly got used to the sensation and the view was tremendous. Cautiously I operated the clutch to swing the turret to starboard. I swayed it back and forth tentatively, but stopped as we began to descend. I watched the ground below come, slowly at first, but then quickening towards me, as we landed.

We swapped kites and took off for base, with me again in the rear turret, much to Pete's amusement. On the return journey – safe in the knowledge that I wouldn't fall out – I swung the turret from side to side and moved the guns up and down. Messerschmitts tumbled out of the sky, and troop trains blew up in smoke. Carried away, I moved the turret from side to side as fast as it would go. It felt as if the whole aircraft was oscillating like a pendulum. It was! "For fuck's sake, keep that turret still!" I didn't know it was dangerous to swing the turret when the aircraft was landing, but Pete took the time to explain it to me very forcefully.

Two days after the Cologne raid, Pete's relief as 'A' Flight Commander arrived: Squadron Leader Erthrowl, quickly nicknamed 'Groundloop'. The squadron took part (without us) in a heavy raid on St Nazaire, Hitler's other U-boat base. We lost two more aircraft. Sergeant Hartrey's aircraft failed to return, and Sergeant Southwood and his crew bailed out over Ireland – lost and out of fuel.

Two nights later another aircraft, piloted by Sergeant Lymburner, did not return from a mine-laying trip. The squadron had lost nine aircraft and forty-one crew in two months and the losses had averaged 7%. It didn't take much of a mathematician to calculate that fourteen ops was the average life expectancy of crews on this new and inexperienced squadron. But nobody talked about the odds, and everyone tried to keep spirits up. There was fear, of course, but it was not a fierce thing. It was not a violent fear, but rather an unhappiness that would sometimes drift away, half-forgotten, but then retrieved quite easily and quite often. The fear was, most often, a constant burden rather than a sharp pain; but then again we had not yet been to the Ruhr.

We were given a stand-down on 14 March, and 'A' Flight quickly organised a party in Darlington. We hired a room in the Fleece and invited our groundcrews, buying them beer all evening from the kitty money – five bob an NCO, ten bob an officer. It was a great success, especially after the 'Muffin Man', and we sang raucously in the bus – three of them from the MT pool – on the way back:

"If I was the marrying kind,
Which thank the Lord I'm not, sir,
For the rest of my life
I'd take me a wife
A Wimpy bomb-aimer,
For he'd press a tit,
And I'd press a tit,
We'd all press tits together,
We'd be all right,
In the middle of the night,
Pressing tits together."

I wasn't at my best the morning after. My head throbbed as I bent over to put on my identity discs – one non-inflammable, the other insoluble, to cater for both emergencies. The light made me blink as I walked out of the billet. The throbbing in my head made my temples pulse in unison. I forced my head up to look through the glare of the day – second nature by now – to assess the possibility of ops that night.

"Don't bother, Smithy," I heard, recognising Mel's Canadian accent as he caught up with me from his billet next to ours. "Ops tonight." The light, scattered cumulus cloud confirmed his words. I felt ropy, but two mugs of bromide-laced tea, and a breakfast of baked beans on fried bread, quickly restored me to normality.

Together, Mel and I sat in the crew room waiting for the inevitable. Pete joined us later from his privileged access to the Flight Commander's office. "We're on tonight. NFT 1130." And, patting me on the head before taking up one of the empty armchairs, "You were pretty lively last night, Smithy."

At briefing, the Wingco pulled the curtain back to reveal the wall chart and I followed the line of the red ribbon – Flamborough Head, Zuider Zee … Essen. People around me groaned, and I felt the blood drain from my face.

The briefing officer was talking and I was listening, but I felt light-headed and detached from my body. The target was the sprawling Krupps steelworks. It had been attacked dozens of times, but remained relatively intact. Tonight the Pathfinders would use a new target-marking aid, dropping red target indicators that would be accurate to within 100 yards. Such accuracy had been unknown prior to this raid, which was to herald an all-out onslaught on the industrial towns in the Ruhr Valley.

Nearly four hundred and fifty aircraft were taking part in the raid, arriving in three waves, first Halifaxes, then Stirlings and Wellingtons, and finally Lancasters. Our wave would bomb between 2115 and 2125 hours from 16,000 feet and all aircraft would continue their bombing run for thirty seconds after release to enable the on-board camera to photograph the bombs' destination.

The briefing officer continued, pointing out the defended

areas. which were shaded red on the wall chart – the Ruhr Valley was one huge, hideous red blotch, with Essen slap in the middle of it – the searchlight belts, and the regions where night fighters would be active.

The Squadron Leader followed, going through the usual warnings about emptying pockets of letters and other personal items, burying the parachute if forced to bale out, "name / rank / number only" to be given if captured, and finally the synchronising of watches. The usual "Good luck" from the Group Captain, then, released of military protocol, the crews dispersed amidst the scrapings of chairs and subdued – quieter than usual – aircrew shop talk. The navigators spread out their instruments, and the Squadron Navigation Officer – a reassuring and slightly fatherly Flight Lieutenant with a DFC – handed out charts and logs. He read out the co-ordinates of the turning points and the planned times of arrival at each of them. We worked on our flight plans in a now quiet and largely empty briefing room.

It was quiet in the Mess too, with the heavy pre-ops atmosphere more noticeable than before. The clink of plates and the scrape of knives predominated, and I ate my egg and bacon mechanically. This peculiar and intense detachment followed us to the crew room and into the bus that took us out to dispersal. "J Johnnie," announced the WAAF driver at her first stop. "That's us," said Pete, and we climbed out onto the tarmac and into the cold night, where 'J Johnnie' stood awaiting its crew. It was an hour before take-off, with ample time to give our instruments a final check, smoke cigarettes and chat to the groundcrew, leaning against the fuselage.

And all too soon, pinning my charts to the table, I heard over the intercom, "Bomb doors closed. Chocks away." We taxied round the perimeter track, five aircraft ahead of us and one behind, with, incredibly, one of those ahead of us uncamouflaged and conspicuous in its silver undercoat. A rising vibration as the brakes held the aircraft against the increasing power of the engines, then the hiss of the brakes being released and the feeling of gathering speed. Fully loaded, 'J Johnnie' lifted herself agonisingly slowly from the runway, barely clearing the hedge that surrounded the airfield. We joined the others in a left-hand circuit, and climbed laboriously to 6000 feet before setting course for Flamborough Head, still climbing.

We hit searchlights and scattered flak at the Dutch coast. I worked on my navigation, but my mind kept wandering to the Ruhr box barrage – a forty-mile-long corridor of exploding shells. And the danger of collision, with four hundred and fifty aircraft going through the aiming point in twenty minutes. At least we weren't going to be below anybody in our wave, not like the Stirlings, who couldn't make our height and would be in danger of being hit by our bombs.

I gave Pete a five-minute warning before the start of the bombing run. "OK, Smithy," he said, "I can see the target. What's the course out?"

"020 degrees for five minutes, then 290 degrees."

Silence for a couple of minutes, then Pete's voice again. "Come and have a look at this, Smithy."

I squeezed through the fuselage and up to Pete's seat to stand transfixed by the sight in front of me. I felt myself say "Jesus."

The sky in front was packed tight with stars. But every star was an angry red explosion. As one spark of red spread out like a bloodstain, then disappeared, another red flash would burn itself into the after image. The pulsing scene ahead was shot with beams of light, dozens of them, cutting white swathes through the red stars.

I couldn't see how anything could squeeze between the livid broken edges of red. Nothing in it could possibly survive. I slumped against the archway and my horrified gaze fell slowly from the murderous sight in front of me to the ground below. Vivid carpets of red and green had been laid by the Pathfinders. Flickering orange flames scarred them, merging with the markers in a mass of colour. Explosions bounced like raindrops on a puddle, and, shimmering over it all, massive bombs spread overlapping patterns of shock waves.

My eyes were drawn back to the sky ahead, tormenting me with what they saw. My mouth hung open, dry, my legs felt weak. I was pulling myself away from the windscreen, willing the aircraft back from the maelstrom ahead.

And then we were in it, surrounded by it. I gripped tight hold of the archway as explosions tossed the aircraft like a fragile bubble on the surface of a cataract. The acrid smell of cordite clung to my nostrils and stung my eyes. Light from a searchlight flashed through the cockpit, filling it with an eerie, deathly whiteness. Smoke swirled past, casting writhing shadows.

Below and to port, a Stirling was coned by a dozen searchlights. Flak was bursting all around it. It dived and climbed, left and right, twisting itself misshapenly and frantically. But it couldn't escape. I watched spellbound until it finally dropped its starboard wing and fell lazily out of the sky trailing fire and smoke.

A startling flash straight in front of us made me duck instinctively. But unbelievably we were almost over Krupps and totally unharmed. "Bomb doors open. Left, left, steady, steady … bombs gone." The yellow light appeared on the panel in front of me. I closed my eyes and started counting, images and sounds crowding my head.

I felt the aircraft bank to port, and opened my eyes. Still the fearful sight of exploding shells. I turned my back on it and stumbled back to my seat, sitting rigid and gazing unseeingly at the chart.

Gradually the sound of muffled explosions lessened, until the only sound around me was the comforting drone of the engines. I went to the astro-dome to look at the scene behind the tailplane. The battle still raged over Essen. The orange ground crackled like burning paper, consuming the last specks of red and green. Smoke and dust seeped high into the sky through the latticework of the searchlight beams. I went back to my plotting table feeling drained and exhausted. I resumed the plot.

Spirits were high in the de-briefing room. All seven of our Wellingtons had returned safely. It seemed miraculous to me, impossible to comprehend how all of us had come unscathed through that frenzy. I was still quiet and didn't join in the banter. The Essen skyline dominated my thoughts.

"Glad you joined, Smithy?" Pete joked on the walk back to the Mess. I looked at him without expression, still numbed by what I had seen.

[5/6 March 1943. Essen. 442 aircraft – 157 Lancasters, 131 Wellingtons, 94 Halifaxes, 52 Stirlings, 8 Mosquitoes. It was on this night that Bomber Command's 100,000th sortie of the war was flown. 14 aircraft – 4 Lancasters, 4 Wellingtons, 3 Halifaxes, 3 Stirlings – lost, 3.2% of the force.

The only tactical setback to this raid was that fifty-six aircraft – nearly 13% of the force – turned back early because of technical defects and other causes. Three of the 'early returns' were from the eight Oboe Mosquito marker aircraft upon which the success of the raid depended, but the five Mosquitoes that did reach the target area opened the attack on time and marked the centre of Essen perfectly. The Pathfinder backers-up also arrived in good time and carried out their part of the plan. The whole of the marking was 'blind', so the ground haze that normally concealed Essen did not affect the outcome of the raid. The Main Force bombed in three waves – Halifaxes in the first wave, Wellingtons and Stirlings in the second, Lancasters in the third. Two-thirds of the bomb tonnage was incendiary; one third of the high-explosive bombs were fused for long delay. The attack lasted for forty minutes and 362 aircraft claimed to have bombed the main target. These tactics would be typical of many other raids on the Ruhr area in the next four months.

Reconnaissance photographs showed 160 acres of destruction with fifty-three separate buildings within the Krupps works hit by bombs. A map from Essen showed the main area of the damage to have been between the Krupps works and the city centre. The local report states that 3,108

*houses were destroyed and 2,166 were seriously damaged.
The number of people killed is given in various reports as
between 457 and 482; at least ten of these were firemen. If the
higher figure is correct, the previous record number of people
killed in an air raid on Germany – 469 in the 1000-bomber
raid on Cologne in May 1942 – was exceeded.*

Small numbers of bombs fell in six other Ruhr cities.]

I lay in bed the next morning, thoughts and recollections
eddying in my head like vapours. "I survived Essen last
night. All seven aircraft had flown through Happy Valley
and returned. Pete isn't scared – he isn't going to die, and if
I fly with him, then I won't either." I got up and went to
breakfast. "Were you frightened last night, Tony?" I asked.
"Shit scared." Good – I wasn't the only one, then.

The squadron was stood down the next night and we got
drunk in the Fleece. We got drunk again the following night,
but then the money ran out and we had to spend the next few
nights in the Mess until pay day.

We were back in the briefing room on the 12th. The curtain
was drawn aside and Mel, sitting next to me, said "Shit." It
was Essen again. I groaned inwardly. It was a replica of the
previous raid, even to the take-off time. I didn't need
briefing, I'd re-lived the last one so many times.

"I can't do it again," I thought. "I'll go sick. I can't bear this
bowel-wrenching fear. Why aren't the others as scared as I
am? Perhaps they are. Perhaps they are thinking about
going sick. But what with?" LMF would be the only possible
diagnosis, and I couldn't bear the consequences of that.
Fear, I began to understand, was expected and accepted. But
cowardice! That was without excuse and exoneration.

The call to attention as the briefing officers left the room
brought me back to earth. I joined the other navigators in
preparing the flight plan.

We took off at 1905 hours, and I worked busily on my
navigation, blotting out thoughts of the flak at the target.
Just after the Dutch coast, fighter flares burst in the sky

ahead of us, hanging lazily on their parachutes. "Tracer ahead at our level," reported Tony from the front turret.

"Yes – I see it," Pete acknowledged. "Keep your eyes peeled for fighters."

Soon the flares were behind us and the first explosion rose above the sound of the engines. "You coming up front, Smithy?"

"Er, no – no thanks, Pete." His chuckle was cut short as he switched off the intercom.

I kept on working hard, calculating the effects of my found winds on the flight plan. I sharpened my pencils, tidied up my log – anything to avoid thinking about what was going on outside, working the crashing sounds into a hypnotic cocoon.

"Left, left, steady, right a bit, steady, steady … bombs gone." Halfway through – soon be out. And after a few more minutes, Pete's voice again: "We're clear of the flak, watch out for fighters." They must have been concentrating on the Lancasters behind us, for we saw nothing of them on our way back to the black sanctuary of the North Sea.

But the squadron had not been quite as lucky as it had been seven nights earlier. Of the eleven aircraft that took off, ten got back to base. The other, piloted by Wing Commander Burnside, had been badly damaged by flak on its run into the target. Its navigator, Pilot Officer Heather, had been killed instantly as shrapnel ripped through the aircraft, and its wireless operator, Flight Sergeant Keen, had a foot torn off. The Wingco carried on and bombed the target, landing his damaged aircraft at Stradishall. He was awarded an immediate bar to his DFC.

[12/13 March 1943. Essen. 457 aircraft – 158 Wellingtons, 156 Lancasters, 91 Halifaxes, 42 Stirlings, 10 Mosquitoes. 23 aircraft – 8 Lancasters, 7 Halifaxes, 6 Wellingtons, 2 Stirlings – lost, 5% of the force.

This was another very successful Oboe-marked raid. The centre of the bombing area was right across the giant Krupps factory, just west of the city centre, with later bombing drifting back to the north-western outskirts. Photographic interpretation assessed that Krupps received 30% more damage on this night than on the earlier successful raid of 5/6 March. Nearly 500 houses were also destroyed in the raid. The number of people killed is variously reported between 169 and 322, with 198 probably being the most accurate figure, made up of sixty-four men, forty-five women, nineteen children, four soldiers, sixty-one foreign workers and five prisoners-of-war.

German records say that one-third of the bombs dropped on this night did not hit Essen and that 39 people were killed in other towns, with Bottrop, just north of Essen, being the worst hit, but these towns were all close to Essen and there was often no clear division between overlapping built-up areas.]

We were on the battle order again four days later and took 'X X-ray' up for an NFT, but the op was scrubbed before briefing.

I was in the Mess later eating beans on toast when I was called out to the Mess vestibule. Pete was sitting there waiting for me. It was strange to see an officer in the Sergeants' Mess. We were only allowed into each other's Mess by invitation, and only on official business.

He looked excited, quite unlike his normal composed self. I sat down next to him with a questioning look. "Got news for you, Smithy. We're posted."

"Posted – how come?"

"You'll never guess where."

"Lancasters?" I conjectured.

"North Africa."

"North Africa! What, the whole squadron?"

"No, just us."

"Just us? But ..."

"Shut up, and I'll tell you."

I leaned back in my chair. "Well, go on then."

"A Wellington squadron in Algeria needs a flight

commander with an experienced crew. We've got four days leave starting tomorrow. We report to Moreton-in-Marsh on 23 March to collect our aircraft, then off to North Africa. Aren't you pleased?"

"I suppose so. Hell, yes of course I am." Whatever North Africa held for us, we wouldn't be going to Happy Valley again. I went back into the Mess to tell Tony. We hurried to the billet for a quick change in time to catch the bus to Darlington. Mel had left earlier for a night with his married woman whose husband was with the Eighth Army in Egypt. My barmaid, Thelma, cried when I told her I wouldn't be seeing her again. Everybody bought us drinks and called us lucky bastards. At closing time Thelma and I went to the park instead of to the dance to say our good-byes. But it was freezing so we ended up at the dance after all.

Tony and I were in good voice on the bus back to camp. No more Essen, four days leave, then the sunshine of North Africa. We felt pretty good.

Mel didn't know until he arrived back at the hut in the morning and we told him the news. He was back in Darlington with me and Tony within two hours. We parted outside the railway station, Tony and I to catch our trains, and Mel to go back to his married woman with whom he intended to spend his leave. "Fucking sight better than the YMCA," he assured us. I'd invited him to spend his leave at home in Salford, but he didn't think much of the idea, having, as he said, "got my feet under the table."

Mother wasn't very happy about me "going all that way" to Africa. "You only volunteered to fly over Europe," she said. I didn't tell her about Essen and the squadron's losses, but I made the usual round of relatives and friends and told them all about ops over Germany as nonchalantly as I could. They thought I was full of courage and it felt good. I didn't tell them of my terror at facing the Ruhr flak.

Hardly before I knew it, Dad was seeing me off again at London Road Station. No parting message this time. He said he thought I'd grown since the last time he'd seen me off eighteen months ago. I felt I had too.

CHAPTER 6

142 Squadron, Blida

The village of Moreton-in-Marsh was an American's dream of England: Cotswold stone, thatched roofs, and tidy green fields. It was quite strange to me too, and only twenty minutes walk from the guardroom. At this camp we met our new bomb-aimer, a little Aussie called Doug Wees – nicknamed Digger. He had a wizened face, a bit like Don Bradman, and wore a navy blue Australian Air Force uniform. He seemed all right, but talked a bit too much about "fucking Poms", and hadn't yet done any ops. I preferred Jim by a mile.

Our aircraft, the one that we would be taking to North Africa, was a Mark III, 'W William'. We had expected a Mark X but it seemed they were all going to the UK squadrons. On the day after our arrival we took it on a tour of England to test its fuel consumption. We took off at 1000 hours and landed eight and a quarter hours later. We did the same two days later and, declaring 'W William' satisfactory, we were ready to go. We were kitted out with khaki on the next day, had two injections, and in the evening were briefed for the first leg of our journey. It was to Portreath, a few miles from Land's End.

We took off at noon on 28 March and arrived two hours later on a beautiful English spring day. It was a small, slightly sparse airfield, with no living quarters for in-transit bomber crews. We slept in tents, and were not very comfortable.

Nobody seemed very interested in us, and we did nothing the next day, just hung around waiting for something to happen. But on the second day we were told to take 'W William' up for an air-test late in the afternoon and report for briefing at 1900 hours.

Our next stop-over was Gibraltar – it couldn't have been

anywhere else – and the delay had been caused by bad weather off the Portuguese coast. Take-off was at 0700 hours.

The route took us way out into the Atlantic, out of range of fighters based in France. After the Scilly Isles our next sight of land should be Cape Finisterre on the north-west tip of Portugal. Five hundred miles in daylight – over the sea – with no Gee or radio bearings. All I had to back up my dead reckoning plot was the sun – one line of position on the chart – and flame floats to check our drift. I was worried at the lack of navigation aids, but I got us there with no problem. After three and a half hours with nothing beneath us but the Atlantic, Cape Finisterre loomed out of the sun ahead. From then on we went down the coast of Portugal – ten miles out to sea – round into the Gulf of Cadiz and through the Straits of Gibraltar. The sun was shining, and the war seemed far away. It was a pleasure trip. And suddenly there it was dead ahead – the Rock. As we had been warned, there were strong air currents on the western side and it was very turbulent on the circuit. We'd also been warned about the length of the runway – touch down halfway along, we were warned, and you'll end up in the sea, and several aircraft had. But Pete put 'W William' down just past the perimeter track – seven and a quarter hours after leaving Britain.

At the control room they didn't know anything about us and practically demanded that we push off the next morning. But it was nothing personal – the parking area wasn't very extensive, and there seemed to be aircraft coming and going all the time. Having little time to look around we had a quick shower and went up on the Rock to see the monkeys and enjoy the view. It was evening by the time we moved down into the town itself. The narrow main street was fascinating and a bit frightening. There were pubs everywhere, each one strangely open to the street. They were full of servicemen, mostly sailors from the warships we'd seen in the harbour as we had circled the Rock. Service Policemen were on constant patrol. At one pub they were breaking up a brawl – boots were going in, truncheons thudded on heads and smashed on flesh. A short way down the street a gang of sailors began to swear at us threateningly. It was a hostile place, and we all decided to call it a day and head back to bed.

We weren't sorry to leave Gibraltar the next day, 1 April 1943, at 1215 hours. It was a three-hour flight over the Mediterranean to our final destination, Blida, eighteen miles south-west of Algiers, to join 142 Squadron. The sea below was a spectacular blue colour, quite a contrast to the dirty grey blackness of the Atlantic.

The squadron was equipped with Wellington IIIs, coded QT, and shared the airfield with its sister squadron 150, and two American squadrons equipped with Bostons. We were all part of North West African Strategic Air Force, under the command of Major General Doolittle, who had led the squadron of B25 bombers that bombed Tokyo in reprisal for Pearl Harbor.

142 Squadron had moved to North Africa from Lincolnshire in December 1942, shortly after the invasion of Algeria – operation Torch – and had spent the last three months bombing Tunis and Bizerta, Rommel's supply ports.

Blida was a permanent station and our billet was a quite respectable brick building on the edge of the airfield. There were no beds in it though, so we were back to biscuits on the floor. Pete dropped by later, driving the A Flight van. He'd quickly slipped into the role of the Flight Commander, and having found out where we were he soon left for the Flight Office. "By the way, Pete," I called after him, "what happened to the previous Flight Commander and his crew?"

"They got the chop," he called back over his shoulder.

On the following day we reported to 'flights' and became operational again. It was 2 April 1943, my twentieth birthday.

A stand-down was announced towards midday; the weather over Tunisia was duff and unfit for visual bombing. We had all come to appreciate bad weather with a very special feeling. The four of us were soon walking down the dusty road to Blida. Every time a vehicle drove past a cloud of sand followed it. The desert was not sandy as we had all imagined, but was really a pale gravel – like a building site just before work begins. The landscape was softly undulating, and as it was difficult to see far, it seemed as if we were in the middle of some vast wasteland. The road, although potholed and fringed with litter, felt like a lifeline that kept us on our route to human habitation. As we walked along it we saw our first Arab. He looked exotic, his robes flowing, as he walked along the road in front of us. Suddenly he stopped, gathered up his robes, squatted down and defecated on the ground. We walked past him trying to pretend that we hadn't seen anything.

Blida was not very big, and it was wholly different from anything that we had ever seen before. The houses, made of dusty gravel, merged into the paths, and the paths merged into the desert wasteland around. There were no street names, just randomly placed buildings and spaces between them. Few buildings were more than two storeys high, and the town seemed to be temporary, as if the whole place might disappear overnight, like a tent town. But it was quite pleasant sipping muscatel at a French-style pavement cafe in the 'main' square.

There was nothing more to see in Blida, so we were back at base by 1800 hours, and in good time for the evening meal. Attached, as we were, to the US Army Air Force, our meals were American – mostly tinned, but better than anything we had in the RAF. And we were treated to delicious American coffee.

We were stood down on the following day, and after lunch I stripped off to my khaki shorts and spent the afternoon sunbathing. After a sleepless night, I spent the next day in sick-bay with sunstroke and sunburn. I lay smothered in calamine lotion, rustling like paper every time I moved. I was discharged the following morning and arrived up at 'flights' as the ops list for the night was pinned up on the notice board. Nine captains of aircraft were listed, and top of the list was Flight Lieutenant Peters.

It seemed unnatural to be briefed while standing around in a marquee. It was very informal and a bit undignified, with no protocol whatsoever. And the briefing took hardly any time at all – Base to the coast, west of Algiers, then a long leg along the North African coast to the docks at Tunis. It was the squadron's milk run. No fighters were expected, and the flak at the target was tiny compared with European targets. But then there was a new hazard for us – mountains up to 7,000 feet. 'W William' had a defective engine, so we took the spare aircraft, 'O Orange'. The bomb load was eight 500lb high explosives.

There were no Pathfinders out here. Each bomb-aimer had to identify the aiming point himself, and each navigator had to get to the target with very few aids. The place in the aircraft formerly occupied by the Gee box was an aching void, and there were very few loop bearings available. There were no flashing beacons except near to the base, and hardly anywhere to put down in an emergency.

But the milk run on a clear cloudless night with so many visual fixes – the sky glowing with stars, the sea shimmering and the contours on the ground textured with moonlight – was not difficult. The flak at the target from not more than 100 guns was almost unnoticeable, and we didn't hear a single crump on the bomb run up to the easily identifiable aiming point at the end of the canal.

We emerged into the Gulf of Tunis after dropping our bombs and turned port 180 degrees onto the long leg back to base. From pinpoint to pinpoint, my plot made its leisurely way due west over territory still held by the Axis. The sound of the engines was comforting and relaxing. With no flak to worry about, no waiting for the relief of leaving the enemy coast, we drank our coffee and ate our rations. We could even joke about having to bale out in this new theatre of war. We'd been told about the treatment we could expect from the Arabs of the region, who resented the intrusive Allies and Germans alike. Whether the stories were true or not was never confirmed, but if they were, there would be absolutely no possibility of fathering a child if they got hold of you.

I got a withering look from Pete at interrogation when I gave a derogatory laugh at the Intelligence Officer's enquiry as to the severity of the flak at the target – juvenile and immature. The silent rebuke was enough for me never to do it again.

But it felt good lying on the biscuits in the billet. If this was to be the pattern of ops in the Middle East, then we were well rid of Essen and its bastard neighbours in the Ruhr Valley.

We were on ops again four nights later, in a very different role. It was a low-level attack on enemy columns retreating along the coast road to Tunis at Enfidaville. Again it was a clear moonlit night with no navigation problems. We found the coast road on ETA, and there they were – German armour and transport making for Tunis. We were carrying a mixed load of six 250lb HE and forty-eight 40lb anti-personnel bombs. We dropped the lot from 1,000 feet amidst a hail of tracer machine-gun fire from the ground. Our bombs straddled the road, and we climbed away with not one bullet-hole in 'W William'. It had been another piece of cake with the odds heavily stacked on our side, though one of the seven aircraft detailed failed to return.

Ops outside the UK were proving much more to my liking. If only there had been something to do between ops, it would have been even better. I missed the pubs and the search for girls. During the day we sat around most of the time. We shared the billet with a crew composed entirely of sergeants who were continually at loggerheads with each other. The bickering between them was constant and interminable, and there appeared to be a lack of confidence in each other. If ever a crew was doomed – this was the one.

Two nights later we made a repeat low-level attack on the retreating Germans on the coast road at St Marie-du-Zit, and the next night bombed their airfield at Tunis.

We were stood down for two days after that, and I set off for Algiers in search of my cousin – Harold Barnes. He was a sergeant in the RASC, and had taken part in the Torch landings. All I knew was that he was stationed in the Jardin something or other in Algiers. I was in the city within two hours of hitching my first lift in the back of an Army truck, my second hitch taking me to the Jardin. Naively, I had no fears about not being able to find Barney – if he was there, everyone would know him. The Jardin turned out to be Algiers's 'Regents Park', and there was not a soul in sight as I walked along a long footpath in the park, in search of my relative. I shortly saw a figure in khaki approaching me in the distance, who would no doubt direct me. The distance between us closed until, at about thirty yards, I recognised Barney. We both stopped at the same time. His surprise was complete. He'd no idea that I was in North Africa, and we punched and pummelled each other in delight.

"What the bloody hell are you doing here?" he shouted at me.

"Looking for you, of course."

"But where have you come from?"

"Blida."

"Where the hell is that?"

He was on his way to Algiers for the afternoon so I joined him, recounting my service to date. The last time I'd seen him was when he was on leave while I was still a civilian, nearly two years earlier.

Algiers was an exotic mixture of Arab and French. We stood at the entrance to the Casbah and peered into its sordid alleys, out of bounds to service personnel. There were sailors in there, but they didn't care for restrictions.

Several times we stopped at pavement cafes on our walk round the city, getting more and more tired. "When do you have to be back?" Barney asked.

"Not until tomorrow night."

"You're in luck then – we're having a dance in the Jardin tonight."

"A dance!"

"Yes. A band, a bar, and guess what – girls. ATS and Queen Alexandra nurses. You couldn't have picked a better day. You'll be all right for a bed in my platoon's marquee."

I was instantly accepted by the platoon, even if I was a 'blue job'. I was Barney's cousin, and that made all the difference. They made a bed for me, fed me, loaned me their gear – and even gave me a shoe-shine.

But there weren't many girls, so we made do with the bar. There were cans and cans of McEwans Export. Cigarettes too. Towards the end of the evening Barney and I sat on some steps – smoking and drinking and talking about home. We'd lived near to each other all our lives, in closely-knit Salford. His father, my Uncle Bill, was the custodian of 'my letter', the one most aircrew left with somebody, only to be delivered and opened 'in the event of my death'. We lived again the test match at Old Trafford where we had seen England score 627 against Australia with Grimmett and O'Reilly. And the one against India when Wally Hammond had scored a majestic 167. And that dreadful Saturday afternoon when Yeovil and Petters United had beaten United 1-0 in the Cup. And the first day of the holiday at Abergele when Barney had scored 392 not out on Pensarn beach for Mother's team against me and Dad. And as his voice became fainter and fainter I finally gave up the struggle to lift up my eyelids for just one more time.

I woke up in a camp bed in a huge marquee in just my underpants. Four grinning soldiers looked down at me. "Come on, Smithy – cha's up." I was thrust a pint mug of army tea – sweet and strong and metallic – to wash away the awful dry taste in my mouth. They gave me breakfast too, from the cook-house – soya sausage and beans. I was impressed with their self-sufficiency. They were much better organised than we were, and they made the best of their conditions. Everywhere was so tidy, quite different from the normal RAF billet.

I left around midday after exchanging addresses. "Hope you make it, Albert. See you in Salford."

"Yeah, you too Barney."

I got a lift all the way back to Blida in a monstrous car driven by a French civilian at speeds approaching that of our Wellington at take-off, leaving clouds of dust in our wake. I rated my chances of surviving the war better than that Frenchman's.

The following night we dropped three 500lb. of explosives and ten canisters of incendiaries on the north quay of the docks at Bizerta. We weren't listed the next night for the milk run to Tunis, when the squadron lost two aircraft. Owing to cross winds at base, two aircraft had been diverted to Maison Blanche, Algiers's civilian airport. One aircraft had crash-landed and was written off. The other never arrived – it was the crew of sergeants who shared our billet and bickered so ominously.

Pete went sick the following day and was taken to the military hospital in Algiers for treatment. To our surprise, transport arrived at the billet to take us to an aircrew rest centre on the coast west of Algiers to await his return. Our quarters were single rooms in a civilian hotel where we were fed French meals and treated as paying guests. We swam and sunbathed during the day and luxuriated in this totally unexpected rest from operations. After eight days of this artificial existence, transport arrived to take us back to Blida. Pete arrived back two days later looking none the worse for whatever ailed him. He offered no explanation and was reluctant to talk about it – it was all a bit of a mystery.

During our absence a new CO had arrived – Group Captain J A Powell – to take over 142 and 150 Squadrons. He was instantly recognised by us all as the Wing Commander in the film *Target for Tonight*.

We were briefed for the aerodrome at Tunis on 29 April and did an NFT in 'W William'. Junkers 52s were evacuating German troops to Italy and we carried a mixed load of high-explosive, incendiary and anti-personnel bombs. The weather made us think of home – grey with thundery showers. We took off at 0100 hours, and dawn was breaking shortly after we left the target. The flak had been surprisingly heavy, evidence of the build-up of retreating Germans and their artillery. On the way back – in the sharp, drowsy light of morning – we saw below an encampment of nomadic Arabs, and Pete decided to wake them up. He dived down on their tents, scattering the camels, and bringing out the Bedouin. They threw stones at us as we swooped down on their tents half a dozen times before taking up the course to base. Pete, and especially Mel, were highly amused, but I grumbled that it wasn't a good idea to antagonise the residents in view of the stories we'd heard about them.

The raid was repeated on the following night. Ten aircraft were detailed and we were the fifth to take off. As we climbed away from the airfield, Mel's voice came excitedly over the intercom: "Aircraft taking off behind us has crashed and exploded!"

We turned back to look at the aircraft burning at the end of the runway, obstructing the take-off of the remaining four. "Must have had an engine failure, poor sods," said Pete before resuming course for Tunis.

There was 10/10ths cloud at the target so we released our load on ETA, and there was a subdued atmosphere when we landed back at base to learn that the pilot and wireless operator had survived the take-off crash, though with horrific injuries.

The squadrons were stood down for the next three days preparatory to moving up to a landing ground at Fontaine Chaud, near Constantine. The American First Army had pushed on that far, and with the Eighth Army advancing up the coast road to Tunis, the last phase of the North African campaign was ready to be played out. We were moving up in support.

'W William' had become a furniture removal van when we went out to her at 0800 hours on the morning of 5 May. The groundcrews had loaded her with all the necessities of life and we were flying it all to a virgin landing ground nearly 300 miles due east. With its domestic load plus seven airmen, 'W William' rose slowly from the runway for the two-and-a-half-hour flight to our new base.

It proved to be a perfect landing strip for the Wellingtons. Forty miles south-west of Constantine, the landing ground spread invitingly below us. It was solid, hard, sun-baked earth, with no grass and with the foothills of the Atlas Mountains rising gently, then ever more steeply, on its southern edge. Pete put us down immaculately with plenty of landing ground to spare.

Our tents had been pitched by American engineers the previous day, and from them we heard the bad news. The administration had indeed found a perfect landing ground for our aircraft, but had failed to notice the hundreds of small oval-shaped holes in the ground, each of which contained the most devilish of God's creatures – a scorpion. True, they weren't the black ones whose stings are fatal. They were, however, the next most obnoxious, the red ones, whose sting meant an emergency flight to hospital in Algiers, and an excruciatingly painful illness. But not only scorpions – there were centipedes as well, eight inches long, with countless poisonous legs.

There was a hurried conference by 'administration', and it was apparently decided that in spite of the hazards nothing could be done to move us on, and here we must stay and test out our new adversaries. There was, apparently, no action to be taken. We were advised that, if a scorpion was found on your body, you should freeze and hope that it would crawl away. For the centipedes the idea was to strike it off from the head (or was it the tail?), otherwise its poisonous feet would dig into your flesh.

With the utmost fear and trepidation, Tony and I, who were sharing a tent, prepared to settle down for the night. I was more fortunate than he. Pete had given me his old camp bed; it had a broken joint on the port side, and the male bit parted company with the female bit at the slightest movement of my body, though this was only slightly uncomfortable. Tony had only a straw-filled palliasse on the ground and his only protection from intruders was the mosquito net that we both had hanging from the roof of the tent. The light came from an oil lamp, also hanging from the tent roof. There was nowhere to put our clothes except into our kit bags, and we decided to sleep in our underclothes and socks. Conditions were primitive, and we both felt very vulnerable – two skinny Englishmen in their underwear huddling child-like in mosquito nets.

On that first night we carefully made our beds, searching every possible entry point for scorpions and centipedes, and we carefully tucked in our mosquito nets, satisfied, hopefully, that we were immune from intruders. We prepared for sleep. But the lamp was still burning, and I, from my privileged position off the ground, had to undo my carefully prepared defensive position to turn it off. I did so with all haste and climbed swiftly back into my camp bed, carefully re-tucking in the ends of my mosquito net. I lay tired, but wide awake, listening for the slightest movement, waiting for the scorpion's sting, until the buzz of the mosquitoes lulled me to sleep. But the heat of the day was replaced by the cold of the night, and I woke up shivering, cursing the thinness of the single blanket with which we had been issued. This was a very miserable first night on our advanced landing ground, and dawn, with its welcoming warmth and light, was a relief.

Wonderingly, we extracted ourselves from our defence, and trudged to the mess tent for our first desert breakfast of porridge – in the desert! – and bacon and sausages. The porridge was brewed in a huge vat, like a cannibal's cauldron, stirred avidly by an airman with a broom pale. The bacon and sausages wallowed around in another huge vat full of evil-smelling fat. It didn't taste too bad, probably because we were so hungry. We returned to our tent, still hungry, and looking forward to lunch.

Inevitably, an hour after breakfast, I felt the call of nature. I hadn't given a thought, not a single thought, to the question of lavatories on our advanced landing ground. And why should I? My life to date, wherever I had been, had included toilets. But there weren't any conveniences here, just a long straight trench about two hundred yards away in the foothills of the mountains. There was nothing to sit on, let alone anything to pull. Urinating was no problem – you were used to company whilst doing this. All you did was to find a little oval hole, stand three feet away and take aim. If the aim was good, after a few seconds out would pop one of the little red bastards, and with a quick stamp there was one less of them to worry about. But it was the other, defecation, that worried me. It's one thing to have a chat with the bloke in the next cubicle, but to squat down in full view of everyone was quite another thing. I was terribly embarrassed to begin with. I felt every eye upon me as I made my first sortie up the hill, self-consciously clutching my pitifully inadequate piece of paper that I'd found after rummaging through my navigation bag. God knows where the next piece was to come from. I made a mental note to conserve every suitable piece of paper that came my way in future. Perhaps the flimsy – but no, it was a little too flimsy. But as with everything else in life, abnormal things become normal if you do them often enough, and after a few days a trip up the hill became as routine as getting out of bed.

We determined to arrange our tent for better protection and a more peaceful night's sleep. No doubt we would be given a day or two to sort ourselves out in our new surroundings and to get accustomed to them. But as we started to plan our day out, a sergeant admin popped his head into our tent: "Ops tonight. You're on briefing at 1700 hours." Just like that. Pete arrived shortly afterwards. The perfectionist as always, he wanted a night flying test of 'W William'. He'd arranged it for 1400 hours. We took off at 1450 hours and flew around for thirty minutes over the brown and yellow terrain below. Those mountains looked much closer to the landing ground from the air. Pete tested the engines, Tony the wireless, Mel his guns, Digger his bombsight. I had nothing to test. Pete made another lousy landing. Digger thought it was "a piss poor effort". I lost count of the bumps, but 'W William' was not damaged, and practice could only improve things.

Briefing was held in a marquee with the heat almost unbearable. The target was Trapani, a port on the north-west coast of Sicily. The Germans were disembarking there after evacuating North Africa, operating around the clock. We had the same bomb load as on our last two ops, high explosives, incendiaries, and anti-personnel bombs. The route took us 200 miles to the coast at Cap Blanc, just a few miles from Bizerta, then 150 miles across the Sicilian Channel to the target – our first Mae West job since arriving in North Africa. Thirty miles from base we ran into 10/10ths cloud and for the next hundred miles we were tossed about in violent electrical storms. Approaching the target the cloud was about 7/10ths, and the coast hard to discern. But the black-out at the target wasn't very good, and there were lights for us to aim at. Digger made a mess of it, dropping most of the bombs in the sea, and it was Pete's turn to think this was "a piss-poor effort". But I was quite happy at the total absence of flak, and the other six Wellingtons clobbered the lights good and proper.

The electrical storms had been following us across the Channel and we met up with them again shortly after we left the target. The propeller tips drew St Elmo's fire around the engines and lightning flashed through the clouds. The sky cleared as if by order twenty miles before our landfall at Cap Serrat, much to my relief, enabling me to get a fix and plot a course to base with a brand new wind.

We touched down in daylight at 0515 hours, and after a mug of tea at interrogation, we looked forward to a few hours sleep before the day heated up. It had quickly become general practice to start clearing the scorpions from the close proximity of the tents by peeing down a hole and clubbing the occupant when it came up for air. Tony and I got one each before going to sleep under our mosquito nets, which served as fly nets during the day.

We were up again by 1030 hours, it being impossible to sleep in the suffocating heat of the tent. Word came round that one aircraft was missing from the previous night's op, and later that it had crash landed on the beach at Cap Oum Achiche. The squadrons were stood down for the night, which wasn't such good news as it had previously been, as it meant an afternoon and an evening of boredom with nowhere to go, nothing to do, and nothing to read. Even the news that hostilities in North Africa had come to an end caused no jubilation, unrelated as we were to the land battle, and now the Mediterranean lay between us and our targets.

Everyone expected Sicily to be the target again at briefing on the next day, but instead we would be going to Sardinia – specifically Villacidro, the main airfield on the island, and its two satellites. From these airfields German bombers harassed our supply ships on their way to the battered and depleted island of Malta. A convoy was making the run between Sardinia and North Africa, and we were briefed to fly a triangle, dropping a bomb on each airfield in turn for an hour – visiting each one three times. Thirteen aircraft were detailed throughout the night from dawn to dusk, preventing the Luftwaffe from taking off for want of a flare path. And we were in our brand new Mark X Wellington – 'N Nuts'.

Digger picked up our exit point at Cap de Fer and I gave Pete the course for the 180-mile leg over the Med. Soon after leaving the coast, Tony dropped a flame float down the flare chute and Mel took a drift on it with his gunsight as it flamed away on the surface of the sea. I shot three stars with my sextant from the astro-dome and got a pretty good triangle. On track, and in a cloudless moonlit sky, I made a good landfall via the two islands off the south-west coast of Sardinia. Digger easily identified the main airfield twenty minutes later. First bomb gone, followed shortly by one on the airfield to the north, and another on the one to the west.

Then we did it again – one bomb on each airfield. Not a shot had been fired at us. This was curious, as the island was occupied by Germans, not Italians, and it wasn't like the Germans to let us off scot free. I felt drowsy, with nothing to do and nothing to worry about. I heard the message "bomb gone", then a sliver of silence, then a massive blast wrapped around me. The noise pressed on my ears and head. I thought, "The bomb's gone off on release!" At the same time a hole punctured itself in the plotting table in front of me. I felt the smell of burnt wood. I turned my head sharply to my right and saw a gaping hole over Tony's radio.

The plane shuddered with pain, then glided, as if pulled by a noose, down and to the right. I thought, "We're going down." The sweat on my forehead was scraped away by the wind that was sucked in through the many shrapnel holes in the fuselage. The rushing air screamed around me.

The electronic flick of a microphone switch. I thought, "It's the order to bale out. Where the hell is my parachute?" Then, all at once, I felt the nose of the aeroplane push up to the left and Pete's voice said, "Sit tight everyone – I think we're all right." We were flying straight and level again. "You all right, Smithy?" Silence. "Smithy – are you all right?" I pushed my hands to each side of my head, and squeezed out a sound. "Tony?" "Yes, Skip." "Mel?" "Yeah, that was fucking close."

Incredibly the shrapnel had missed us all, and the vital parts of 'N Nuts' were virtually intact. The crew steadied itself quickly.

Within minutes we were alive and in control of the flight. I plotted the course to the target, and we bombed both airfields.

As we turned away from the target, I began plotting a course over the sea and back to base, and Pete called for a damage report. Each of us reported holes in the fabric around us, but no important damage. I reported the hole in my plotting table. As I said it, I shook my head, thinking how close it was to my penis and balls. My head jerked into a nodding motion as Pete replied, "Good job it missed your old man, Smithy."

As we chattered on the intercom, we worked out that the flak burst must have been ten or twenty feet above the aircraft. The German gunners must have been plotting our course, and, with skill, had fired a shot that should have brought us down. "Bloody good shot," Pete said. His words were the last spoken until, two hours later, we began our landing routine.

The op had been our closest to disaster since we'd joined 142 Squadron, and definitely a 'shaky do' in our brand new aircraft. Pete had been like a man with his first Rolls-Royce at take-off, but we were already calling her 'J for Jinx' as we left her standing at dispersal. We moved away quickly.

We discussed her interminably for the whole of the next morning. Aircrew, almost without exception, were intensely superstitious, and once an aircraft had been branded a jinx it took a lot of convincing that it wasn't. "She hardly blinked an eyelid when she was hit," Digger said emphatically, in reply to the hate we were building towards the aircraft. "She's fucking jinxed," grunted Mel, letting wind noisily before making his way up the hill.

We were on ops again the next night – in 'N Nuts'. We couldn't believe she was ready to fly again, so we went to dispersal to have a look at her. All her holes had been patched, doped, and painted – and my table had been replaced. The fitters were running up the engines when we arrived. They sounded clear as a bell. She looked young and fit – her paintwork immaculate. Even Mel grudgingly agreed that she looked good, but said "Well, we'll see, won't we?"

CHAPTER 7

'N Nuts'

The target was Palermo, the capital town and major port of Sicily. Twelve aircraft were detailed and all took off for the five-and-a-half-hour round trip in wet and blustery weather. But it was clear at the target and there was moderate flak over the town as we approached it on track. Pete decided to run in from the sea and bomb from 6,000 feet on course for base. Digger made up for his miss at Trapani and straddled the docks, starting a fire on the quayside.

The weather deteriorated on the return journey and we were in cloud until thirty miles from base, but my wind was accurate and the flare path spread out dead ahead of us five minutes before ETA. Only five of the twelve detailed aircraft managed to find base on return; five landed on the emergency landing ground at Bone, and another on the airstrip at Biskra. The remaining aircraft, 'X for X-ray', could not find a landing ground and the crew had to bale out near Montcalm. They all survived and were picked up; the rear-gunner had two broken legs and the bomb-aimer had fractured ribs.

Stand-down was announced early on the next day, so we went to the stream to do our laundry and have a wash down. After lunch we sat around talking in the briefing marquee until tea time, when several left to join the group around the 'entertainment', an arranged fight between a scorpion and one of the monstrous spiders that were common up at the trench. They were thrown into a biscuit tin – the spider first, then the scorpion. It was all over in seconds – the spider dead from the scorpion's sting. But there were no spoils for the victor. The scorpion was then put into the middle of a circle of flaming petrol where it killed itself with its own sting when it could find no escape from the flames. I only watched this 'entertainment' once – that was enough.

Tea was bully beef, beans, potatoes and a jam puff – as always. Lunch was bully beef, cheese, biscuits and jam. But there was always lots of tea – strongly laced with bromide. Several of the older aircrew, those in their mid-twenties, and mostly married, seemed to be suffering badly from the lack of sex, and the bromide appeared to have no effect on them. But it seemed to work for the younger ones like me, for whom sex was still unknown. I hadn't seen a woman for over a month, and it didn't seem to matter.

The stand-down lasted for just one day. On 11 May 1943 we were briefed for Sicily again – Marsala, another port on the western coast of the island south of Trapani. The sky was clear of cloud and of flak. By 0130 we were already back at base, tucking in our mosquito nets ready for sleep.

It was raining when we awoke in the morning. The flies had disappeared, and we stood outside enjoying the coolness. I closed my eyes and saw the reassuring greyness of Salford streets. But within minutes the sun was back, and with it our first sirocco, a miniature whirlwind spiralling into the sky and heading straight for us. But then it veered away, leaving us with a cloudless sky overhead and towering clouds over to the north-east. The flies came back.

We were on the battle order again that morning. Briefing had become much more civilised by now. There were tables and chairs, where the others in their crews sat and watched the navigators doing all the work. If I hadn't been good at maths I would have been a pilot and would have missed all the difficult work.

This was my 22nd op, and I expected an attack on another Sicilian target – but it wasn't. It took us seven and a half hours to fly there and back to the marshalling yards and docks at Naples. It was an exhausting trip. At the bottom of the ladder I fumbled for a cigarette, lit it, and dragged in its comforting smoke.

At briefing, nearly nine hours earlier, the intelligence officer had been quite encouraging, predicting moderate and inaccurate flak at the target. The Met officer apologetically offered us fronts and occlusions straddling the route across the Tyrrhenian Sea, and little certainty as to how fast and in what direction the weather system was moving. Eight hundred miles over the sea with the fronts and occlusions veering the winds several times, and with only astro shots and flame floats as aids, navigation was going to be abnormally difficult.

As we took off I glanced at my astro watch – it had stopped. Astro shots entailed measuring the altitude of a star and noting the exact GMT on the astro watch. An error of a second in the watch meant an error of three miles in the line of position on the chart.

"No, I didn't forget to wind it," I countered testily at Pete's question after I told him. Mel joined in: "I've got a good watch, and I synchronised it at briefing." Dubiously, I accepted the offer and we pressed on, hoping that Mel's watch was as good as he said it was. It probably was, but he'd only synchronised the minute finger – hadn't even looked at the second finger at the end of the count. Anyway we couldn't turn back and land with a full bomb load and extra fuel tanks, so we grudgingly continued on our 400 mile journey.

As soon as we left the coast at Cap Serrat, I asked Pete to hold the plane straight and level while I took astro shots. When I plotted the three lines on the chart they made a triangle all right – but nearly a hundred miles away from the coast of North Africa. Mel's bloody watch! Astro shots were useless tonight.

All I could do now was to check the drift. Tony dropped a flame float, and Mel trained his gunsight on it. "Nine degrees starboard," he reported. "Balls," I replied. "Get stuffed," he countered.

Pete broke into the argument. "Are you quite sure it's starboard, Mel? Smithy is expecting a strong drift to port."

"I know fucking starboard from port," said Mel.

"Perhaps the float had a faulty fin," suggested Pete. "Chuck another one out, Tony."

"Float gone," reported Tony. There was a long silence,

then the click of a switch. "Eight degrees." Another pause. Then a triumphant snarl. "Starboard!"

"OK, Mel. I'm sorry," I apologised.

We must be miles off track already. "What are you going to do, Smithy?" Pete queried.

"It's these fronts and occlusions," I said. "What's the cloud look like? Does it look like a front?"

"Not particularly."

I thought for a while. "Think I'll use nil drift. What do you think?"

"Yeah, so would I." It would be another two hours before we were proved right or wrong.

An hour later we tried another flame float. Three degrees port. Well, could be worse.

Twenty minutes short of ETA at Naples there was flak in the sky twenty degrees to starboard, so we changed course towards it. I was careful to keep my air plot going on my chart – the compass courses we'd flown since take-off – so that I would be able to get a mean wind when we pinpointed the coast of Italy.

Digger began to have problems too. "That's not Naples they're bombing – it's Salerno. They've got the wrong bay."

"Are you sure Digger?" from Pete.

"Think so. Yes, yes. They're in the wrong bay. I can see the target."

"OK Digger – bomb doors open."

"Ten degrees port."

"OK steady."

"Right – steady, steady – good – steady – bombs going – bombs gone." At last I had a pinpoint – Naples. Mean wind – 135 degrees, 9 knots. Well away from the forecast, but something to use for the return journey.

I felt the aircraft leaning to the right to take up the course out of the target area immediately after bombs gone. After I'd agreed it with Pete, I changed the flight plan for the return journey to take us a mile off the coast of Sicily with the hope of getting a pinpoint after 200 miles. The new track took us out over Capri, which didn't have much relevance until the flak from the island started to burst around us. It wasn't unduly close, but there was enough of it to persuade Pete to swing away to port and put the revs up for a few minutes until it died away. Already my airplot had taken a knock.

Straight and level again at 6,000 feet, I asked for a flame float but there was 10/10ths cloud below so I was out of luck. I asked Tony to try for a loop bearing on Bone, but the signal was too faint, and anyway I didn't have much faith in loop bearings from past experience.

Just before ETA off the Sicilian coast we started to descend and broke out of cloud at 3,000 feet. "Can you see anything, Digger?" My heart sank when he replied "Not yet." Obviously west of track, I deducted five degrees from the next leg to North Africa. We couldn't miss that and we'd get a pinpoint on our landfall. But approaching ETA for the coast we ran into cloud, and when we got below it we were already over land – black and anonymous. We must be ahead of my plot, but how far? We turned on to the last leg of the flight plan – ETA base in fifty minutes. Tony got me two loop bearings – from Bone and from base – but the position lines were too acute and crossed near Tunis.

Three hundred and fifty miles on dead reckoning without a fix and with a weather system veering the wind through 180 degrees – flying at 3,000 feet under the cloud ceiling, with mountains ahead topping 7,000 feet – fuel for little more than an hour's flying time. The silence on the intercom was excruciating. Four pairs of eyes strained into the darkness. Mine moved from chart to minute-hand interminably. Five minutes from ETA I could bear the silence no longer. "Still nothing, Skip?"

"No – what do you want me to do?"

"I'm pretty sure we're ahead of my plot, and with those mountains only three minutes after base, I'd say change course 180 degrees. After two more minutes, try to home on to the base loop." I had nothing else to offer.

"OK Smithy – tell me when."

Two minutes later we were turning through 180 degrees with Tony at his set, and me taking his place at the astro-dome. "Loop bearing base – 285 degrees," I heard Tony report, the port wing dropping to take up the course. As we settled on 285, Pete's microphone clicked on: "We've less than thirty minutes fuel left. Commence parachute drill after..." Digger's voice burst in excitedly: "Flare path, flare path – port 20 degrees!"

"Well done, lads," I heard over the intercom. "Thank God," I mumbled to myself, as I shut my eyes tightly, and felt them begin to fill with water.

My first thoughts when I woke up in the morning were of the previous night. I didn't want to fly again – but I was all right by lunchtime. With typical aircrew logic, we had decided that after last night 'N Nuts' was indestructible and that, therefore, so were we as long as we flew in her. It was easy to convince ourselves and there were no dissenters.

Even so, we were happier that night to be going to Cagliari instead of Naples on our fifth op in a week. The capital of Sardinia lay in a gulf on the south-east coast of the island and was a short trip by North African standards. Ten aircraft took off to bomb the dock area with 4000lb of high explosive in each bomb bay.

With the second finger on my new astro watch rotating reassuringly, we had a perfect exit at Cap de Fer and had sight of our landfall at Spartivento long before ETA. From 6,500 feet the target lay prostrate below us. Just as we commenced our run up to the aiming point we could see on the ground ahead a huge billow of flame and smoke as the bombs of a plane in front hit the oil storage tanks. Our bombs hit the dock area just short of the aiming point. The flak had been negligible, and we had the flare path at base in view dead ahead five minutes from ETA.

The squadrons were briefed for Palermo the following day, but we weren't on. We did our washing and spread it out on the tent canvas to dry. In the evening there was an issue of beer – two bottles each of McEwans Export – just enough to whet the appetite. One night on, one night off seemed to be the routine at Fontaine Chaud, and we were briefed for Trapani on 15 May. We flew out over Bizerta – unmistakable with its two inland seas. Like Cagliari, the raid was easy except that we collected two small flak holes over the target. As we were leaving the area somebody must have hit the gasworks. There was a tremendous white explosion – quite unique. One aircraft failed to return, but we were safely back and tucking in our mosquito nets by 0200 hours.

I was on the point of turning off the lamp when Tony, who was all tucked in and lying down, shot out of his cocoon with such skill and speed that it had to be seen to be believed. There, high up on the inside of his net and makings its way down towards his bed, was a centipede. He had seen it as he had turned on to his side to go to sleep.

Now we had to get it! It's quite difficult to dislodge a centipede from the inside of a mosquito net, especially in the confines of a two-man tent with bedding on the floor and with only the light from a flickering lamp to keep track of its movements. We discussed our strategy, sitting feet up on my camp bed; it groaned at the double load. Two bricks would be the remedy, but bricks were non-existent at Fontaine Chaud. Two books wouldn't do – centipedes were tough to kill. We watched it crawl closer and closer to the ground. Gently we pulled the mosquito net away from the bedding to allow it access. Leisurely, it levelled off on the ground and started to make its way out of the tent. I stalked it with the blade of a spade, took aim, and missed by a mile, at which point it sped off into the night. We re-made our beds, crawled back in after I had turned off the lamp, and knew nothing more until the heat of the day woke us up.

We weren't on the list for the next night – 16 May – but were told to stand by in case we were needed to make up a crew and to attend the briefing. "Why might we have to make up a crew?" we asked Pete when he joined us to walk to the briefing marquee. "In case somebody doesn't want to go." Ask a silly question, I thought, but in fact two aircrew exercised the option not to go on the op when the target was disclosed – Rome. Not bombs. Even the non-Catholics might not have been too happy about bombing Rome. The sea-plane base on the coast was the target for the bombs, and Rome for the leaflets. One pilot and one rear gunner elected not to go, and a volunteer rear-gunner was called for. Mel's response was to offer two fingers, but there were two volunteers – short on ops from the rest of their crews – who tossed for the privilege of a guaranteed flak-free trip.

"As only one pilot has expressed a wish not to go," announced the briefing officer, "there is no need to ask for a volunteer as Flight Lieutenant Peters will be taking his place." At which, four pairs of eyes on the right of the intrepid volunteer swung slowly and reprovingly in his direction. Sheepishly, forcing a smile, he accepted our admonishment. And in the early hours of the next morning, as if to make amends, he stuck his head into our tent. "Tony, Smithy – I'm back."

At briefing the next day we had a distinguished visitor. General Doolittle was going on the raid with Squadron Leader Matthewman, one of the eight crews detailed. The target was Alghero, a small port on the north-west coast of Sardinia. It was a low-level, all-incendiary attack on the town itself. There was medium cloud at about 10,000 feet when we arrived at the recommended bombing height of 3,000 feet with the target easily identifiable in the moonlight. The favourable conditions, a total absence of flak, and an American general observing the attack, was the perfect setting for Pete to display his professionalism. We did a dummy run across the town at 2,000 feet through a hail of incendiaries from the aircraft above us. A large fire had sprung up in the centre of the town by the time we had made a wide turn to port to make our run up to the target to be the last aircraft to bomb. Over the intercom, we heard Pete tell Digger that we were going down to 700 feet and to set the height on his bombsight. Nose down and with full revs, we levelled off and laid a carpet of incendiaries across the fire before climbing away in a steep banking turn up to 5,000 feet for the return trip.

With no feeling of satisfaction at the totally one-sided confrontation, there was an embarrassed silence on the intercom, broken only at landfall on track with a change of course for base. No one spoke in the truck that took us to interrogation, but nobody was complaining at having chalked up another op – my 25th.

By noon the next day the fire raid on Alghero had been forgotten with practically all the non-commissioned personnel beginning to experience the miseries of dysentery. I had had to go up to the trench as dawn was breaking, to find others with the same problem – acute diarrhoea, pain in the bowels and a feverish temperature. The symptoms spread rapidly. Weak, pale-faced men shuffled round the camp aimlessly.

For the next three days the smell, the heat and the lack of water with which to clean ourselves added up to abject misery. We felt drained of energy and spent our time lying on our beds awaiting the next spasm, desperately hoping that next time we would be able to make it up to the trench before the warm ooze again stung our sore backsides. The smell in the camp rose. From my bed I watched miserably as others hurried up the hill, some disconsolately making their way back to their tents with short, slow strides, having failed to make it up the hill. I had to make the 'run' about every two hours – sometimes I made it, sometimes I didn't – returning every time to collapse back on to my bed, miserable and exhausted. Every sortie up the hill was accompanied by encouraging shouts from those lying in their tents awaiting their turn to take the stage.

Medicine came round three times a day – white powder in a liquid suspension. We had to whisk it around in our mugs and down it before the powder sank to the bottom. As it settled in our stomachs there were rumblings and an abundance of wind. But gradually it worked and it became increasingly less difficult to make it up to the trench.

Pete didn't get it, nor did most of the other officers – evidence of its source in the food in the Other Ranks' Mess. Pete visited us daily, and on the third day, by which time the symptoms had begun to subside, arrived with news – both good and bad. His promotion had come through – acting Squadron Leader Peters – already sporting the extra bar on his shoulder tabs. That was the good news. The bad – we were on ops that night. I protested that I was still feeling as weak as a kitten and hadn't eaten for three days. Pete shook his head as he said, "Briefing 1400 hours – I'll see you there."

Take-off was at 1900 hours in an old Mark III Wellington, 'J Johnny'. 'N Nuts' had a mag drop on one of its engines and was u/s. I was hoping it would be a short trip, but it was another intruder patrol – this time on the airfields in Sicily – six and a half hours from take-off to landing, with a maximum load of eighteen 250lb high explosives. Soon after we left the coast behind I felt the familiar contractions in my bowels. I made my way to the Elsan by the main spar, hurriedly punching the release mechanism of my parachute harness and untying the Mae West tapes on the way. Several times during the next six hours I followed the same ritual – harness and Mae West discarded and done up again – before returning to catch up on my plot. Once, when I returned shakily to my table and plugged in my intercom, I heard Pete's voice: "Where is he?" meaning me. "On the Elsan." "Not again." "Again." "Tell him to pull his finger out and give me a course."

Otherwise the raid had been uneventful with no opposition from the ground and forecast winds unusually accurate, requiring little divergence from the flight plan. But I felt limp and weak-kneed as I climbed down the ladders six hours and ten minutes after take-off. I refused to go to de-briefing and slunk off to my bed, where, fully clothed and uncharacteristically brave about the scorpions and centipedes, I knew nothing more until Tony woke me with a mug of tea eight hours later. It was mid-morning and, though hot and sweaty, I felt surprisingly good after my wretched state the night before.

The medicine that we had been given had done its work well, and everybody was eating meals and returning to normal. Normal, that is, except for a total absence of bowel movement. The first indication that everything was not as it should be was the lack of movement up at the trench. The powder suspension had done its work too well and we were all seized up. We felt the need to go, but visits to the trench were long, painful and uneventful. The dung beetles queued expectantly and fought for their trophies, dragging them off to their holes before we had time to kick in the sand. We were quickly issued with opening medicine, which soon had the desired effect.

Our basic diet, consisting as it did of bully beef, porridge and potatoes, was not conducive to a normal throughput, with vegetables and fruit non-existent. So it was a major event when, on the next night, we had a stand-down and Pete drove us to Batna in his Flight Commander's van for dinner to celebrate his promotion. The food at the French restaurant was unusual – the gravy in particular tasted milky – but it was good. And Pete paid for everything. We got very drunk on wine and brandy and sang all the usual songs on the bumpy road back to camp. I felt pretty ropy the next morning, but after I'd been sick in the trench I managed to eat the breakfast of porridge and fried bully beef with the help of the inexhaustible supply of hot tea.

With 26 ops in our log books we were approaching the magical 30 and the end of a tour, but a tour out here was more open-ended. It was a minimum of 30, and a few more, depending upon the military situation. Knowing Pete as we did, we held out little hope of the few more being only two or three. But since the fall of Tunis, flak at the new targets had been either light or non-existent, so even the navigators' union had little to say about the 'few more'. Even less so after our next op.

It was to Pantellaria – the island between Tunisia and Sicily, still held by the Axis. Four hours and ten minutes from take-off to landing, and with the small harbour devoid of shipping, it seemed hardly worth the effort and a waste of nine 500lb high explosives. There were a few flak bursts, but nowhere near us, and all twelve aircraft detailed returned safely, though one had to land at Biskra.

The boredom of life at Fontaine Chaud was the main burden. Ops to places like Pantellaria were even to be looked forward to – something to do and pleasantly tiring, resulting in a good night's sleep to pass away the hours of darkness.

The starboard engine had misfired on the return leg from Pantellaria, so we had to take the plane up for an NFT before being briefed for the next night's op. The target was Olbia on the north-eastern tip of Sardinia. It was a boring six-hour stooge over the Med and the length of the island. Ten aircraft were detailed to bomb the docks and shipping from 6,000 feet, with the weather good but hazy over the target. Six or seven fires were started and there was one big explosion. Three ships in the docks were set on fire in the face of little opposition, and Tony spent the time over the target chucking bundles of leaflets down the flare chute.

CHAPTER 8

Kairouan

The following day – 25 May 1943 – the squadrons were stood down in readiness for a move the next day to a new landing ground 200 miles due east, outside Kairouan. We were overjoyed to be leaving the scorpions of Fontaine Chaud. Glad too to be leaving the foul trench, the smell from which drifted into our tents when the wind was in our direction. A sack of mail arrived during the morning – three letters for me, to be enjoyed and re-read over and over. But there was bad news from home: Paddy was missing from a raid on Kiel on 4 April. From OTU his crew had gone to a Halifax Conversion Unit before being posted to 51 Squadron at Snaith in Yorkshire. He couldn't have done more than three or four ops before he got the chop – one of twelve aircraft lost on the raid. We'd have probably got the chop too by now if we'd stayed at Croft. Poor old Paddy. I was surprised that I didn't feel a sharper pain at his loss. Rather, I felt sadness that made my stomach feel light. Somehow I'd always known he wouldn't make it. The 'few more' in North Africa seemed very preferable to the terrible flak and death over Germany.

Kairouan looked attractive from the air as did all the North African towns – bleached white and clean by the sun. We touched down at our new base at 1055 hours, leaving the plane to be unloaded. We were allocated our respective tents – spread haphazardly around the cookhouse. There was little or no improvement on the amenities of Fontaine Chaud. In fact, they weren't as 'good', with no nearby stream to wash our clothes, and – with large areas of brush-like vegetation, brown and uninviting, nearby – a trench was deemed unnecessary. We just made our way into the vegetation when the time came, but at least there was a bit of privacy. This was a welcome development for me as I'd never really come to terms with the degradation of the communal trench.

The ground was free of scorpions – another major advantage – but there were reputed to be snakes in the brush. They were thought not to be poisonous! On the other hand, the area was prone to an energy-sapping high humidity and to the scorching winds of the siroccos. A vile smell occasionally pervaded the air, and the only water came from the water wagons. It was strictly rationed, and we could only wash away the baked and rough sand during the occasional trip to the sea at Sousse thirty miles away.

We discovered the source of the smell when some of us walked into Kairouan on the day after our arrival. Kairouan – the third holiest city – had been well named by the American soldiers who'd passed through it ahead of us: 'The Holy City with the unholy smell'. White and clean from the air, it was dirty yellow and mildewed on the ground. The basic industry was obvious – every other stall housed a carpet maker. The repeated warnings against buying any of the food on sale were superfluous. The kebabs were encrusted with flies, vigorously whisked away from time to time for the benefit of a prospective customer. They zoomed in again in their squadrons when the whisking stopped. The Arabs were unfriendly and eyed us with suspicion, and I only went back there once – to buy a porous jug to keep my water ration in.

The Arabs visited the camp from time to time with eggs to barter for tins of bully beef or anything else we had to offer. The Kairouan flies visited us too – but they became resident. They'd been bad enough at Fontaine Chaud, but here they were unbearable. During the day they tormented us, and as dusk fell they settled on the inside of the tent roof in a thick black mass. And as the flies dozed off, the mosquitoes woke up and buzzed around, forcing us to seek the protection of our nets long before bedtime. So if we weren't on ops, we went to bed and tried to dream of pubs and girls.

Inevitably, the conditions – hot, humid and boring – provoked discord among tent mates. We felt ill-tempered, and bickered over the least little incident. But we never – or nearly never – came to blows, and animosity disappeared as soon as we took up our positions in the aeroplane, which we did two nights after our arrival.

It was another intruder patrol on Sicilian airfields. Another busy night for me with numerous short legs and several changes of course over Sicily, made worse by Pete's evasive action to avoid the flak at two of the airfields. We missed one of the turning points so we unloaded two bombs at the next one. Otherwise, the op was uneventful and we landed back at 0420 hours.

During our absence the Luftwaffe had come to our camp, dropping three bombs near the Mess without damaging anything but the brush. We were asleep by 0530 hours, and took off again fifteen hours later at 2050 hours for the short trip to Pantellaria, now only an hour's flying time away. With fuel tanks only a third full, the bomb bays were packed with five 250lb high-explosives to drop on the garrison below. Back at base we had a cup of coffee while the plane was being refuelled and re-armed, then took off again back to Pantellaria. Two ops in five hours – numbers 30 and 31. "Is that it, Skip?" I asked. "Tour expired?" His grunt was non-committal.

We missed the next night's raids on the same target, but we repeated the double dose the night after, getting a good view of the flak over Sousse on the way back. We couldn't understand the current obsession with Pantellaria, which didn't seem to pose any threat to the forthcoming assault on Sicily. But nobody was complaining, and we thought the obsession was over when we were briefed for Reggio after the statutory night off.

The target, on the toe of Italy, had flak bursting over it as we approached it from the Straits of Messina. The track had taken us the length of Sicily and over Mount Etna, but the volcano was indiscernible from the black ground mass below us. The raid was a heavy one by North African standards, with more than sixty Wellingtons taking part. We had been joined around Kairouan by the Wellington squadrons that had moved up from the Western Desert with the Eighth Army. We were first in with incendiaries – and leaflets – and straddled the aiming point east to west. The desert squadrons followed up with 500-pounders, at which time the flak gunners must have retired to their shelters to leave the sky over the target clear and unblemished.

We were stood down for two days after the Reggio raid and the four of us hitched a lift to Sousse for a long cool swim away from the flies and the smells. We got back to the landing ground in mid-afternoon in time to see one of the Wellingtons a mass of flames at its dispersal. Its navigator had left the colours of the day cartridge in the Very pistol on the top of the fuselage over the navigator's cubicle and the heat of the sun had exploded it. The fire burned for half an hour before it was put out, with the Wellington written off.

After the stand-down we were briefed for another double-dose raid on Pantellaria, and landed back at base from the first attack at 2320 hours. The customary hour between landing and take-off was extended to two, then to two and a half, at the end of which Squadron Leader Peters and crew took off last with General Vandenberg, Doolittle's deputy, in the co-pilot's seat as an observer. He was a tall, striking man, later to become Chief of the American Air Force. Pete had to show off, of course. He aborted the first bombing run and went round again, giving Digger a longer run up to be sure of his aim. Our Aussie caught the mood and obliged with a direct hit on the harbour. On the way back our guest stood behind me, watching me work on my chart, and as Digger identified our landfall dead on track, gave me a big American slap on the back. After we landed he thanked us, complimented us on our performance, and told us that our crew had been recommended to him out of the forty-plus Wellingtons on the raid.

Three days of inactivity followed – stood down, not listed, stood down. On the stand-down days we swam in the sea at Sousse, and on the other day sweated it out in the heat and humidity of the Kairouan plains. On 10 June we were first on the battle order for yet another double on Pantellaria.

There had been heavy thunderstorms in the afternoon, but the sky was clear as we took off behind Group Captain Powell. We landed back at base at 2250 hours, and were airborne again at 2355 hours – straight into a thunderstorm. For ten minutes we bounced around through the lightning flashes before emerging into a star-filled, moonlit sky in ample time to pinpoint our exit from the mainland. It was only twenty more minutes to the, by now, undefended target. Relaxed and laid back as we approached the island, we were totally unprepared for Mel's voice on the intercom: "Jesus Christ – it's a fucking fighter."

Pencils, protractor, dividers and my coffee flask flew off the table as we dived to starboard at Pete's instantaneous reaction. A steep climbing turn to port glued us to our seats.

"Where is he?" Pete barked.

"Lost him – he went over us," replied Mel, embarrassed at his late sight of the Focke-Wulf. Straight and level again, calm restored, Digger took over for the bombing run. I spent the next ten minutes, including the bombing of the target, on my hands and knees on the floor collecting my gear. My protractor had disappeared without trace. I crawled under the table, shining my torch along the side of the fuselage, feeling along the cables and controls for the vital square of celluloid, and there I found it, lodged between the back of the table and the side of the aircraft. As I retrieved it, I was joined on the floor by Tony with his notepad and pencil, and a scribbled note: "Skip wants to know where you are!" Crawling back to my seat I plugged in and reported my movements, indignant at the inference of deserting my post, by which time we were back in the thunderstorm, the turbulence diverting Pete from further admonishment. Down to 5,000 feet at ETA landfall, we were still in it and still descending. At 3,000 feet we came out of cloud expecting to see the flare path ahead of us with only five minutes to go to ETA base. No flare path, but a burning aircraft on the ground away to port, heavy flak over Sousse behind us, and tracer on the ground below us. Then over the R/T, the instruction: "All returning aircraft orbit beacon."

Lights on, we circled the beacon, other lights already there ahead of us. "Must be intruders around," Pete advised us, adding to the feeling of apprehension at this unexpected turn of events. Nothing to do but sit and wait for further instructions. Mel's voice broke the silence, reporting flare path lights on to port. An immediate relaxation of the tension as the R/T became alive with voices requesting permission to join the circuit. And, shortly, the comforting sound of the engines throttling back as the tyres of 'N Nuts' met the runway.

At debriefing, Mel's sighting of a fighter was verified. Two other crews had been shot at over the target without either being hit, and two aircraft of the Desert Squadrons failed to return from the raid. The thunderstorm had swamped the tents' area in our absence, and in the morning the ground steamed as it dried out. I drew a protractor from the navigation section to replace the spare that I should have had in my navigation bag but which I'd lost weeks ago.

The day after, 12 June 1943, was marked by the news, early in the afternoon, that Pantellaria had surrendered, so it was said, to the crew of a Wellington who had parachuted on to the island after being shot down by a FW 190. The news held little significance for us, used as we were to Allied successes in North Africa, and with no ops scheduled for the night and the temperature having dropped pleasantly, several of us started an impromptu game of cricket on the edge of the landing strip. I was batting, and just beginning to enjoy myself at the expense of the mediocre bowling I was facing when Pete's van suddenly appeared and parked at square leg. He got out, followed by Tony, Mel and Digger and they leaned against the van, watching the game. They all seemed to be in exceptionally good spirits, and Tony and Mel gesticulated jubilantly as I looked in their direction. It couldn't be my batting that was the cause of their exuberance, I thought. I was a pretty fair opening bat, but a bit of a stonewaller. I leaned on my bat and jerked my head enquiringly in their direction, at which Mel cupped his hands to his mouth. "We've finished, we've finished!"

I straightened up, hardly daring to believe what I thought he was saying. "Ops?" I shouted back. "Yes, we've finished," his words loud, clear and triumphant. Flinging my bat into the air, the game forgotten, and with exhilaration surging joyously through my shouts of "Bloody hell, bloody hell!" I ran towards the van and the four beaming faces of my crew. Tour and innings – "Retired undefeated".

CHAPTER 9

The End of the Tour

U nable to go to sleep, I lay awake in the dark on my camp bed. *Tour expired and going home.* My cheeks felt light and happy as pictures filled my head: going to bed and getting up at the same time every morning; no more flak; pubs; girls; warm baths; laundry; newspapers; armchairs; running water; Tommy Handley on the radio; a real bed with sheets; decent cigarettes; coal fires; no more flies; no more foul smells; ties (I'd forgotten how to knot one); water closets; proper meals.

The following morning was like the end of a school term. We packed our kit bags and returned official items. I handed in my sextant, astro watch, escape kit and instruments to the navigation section and was ready to go by 1000 hours. We didn't actually leave for the transit camp at Tunis until the next day at 0900, but it didn't matter.

Sitting amongst our kit bags in the back of an open truck, we watched the Kairouan landing strip disappear into the distance. A lone Wellington, obviously on a night flying test, with flaps and wheels down, flew right over us and landed. The plane seemed to bid us farewell. The tour had been five months and one day – from Terschelling to Pantellaria – two tiny insignificant islands more than a thousand miles apart. Sixty-six times we'd taken off and landed, flown nearly 50,000 nautical miles, 257 hours airborne, and unloaded seventy tons of high explosives and incendiaries. With good-humoured smiles, we relaxed leisurely in the back of the truck, the hot sun warming our tanned faces and bleached hair.

The driver said we were just a mile from Enfidaville, which we had bombed the month before. I looked out of the back of the truck, and glimpsed a bomb crater. I stood and held on to the stanchion at the back. As I looked, the number of bomb craters, filled with mud and debris, increased. Then I saw a twisted German tank beside one of the craters, then horribly burned-out German trucks. For the next mile the number of craters, twisted tanks, and horribly burned-out trucks increased.

Near Hammamet we passed several graves by the side of the road, British and German helmets resting on makeshift crosses, and further on a crashed Junkers 52, lying broken and twisted on the edge of an airstrip. We drove on along the coast road, skirting the Gulf of Tunis – then into the city itself, and for me, a lifelong townie, the welcome sight of bricks, mortar, stone, concrete and cement. Tunis, part French, part African, and strangely unbruised by the recent passage of two armies, had wide boulevards, parallel roads with tree-lined pavements, stylish apartments, bistros and cafes, ill-disguised men's urinals – and elegant French women. It had a fascinating feel about it, contrasting sharply with the sand, bare rock and featureless horizons that had bored us for the past few months.

Our in-transit quarters in a commandeered hotel were unspectacular, sparsely furnished with just a bed, table and chair in tile-floored rooms. But after the past two and a half months of tent life it was luxurious. We arrived in the early evening and, after unpacking our kit bags for the first time since Blida, stretched out comfortably on our mattressed beds, prior to savouring our first evening back in civilised surroundings.

By eight o'clock the five of us – washed, shaved, and in our crumpled best blue – were leaving the hotel for the short walk to the city centre. Pete paid for a meal in a corner cafe, after which we moved along to the nearest bistro for the serious business of getting drunk for the first time in three months. We'd been paid before leaving Kairouan, so there was little to hold us back. We jostled good naturedly in the bar, taking it in turns to pay for rounds of bottled French beer. We became attached to an American Boston crew – halfway through their week's leave – and swapped stories, we of our ops and they of their missions. Between beers, they offered us sips from the hip flasks that they all carried. The contents – crude and home-brewed by themselves – took our breath away and burned our throats. But eventually its anaesthetic effect soothed the burning in our gullets.

By midnight, with no sign of time being called, we had swapped tunics and forage caps, exhausted our repertoire of lewd jokes, and were singing 'Ops in a Wimpy'. Raucously, and through the dense cigarette and cigar smoke, the Americans joined in the chorus at the invitation of "All together now!"

"Ops in a Wimpy, ops in a Wimpy,
Who'll come on ops in a Wimpy with me,
And they sang in the flames
As they pranged upon the hangar roof
Who'll come on ops in a Wimpy with me."

Around one o'clock it broke up. Two of the Americans made their way to a nearby brothel, and the rest of us stumbled uncertainly back to base. Smashed, and giggling like schoolgirls, we prepared for sleep, discarded clothing littering the floor, and fell into our beds. Somebody switched off the light, at which my bed began to float erratically. The foot end took off, banked gently to starboard, then to port, and dropped sickeningly into a shallow dive before bringing up its nose and repeating the manoeuvre. And gradually on came the nausea, in wave after sickening wave. I dragged myself to the open window, cut my lip as I fell against the sill, hauled myself up to lean out and vomited into the night, before falling back on the floor as consciousness ebbed away. It was still dark when my senses struggled to return, the mosquitoes buzzing joyfully over me. I crawled back to my bed and back to oblivion.

I woke up with the mid-morning sun shining directly into my blood-red eyes. Only Mel, more used to bad liquor than the rest of us, was up and about. "Christ, Smithy," he said as he looked up at me. "Shut your eyes or you'll bleed to death." I felt terrible. I was covered in mosquito bites, but even worse, I had difficulty in swallowing. I moved on uncertain legs to the wall mirror and peered into my open mouth, there to find my epiglottis – monstrously elongated – lying on the back of my tongue. Mel was impressed by its size, evidenced by his one and only known expression of astonishment: "Fucking hell!" Later, at the sick bay, the MO was less impressed, lectured me on the dangers of drinking unknown concoctions, and dismissed me, shaking his head disapprovingly.

In the evening, my epiglottis back to its normal size, I walked around the fascinating centre of Tunis, having declined to join the rest of the crew on another bender. In bed by ten o'clock, I was tipped out on to the floor around midnight by my crew mates on their return from the bistro, and I knew that the least sign of resentment on my part would result in further humiliation. I kept my peace until the merriment abated, as it did quite quickly after Mel had left to visit one of the brothels in the vicinity. I hoped he knew where the Early Treatment room was, but he always did.

We took the train the following morning to Carthage, the old Roman city a few miles up the coast. We walked down the narrow streets – rutted by the wheels of the chariots – and marvelled at the ruins of the ancient stone buildings with their mosaic floors and underfloor central heating. We sniggered at the symbol carved in the stone pillars of what had presumably been the entrance to a brothel. Then on to the amphitheatre where we sat on the tiered steps and looked down into the arena where men had fought to the death. On the way back to Tunis we saw the remains of the hangers at El Aouina airport – the milk run of two months ago. And back at the billet we learned that we were moving out the next day to the aircrew transit camp at Surcouf, on the coast six miles east of Algiers, to await the troopship back to Britain.

In the morning a truck arrived to take us to El Aouina, where, after our transit papers had been examined for fully two seconds at the guard post, we were dropped off on the tarmac beside a Douglas Dakota DC3, its crew of Americans awaiting our arrival. We took off at 1210 hours, piloted by Lieutenant Mitchell, for the two-and-a half-hour flight to Maison Blanche. He flew us over El Aouina to show us the filled-in bomb craters and the remains of German aircraft piled in the aircraft cemetery. With no work to do, we peered through the portholes, smiling and relaxed, enjoying the flight and feeling very much our VIP status, with an aircraft laid on to take the five of us on the first stage of our return to Britain. Pete flew it for a while at Lieutenant Mitchell's invitation, and I swapped cigarettes with the navigator at his plotting table, renewing my acquaintance with the American course computer. And, coming into Maison Blanche, we stood up front, intrigued at the DC3's cat-like purring approach to the runway.

Our new billet at Surcouf was in the annexe of a holiday hotel, very comfortable, and only two minutes walk from the hotel situated on the edge of a superb Mediterranean beach. It was surprisingly and totally French, in the middle of a European war, with resident holidaymakers. This was an unexpected and blissful return to normal life. Breakfast, served in the morning room, began with fruit juice, followed by a delicious creamed porridge, then hot croissants, butter and jam, and jugs of French coffee – with cream!

We joined the holidaymakers lying on the beach, several of them women, but unfortunately none seemingly available except one, with whom Pete soon became friendly. She had a caravan in the grounds, and we saw little of Pete for the next few days without her at his side, his already adequate French becoming more and more impressive. The rest of us spent our days swimming out to the raft moored twenty yards from the beach, the Mediterranean tide never more than two or three inches from high to low. Occasionally we hitched into Algiers where I again found Barney, still in the Jardin.

Pete's new friend disappeared from the scene at the end of her holiday, and he joined us swimming between the beach and the raft. He soon became bored with this aimless pursuit, and I, being the baby of the crew and the object of his misplaced affection, took the brunt of his boisterous search for fun around the raft. He would push me down to the seabed and leapfrog over my head. He thought I enjoyed it but I didn't, as he was too powerfully built for me to be able to hold my own in the horseplay. After a week of his frivolity and several near drownings, I was finally set upon on the raft by him and Mel and stripped of my trunks in full view of the audience on the beach. Near to tears, I had to swim away and make a dash up the beach to the annexe, desperately trying to hide my private parts from the amused onlookers. Later he was full of apologies at my obvious embarrassment, but I'd had enough, and that was the end of my days on the beach in front of the hotel. The next bay only a few hundred yards away was equally idyllic and almost devoid of holidaymakers, and for the rest of our stay at Surcouf I swam from there. Pete tried to entice me back with promises of good behaviour, but I was unable to face again the spectators who had witnessed my humiliation.

The war seemed a long way away during our stay at Surcouf, which went on and on. Troopships from Algiers to Britain were infrequent and for obvious reasons we were given no information as to when the next one would be. Twelve hours' notice would be given to move out, we were told, but with no hint of a likely date. And after two weeks of waiting, time again began to hang heavily on our hands. Our money had run out, and with no sign of a pay parade, our evenings were sober and endless. But letters from home were catching up with us, even one from Pearl, forwarded on from Salford. Barney arrived one day with the news that he too was waiting to go back to Britain. He had been recommended for a commission and posted to Officer Training Unit in England. Another diversion was when a body was washed up on the beach in my bay, a gruesome sight – it had obviously been in the sea for a long time.

It was seven long weeks before movement orders came through. At last we were on the move again, and within six hours of packing our kit bags we were climbing up the gangway of the troopship moored at the quayside of Algiers. Two days later, at dusk, our ship moved out into the Mediterranean to take its place in the middle of the convoy bound for Gibraltar.

Forty-eight hours later the Rock, looking much more imposing than it had from the air, stood out proud and majestic against the setting sun as the ships of the convoy, line astern, steamed into the harbour to drop anchor amongst the impressive array of shipping already there. Dominating the scene was the grey hulk of a battleship, its huge superstructure towering arrogantly over its neighbours, its massive guns pointing menacingly out to sea. We gazed at it in admiration of its splendour all the next day, hardly giving its attendant cruiser and its screen of destroyers a second glance. Some said it was the *King George V*, but nobody seemed to know for certain. We thought she had started to move further into the harbour at dusk on the evening after our arrival, but instead it was us moving out to sea, and as night fell we could pick out the lights of Tangiers on our port side.

We sailed due west out into the Atlantic with Polaris on our starboard beam. At dawn the sun rose dead astern, confirming our unchanged course, and again as night fell Polaris twinkled away at right angles to our heading. Some time during the night we must have changed course, for in the morning the sun rose on our starboard side. The Atlantic was again as calm as a park pond, our main concern being the thought that our course would take us past the Bay of Biscay and across the U-boat lines to and from Lorient and St Nazaire. But our troopship, one of the 'Empress' boats, seemed to be making good headway, and presumably, as she didn't need the protection of a convoy, could outpace any U-boat.

She wasn't, however, outpacing the smudge of smoke that appeared on the horizon dead astern on our fifth day out. We watched in dismay as the smoke gained on us, expecting at any second to see the muzzle flash of a pocket battleship's guns, and hear the whistle of its shells on their way to blow us out of the water. Our agitation increased as the ship took shape, eliciting an overdue announcement over the tannoy that our pursuer was another troopship on its way to Britain. It was bigger and faster than we were, and eventually passed us about a mile to starboard. Barney was probably on it, as I'd been unable to find him aboard our ship after several searches.

After nine days at sea we crowded the rails at the shout of "Land ahead" on the port quarter, and for the next two hours watched the south coast of Ireland grow ever greener as we entered St George's Channel, with Wales appearing almost unnoticed to starboard. Out of danger and with Britain in sight, spirits were high at supper that night, and most of us slept contentedly in our hammocks, to be up, dressed, and on deck again at first light. Now at half speed and with a pilot aboard, we entered the Mersey, passing the naval guns on their platforms guarding the mouth of the estuary, finally tying up at Princes Dock at breakfast time on a September morning in 1943.

The Mersey was busy as we leaned on the rails enjoying our first glimpse of England after an absence of six months. The ferry boats hurrying to the pierhead from Seacombe and Woodside were packed with workers, mostly women, who waved enthusiastically back at us in response to our wolf whistles. Merchant ships streamed past us all day in both directions, skirting the two cargo ships that had been sunk in mid-river months ago in an air raid. A submarine came out of Cammell Laird to make its sinister way past us, past New Brighton, and out to sea. We whispered our "Good lucks" and wouldn't have changed places with them for all the tea in China. Barrage balloons in their dozens swayed at the end of their cables on both sides of the river and from every ship in the docks. And as I looked over towards Wallasey, I wondered just where my parents were, and whether one of the houses that I could see would be their home. The last letter I had received from them had told me of their impending move to Wallasey, brought on by Dad's philandering – he had run off with a woman to Wallasey, and my mother had followed and evicted the other woman. My mother could be very imposing.

But there was to be little time to dwell on the problem of how to find them without going to Salford first to discover where they were. At reveille the next morning the tannoy instructed us to assemble with our kit at our appointed station, amidships on the starboard side. After roll call we, and other tour-expired aircrew, trod our way gingerly down the steep gangway to the quayside and to a waiting train, which took us round via Runcorn to the RAF transit camp two miles from West Kirby. We were advised not to leave camp as we would be moving out first thing the next morning. We enjoyed a fresh water shower for the first time in nearly two weeks and slept well, back in familiar surroundings. In the morning buses took us to West Kirby Station, and almost twelve hours later we were assembling on the station platform at Bournemouth to be told our billets.

The seaside resort, even in its wartime austerity, looked pretty good to us after North Africa, and on the train journey England had looked greener than any of us had ever seen it before. Our billets were pretty comfortable too – up the hill in one of the luxury blocks of flats. At last we could unpack our kit bags – take our crumpled uniforms to the cleaners and our other clothes to the laundry. And at last we could spend an evening in a real pub, drink real beer, and luxuriate in our still novel eminence – a tour completed, and screened from ops for at least six months – probably twelve – and possibly, with a bit of luck, for the rest of the war.

We went on leave three days after our arrival at Bournemouth. I'd tried to ring one of the neighbours in Salford who had a telephone, but every time I tried there were no trunk lines available. So I had my railway warrant made out for Salford, to arrive there late in the evening – totally unexpected. I left for Wallasey the next afternoon armed with an address – 23 Danehurst Road – and three hours later I was on one of the ferry boats that I'd looked down on from the rails of the troopship less than a week before.

Five days leave – two days already gone – began with mother's tears and several pints of beer with Dad in the Nelson, only fifty yards away from Danehurst Road. Glad as I was to see them both, girls were more on my mind the next day, which, so the soldiers from the rocket site on the golf course behind Danehurst Road told me in the Nelson at lunchtime, was a Saturday. They recommended the dance at the Tower Ballroom that night as an ideal and plentiful supply of the objects of my desire for female company, and so it was. Girls – lots of girls – ringed the ballroom when I arrived there in the evening with a crisp five-pound note from Dad in my pocket. Lots of servicemen too, but with my brevet, sergeant's stripes, Mediterranean tan and sun-bleached blonde hair, I had a head start on the pale-faced soldiers who manned the heavy guns along the promenade and the hollow-eyed sailors from the destroyers, docked on Merseyside for a few nights before resuming their battle with the U-boats in the North Atlantic.

I lolled against a pillar smoking Senior Service cigarettes from a twenty packet, sizing up the talent. Two delicious blondes took my eye and I moved round towards them to await the opportunity, as soon as the band started a new dance, of requesting 'the pleasure of this dance'. I set course at the first note from the band. A sailor beat me to the nearest of the two, but I beat another sailor to the other one by two yards. He called me an 'RAF bastard' later in the evening down in the gents toilet.

It was a fox-trot, a dance I'd never really got the hang of with its slow-slow-quick-quick-slow tempo, but the girl didn't seem to mind when I stepped on her toes. She was seventeen and good looking by anyone's standards, with long curly fair hair and a flawless peach complexion, blue eyes, and perfectly contoured lips under red lipstick. Her full figure, the like of which I'd dreamed about under the mosquito nets of Fontaine Chaud and Kairouan, pressed breathtakingly against my chest in the constant collisions of the crowded dance floor. Nervous at first, as I always felt with a female stranger, her easy, instantly friendly manner was relaxing and encouraging, and I could hardly believe my luck when at the end of the dance she invited me to join her group of friends, holding my hand to guide me to their table. The rest of the evening couldn't have been better for a repatriated airman starved of women. I didn't miss a dance, either with my prize or her several friends, and flatteringly, at the first note of the last waltz, she took my hand again and guided me on to the floor. We danced it cheek to cheek, and I walked her home, my arm around her waist. I kissed her on the lips on her doorstep and arranged a date for the following night, before walking euphorically the two miles to Danehurst Road.

We met outside the Capitol cinema on our date, and sat in the back row with my arm over her shoulder. I took her home on the last night of my leave to meet my parents, and from then on we wrote to each other every day. As Dad always professed to knew would happen, Drus and I were married eighteen months later at St Hillary's Church in Wallasey.

Back in Bournemouth it was nearly a month before our records caught up with us, and shortly afterwards posting orders arrived. Mine were to proceed to RAF Market Harborough in Leicestershire and report to the Navigation Section. The rest of the crew had similar postings to various Training Command stations as instructors, and though we promised to keep in touch, we inevitably didn't. I never saw any of them again.

The Operational Training Unit at Market Harborough was a facsimile of Chipping Warden. My duties were those of a 'shepherd' and instructor, shepherding five of the pupil navigators through the course, and instructing the bomb-aimers on dead reckoning navigation and the Gee box. Gee had superseded all other navigational aids by now, and I had to go away for a two-day refresher course.

There were few privileges available to the staff aircrew at OUT – the same Nissen huts and cold water ablutions that I had left seven months before at Croft, but there was at least the reasonable assurance that I could look forward to a period of comparative safety. I enjoyed the shepherding aspect of the job, but the lecturing was boring and unrewarding. The bomb-aimers appeared to be either dim, or disinterested in the subject of navigation, which was perhaps to be expected since it wasn't what they were going to do on ops.

Little had changed during my months in North Africa, and the course was precisely the same as my own had been at OTU. The Wellingtons were still the ancient Mark 1 Cs, but, with the demise of operational Wellington squadrons, were replaced by Mark Xs two months after I arrived. I flew again for the first time in seven months on 5 January 1944 on a day cross-country as a staff navigator with one of my five pupils. The pilot was u/t, but he had an ex-operational staff pilot in the co-pilot's seat, which was reassuring. As staff navigators flew infrequently, I was airborne on only four occasions during the month, each time on a day cross-country. The other working days were spent either in the shepherds' room or the lecture room and the evenings in the Mess, the billet, or Market Harborough.

CHAPTER 10

The Phantom Pisser

M arket Harborough probably hadn't been very stimulating in peacetime, but in wartime January 1944 it was stiflingly boring. There weren't any operational stations nearby, so the pubs were as quiet as the tomb. The NCO instructors shared a Nissen hut and we spent most of our leisure time, if not in the Mess, playing cribbage in the hut – me, Snowy Hudson, Billy Bunting and anyone else who was foolish enough to take us on. We played it for hours, frequently until two or three in the morning. A ha'penny a point didn't sound a lot, but a run of bad luck resulted in the writing of IOUs until the next pay parade. There wasn't any great skill in the game once you knew its rudiments, but Snowy was such an agreeable guy that we forgave him his incredible luck at the game.

Some weeks after I took up residence in the staff hut, a peculiar and disturbingly mysterious happening occurred on three or four occasions. With a full house we numbered ten, but with leave and unofficial sleeping-out in a Market Harborough bed – I was never so lucky – it was normally five or six of us who gathered together to play cards, write letters, or sew on buttons and the like. Two or three nights a week, as funds allowed, we spent drinking in the Mess and it was after a heavy session that the phantom pisser struck for the first time. His mark was discovered the following morning – a monstrous pool of urine on the floor of the hut. We were incensed at the desecration of our billet by an outsider. It couldn't have been one of us, we'd all gone to bed drunk and knew nothing until the light of day.

He struck again a few nights later after a party in the Mess, this time in a locker, and after another binge, on one of the beds.

I was roughly awakened the morning after the late-night drinking session by someone calling me a bastard. I was dismayed at his hostility, but not after he told me that I had got up during the night and emptied my bladder all over his bed. I denied it heatedly, but a sleepy-eyed Snowy, still in bed, verified my guilt. Full of shame, I apologised and protested my lack of intention. But it took a long time to live it down. Forever afterwards I took great care, no matter how late, to make the urinal my last stop before going to bed after a session. Eventually it was all forgotten.

Back to normal, the easy friendship of the billet was resumed. The routine of the nine-to-five working day, at first savoured after the uncertainty of life on ops, took on its own uncertainty. Sometimes we flew without a staff pilot, which was unsettling. Fundamental flying errors by u/t pilots were far from unknown. It was not uncommon for a flustered novice, when aborting a landing, to pull up the flaps instead of the undercarriage – which lurched the plane forwards. And there was the occasional panic, as on the evening of 20 February. Three of us – me, Snowy and another staff navigator – were in the billet when the duty officer burst in looking for a staff navigator. "One of you is needed for a Bullseye." Dressed and ready to go out, Snowy and the other navigator were out of the hut in a flash, leaving me, in my shirt and underpants, the only remaining candidate. "Sorry Smithy," he said, "not your lucky night." He offered me a cigarette, which I smoked as he sat on Snowy's bed and I reluctantly pulled on my battledress. A shepherd bomb-aimer – I knew him well – he apologised for being the unwilling and unwelcome envoy.

We rode together on our staff bicycles to the briefing room, where he produced me triumphantly before retreating to the warmth and sanctuary of the Mess. The Bullseye – a feint attack by crews from OTUs and Heavy Conversion Units – was designed to draw the German night fighters away from a main force attack on Stuttgart. We were briefed to fly the North Sea leg to the Dutch coast, indicating an attack on a target in North Germany, before turning back for base. The staff pilot of our crew, also commandeered and another Smith, had been equally as reluctant as me to take part, especially after hearing the Met forecast of the very worst of conditions over the North Sea. Snow clouds were forecast from 4,000 to 20,000 feet, and I had the impression from his remarks that we might have to return early due to heavy icing. In the event we did, and as he put it so succinctly on our way back to the Mess, "Fucked if I'm going down in the North Sea on a fucking Bullseye after thirty fucking ops." I couldn't have agreed more.

The rest of February passed uneventfully, as did March, and on 2 April I had a quiet evening in the Mess to celebrate my twenty-first birthday. I didn't dare announce the occasion, knowing as I did that, had I done so, I would have had to do the 'Muffin Man' in the Mess, with, inevitably, my trousers being torn off and thrown out of a window. And lying in bed that night, I decided to volunteer for a second tour of ops.

I had been thinking about it for a week or two. Almost ten months had passed since I had been screened from ops, and after another two months I might be posted back, though all the other staff navigators had been off ops for considerably longer than a year. I had been listing the debits and credits. If I didn't volunteer and I was recalled for a second tour, it would almost certainly be to a heavy bomber squadron, Lancs or Halifaxes, a prospect I viewed with cold fear. On the credit side, should I volunteer, I could choose the Mosquito. Now in service in several different roles, it had far fewer losses than the heavies. Some aircrew even rated the chop rate on OTUs higher than on the Mosquito squadrons. So, with ostensibly nothing to lose, I volunteered on 3 April for a second tour on Pathfinder Mosquitoes.

CHAPTER 11

Signing Up Again

I n the shepherds' room they thought I was mad when I told them that I was off to the Adjutant's Office to volunteer for a second tour, Billy Bunting amongst them. In the event, it proved to be the right decision, and good-natured Billy, later recalled for a second tour with a Pathfinder Lancaster squadron, didn't survive the war.

I heard nothing further about my application for nearly two weeks. Then, on 16 April I was told to report to the Medical Section for a decompression chamber test. This meant entering the chamber, which was then sealed and the pressure inside reduced to that at 35,000 feet, and remaining there for two hours. It took half an hour to 'climb' to 35,000 feet. With me in the chamber was a medical orderly, there to look after me if I developed the painful symptoms of exposure to high altitude. After we had been at 'altitude' for 15 minutes, it was the medical orderly who developed the symptoms. I turned up his oxygen supply and the controller, peering through the window of the chamber, started to bring us down again. Slowly the altimeter needle in the chamber wound its way anti-clockwise, and at 20,000 feet the orderly recovered. The test, having been aborted, had to be done again on the following day.

I 'took off' again in the chamber, with another orderly, twenty-four hours later. This time all went well and my log book was duly endorsed: "This is to certify that Flight Sergeant Smith has passed successfully the test for Mosquito Light Bomber Squadron and Photographic Reconnaissance Unit in the decompression chamber at RAF Market Harborough on 17.4.44. Signed S H Robinson S/L SMO."

A few days later I had the big aircrew medical. Blowing up the mercury in the tube again proved difficult, no doubt due to the twenty or so cigarettes I'd smoked daily since shortly after I had joined up. But as always, I was passed 'Fit aircrew'. I was a mere 129lb – nine stone three pounds – and nearly six feet tall.

A day later I flew as staff navigator with Flight Lieutenant Ken Letford, one of the characters of Bomber Command, on an extraordinary errand to Sandhurst to arrange a meeting with a friend who was stationed there. We didn't land – it was all done over the r/t as we circled the Army's Academy. I listened spellbound to the conversation. It had obviously been done before, as there was no indication of surprise or indignation from the ground at this blatant misuse of a military aircraft. The arrangement for the meeting confirmed, we returned to base – mission completed.

Three days later I went on two weeks leave – two whole weeks – prior to my posting. Drus met me at Lime Street Station in Liverpool with the news that she had received her mobilisation papers from the ATS and was awaiting call up. We met every night, danced at the Tower Ballroom Wednesdays and Saturdays – and as leave drew to a close, I borrowed thirty quid from Dad, bought a ring, proposed, and was accepted.

Fourteen days had never gone so quickly, and on 22 May 1944 I was on the train from Lime Street Station bound for 1655 Mosquito Training Unit, Warboys, engaged to be married and soon to be back on ops.

I arrived at Warboys in the late afternoon via Huntingdon, the headquarters of the Pathfinder Force. The ubiquitous RAF van arrived in response to my telephone call to Warboys, and dropped me outside the Adjutant's office, where I was actually welcomed by the Adjutant, before being shown to my billet – a drying room, with two beds squeezed into it. The corporal who took me there was totally disinterested at my perplexed disbelief at this makeshift accommodation, and with a departing wave, let in the clutch and drove away. Reluctantly, I chose one of the beds and started to unpack my kit bags. Halfway through this task the door opened and in came another corporal, escorting a Warrant Officer pilot who looked as perplexed as I had been.

"Is this it?" he asked me quizzically.

"'Fraid so," I replied. "At least it's select."

I wasn't particularly pleased with my room mate at first sight. He was big and a little blustery with an unmistakable Yorkshire accent. The only Yorkshiremen I had ever felt any comfort with were Herbert Sutcliffe, Maurice Leyland and Hedley Verity, and only then when they were playing for England. But it quickly became evident that he was intent upon seeking the same pleasures as I was – beer and girls. By agreement, we decided to waste no time in hanging around the station, so after we had unpacked, and not being required to report to 'flights' until the next morning, we moved out to hitchhike to Huntingdon. Hitchhiking wasn't difficult. Every vehicle stopped to pick up servicemen, and the first car along, a Jaguar, driven by a civilian, pulled in to pick us up.

"You going to Huntingdon?" we asked.

"No, St Ives," he replied. So St Ives it was.

He parked outside the Golden Lion in the main street and joined us for a drink at the bar. He bought the round, couldn't stay to accept our reciprocity, and after wishing us good luck, went on his way.

We moved, with a pint tankard each, to two armchairs at a table, and filled each other in on our careers to date. We were on the same course, and thoughts of crewing up entered my mind. But this time crewing up entailed more of a decision than it had at Chipping Warden. I hadn't had much choice on the last occasion I'd crewed up, and I was a bit wary of making a premature decision. As he hadn't done a tour of ops, he didn't seem to be aware of the haphazard crewing-up procedure. He had been instructing on Blenheims ever since he had qualified as a pilot, so obviously he must have been exceptionally good. But could he cope with the Ruhr flak having never seen it before, and was he another press-on-regardless type like Pete? He didn't even know what Gee was when I told him that I'd been a Gee instructor, but he appeared to be duly impressed.

But the more urgent matter was the couple of WAAFs who were sitting drinking at the bar. We moved over to join them and bought them a drink. We took up stools on either side of them and swapped names. Johnny sat next to the dark-haired one – Celia – and I took up the stool next to the fair girl – Joan. They were stationed at Warboys and worked in the Orderly Room – handy friends to have on any RAF station. We were getting along famously when we were joined by a commissioned pilot who sat on the stool next to me. He was also on our course and after we had chatted for a while he began asking me what I'd done before Warboys. I thought to myself, "He's looking for a navigator to crew up with," and sure enough, seemingly satisfied with his enquiries, he suggested we crewed up.

I had to make an instant decision. He was a southerner, pronounced bath as 'barth', waved my cigarette smoke away as I exhaled it, and drank half pints! Pleading the call of nature, I moved towards the gents, nodding to Johnny to follow me.

"That pilot has just asked me to crew up with him," I disclosed as we stood at our respective urinals.

"Just like that?" he asked.

"Just like that," I replied.

"And did you?" he asked. I hesitated. The other pilot had done a tour on Halifaxes – must have come through a few dicey do's on those. But I couldn't see myself throwing in my lot with someone who drank half-pints. My mind was almost made up for me – "No, I didn't. What about us? Should we crew up?" Buttoning up his fly and grinning broadly, he agreed immediately. We shook hands on it, returned to the bar, and I told the pilot officer the news. He left without finishing his beer.

We spent the rest of the evening chatting up our new-found friends, and at closing time they offered us lifts back to camp – on their girl's-type bicycles without crossbars.

The girls sat on the saddle, and Johnny and I pedalled. I couldn't get the hang of it at first, and we soon lost sight of the other two. I finally got the rhythm and about an hour later braked to a thankful halt outside the Orderly Room, where, after kissing Joan goodnight, I walked back to the drying room. There was no sign of Johnny and I was fast asleep before he arrived back.

So our first night at Warboys had been very satisfactory. I'd got myself a pilot, and a date the next night with the delightful little Joan. For Johnny the evening had proved to be even more significant. He had gained a navigator, and his future wife. Johnny and Celia were married less than a year later.

After the usual day of settling in and reporting to the various sections, it was back to the classroom to learn how to become an Oboe Pathfinder navigator. The instructor was a Flight Lieutenant – Paddy O'Hara. He announced impressively that Oboe Mosquitoes now opened all Bomber Command main force raids within their range. This was news to all of us, having been submerged for a year or more in Training Command. It took less than a week to teach us the theory and operation of this newest, more effective, and most secret means of placing target indicators with previously unthought-of accuracy on enemy targets.

Situated in the nose of an aircraft, the Oboe equipment consisted of a repeater and two receivers. The signals to the aircraft emanated from two radar stations situated near the South Coast of England. The distance from each station to the target was meticulously calculated and marked off on the appropriate radar tube on which signals were received back from the repeater in the aircraft. The pilot's signal was transmitted by the tracking station – codenamed the 'cat' – its purpose being to maintain the aircraft on an arc that was at all points equidistant from the station, as was the target. Since the target lay on the arc, the aircraft would eventfully pass over it. It was like flying along a curved 'railway line'.

The navigator's signal came from the other radar station – the 'mouse' – which transmitted a letter to indicate which 'railway station' the train was passing through on its way to its destination. The navigator's function was to navigate the aircraft so as to arrive, at a pre-determined time, at a point on the pilot's arc that was precisely twelve minutes flying time from the target. The timing was crucial. If the aircraft on its way to the turning-on point on the arc was ahead of its time, it lost time by doing a dog-leg. This entailed turning forty-five degrees to port for two minutes, then ninety degrees to starboard for another two minutes, then forty-five degrees to port to resume the original course. If the aircraft was behind time we would have to put up the revs, turn up the boost, and get a move on. Johnny didn't like dog-legs and usually did an orbit instead. This usually lost us more time than we had to spare, so we had to increase speed to catch up again.

About five minutes from the point where the aircraft turned on to the 'railway line', the navigator laid aside his charts and clambered awkwardly down to the nose of the aircraft to switch on the receiver. If you were first down the run to the target you would shortly hear your individual call sign as the radar stations called you in. On hearing your call sign, the navigator switched on the repeater, testing the receivers to ensure that both his own and the pilot's signals were audible. If the aircraft had turned precisely on to the 'railway line', the tracking station signalled the fact by sending out a steady uninterrupted signal to the pilot. It sounded like a note from an Oboe instrument – hence the name.

The width of the curved 'railway line' was twenty-five yards. If the aircraft was to starboard of the line, the tracking station transmitted dots, and if to port, dashes. On hearing either dots or dashes, the pilot would correct his heading to bring the aircraft back on to the line. As the aircraft approached the line, the dots or dashes became fainter and fainter, and the steady signal louder and louder, until when inside the twenty-five-yard corridor, the dots or dashes completely faded out. Flying the aircraft at precisely the briefed altitude and airspeed, the pilot settled on his curved track, adjusting his heading as the dots and dashes dictated, while the navigator waited for his own signals. Ten minutes flying time from the target, the releasing station transmitted the letter A – a dot and a dash – repeated three times. As the run progressed, the letters B, C and D were individually transmitted at intervals, indicating eight, six and three minutes to the target. To keep Johnny informed of our progress I would trace the appropriate letter on the windscreen with my finger. At point D the pilot opened the bomb doors and the navigator took the bomb tit out of its retainer on his side of the aircraft. If the run was ultimately completed, the release signal – five dots and a two-and-a-half-second dash – was transmitted three minutes after D. I would indicate the start of the seven-and-a-half-second release signal by a dramatic raising of my left arm in front of Johnny who hastily made any small adjustment of his heading to that given at briefing. At the end of the two-and-a-half-second dash signal, the bomb tit was pressed, releasing the markers, and automatically switching off the repeater, indicating to the 'cat' and 'mouse' stations that a 'cope' had been successfully achieved.

After a week in the classroom, we started practising the exercises in the air initially in an Oxford, much slower than the Mosquito, giving the u/t crews more time to digest the progress of the aircraft down the run. We navigated to the turning-on point, usually somewhere up in Scotland, switched on, flew down the run, and pressed the tit at the end of the release signal. The Oboe ground stations were able to evaluate from the signals the degree of success of the marking, so each crew's progress towards the required efficiency was monitored on every exercise.

We flew on an operational exercise almost every day, and in between I collected another famous name in my log book, that of the station commander, Group Captain John Searby, the RAF's first Master Bomber and the controller of the massive raid on the V2 rocket research establishment at Peenemunde. I had been detailed to report to the watch office and prepare a flight plan for a trip in an Oxford to

Stanton Harcourt RAF station some sixty miles away, east of Oxford. Johnny was flying dual in a Mosquito at the time. I was taken out to the station at Oxford to await the pilot, which was extraordinary, but became obvious when the pilot arrived, driven in a camouflaged saloon car flying a pennant on its bonnet. "Bloody 'ell – it's the Groupie," I murmured to myself, springing to attention as he stepped out of his car followed by a Flight Lieutenant pilot. I needn't have worried. He had a friendly, no-nonsense attitude that was reassuring. He flew the Oxford to Stanton Harcourt, and went off, driven away in a waiting car, and the Flight Lieutenant flew us back to Warboys.

CHAPTER 12

Mosquitos

After a week or so Johnny went solo, and on the same day, with him in the pilot's seat, I experienced the sheer joy of flying in a Mosquito. It was very different from the Wellington. The navigator sat beside the pilot, on the starboard side, looking ahead through the windscreen. From now on my plotting table would be a wooden board resting on my knees, with clips on it to hold the chart. Situated on my side of the cockpit were the oxygen connection, intercom plug, bomb release tit in its retainer, parachute holder straps and a receptacle for navigation instruments. A few feet away, immediately in front of the navigator, was the Oboe equipment, packed in the nose. The Gee box was on a shelf behind – you had to swivel round to operate it, which was slightly uncomfortable. The cockpit was very cramped – there was no movement that did not mean brushing against something. But there was enough space to move around. A hinged hatch under the nose opened downwards to allow the crew access to the cockpit by way of a metal ladder that was housed – easily accessible from the ground – under the floor. With the crew in position, the bottom hatch was closed by the groundcrew (it could be opened again from inside), and the hinged floor over it released from its clip in the aircraft's side to drop down. Exit from the aircraft in an emergency was either by way of the bottom hatch, or the roof of the cockpit, which flew off when the handle holding it in place was turned.

It was just a short flight, in daylight, to Upwood and back, to pick up something or other – twenty minutes flying time. I thrilled at the sensation of speed as the Mosquito accelerated along the runway, lifted its nose halfway along and skimmed the hedge surrounding the airfield.

But I didn't like the landing ten minutes later at Upwood. The ground just short of the runway fell away into a hollow, which we appeared to sink into, only to shoot up again, then down towards the runway halfway along. I looked hard at Johnny but the expression on his face was unconcerned. Then there came a totally unexpected series of explosions from the engines as the throttles were pulled back – this further depleted my composure, until the comforting screech of tyres on tarmac and the feel of the brakes restored it to normal. Taxiing round the perimeter track, Johnny looked over at me. "Did you enjoy that?"

"Enjoy what?"

"That landing."

"Should I?"

"Didn't you notice?"

"Notice what?" then quickly, "no, don't tell me." Ignorance is bliss. As for the explosions from the engines as we landed, nobody had warned me of those. They were backfires from the Rolls-Royce Merlin engine exhausts as they were throttled back to land – for ever afterwards the most welcome of sounds.

From then on we did ops exercises in Mosquitoes almost every day, and most evenings we met Celia and Joan and went to Warboys village.

Our foursome had blossomed into a mutually enjoyable friendship, and with the Mosquito and regular female company, June 1944 was most pleasurable. We usually spent the evening drinking in the Ship. It was about three miles from camp, and Johnny and I usually managed to borrow a bicycle each. There were two or three haystacks in the fields just off the road to Warboys village, conveniently situated for spending an hour or so in on the way back to camp from the Ship. And, come to think of it, sometimes in the reverse direction, depending on the mood of the moment.

The four of us 'got' a 24-hour pass, which we spent in Cambridge. The girls provided the stamped passes, and we signed them after Johnny had suggested to the course instructor, whom we know, that we might be overlooked for the day's flying programme. Armed with our passes, we scrounged a lift in the morning truck to Huntingdon and took the train to Cambridge. We spent the day admiring the splendour of the colleges, and the evening in the pubs drinking and singing with the operational aircrew from the nearby squadrons. Tired, hungry, and with a hangover settling in, we spread ourselves out in the station waiting room to await the three o'clock milk train to Huntingdon. It took it more than two hours to pick up the milk, with the constant drone of aircraft overhead. It was the morning of 6 June – D-Day – and as dawn broke we watched them from the square in St Neots, their black and white D-Day markings clearly visible under the wings, on their way to Normandy. We'd missed it by a month.

A few days later Johnny collected his motor cycle from St Neots station, sent by his father who ran a garage and petrol station in Middlesbrough. It was a Manxman – a fearsome thing with God knows how many horsepower at its disposal. On the evening of its arrival he took Celia out for a spin to nearby Ramsey, promising to collect me at the Ship at closing time. I'd gone there by myself, Joan having refused to have anything more to do with me after I'd told her that I was engaged to be married. By now I was almost the resident pianist at the Ship with a repertoire of the times – 'In the Mood', 'Roll Out the Barrel', 'White Cliffs of Dover', 'Home' (always good for a few sniffs and hankie-dabbing from the WAAFs), 'There'll Always Be an England', 'Who's Taking you Home Tonight', 'Hang Out the Washing on the Siegfried Line', 'Run Rabbit Run', 'Underneath the Arches', 'We'll Meet Again', 'Chattanooga Choo Choo', 'Ops in a Wimpy', and by popular request towards ten o'clock, 'Oh, Please don't Burn our Shithouse Down'.

Outside the Ship at closing time there was no sign of Johnny, so muttering obscenities I set off to walk back to camp. I had walked for about two miles, with another mile to go, when I was approached by a vehicle that failed to stop when I thumbed it. As it passed, I recognised it as an ambulance. Twenty yards behind it was Johnny on the Manxman with no lights and a bloke on the pillion seat.

"Smithy?" Johnny enquired as he stopped. Fencing off my furious response of "Where the fuck were you at closing time?" with "I'll tell you later. Climb on behind this bloke," he moved on to the petrol tank to make room. Three on a motor bike was quite normal at the time. But the bloke on the pillion had had enough, preferring to walk the rest of the way, and stood watching as Johnny let in the clutch with me on the pillion to pursue the disappearing rear lights of the ambulance. I didn't blame him after I'd heard the full story from Johnny as we sped off into the black night.

He was a Flying Officer navigator who had been quite happily making his way on foot back to camp when he was hailed by Johnny, who thought he was me, riding a motor cycle without lights, on a dark night on a road without markings or cat's-eyes. Accepting the offer of a lift, he had clung on desperately as Johnny sped off into the darkness to catch up with the ambulance that had passed him earlier. "Must catch that ambulance," Johnny explained, "my girlfriend's in it. We crashed about an hour ago. She's unconscious, my lights are gone and the front forks are bent." At which point I appeared as a dark shadow at the side of the road.

In the event we lost the ambulance and, not knowing where it was bound, juddered our way on the bent forks to the drying room. Celia returned to camp the next day from the hospital in Huntingdon with stitches in her scalp, but otherwise none the worse from her contact with the road. With the front forks realigned and the lights repaired unofficially by the MT section, she was on the pillion of the Manxman again within a week. My own experiences on the pillion were without incident, but none the less hair-raising, and I later rated my chances of survival higher sitting beside Johnny in a Mosquito over the Ruhr than sitting behind him on the Manxman on the narrow winding roads of Huntingdonshire.

Just four weeks after D-Day we did our final night

operations exercise and finished the course. Our training at 1655 MTU had lasted precisely six weeks, during which time we had simulated the marking of a target by Oboe twenty-two times, nine in Oxfords and thirteen in Mosquitoes. We were both given exceptional assessments, and mine read, "This navigator's work has been above average throughout. Very keen and hardworking, he should be an asset to the squadron. Easily one of the best navigators we have ever had on this course."

"Must have had some bloody awful ones, then," Johnny said when he saw it.

We learned of our posting the next afternoon. There were only two Oboe squadrons – 109 at Little Staughton and 105 at Bourne – both a few miles from St Neots. Until April 1943 both squadrons had been stationed at Marham, but as the value of the new marking technique had become evident, they had taken up separate residences as a precaution against an assault by the Luftwaffe. The first occasion on which they had marked for the main force had been on 5 March 1943 – the night Pete had invited me up front to view the sky over Essen.

Newly qualified:
Albert Smith, Miami, 1942
(*I. Smith*)

Sgt J. K. B. Veal ('Paddy'),
51 Squadron (*I. Smith*)

427 Squadron crest
(MH2278 *Imperial War
Museum*)

Albert Smith in his first flying kit,
Paignton (*I. Smith*)

A typical scene of Wellingtons in preparation for a raid. These are 149 Squadron aircraft. (HU44865 *Imperial War Museum*)

Left 142 Squadron crest (*Crown Copyright*)

Above A Wellington testing its engines in the desert (CM2940 *Imperial War Museum*)

Below A battle-scarred desert Wellington between operations (ME6294 *Imperial War Museum*)

Right 109 Squadron crest (*Crown Copyright*)

Above Albert Smith (left) and his pilot
Johnny Liddle, Little Staughton, 1944 (*I. Smith*)

Below B Flight, 109 Squadron, 1944 (*I. Smith*)

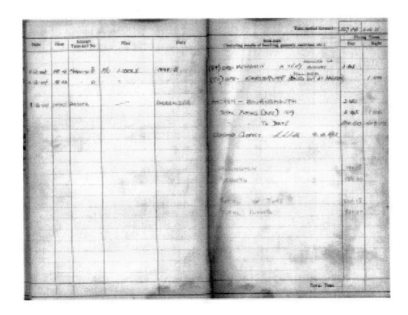

Extracts from Albert Smith's logbook: the fateful final mission including a summary of flying hours (*above*), and a brief summary of Albert's service with no mention of 109 Squadron (*below*) (*I. Smith*)

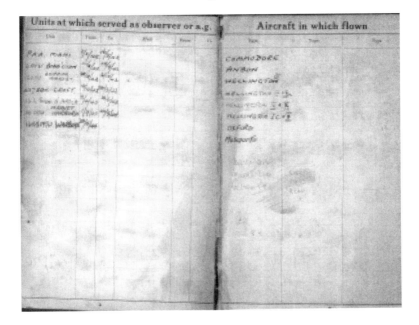

Just married, February 1945 (*I. Smith*)

Albert Smith visits the grave of Pilot Officer Eckton, Guidel Lorient
(*above left*), and the field where he crash-landed (*I. Smith*)

Below The author, his family and members of the archivist organisation
Heemkundekring Saint Tolbert visiting the Mosquito crash site.
Left to right, Ian Smith (co-author), Dolf Baltus (Secretary), Albert Smith,
Peter Sparla (Director), and Stephen Smith (*I. Smith*)

CHAPTER 13

Pathfinders

Our posting was to 109 Squadron, one of the original units of the Pathfinder Force. Its badge was 'a panther rampant, incensed' and its motto 'Primi Hastati' – the first of the legion. So, after a week's leave, I arrived at St Neots Station to make my own way to Little Staughton on 13 July 1944 for my second tour of ops. I was boyishly proud to have made it into the Pathfinder Force to join the so-called elite crews of Bomber Command. But now that the moment had arrived, I was beginning to feel scared at once again having to face the flak over German targets.

On arrival at the squadron we learned that most of 109's crews were commissioned – in fact, Johnny and I and one other crew were the only ones who weren't. But the Sergeants' Mess was heavily populated by aircrew NCOs of 582 Squadron, a Lancaster Pathfinder Squadron that shared Little Staughton with 109. I felt very much an onlooker on that first evening in the Mess. 582 Squadron were on ops and the Mess was packed with crews noisily chattering and clowning over their operational bacon and egg, with those who weren't able to chatter and clown sipping their coffee quietly and wishing they weren't going on ops that night. I recognised immediately the extraordinary atmosphere of pre-op tension. I could sense their apprehension and doubted again the wisdom of my decision to volunteer for a second tour. But these were Lancaster Pathfinder crews with far less chance of completing a second tour than had the crews of 109.

They left in twos and threes and gradually the Mess took on its more normal atmosphere, with the crews who weren't flying behaving as if the war was no concern of theirs. And for them, on the night, it wasn't. They had quickly learned that that was the only way to treat a night off, for in twenty-four, forty-eight or seventy-two hours they would be back in the war, until either they finished their tour or they got killed. Two or three pints in the Mess for Johnny and me that night, then back to the billet for an early night, with Johnny unusually subdued after his first taste of pre-op tension in a Mess at operational meal time.

But his silence didn't last long. He was his usual ebullient self the next morning at 0730 hours. I liked to doze for a while before getting up, but he didn't. When he woke up, he got up. And if I wasn't awake, I very soon was. He was noisy in the mornings, and I used to lie in bed cringing and waiting for the next clump, bang, crash or whistle. I hated him for the first five minutes of every morning for the next five months, during which time we became, as with all Mosquito crews, part of each other's lives, with a tensile bond forged of mutual dependency. From that day on we became as one – Liddle and Smith.

When we reported to 'flights' on our first morning, it was evident that this was a squadron of which anyone could count himself privileged to be a part. The crew room had a relaxed and friendly atmosphere with the crews lounging about in armchairs, the air heavy with cigarette smoke, a constant hiss of conversation, and now and then an outbreak of horseplay. Many of its occupants wore the DFC, with here and there a DFM and a DSO. We were instantly recognised as 'new bods' and two or three came over to welcome us and show us to the B Flight Commander's office. The Flight Commander was a Wingco with the DFC and Bar – Wing Commander Peter Kleboe – boyish, clean cut, effervescent, a typical Guy Gibson type with more than a hundred ops to his credit. After a few minutes it was as if he had known us for years. We were instantly Johnny and Smithy. We were smoking our first cigarette together when ops orders arrived and we were kicked out with apologies.

The ops orders were what the crews in the crew room had been waiting for. Soon the battle order for the night was posted on the notice board, and those who were 'on' made their way to their respective flights for briefing times and night flying test requirements. After a while those not on ops dispersed, and Johnny and I were left alone in the crew room to await instructions. I went off to the navigation section to collect an astro watch and the rest of my equipment, together with the familiar green navigator's bag to hold it all. When I got back to the crew room it was to learn that we were taking Mosquito 'O Oboe' for a night flying test at 1630 hours, prior to taking her up again around midnight for an hour or so on local flying to get the feel of the area around Little Staughton and the voices from the control tower. Camouflaged brown and green on top with a black underside for night flying, 'O Oboe', a veteran Mark 9, behaved immaculately, as she later did on the several ops we did in her.

The next morning we made breakfast in the Sergeants' Mess with minutes to spare. As we had been flying after midnight we weren't due up at 'flights' until 1030 hours, so we had a leisurely after-breakfast smoke in the Mess. In the afternoon we did a training exercise on Otmoor, one of the RAF's bombing ranges. We flew a practice run down to the aiming point, the same as we had done so many times at Warboys, landing back at base at 1725 hours. Flying always seemed to make me hungry, and I was looking forward to tea in the Mess as we landed – until, as we passed the Wingco's open door on our way to the parachute section to return our parachutes, he called after us, "You're on tonight." We stopped after a few more paces – as it happened, by the notice board in the corridor.

"On? On what?" I enquired of Johnny, querulously. We turned our heads toward the notice board. Two solitary names – Liddle and Smith – briefing 2030 hours.

As we stared at our names and at each other the Wingco came out of his room on his way to the Mess. "Thought you'd like to get operational as soon as possible," he said. "Good luck – hope you cope," and left us to it.

"Bloody hell, they don't waste much time do they?" mumbled Johnny. I nodded slowly in agreement.

I forgot about tea as the old familiar feeling in the pit of my stomach drove away the hunger. It was still there at the briefing, but slightly relieved when the target was disclosed. It was Acquet, in nearby France. We carried four 500lb bombs, and in the event the operation turned out to be one of the most abysmal by any Oboe Mosquito in the short history of the Pathfinder Force.

The target was a flying-bomb launching site in a forest in the north-west of France, a very short trip indeed. I had Gee all the way to the turning-on point, and as we neared it I clambered down into the nose and switched on the receiver. The signals were such as I'd never received before. They had always been so clear and identifiable on the ops exercises, but these were almost inaudible, with lots of crackling and dots coming and going. This was on Johnny's tracking signal. Mine was even worse, totally unrecognisable. I stared at the equipment non-plussed, and more so to see Johnny peering down at me from his seat. With the receiver on I couldn't hear what he was yelling into the intercom, but I could guess from the look on that part of his face that was visible between his mask and his helmet. I would have given odds on that it was, "What the fuck is happening?"

I switched over to the intercom and we held a conference while we did an orbit during which I switched back to Oboe. Dashes, clear as anything, but as Johnny instinctively turned to starboard, they faded again to be replaced by the crackling. We tried another orbit, then another, then decided belatedly that we weren't going to cope and would have to abort and return to base. I had no idea to within fifty miles or so where we were after our futile attempts to find the signals. I had been in the nose for more than fifteen minutes, during which time we had flown several courses, none of which I had been able to plot, and there was a strong wind that veered fifty or so degrees. But with the reassuring knowledge that the Gee signals would be discernible, I climbed back into my seat, placed my plotting table in position and swung the shaded light over the chart.

I'd given Johnny a course of 270 degrees pending our first

Gee fix. It was a foul night and we were in continuous cloud as we lost height for the homeward leg. I switched on the Gee set – and there was a blue flash at the back of it, followed by smoke, leaving me looking at a blank screen. The set had blown. It had happened to me twice before, but never at such a bad time. I didn't know where we were, we were in cloud, and I had no dead reckoning plot.

"What course do you want me to fly?" asked Johnny.

My immediate intention to snarl back "How the fuck should I know?" was cut short as I realised the reasonableness of his question. "315," I replied – couldn't miss the whole of the UK on that – "and try to get under the cloud. The Gee's blown and I don't know where we are."

"Jesus!" was his justifiable response.

So we flew on in silence, coming down through cloud. I switched on the IFF and at 1,500 feet we broke cloud. Pretty bloody low. It was dark too, very dark, as we peered nervously ahead, to port and to starboard looking for a beacon. Nothing at all, absolutely nothing. We sped on, the aircraft pitching violently in the turbulence under the clouds. Then suddenly – searchlights dead ahead of us. Thank God for the presence of mind of the searchlight crews, I thought, as we picked our way between the two balloons – 315 degrees had been a lucky guess, for as we tried to raise base on the RT we got an immediate response, and a course to steer to the beacon. Ten minutes later came the welcome sight of the red flashing light on the ground, and within minutes of flying over it we were on the circuit at Little Staughton.

[18/19 July 1944. Acquet. 62 aircraft – 51 Halifaxes, 9 Mosquitoes, 2 Lancasters – of 4 and 8 Groups bombed a flying-bomb launch site but photographs indicated that no new damage was caused. 2 Halifaxes lost.]

Not looking forward to de-briefing, we climbed down the ladder at dispersal. Sitting at the table with the Intelligence

Officer in the de-briefing room, we told our sorry tale. "I couldn't get an audible signal when I switched on," I explained confidently.

"Not even when you tried to tune it in?" queried the interrogator.

"Tune it in?" I responded. "Nobody ever told me at Warboys that it had to be tuned in."

And so far as I was aware, nobody had. Every time I had switched on in the exercises there were the signals, loud and clear.

The next afternoon at 'flights' there was an inquest on our fiasco, and I re-iterated my assertion that at no time during the course had I been told that it might be necessary to use the fine tuners to obtain the signals on ops. The fact that I hadn't done so was accepted as proof of my ignorance of the procedure. Telephone calls were made to Warboys, and I was taken out to a Mosquito to be belatedly instructed on my deficiencies. No doubt I had dozed off during the crucial lecture, but then that was not unknown, and I understood that the training manual at 1655 MTU was strengthened to ensure that every navigator on future courses knew his stuff concerning fine tuning on ops.

That night we both sat glumly in the Sergeants' Mess, dismayed that our first op had been such a failure. We were not at all surprised to find that we were on the ops list the following morning. Nine other crews were listed, well experienced ones who would obviously be marking a target for the heavies. Where we were going to fit in on the night's ops was a matter for conjecture – probably to a different target, carrying bombs again to see if we knew what we were doing after our miserable performance the night before. But nothing of the sort. Obviously our assessments at the end of the course at Warboys were enough to dismiss Acquet as a one off, for we were one of the four Mosquitoes detailed to mark a launching site at Andersvelck in northern France for a force of Lancasters and Halifaxes.

Take-off was at 1955 hours, giving us broad daylight almost there and back. We were desperate to be absolved from our failure of the previous night – and we were, totally. The op was as near perfect as it was possible to be. I received the same inaudible signals when I switched on the receiver, but with very little oscillation of the fine tuner they became as clear as any that we had received on our ops exercises over Britain. We coped, dead on time, and with only a forty-five-yard error. With a cloudless sky over the target, we stood off after marking to see our red TIs burning in the wood with the bombs from the heavies exploding amongst them. We landed back at base at 2200 hours with broad smiles, shortly to savour the pleasure of the rum and coffee at a relaxed interrogation in the de-briefing room.

[20 July 1944. V-weapon sites. 369 aircraft – 174 Lancasters, 165 Halifaxes and 30 Mosquitoes – attacked 6 flying-bomb launching sites and the V-weapon site at Wizernes. All raids were successful except the small raid by 20 aircraft on the Forêt-de-Croc site where the Oboe leader Lancaster was shot down on the bombing run and the bombs of this force all missed the target. This was the only aircraft lost.

The unsuccessful attempt on Hitler's life at his headquarters in East Prussia took place on this day.]

CHAPTER 14

Coping

In the morning we were looking for some sort of praise up at 'flights', but nobody there appeared to be even aware that we had coped for the first time. And as we learned in the next few weeks, a 'cope' was expected every time unless there was a technical failure of the equipment or the aircraft was shot up. It was a sobering lesson to digest; that failure must be 100% 'not your fault', and after our elation our spirits were down to earth again after the next week of ops. In seven days we did four of them, all bombing raids on nondescript targets – the railway yards at Aachen and Somain (twice) and the night fighter base at St Trond. We coped on the first two, and failed on the others, once due to loss of the tracking signal, and the other because we very nearly bought it on the way to St Trond.

[21 July 1944. Support and Minor Operations. 107 aircraft from training units on diversionary sweep, 27 Mosquitoes to Berlin, 8 to Frankfurt and 5 to Aachen, 36 RCM sorties, 46 Mosquito patrols, 4 Halifaxes mine-laying off Brest and Lorient, 12 aircraft on Resistance operations, 4 OTU sorties. No aircraft lost.

25 July, 1944. Minor Operations. 21 Mosquitoes to Berlin, 15 to Mannheim and 6 to Somain, 28 RCM sorties, 37 Mosquito patrols, 4 Halifaxes mine-laying off Brest, 5 Halifaxes on Resistance operations. 1 Mosquito of 100 Group lost.

26 July 1944. Minor Operations. 30 Mosquitoes to Hamburg, 11 to Somain and 2 to Saarbrucken, 6 RCM sorties, 23 Mosquito patrols, 6 Lancasters mine-laying off Heligoland, 6 aircraft on Resistance operations. 1 Mosquito lost from the Hamburg raid.

29 July, 1944. Minor Operations. 30 Mosquitoes to Frankfurt (though some bombs fell in Mainz 20 miles away, killing 8 people), 9 to St Trond and 4 to Coulommiers (these last 2 targets were German night fighter airfields), 13 RCM sorties, 6 Mosquito patrols, 9 OTU sorties. No aircraft lost.]

For me, the op had been progressing perfectly. Gee was quite exceptional and every time I computed the wind it was the same. On track and on time, I began to notice the aircraft's extraordinary conduct. It was behaving like the high-speed elevator in the Empire State Building – first rising then descending vertically. But I thought little of it, used as I had become to turbulence in poor flying conditions. What did concern me was the position of the next Gee fix, which showed us way off track. On checking the compass and altimeter readings, I wondered what the hell Johnny was up to, and how the hell he expected me to navigate unless he held height, speed and course. I thought his oxygen supply had failed. He was behaving like a madman, frantically shoving the stick back and forth and turning it left and right to its full extent. I leaned across to him, tested his oxygen connection and the needle on the supply dial. They were both normal. Anger replacing concern – I flicked the switch on my mask.

"What the fuck are you doing?" No answer. He must have cracked up. "Johnny!" I screamed into the intercom. Again no answer. Then, in the middle of his extraordinary antics, he snatched one hand up to his microphone. He yelled into it, "Put your parachute on!"

Fear instantly replaced my anger. I hurriedly, fumblingly clipped on my parachute, and sat tense and wide eyed. "What is it?" I asked, tightly.

"Cu-nim. All my instruments have gone!" he shouted back. Then I noticed. With the stick full forward we were shooting up, and with it back in the pit of his stomach, falling like a stone. The plane stuttered and lurched forward. Then it sank, and my organs felt light. Then it hiccoughed back into the sky. I was being tossed in my chair

– the safety straps jerking me into position. I began to shake. I looked at the altimeter. The needle was whizzing round frantically. It stopped at 2,000 feet, then set off again, stopping at 5,000 feet. We had been at 28,000 feet. It started to unwind again – 4,000 – 3,000 – 2,000. God we're going down! I heaved up the floor, and felt for the handle on the bottom hatch.

At 1,800 feet we broke cloud. Still we were yawing and pitching – sliding through the sky as if we were being bounced forward by the strings of a puppeteer.

Johnny picked up a visual horizon and the propellers lost their blue surrounds. The plane became firmer and steadier. "OK, Smithy – put it back – we're out of it." Straight and level again with no hope of getting back to operational height, we aborted and set course for home. We had flown unwittingly into the top of a towering cumulo-nimbus bank of cloud in which we had nearly lost our wings. They'd stayed on, and we had the instruments back. Relief. But the evening had not yet finished.

Our load that night had been six 500lb bombs – four in the bomb bay and one under each wing. Normally we brought them back if we failed to cope over occupied territory, but not the wing bombs. They had been known to fall off on landing, so they had to be jettisoned. Safely over the North Sea I selected the two switches, opened the bomb doors to complete the circuit and pressed the tit, feeling the usual lurch as the bombs fell away. Bomb doors closed again, the return journey was free of incident, and Johnny put the Mosquito down sweetly on the main runway. As we started to taxi along the perimeter the voice from the control tower called us up on the R/T: "Presumably," it said, pausing a little to give emphasis to the supposition, "you are unaware that you are still carrying your wing bombs." There followed instructions to taxi slowly to a dispersal on the far side of the airfield. It took us twenty tortuous minutes. My breathing was shallow. Both of us moved, even turning to glance at each other, with slow, quiet and deliberate gestures. Johnny caressed the plane to the designated area.

His braking was smooth, his turning was gradual. Finally we came to a smooth slow half at the dispersal. Gingerly, we climbed down the ladder, craning to see the two huge, black bombs hanging from their hooks under the wings. Whether the armourers had given me the wrong numbers or I had selected the wrong two was never known – nor did we care. The two bombs had stayed on, which was all that mattered. My shoulders and neck ached.

Again, nobody seemed to be very interested in our 'dicey do' – merely dismissed as 'one of those things'.

The next morning we were recommended for commissions, and forgot our troubles of the night before.

The process of becoming commissioned entailed four interviews, the first with the Flight Commander, Pete Kleboe, the second with the Squadron Commander, Wingco George Grant, then the Station Commander, a Group Captain, and finally with the Group Commander – Air Vice Marshall D C T Bennett. The first one was of minimal duration, all of two minutes, immediately followed by the second – twice as long. Two days later a civilian appeared in the crew room asking for Liddle and Smith. He turned out to be a tailor from Cambridge, come to measure us for our uniforms; he would get the £50 uniform allowance that went with the commission. We thought he was unaware that the two higher-up interviewers had still to be seen, but he was not in the least put off when we told him so. He took his measurements, professing his confidence that we would be commissioned within a month. It was the first time that I had been measured by a tailor and I didn't much care for the inside leg part. We had our interviews with the Groupie later the same day.

On the first day of August we marked by night for a force of heavies – our first time. The target was a launching site at Oeuf-en-Ternois, about twenty miles into France from Le Touquet. Airborne at ten minutes past midnight, it was like the 'grope' at OTU, dark and stealthy, no flak, and just a few subdued flashes from exploding bombs. Like burglars in the night, we stole silently away, heading straight for base.

*[31 July 1944. Flying-bomb sites. 202 aircraft – 104
Lancasters, 76 Halifaxes, 22 Mosquitoes – of 1, 6 and 8
Groups attacked two launching and storage sites, but only at
the Forêt de Nieppe storage site was effective damage caused.
1 Halifax and 1 Lancaster lost.]*

In the 'grope', a ground simulator of night ops, fog on
return was sometimes reproduced in the exercise, but
nothing like the pea-souper that spread out below us as we
approached base on our return from Oeuf-en-Ternois. It was
eerie, down at 5,000 feet, with below us a grey carpet in the
light of the moon, extending in all directions. On calling
base we were instructed to divert to Hartford Bridge, which
I quickly found on my chart. Ten miles from our diversion,
the carpet lay unbroken below us – fitted wall to wall. But
RAF communications had got it right. Almost directly over
the airfield there was a black hole in the carpet just big
enough to drop into on a tight circuit and pancake on the
runway.

Three other Mosquito crews joined us in the watch office
to be interrogated by an Intelligence Officer, dragged from
his bed to de-brief us and prepare a report for group. And
soon we were being served sausage and chips by a WAAF
corporal wearing her greatcoat over pyjamas, and not at all
pleased to see us. No worse nor better than most other
diversions, Hartford Bridge supplied us with the usual
damp billets set aside for such occasions. And after a cold,
uncomfortable night we took off for base at 0700, not even
waiting for breakfast. By 0830 we were between our own
sheets with the curtains drawn until noon. Up at 'flights' in
the afternoon, we were gratified to learn that our marking
error had been a mere four yards, but not overjoyed to be on
the ops list again.

It was a daylight take-off at 1925 hours – and another
launching site at Belle Croix, again only twenty miles into
France, and just 105 minutes from take-off to landing. The
V1 assault on London was at its height, an ill-wind for the
capital, but blowing good for us, with short trips to lightly

defended targets. To compensate for our easy rides the numerical system of determining a tour in Mosquito Pathfinders was replaced by a points system – two for the launching sites and five for other targets. The change was of little concern to Johnny and me at the time, with our tour just begun, and appeared not to concern our more operational colleagues either, to whom it appeared to be of academic interest only. Apparently 'one carried on until one felt that one had had enough', as I was informed by a Flight Lieutenant navigator when I asked his opinion.

We commenced the run down to the Belle Croix launching site from over the English Channel. England to starboard and France to port and ahead, the green, moist fields of England contrasting with the patterned, paler ones of France. We were on Channel 1 – there were two Oboe channels – and we spotted the Mosquito on Channel 2 about fifteen seconds ahead of us. His markers fell away as I sat with my thumb on the tit waiting for our own release signal. Banking steeply to port after we had dropped, we saw our red TIs burst close to those already burning on the ground. Within minutes both sets of TIs had been smothered with bombs from the bomber stream behind us.

[1 August 1944. Flying-bomb sites. 777 aircraft – 385 Lancasters, 324 Halifaxes, 67 Mosquitoes, 1 Lightning – to attack numerous targets but only 79 aircraft were able to bomb; Bomber Command records do not state why the remaining sorties were abortive, but poor weather conditions was the probable cause. No aircraft lost.]

Knocking out a launching site presented no problems whatsoever, after its location, usually hidden in a forest, had been detected by the French Underground. But they were so numerous and so quickly replaced that there had been no decrease in the number of flying-bombs falling on London, said to be a hundred a day. So, four days after Belle Croix, a move was made to cut off the supply of bombs to the sites by means of a massive attack on a storage site at St Leu-d'Esserent by nearly 750 Lancasters and Halifaxes. We were one of eight Oboe Mosquitoes detailed to mark the aiming points.

The flying-bombs were stored in underground caves, used by the French in peacetime to grow mushrooms. Roads and railways led into the caves through tunnels carved into the rock face on the northern side of the river. The depot, thirty miles north-west of Paris, and heavily defended by flak batteries, had been attacked before, but was still the main source of supply to the launching sites. On this raid two aiming points had been designated. The first markers, red ones, were aimed at the roads, railways and tunnel entrances, and the majority of the heavies were briefed to bomb them on the same heading as the roads leading into the tunnel. This part of the attack was scheduled to last for twelve minutes, at the end of which green markers were dropped by two Mosquitoes directly over the underground caves. Standing off and waiting for the green markers were other Lancasters carrying 12,000lb earthquake bombs, expected to penetrate the surface and explode in the caves, causing the earth to subside and cave in. Having been one of the markers for the first phase of the attack, we saw nothing of the earthquake bombs, but learned at de-briefing that the Master Bomber on the raid had declared the raid an outstanding success.

[5 August 1944. Flying-bomb sites. 742 aircraft – 469 Halifaxes, 257 Lancasters, 16 Mosquitoes – of 4, 5, 6 and 8 Groups attacked the Forêt de Nieppe and St Leu-d'Esserent storage sites. Bombing conditions were good. 1 Halifax lost. 31 Lancasters and 8 Mosquitoes of 8 Group attempted to carry out small 'Oboe Leader' raids on 4 launching sites but only 9 aircraft succeeded in bombing. None lost.]

It was a blazing hot summer's day as we emerged from de-briefing around 1500 hours. An ideal day for a swim, so we hitched a lift to the River Ouse on the edge of St Neots. Johnny had no petrol for the Manxman, which was a relief.

We stripped off and swam in the river, then sunbathed on the bank until opening time, when we made the short walk over the bridge into St Neots. This was a pleasant little place, the size of a largish village with four or five 'olde worlde' pubs. We stopped at the first one – the Bridge. First in and last out, we were both feeling pretty pleased with ourselves and pleasantly under the influence of a few pints of wartime mild beer – they'd run out of bitter. We rode back to camp in one of the assorted vehicles in the convoy weaving its way back to base. Usually without lights, still less taxed and insured, most emitted exhaust fumes smelling suspiciously of high octane aeroplane petrol. It didn't do the cylinders much good, but as most of the cars were on their last legs anyway and strictly for local use only, it didn't really matter. I nearly bought a little Austin 7 for four pounds, but didn't because Johnny was in the process of arranging for one of the second-hand cars in his father's garage to be 'loaned' for the duration. It was fortunate that I had kept my four pounds in my pocket for we saw the little Austin 7 a couple of weeks later abandoned and ready for scrap in the ditch on the road to St Neots. It looked like the springs had gone, not surprising with its normal load of seven or eight passengers.

CHAPTER 15

Back to the Ruhr

Having been one of the few 109 crews on the St Leu-d'Essercnt raid the day before, we thought we might not be on the next night, but we were listed to fly 'Q Queenie' on a night op – briefing at 1600 hours. We had flown in 'Q Queenie' on the Oeuf-en-Ternois and Belle Croix ops – each time with only three markers; she had a u/s hook on the fourth, but the groundcrew lads had repaired it in time for the op on the night of 6 August. At the briefing, familiar as we were with the red ribbon making its way to the South Coast, it was – for me – a heart-stopping, shuddering moment to see it stretch horizontally to a turning-on point north of the Ruhr Valley, then down to the target – Castrop Rauxel – lying between Essen and Dortmund, and deep inside the Ruhr flak belt. I recalled Pete's invitation on my first flight to the Ruhr in March 1943 – "Come and have a look at this, Smithy" – and the horrendous bloodstained sky that had throbbed out in front of me. Johnny was unaffected by my white-faced fear of the trip. For him it had all been nice and tidy so far except for the night of the 'cu-nim', and he'd never seen the Ruhr flak at its most ferocious. It must be still there – probably more intense than ever – but let's hope it won't be as bad at 32,000 feet as it had been at 16,000.

The target was the synthetic oil plant on either side of the Rhein Herne Canal, which was to be attacked by a force consisting entirely of Mosquitoes. Four Pathfinders, all from 109, were to open the proceedings, followed by thirty-six Pathfinders marking, bombing and photographing, and, for the triple purpose, carrying two 500lb bombs, one green TI and a photoflash, with a camera beside them in the bomb bays. We took off at 1940 hours towards the gathering dusk in the east, exiting the coast at Orford Ness, on a heading for the Zuider Zee.

Again there was the feeling of stealth as we stole into enemy territory, conscious that the only other aircraft anywhere near us would be the other Mosquito, marking at almost the same time as us on the other channel. Aware too, that with no main force we would be an isolated blip on the radar screens six miles below us, our height, speed and heading being passed to the flak batteries on our track. They would know that we were Mosquitoes, and that, as their night fighters couldn't catch us, flak was the only way to stop us. I imagined the shells, primed to explode at our height, already loaded – the barrels following our track and moving ahead of us like a shot-gun moving ahead of a pheasant. How could they miss?

Point A was just outside the Ruhr flak belt. But B wasn't. I expected the flak to start arriving at B, but there was still no sign of it even at C – just a few aimless searchlights. Probably they were going to put up a screen round about point D. I frowned and watched the seconds on my watch, waiting for the explosions as we approached it. My heart raced with dull thuds. Any time now – wait for it.

Then, nothing. The aircraft banked gently in the direction of Holland, Johnny waved his hand indicating an abort, and I switched off Oboe and on to intercom. "Signal's gone," he explained, re-setting his gyro-compass for the course home. It was our first technical failure, and while I was relieved to turn off the run, it did seem a bit of a wasted effort. But we had several technical failures ahead of us – usually from loss of the tracking signal round about D. But inevitably, somebody, as on this raid, managed a 'cope'. As we had a look back at Castrop Rauxel, two green TIs were burning on the ground with bombs exploding around them, and as we were still over Germany, I selected the two bomb switches and let them go.

[6 August 1944. Castrop-Rauxel. 40 Mosquitoes attacked the synthetic oil plant; a large fire was seen. 1 Mosquito lost.]

So we had chalked up another op, and a significant one for both of us. I'd been back to the Ruhr and Johnny had been to Germany for the first time, without a shot being fired at us. He thought it had been a bit of a yawn, and so it had. He must have thought I'd been shooting a line about the Ruhr flak, but it wasn't very long before he was to see it in its full glory.

CHAPTER 16

Regular Coping

We were up early the next morning, vigorously polishing our buttons and shoes, and pressing our uniforms. We were off to Pathfinder Headquarters – Castle Hill House in the town of Huntingdon – for our interview with Air Vice Marshall D C T Bennett. Few of the aircrew had ever seen him, not even a photograph of him in the papers, and, as with all the unseen commanders, the myths and legends had been added to the stories even over the time that I had been listening to them. So we were apprehensive as we stood outside the lovely old country house that housed PFF Headquarters staff. We went in and were ushered into a little waiting room containing six tip-up chairs and nothing else. I nervously felt for my Woodbines, but before I could light up, a delicious WAAF corporal opened the door and asked Johnny to follow her for his interview. We had been there less then three minutes. He must have been waiting for us.

I got up off the chair and gazed nervously out of the small window on to the High Street. I felt again for my Woodbines, but thought it might be insubordinate to light up so near the AOC. He was a non-smoker. I was still gazing out of the window when Johnny rejoined me – just about five minutes after he'd left the room. The WAAF corporal asked me sweetly to follow her along the corridor. Poor Johnny, I thought. Only five minutes, four in fact after deducting the time to walk there and back – the AOC must have quickly decided that he wasn't officer material. If he wasn't, then I probably wasn't either. Well, I didn't really want a commission anyway, I thought, as the WAAF (she really was a smasher) opened the door of the AOC's office, and startled me with a whispered, "Good luck."

"Flight Sergeant Smith, Sir," she announced.

The room was simple. It had a carpet of sorts and quite a large desk with a couple of filing cabinets and two uncomfortable-looking chairs. I took in the details as I marched in, stiffly coming to a drill-style halt and saluting. The little man with neatly trimmed black hair, seated on the other side of the big desk, smiled kindly. "Stand at ease, Smith," he said in a quiet, gentle voice. I smiled too. He looked down again at the papers that he had been studying when I marched in. He looked up fleetingly. "How do you like the Mosquito?"

"Very much, Sir." (What a bloody inadequate answer.)

"How many operations have you done so far?"

"Forty-eight, Sir." I thought it better to merely answer questions rather than to volunteer additional information.

A short pause as he turned over one of the sheets of paper on his desk to continue his reading. "Good – and – er – in what aircraft?"

"Thirty-eight in Wellingtons and ten in Mosquitoes, Sir."

Another – longer – pause as he finished the page he was reading and turned it over. I had the impression that his thoughts might be wandering, as I could not imagine my records being that interesting.

"Yes," he said, looking up again briefly, the gentle smile once more on his lips. "And what is the distance between lines of longitude?"

"Sixty knots, Sir." (What a simple question – I'd learned that at my first navigation lesson back at ITW.)

"Knots?" he mused.

"Yes, Sir."

"Are you quite sure?"

"Yes, Sir."

A pause – then, "Don't you mean nautical miles?"

Bloody hell. I've fluffed it. Of course it was nautical miles. Knots were nautical miles per hour. "Of course, Sir – sorry," I mumbled, totally confused at having made such a fundamental error. And for the first time since I had entered the room he leaned back in his chair, put his hands on his desk and fixed me with a paternal smile, obviously aware of my confusion.

"Of course you meant to say nautical miles, didn't you?" he said. "Return to your squadron, Flight Sergeant Smith – goodbye – and good luck," and before I had finished my salute and about turn, he was again engrossed in his papers.

I joined Johnny back in the waiting room. The WAAF corporal was waiting to show us out, and he was chatting her up. She was friendly but quite obviously inaccessible, and as I returned she got up and guided us out of the house, waving us goodbye, a nice unusual gesture from a service person.

Back in the High Street to await the return of our transport, we looked at each other sheepishly. Neither of us felt that we had been particularly impressive, and even the AOC's disarming manner had not completely allayed our awe at being alone with him. Feeling a bit deflated, we had our WAAF MT driver drop us off outside the Bridge in St Neots. We had to hang around for two hours until the pub opened – then decided to stay until closing time. Johnny had to pay all night. I was flat broke, but I gave him one of the two pints I had bought for me for playing the piano. He was broke too at the end of the night and poverty stared us in the face.

I tried to recall the day's events as I lay in a drunken state in the back of an open truck on the road back to base. I had seen the founder of the Pathfinder Force. I'd gone through at least eight pints of beer with only sevenpence in my pocket at the outset. God knows how I had come by the crumpled packet of Players Medium cigarettes in my tunic pocket with still seven in it. And God knows who the little WAAF was who nestled in my arms in the back of the truck. It stopped to let us all off in the little country road that shortly led to the guard room. Everyone dutifully halted on the challenge of "Halt, who goes there?" from the guard on duty. We giggled as I helped the little WAAF fasten up her shirt buttons – it had been warm in there – before she joined two of her mates on their way to the WAAFery. The next thing I remembered was waking up on my bed fully clothed, cold, light on, and the time 0330 hours. My head throbbed as I discarded my uniform on the floor and climbed between the sheets.

I woke up at 0730 hours. I could taste the beer on my dry, big tongue. A pain flowed through my head to the bridge of my nose. Johnny went for breakfast, but I couldn't face it. By the time he returned at 0830 hours I'd been sick and was beginning to feel better. Up at 'flights' by 0900, our tailor arrived shortly afterwards to give us our final fittings, promising delivery within a week. I had given up protesting at his optimism, but hoped that it would prove to be well founded. Prior to joining 109 a commission hadn't been important, as the large majority of Bomber Command aircrew were NCOs like myself. But here it was different. We were cut off from the other crews during off-duty hours, and they seemed to use the Officers' Mess much more than we used the Sergeants'.

After the final fitting I sank into one of the armchairs in the room, hoping to sleep off the remainder of the previous night's alcohol. I made a mental note to seek out the little WAAF who had appeared late on the scene. She had helped me unfasten one of her shirt buttons that had proved stubborn, and had displayed distinct possibilities. I felt myself slipping away into oblivion, but the bliss was short-lived. Johnny was shaking me impatiently.

"Night flying test, ten minutes."

"Shit," I grumbled, dragging myself off to the locker room, then to the nearby parachute section to collect a parachute.

It was the shortest NFT we ever did, just one circuit and down again. Johnny had reported the aircraft – 'J Johnnie' – unserviceable after we had landed her in from St Leu-d'Esserent, and she was still u/s. But we were still on the ops list for the evening. We took off in 'L London' at 1805 hours with four red TIs to mark a 'buzz bomb' launching ramp at St Philibert Ferme for a small force of Halifaxes. We coped, albeit with a marking error of 105 yards, and the Master

Bomber directed the bomb-aimers to aim their bombs at the markers north of ours. The op took us just ninety-eight minutes, and nobody fired at us.

[8 August 1944. Flying-bomb sites. 58 Halifaxes and 20 Mosquitoes of 4 and 8 Groups attacked 4 launching sites; the bombing was accurate. 1 Halifax lost.]

Hopes of a quiet evening, catching up on my letter-writing, which I had been wanting to do for several days, were dashed when the battle order was posted around lunchtime the next day. The target was Acquet – how could we ever forget the name? But this time we weren't beginners, and were marking the launching site for the heavies – sixty Lancasters. We did too, with an error of only forty-five yards.

It was nearly midnight as we turned away from Acquet, still feeling far from our best after the previous night at the Bridge. So Johnny put the nose down and we came back downhill all the way. And as I climbed into bed after my fiftieth op it was beginning to look as if volunteering for Mosquitoes had realised my hopes of keeping clear of the real action taking place below us.

[9 August 1944. Flying-bomb sites. 311 aircraft – 171 Lancasters, 115 Halifaxes, 25 Mosquitoes – of 1, 3, 6 and 8 Groups attacked 4 launching sites and the Fort-d'Englos storage site. All targets were accurately bombed and no aircraft were lost.]

We couldn't celebrate my half-century for a while as we had no money. But there was a touring ENSA show on the night after Acquet. Usually we avoided them like the plague, but with nothing else to do we went along. It was the usual stuff. "I say, I say, I say – my wife's gone to the West Indies." "Jamaica?" "No, she went of her own accord." But there was a big blonde dancer with a bouncing bust who attracted the inevitable wolf whistles and the coarse remarks about nipples like football studs. The troupe had cocoa in the Sergeants' Mess after the show. The dancer didn't look half as good close up without her make-up, and even looked a bit top heavy. Drinking my cocoa, it struck me how much fitter I felt after two whole days free of alcohol, and I resolved to do it more often. It would have to wait though – tomorrow was pay day.

But we didn't get our pay that afternoon. At precisely the time fixed for the pay parade, 1430 hours, we were taking off with our four red TIs, which were hopefully going to cascade precisely on the major railway network at Douai in France. Signals were clear as a bell, and with the instruments showing exactly the briefed heading, altitude and airspeed when I pressed the tit on release, we had to be pretty close to the aiming point. So with our pay waiting for us back at base we didn't even take a backward glance, and I was packing my green navigation bag by 1630 hours as we taxied round to dispersal. 'L London' was proving to be our lucky aircraft. We'd done three ops in her and coped on each occasion.

[11 August 1944. Railway targets. 459 aircraft – 270 Lancasters, 169 Halifaxes, 20 Mosquitoes – of 1, 3, 4 and 8 Groups attacked 3 railway yards and 1 bridge. Forces of between 133 aircraft and 142 aircraft attacked Douai, Lens and Somain; the bombing at these targets started well but ground features rapidly became covered by smoke and dust. 1 Halifax lost on the Somain raid. 49 aircraft attacked the Étaples railway bridge without loss and claimed direct hits on the bridge.]

The seven o'clock bus to Bedford that night was packed as it always was when there was a dance at the Corn Exchange. Somehow we missed the bus back to camp and had a rotten hitch-hike, walking for ages before we were picked up. I fell into my pit around two o'clock absolutely exhausted. We'd been up early, done an NFT, then an op, drunk six or seven pints, danced for two hours and walked a couple of miles.

We both missed breakfast and were late up at 'flights' – to resume our slumber in the crew room. No night off, though – not even the afternoon. Briefing was at 1800 hours, which meant a late take-off, and our aircraft for the night – 'K King' – needed an NFT, so we had to go back to 'flights' in the afternoon. The target was another 'buzz bomb' site in France at La Breteque, and all was going like clockwork until point C, where both our signals went off the air. "Technical failure," the Intelligence Officer told us at de-briefing. It was frustrating to have got so far and failed, then to be blandly told that the ground equipment had failed. 'Copes' had been falling off recently and there was a suspicion that the Germans were interfering with the signals, though if they had been able to, they would have done it every time. But we had another two points, and after we had scrounged a second rum and coffee, our frustration had evaporated by the time we had cycled the mile or so to the hut – that is, Johnny cycled and I coasted, my chain having come off. It had been doing so frequently of late, and it was difficult to get it back on again. So I had to cling on to Johnny's shoulder while he pedalled and I free-wheeled. I went to sleep with his exhortation about "fixing the fucking chain", the last thing I remembered until morning.

[11 August 1944. Flying-bomb sites. 40 Halifaxes and 12 Mosquitoes bombed 2 launching sites and a storage depot. No aircraft lost.]

Not listed the next day, we had, at last, a full day off to ourselves. I wrote my letters and, as both of us felt like an early night, we cycled to the little pub – just a bar, nothing else – on the St Neots road, for two or three pints with our farm-labouring friends who seemed to spend most evenings there – they were always there whenever we called in for a quick drink. We left before closing time and were in bed by half past ten.

In the morning we had an early call at 0700 hours, and a briefing at 0900 hours. I skipped breakfast, preferring to wait for the operational meal, but Johnny was hungry and just made briefing after a bolted breakfast.

The target was 48 degrees 57½ N, 00 deg 16½ W, which were the co-ordinates of the tiny French village of Fontaine le Pin in the Normandy battle area. A week earlier, on 7 August, the German Army had committed itself to making a desperate attempt to reach Avranches on the west coast of Brittany, hoping to cut the Allied armies in two. The advance had been halted by 12 August and turned into a retreat. The German armour was withdrawing through a narrow corridor between Falaise and Argenton with the US First Army in hot pursuit. Falaise, and its approaches from Caen, were being bitterly defended by the left flank of the German divisions from attack by the British Second Army, and Argenton, by the right flank, from attack by the US Third Army. The Allies were trying to close the gap, hoping to trap the bulk of the Germany forces in the pocket between Falaise and Argenton.

The main defending German armour had been concentrated on its more threatened left flank, holding off the British divisions on one side of the road to Falaise, and the Canadian divisions on the other. The Allies had ground to a halt in the face of determined resistance by the German armour, which was dug in in roughly a straight line east to west, just north of Falaise.

At the briefing, which was quite the most detailed I'd ever attended, we were told the background to our marking – quite unusual. Seven German strong points holding the slanting line of defence were to be attacked in turn for fifteen minutes each, with an interval of five minutes between each attack to enable the smoke and dust to clear before the next aiming point was attacked. Each wave of bombers was to have its own Master Bomber, and was under instructions to adhere strictly to his directions in view of the close proximity of our own troops to the aiming points.

We were marking the sixth strong point, and at point B we could see the bombs from the fifth wave still exploding on the ground. Our instructions were to abort if we weren't exactly on the briefed height, speed and heading on release. But we were having a superb run, Johnny having settled on the curved track almost immediately, and we dropped our markers untroubled by flak. The heavies weren't under fire either.

We couldn't see our own markers cascade down, but three minutes after release we heard the Master Bomber ordering the heavies to aim directly at the yellow marker from their height of 3,000 feet. Banking around the target, we could see our markers being smothered with high explosives, dust spreading in all directions. I looked at Johnny. He grinned back. "Jesus, wouldn't like to be under that lot," he said, turning on to the unfamiliar homeward course of 010 degrees. It took us over London, with the Houses of Parliament quite clear – it was the first time I'd seen them from the air.

[14 August 1944. Normandy Battle Area. 805 aircraft – 411 Lancasters, 352 Halifaxes, 42 Mosquitoes – to attack 7 German troop positions facing the 3rd Canadian Division, which was advancing on Falaise. 2 Lancasters lost. A careful plan was prepared with Oboe and visual marking, and with a Master Bomber and a deputy at each of the 7 targets. Most of the bombing was accurate and effective, but about halfway through the raids some aircraft started to bomb a large quarry in which parts of the 12th Canadian Field Regiment were positioned. This mistake may have been caused by the yellow identification flares that were ignited by the Canadians. It was unfortunate that the target indicators being used by the Pathfinders were also yellow. Bomber Command crews claimed that the Canadians used the yellow flares before any bombs fell in the quarry; the history of the Canadian units says that the bombs fell first. The Master Bombers tried hard to stop further crews bombing in the wrong area but approximately 70 aircraft bombed the quarry and other nearby Allied positions over a 70-minute period. The Canadians took shelter in their slit trenches and most emerged unscathed though shaken, but 13 men were killed

and 53 were injured and a large number of vehicles and guns were hit.]

De-briefing was a hubbub. Practically the whole of the squadron had been on the marking. There was a queue to be interrogated, with the word being passed round that some bombs had fallen on Canadian troops. This was confirmed by the Intelligence Officer when it came to our turn to sit at his table. Relieved at his assurance that it hadn't happened at our aiming point, we weren't unduly elated at hearing of our marking error of seventy yards, even if it was within the limits for the day. We heard little of the casualties suffered by the Canadians. (This was believed to have been the first occasion on which Bomber Command aircraft had hit friendly troops during the Battle of Normandy. The Canadian artillery regiment was machine-gunned by RAF Spitfires and USAAF Mustangs the following day!)

Two days later the newspapers were full of the news that Falaise had been taken and the gap closed, with dozens of tanks and thousands of Germans trapped in the pocket. It was all of fleeting interest to us, with momentary sympathy for the dead Canadians and total indifference for the dead Germans. Two more points and one day nearer to leave was all that really mattered, and as for everyone else on the op – as far as I knew – it was the same.

I was flying again on the following afternoon, but not with Johnny. One of the squadron pilots, Flying Officer Ralph, had been detailed for special duties over the range at Otmoor, but his navigator was unavailable. Pete Kleboe found me sitting in the crew room. "Smithy – show Ralph here the way to Otmoor and back, will you?" A bit peeved at first, I didn't really mind. Ralph was a pleasant enough bloke and we were only airborne for half an hour. He was the only other pilot I ever flew with during my tour with 109, an extraordinary coincidence as it turned out.

After we landed it was my intention to go straight to the Mess for tea, then to the hut to polish up prior to going on a week's leave at the crack of dawn. But it wasn't to be – there was a briefing at 1900 for four crews, including Liddle and Smith. Several crews had been on ops during the afternoon, and ours looked rather like an afterthought or a follow-up. It was a follow-up.

During the afternoon, 109 and 105 Squadrons had marked several night fighter airfields in Holland and Belgium for more than a thousand Lancasters and Halifaxes. The bombing of Germany by night had been largely pigeon-holed since D-Day, so the afternoon's raids were a clear indication to both us and the Germans that a change was in the offing. One of the airfields bombed in the afternoon had been Venlo on the Dutch side of the border with Germany. But the bombs must have missed the runways, since the night raid by the four Mosquitoes was a precision bombing exercise to put them out of action. All four coped, and we had an error of only sixteen yards, as we were told at de-briefing. But we weren't too interested and went straight to the hut, skipping the post-op meal. In bed for 0200, we were on the road by 0800 hours.

[15 August 1944. Minor operations. 32 Mosquitoes to Berlin, 8 to Venlo airfield and 9 to various Ruhr targets, 1 RCM sortie, 7 Mosquito patrols, 6 Halifaxes mine-laying off La Pallice. No aircraft lost.]

In the summer of 1944 it took most of the day to make the journey home. Johnny was going up the A1 to Middlesbrough on the Manxman. He offered to make the short diversion to Sheffield to drop me off at the station there to catch a train to Manchester, where I was going to spend the first two days of my leave. It seemed a good idea at the time, but it finished me once and for all from any desire to own a motor bike. I arrived at Sheffield with a sore bottom, nervous exhaustion, and untold relief at parting company with the Manxman and the lunatic on the front seat.

Nobody I knew was home on leave on my arrival at Salford, so I had nobody to drink with. I pressed on to

Wallasey on the second day. Drus was still working at C&A in Liverpool, awaiting her call-up into the ATS. So the rest of the leave was very pleasant indeed, drinking at lunchtime, dancing, picture-going and drinking in the evening, and lying in bed every morning until it was time to get up for the lunchtime drinking session. Almost before I knew it, I was on the midnight train from Lime Street. It was packed and I had to sit on the floor in the corridor all the way to Rugby.

CHAPTER 17

Commissioned

The tailor had been right. Our commissions had come through during the leave. Transport was laid on to take us to Cambridge to collect our new kit. It was ready and waiting for us – a tunic and two pairs of slacks, a raincoat, a beautiful crombie overcoat, two shirts, four collars, a peaked cap and a forage cap, two pairs of socks, a pair of shoes, two ties, leather gloves, brevets and shoulder tabs. Forty-three pounds nine shillings and tenpence the lot, with six pounds ten shillings and tuppence change out of our £50 uniform allowance.

Back at base we packed the rest of our gear and moved into new billets – very superior to the ones we were vacating. It was a room in a block of eight, with curtains and polished floors, the first lit every evening by WAAF orderlies. We had an eighth share in a batman to look after our uniforms, see to our laundry and deal with any of the other domestic chores we'd had to do ourselves for the last three years – in fact, for all of our lives so far. Self-conscious in our brand new uniforms, we made our way to the Officers' Mess, and into another world.

The Mess was spotlessly clean and tidy, with the scent of furniture polish. I was worried that someone might stop me and ask what I was doing there. When someone held a door open for me, I thanked them four or five times. In the entrance foyer an orderly in a white jacket sat at a table to receive or give messages or information to the 'gentlemen' of the Mess. The very large ante-room was carpeted and furnished with writing tables, deep comfortable armchairs, standing ashtrays and occasionasl tables. I was intrigued at the line of footmarks that went up one wall, across the ceiling, and down the other wall.

A large open fireplace dominated the far end of the room

with an arc of armchairs facing it. Off the big lounge was the bar. There were high stools and beer mats, the latter practically extinct in pubs since the start of the war. Stewards, two of them, waited for those officers too tired or too lazy to make their own way to the bar to request delivery of drinks to their armchairs. You could pay at the time for your drinks or sign a chit and pay at the end of the month. All notices on the notice board referred to either 'officers' or to 'gentlemen'.

The dining room was equally impressive, with polished tables, not at all like the unstained trestle types we had been used to. There were also tablecloths and placemats at mealtimes, and the smell of cooking, untainted by the background odour of oil and glycol. The food, served by hand-picked WAAFs in white coats, was infinitely superior to any I'd seen in wartime Britain. Eating times were different too. We still had breakfast, but now, instead of dinner, tea and supper, we had lunch, afternoon tea and dinner, late in the evening.

The behaviour of the occupants of the Mess was also different. It was more relaxed and self-assured, with never a raised voice, and there was lots more vociferous, barking laughter in the evening. There were some delightful WAAF officers, very smart and attractive in their tailored uniforms. They mostly seemed to disappear after dinner.

But despite my fumbling self-consciousness, it was a friendly place, in which we were quickly accepted and put at ease. Within two or three days we had forgotten our shyness and quickly felt much more in touch with life at the top end of the station, and also more informed, on account of the shop talk, opinions expressed and 'gen' passed around. There was very little bad language in the Mess, with WAAF officers frequently within earshot, and never again did we need to go without a pint. All you had to do was sign a chit.

We were being saluted all the time outside the Mess, a bit embarrassing at first. I got an early one from the Station Warrant Officer, no less. A week or two earlier he had eyed me disdainfully in the Sergeants' Mess as I sang the solo part of 'There were Three Jews from Jerusalem'. Yes, life had certainly taken a change for the better, I thought, as I laid my head on a cased pillow after a luxurious hot bath, slipping off to sleep for the first time as Pilot Officer Smith 182405, leaving Fight Sergeant Smith 1438275 behind for ever.

We were given two days stand-down to effect the transition, and as a result missed the first ever daylight raid in strength by Bomber Command on Germany, on 27 August 1944 – the target Hamburg. The seven crews who marked the target, with seven other crews from 105, were instant, if short-lived, celebrities. An Oboe run into the Ruhr in broad daylight had previously been thought suicidal, but while they had received the individual attention of the flak batteries towards the end of the run, the flak had been dispersed and ineffective at the Mosquitoes' height. The heavies had had full fighter cover from Spitfires there and back, and the Luftwaffe had stayed away. There were obviously going to be more like Hamburg.

In the meantime, Johnny and I resumed our contribution on 28 August with a daylight sortie on L'Hey, another flying-bomb launching site. We marked it from 22,000 feet, and we could see the Lancasters 10,000 feet below queuing up, waiting for the markers. They were early owing to a wind change, which many hadn't had time to correct for on the short trip to the French coast. We were actually shot at near the end of the run. The bursts were quite close but we were undamaged. I didn't like it nevertheless.

[28 August 1944. Flying-bomb sites. 150 aircraft – 77 Halifaxes, 48 Lancasters, 25 Mosquitoes – carried out small 'Oboe Leader' raids on 12 sites. Most of the targets were satisfactorily hit. This was the last of the long series of raids on the German flying-bomb launching and storage sites in the Pas-de-Calais area, which was captured by Allied ground troops a few days later.

There was one aircraft casualty. A 550 Squadron Lancaster, which had just bombed the Wemars/Cappel launching site near Amiens, received a direct hit from a flak battery near Dunkirk. The Lancaster went down in flames and exploded. The pilot, Pilot Officer S C Beeson, and 3 other members of the crew escaped by parachute, but the wireless operator and the 2 gunners were killed. Sergeants J K Norgate, H S Picton and J A Trayhorn were thus the last fatal casualties in Bomber Command's campaign against the V-1 flying-bomb.]

But it was another lovely day and we were in the best of spirits on the way home. I flew the aircraft almost back to the South Coast. I had taken the pilot's seat of the Oxford several times at Warboys and Johnny had shown me how to fly it straight and level. It was more difficult changing seats in the cramped cockpit of a Mosquito, and the aircraft dropped a wing and slipped away to port in the middle of the change-over. Johnny, from the navigator's seat, brought her back to an even keel and back on course, then left me to enjoy the delight of flying a Mosquito. It was very foolhardy and fraught with danger, but it didn't occur to either of us that anything untoward could happen to us in an empty cloudless sky. And, of course, we didn't mention it at de-briefing. It was probably a court martial offence.

We had spent the first two evenings in the Mess noting all that was going on, reluctant to do anything that might be considered 'putting up a black'. But after nearly a week our timidity had evaporated and we were joining in the life and style of the Mess, especially in the loud and frivolous buffoonery that frequently developed late in the evening if the extroverts – of which there were quite a few – had been drinking at the bar. I'd noticed that one or two pieces of furniture looked a bit the worse for wear, and I quickly found out why. It was used as a barricade behind which the defending team attempted to defend its territory from the attacking team, massed on the other side. Anything was allowed, except punching, and the battle was over when the attackers reached the wall behind the defenders.

The footsteps up the wall and along the ceiling were another popular event. It was done with soot from the fireplace on the soles of shoes of anyone willing to volunteer for the hazardous task of scaling the stacked tables – assisted by his many helpers – to lie on the top one and plant his feet on the ceiling. Everyone else stood around the stack waiting for the inevitable moment when the planter, his helpers, and the tables came crashing down to land on the armchairs congregated around the climb. Somehow you didn't seem to hurt yourself when you were drunk.

On the last day of August Johnny and I had intended to go to Bedford in the evening to join the Key Club, but thought that it might have to be put off for a day when we found ourselves on the list posted shortly after 0900 hours. As it happened, though, we were on early and were back from St Riquier, a flying-bomb storage depot near Abbeville, in good time to change and catch the bus into Bedford.

[31 August 1944. V-2 rocket stores. 601 aircraft – 418 Lancasters, 147 Halifaxes, 36 Mosquitoes – to attack 9 sites in northern France where the Germans were believed to be storing V-2 rockets. 8 of the sites were found and bombed. 6 Lancasters lost.]

Resplendent in our new uniforms and peaked caps (I was dying to wear the overcoat but it was midsummer), we sallied forth into Bedford and the Key Club. It was a small club with membership restricted to officers. It cost nothing to join, and after filling in an application form we were each issued with a key to the front door, downstairs from the club and fronting on to the street. It was a condition of membership that the door was shut after you when entering or leaving. It was a classy joint with a tremendous stock of alcohol considering it was wartime Britain. The RAF Officers were heavily out-numbered by those of the

American Air Force, but there was never any resentment, even if they did have money to burn and all the smart girls in tow. Their uniforms, too, made ours look plain by comparison. "How the hell d'yuh find the target in the dark?" they would ask. But we couldn't tell even our Allies about Oboe, so we just said, "Radar." We gathered that they probably had Gee in their aircraft, but that once out of range it was visual fixes and visual identification of the target. They gave us graphic descriptions of their long treks in daylight formations deep into Germany, harassed by ME 109s after their fighter cover had run out of range. Their losses were far greater than ours so we didn't envy them their more luxurious lifestyle. A lot of them were stationed at Kimbolton, just a few miles from Little Staughton. We saw their Flying Fortresses almost daily.

On that first night we stayed in the club until time for the bus, and returned to the Mess in high spirits to find it quiet and subdued. Two 109 crews were missing – one from Cologne and the other from Leverkusen. Two in one night – it was unheard of. One of the missing navigators was Freddie Waterman, a jovial Canadian who, with his pilot, Henry A'Court, formed a very popular crew. The other crew were Flight Lieutenant Shaw and his navigator, Flying Officer Bradley. They weren't in B Flight, and we didn't know them as well as the other two, but it was a bad night for 109.

There was no stand-down for us the next day. We had an early call – briefing 0900 hours again. It was exactly 1200 hours when I wrote "Airborne climbing" in my log, prior to setting course for Lumbres, another storage depot near St Omer. Our marking height was 22,000 feet, almost low-level for us. The further into Europe we went, the higher we had to fly, owing to the earth's parabola. And the further we went, the more risk there was of a technical failure. We certainly shouldn't have had one on Lumbres, almost on our doorstep, but we did. The 'cat' signal faded away at B so we did a couple of orbits in the hope that it would reappear. It didn't, so we flew down the run behind a 105 Squadron

Mosquito until it dropped its TIs and we flew back with it to Bourne, which looked even more rural than Little Staughton from the air.

[1 September 1944. V-2 rocket stores. 121 aircraft – 97 Halifaxes, 15 Mosquitoes, 9 Lancasters – of 4 and 8 Groups bombed storage sites at Lumbres and La Pourchinte without loss. Both raids were successful, the Lumbres attack particularly so.]

We landed back at base shortly afterwards, relishing the familiar surroundings as we taxied to dispersal. Little Staughton had become home to us in a very short space of time. It was in the soft folds of the Huntingdonshire countryside, and it was a glorious summer. We felt well pleased at being part of the Pathfinder Force and rejoiced in the recently acquired luxury of the Officers' Mess. Ops too, apart from one or two exceptions, had been very bearable, with skies free of flak, and the points mounting up quickly. And Johnny now had Celia there too, having somehow got her posted from Warboys. I had traced the little WAAF again, and as summer began to give way to autumn, life just couldn't have been better.

On 3 September 1944 the war was five years old and I'd been in the RAF for three of them. The following day, Sunday 4 September, I went to Holy Communion in the station Chapel. Every RAF station had a chapel, even the hastily constructed wartime ones. They were usually huts with an altar at one end – a table draped in purple cloth – with a cross and chalice on it. Some had chairs for the congregation, others six-foot forms. I had celebrated Holy Communion every month since I had reported to Arcytarcy three years ago. Congregations were usually sparse; sometimes I was the only male celebrant among a dozen or so WAAFs. On one occasion I was late and the Padre had started the service on his own. And I always said a silent prayer before take off, even on an NFT. Nothing sophisticated: "O Lord, please bring me safely through this flight", and a little "Thank you, God" as we landed. It had worked so far, occasionally with odds on against.

By coincidence or otherwise, Johnny and I weren't on the ops list for the next five days after I'd been to Communion. We swam in the river in the afternoons and I caught up with my letter-writing in the Mess. Up at 'flights' we had time to read *TEE EM*, the training magazine featuring Pilot Officer Prune, an imaginary pilot with a huge handlebar moustache. He was always 'putting up blacks' and we were expected to profit from them. Every month, somebody – the one who'd put up the biggest black during the month – was awarded the Golden Order of the Irremovable Finger. I didn't know what the connection was until somebody explained it. If you kept your finger in, you couldn't get anything else in, so you had to get your finger out. I still didn't really understand it, but I sort of got the point – if you wanted to succeed, you had to get your finger out. Johnny thought I should have got the award after the Acquet trip, but he was only joking – or so he said.

Our days of leisure couldn't go on for ever, but it was a surprise to be detailed to bomb Emden with five other Mosquitoes on 8 September. The most western of the German ports, right up near Denmark, we had thought Emden was out of Oboe range, and thought the op was probably to find out whether it was. Certainly the signals were pretty ropy when I switched on and they didn't get any better. We had been briefed to drop our bombs on ETA at the release point if the signals faded, so we did, hoping they hit something more than a ploughed field. It had been a late take-off and a long trip – by Mosquito standards – of three hours, so we were tired and glad to get to bed around 0300 hours.

[8 September 1944. Minor operations. 45 Mosquitoes, 6 to Emden and 3 to Steenwijk, 13 RCM sorties, 13 aircraft on Resistance operations. 1 Stirling on a Resistance flight was lost.]

Still sleepy from our lie-in, on arrival at the Mess for lunch Paddy O'Hara – back on the squadron for yet another tour – greeted us with "You're on again tonight."

CHAPTER 18

Back to Germany

The target was Munchen Gladbach, and my fifty-ninth op. It was on the edge of the Ruhr flak belt and had been Guy Gibson's last target – he'd been killed on the way home. It was an innovation night for Oboe. Owing to the frequent failures of the technical equipment, someone had come up with the bright idea of sending two aircraft on the same run – a primary and a reserve. The primary proceeded as normal, but the reserve aircraft was briefed to arrive at the turning-on point one minute after the primary, then to fly down the run on dead reckoning, listening to the primary's signals. Should the signals fail, the ground station would then call in the reserve, who, if his dead reckoning was right, should be close to the 'railway line' and would take over the run.

We were flying as reserve to Flight Lieutenants Gartill and Burnett – take-off 2200 hours. The op was put back two hours, and as we went into the crew room to prepare for the midnight take-off, it was put back another two. Again, we stowed away our gear and went back to the Mess, returning to the crew room at 0100 hours for take-off at 0200. At 0130 we were assured that the further delay of another two hours would be the last.

I felt pretty bloody fed up. The time between the operational meal and take-off was always my worst time, no matter where the target lay. It was the waking equivalent of being unable to sleep due to recurring thoughts and images – always the same ones. I would live through, wide-eyed, the details of the 'slow' seconds, as we would come on beam. The flak would start exploding in my mind. The explosions would get closer and closer. The thoughts and images in my mind would become more jumbled, louder, and more

380

threatening – more like dark, swirling colours than distinct images. Then the dream would evaporate as someone would ask me something, or I would mechanically pick up a newspaper – the thoughts and images would go, leaving an empty fear.

On this occasion the wait had gone on for seven hours. I was so hungry that I had already eaten my operational chocolate ration, and I sat hoping that the op would be scrubbed.

No such luck – and we took off with rumbling stomachs at 0350 hours. Approaching the turning-on point, dawn was beginning to burn jagged edges on the horizon. We listened in to the primary's signals, as we followed him down the run. A – then B, followed by the thrice-repeated Morse letter C. If the signals faded now it would be difficult to settle on the run sufficiently well to achieve a 'cope'. D sounded shortly afterwards in my earphones and, three minutes later, the release. So, not required – and not at all resentful – we turned on to 270 degrees at the end of the two-and-a-half-second dash and were switching off our engines in dispersal as the primary was calling up the watch office for permission to land.

[9 September 1944. München Gladbach. 113 Lancasters and 24 Mosquitoes of 5 and 8 Groups carried out a devastating raid on the centre of this target without loss.]

We weren't on again for three days, during which Freddie Waterman and Henry A'Court arrived back. They'd had to bale out over France and the Americans had brought them back to the UK. The other two – Shaw and Bradley – were also safe and on their way back, and were probably going to be needed by the look of things.

Every operational aircraft in Huntingdonshire seemed to be taking to the air. It was common knowledge that Harris, C-in-C of Bomber Command, was impatient to be back to his primary targets – the German towns. Forced to concentrate his squadrons for the past two months on the launching sites and storage depots, the oil dumps, and the marshalling towns and junctions of the German land forces, he considered these only diversions from his main plan – to obliterate and lay waste the German cities. Now that the Germans were retreating into Germany, Eisenhower's control over Bomber Command had been relinquished, so it was back to Germany – and with a vengeance.

The assault began on the morning of 10 September 1944 while Johnny and I were still in bed after our trip to München Gladbach. We were woken up by the rising din of Fortresses – hundreds of them – joining up in their formations on their way to the Dutch coast. The noise reached a crescendo, and the windows rattled. I could hear Johnny's voice, but couldn't make out the words. The noise drifted away leaving a deeper, but troubled quietness. We went back to sleep, but were woken up again by another lot.

It was the same the next day – Sunday 11 September. There didn't seem to be quite so many on the Monday, but they were back to full strength on the Tuesday.

The RAF was out in strength too, but we saw little of the Lancasters and Halifaxes over Little Staughton. Everyone on 109 seemed to be on ops except us, and the 582 crews kept the mess cooks busy with their frying-pans; they must have been sick of the sight of bacon and eggs. And we joined in on the Wednesday – a day on which 2,000 Allied aircraft bombed Germany.

Briefing was at 1000 hours, the red ribbon stretching unwaveringly to Essen in the heart of the Ruhr. And in broad daylight. As I strained my eyes, I saw it wasn't Essen, but Gelsenkirchen – as close to Essen as Salford is to Manchester. The aiming point was the big oil refinery on the edge of the city. It had been bombed on several occasions but was still refining. Now it was to be the first target to attract a full-scale Bomber Command attack in daylight. The decision to go into Germany in daylight had been taken, so we were told, because Fighter Command was now able to provide cover for the heavies all the way to the target from its new airfields in France. And there had been a marked reluctance on the part of the Luftwaffe to show itself in daylight. But there was still the flak.

My alarm at the sight of the red ribbon jumped to a quiet panic on learning that we were first down the run. We were the primary, with Pete Kleboe and his navigator – Paddy O'Hara – our reserve. They were so totally unaffected by the briefing that I wondered if they knew about the Ruhr. But of course they did – they'd both been there several times. Perhaps that was why. Perhaps familiarity had bred contempt, I reasoned. I tried to mimic their calmness, but it was hopeless. Gone was my smugness of only a week ago. A wave of despondency swept over me. The squadron CO, Group Captain Grant, was speaking but I wasn't listening. I looked at him with envy. A rather quiet man, Canadian, DSO and DFC, he had no need or inclination to brag about his achievements – they were manifold. By his side was Wing Commander Law – again, DSO and DFC – universally liked and respected. Impossible to imagine his ever being in a flap. I envied him too. I looked round the room at the others – Kleboe, Cobbe, Cummings, Thelwall, Palmer, Spedding, Rimmer, Finlater. I felt like a boy among men. What was I doing among these people – they so self-confident, self-reliant and seemingly without fear. And me so utterly devoid of such qualities. I didn't belong there. Why wasn't I sitting at a desk in the accounting section, scratching away with pen and ink every day from 8.30am to 4.30pm, and looking forward to a quiet evening in the NAAFI, cocoa for a nightcap, and bed for 10.00pm. That's where I belonged. But a dig in the ribs from Johnny at synchronisation of watches brought me back inescapably to the ribbon on the wall.

At 25,000 feet approaching the Dutch coast in 'P Peter' we saw below us the Fortresses coming back. They seemed to be everywhere, with their escorts, the Thunderbolts, Lightnings and Mustangs, flanking them with their protective shield. Wherever they had been, there were enough of them to have tested the Germany fighter resistance – still a powerful and efficient force – to the full. But for the moment, it was our turn.

The daylight system of primary and reserve differed from that of the night. The two aircraft flew down the run in formation after joining up with each other at the turning-on point. We were looking out for Pete and Paddy after we had reached 32,000 feet but they were nowhere to be seen. Instead, directly ahead of us and many miles away, a plume of white smoke rose from the ground and up into the sky to a height far and away above our ceiling. Obsessed as I was with flak, I was convinced that this was some new form of threat that would come bearing down on us from above and blow us out of the sky. But it wasn't aimed at us – it was on its way to London. I had seen the very first V2 rocket to be launched against the capital.

I packed away my gear and clambered down into the nose. The sky was cloudless and I could see Germany stretched out below us, and now, fifty yards behind and to starboard – our reserve. I could see the heavies and their fighter escort approaching the target as we moved ahead of them at point A and on to B. The flak, if it was going to be concentrated on us, should start arriving a minute or so after B. In fact it was only thirty seconds on my astro watch before the virgin sky ahead of us was horribly transformed into hideous pock-marked flesh. Within seconds 'P Peter' was rolling unsteadily inside the pin cushion, and into a world of red and black hostility – the reds translucent and murderous, the blacks lingering and intimidating. They struck at us without warning, anonymous from breach-block to sky six miles above. The plane tried to ignore them, impervious to the blasts and body blows from the reds, returning unerringly to her course, coaxed and cajoled by Johnny. White-knuckled hands clutching her controls, he focused aggressively on the instruments in front of him. Height, speed, heading – the crucial ingredients – were brought back time and again to perfection, the merest hint of dot or dash instantly extinguished. Braced tense in my seat, I followed his gaze, preferring the familiar friendly scene inside the cockpit to that of the blacks rushing at us and past us at 300 miles an hour. Light-headed, hardly breathing, I tightened my mask and turned up the oxygen. Where the hell was C – it seemed ages since we'd left B. I flinched at every bang, defenceless against the onslaught. Dah-di-dah-di. Dah-di-BANG. Dah-di-dah-di. Still another five excruciating minutes to release. The bursts seemed to be moving ahead of us a bit with not quite so many around us. Suddenly I remembered our reserve, and turned to look for it. It was still there, tucked in close – close enough for me to see holes in the fuselage. It flipped a wing up, tossed by yet another near miss, then fell away underneath us out of sight. Seconds later, as the first D came through, I instinctively reached for the bomb tit, but as I did so we banked steeply to port, climbed then dived, lifting me off my seat. I thought we were going down and glanced wide-eyed over at Johnny.

Holding the stick over and forward with his left hand, he was waving his right hand indicating an abort, and shaking his head. The sky around us was suddenly unblemished. I switched over to intercom. The needles on the instrument panel were spinning around as, nose down, we headed on to 090 degrees – into Germany – but out of that hateful place, the Ruhr. Then Johnny's voice on the intercom: "Signal died on me – you all right?"

"Yes – are you?" And conscious of the anxiety in my voice, he turned his head in my direction – a nod of the head and a wink of an eye was all that was needed in reply. I looked at him again. He'd flown 'P Peter' down that horrendous run with classic quality, seemingly insensible to the imminence of the direct hit that would have blown us apart. Little more than a year older than me, he had become one of the men.

[13 September 1944. Gelsenkirchen. 140 aircraft – 102 Halifaxes of 4 Group and 28 Lancasters and 10 Mosquitoes of

8 Group – attacked the Nordstern oil plant. Large explosions were seen through the smoke-screen. 2 Halifaxes lost.]

Our groundcrew, lying on the grass at dispersal awaiting our return, watched us taxi round the perimeter track to join them, then moved in as the engines were cut. They opened the bottom hatch and took out the ladder, put the chocks under 'P Peter', and started counting the holes. Her tail had been peppered, as had the rear of the fuselage, but the wings, cockpit and engines were undamaged. We climbed down the ladder in time to see our reserve touch down. We already knew that they were all right – we'd heard them call up the watch office as we were in the funnel. We sat on the grass with the groundcrew, smoking cigarettes, waiting for the MT van, telling them about the raid and the flak, not unduly displeased that it had all been in vain, with the markers still nestling in the bomb bays. The crew on the other channel must have coped. Markers had been burning three minutes after our abort.

The groundcrew lads were in the cockpit and on the wings of 'P Peter' even before our transport had left the concrete circle to pick up the Wingco and Paddy at their dispersal. We were looking forward to swapping stories. They would have heard the 'cat' signal fade at D, too late for them to be called in to take over, and would have turned for home at the same time as us. We hadn't seen them after they had seemed to fall away underneath us out of control.

They greeted us with wide smiles, and threw their gear into the van before climbing in beside us. They had been damaged more than we, with big holes in their fuselage and ailerons. And Paddy had been demoted in flight. He was full of it. The flak burst that had blown them under our tail had sent a piece of shrapnel through the back of the cockpit canopy behind Paddy's head, and had torn away one of the bars of rank on his left shoulder. On his right shoulder he was a Flight Lieutenant, on his left only a Flying Officer. Already his vivid imagination was running wild with embroideries on the story that he would now recount for years to come – of how the Germans had demoted him. Six inches to the right of his shoulder tab was the back of his neck, but that didn't seem to have occurred to him at the time. If it had, he didn't mention it.

At interrogation I expected them to join me in an expression of disapproval of raids on the Ruhr in broad daylight, but they seemed to have relished the bumpy ride. And the crews behind us had reported only moderate flak at their height, and those behind them hardly any at all. So it was at least consoling to learn that once the markers were down, those behind had been comparatively untroubled. And we wouldn't be first down next time. I had my usual post-'dicey do' depression in the Mess after dinner, and as a raucous evening was beginning to develop, I left early and went to bed. God, how I hated the Ruhr Valley. And my story of the white vapour trail from ground level to well over our height had received scant interest from the Intelligence Officer. If he knew what it was, he wasn't saying, and I was the only one who seemed to have seen it. Within a week everybody had seen them.

But as normal, my memory had conveniently decided to put the previous day behind it and I enjoyed breakfast in the Mess the next morning. There was a choice of tea or coffee, and I lingered over the decision. I was hoping to have the day off so that I could collect the bicycle from St Neots that Dad had sent me to replace the one I'd been issued with – much to Johnny's relief. Up at 'flights' it was a full house with nobody having been on late the night before. About ten o'clock Johnny and I were called into the Flight Commander's office and presented with our Pathfinder wings. They were awarded 'temporarily' after about ten marking ops, and if you progressed to the veteran stage and near the end of a tour, you got a permanent award with a certificate to prove it, signed by AVM Bennett. We were delighted and couldn't wait to get them up. With no ops listed by lunchtime, we went back to the hut after we had eaten to put the new badge on our tunics. It was in the shape of an RAF eagle and went on the flap of the top pocket on the left side, under the flying brevet and medal ribbons. They weren't worn with battle dress, in case you had to bale out and were captured – the German interrogators had a special interest in Pathfinder aircrew. Johnny was going to take me on the Manxman to St Neots to collect my bicycle and Celia was coming with us, sitting in the middle. I always enjoyed that.

CHAPTER 19

Friendly Encounters

We were stood down late in the afternoon, so, changed and sporting our Pathfinder wings, we picked Celia up at the WAAFery and made for St Neots railway station. The new bike – second-hand new – was a cracker. It had three gears and a complicated chain arrangement, which Johnny viewed with some apprehension. I was going to ride it back to the aerodrome, six or seven miles away, so I left them after a pint and pedalled off over the bridge. I stopped off at the little pub to show them my new bike and my badge and they bought me a pint on the strength of them. I'd already forgotten Gelsenkirchen.

There was a decidedly autumnal nip in the air the next day, just what I'd been waiting for – a chance to wear my greatcoat. It was the most luxurious coat I'd ever had by a long way, with a stiffened epaulet on each shoulder, huge lapels, and a buckled belt. And the peaked cap really set it off. We had taken the wires out and left the caps trussed up with string for a few days so that the front stood up straight and the sides hung down. They looked more military that way and almost everybody did it – except for the adjutant. I caught the bus into Bedford. Now that Johnny had Celia around, I had to go scouting for girls alone. I made for the Key Club. I wasn't happy about leaving my greatcoat in the cloakroom, but I couldn't wear it at the bar. I combed my hair in the mirror and pressed the little wave into place at the front – I'd had to run my finger round the jar of Brylcreme to get enough out. I lit up a Gold Flake and, one hand in trouser pocket, took a high stool at the little bar. Pint tankard in hand, I looked around the room. There were about a dozen officers and five or six girls, including a stunning brunette. I had seen her there before, and at the dance, in the company of a Flight Lieutenant from 582 Squadron. He was a pilot, a tall, good-looking Clark Gable type. They seemed to be having a row and she looked over towards me. I hastily turned my eyes elsewhere, pretending I hadn't been looking. A minute or so later, out of the corner of my eye, I saw here get up and walk towards the bar. She sat down next to me, and we smiled at each other.

"Are you going to dance?" she asked, as I thought, by way of conversation.

"Er – yes – I am, as a matter of fact."

A short pause, then she said, "Would you like to take me?" I couldn't believe my ears – it sounded too good to be true. On the point of replying "Not arf," I remembered my new status. "I'd be delighted to, but what about your pilot friend?"

"He's a beast," she retorted, and moved her stool closer, as her friend made for the door. She turned her back on him and smiled sweetly at me as she sipped her gin and tonic.

She was wearing a pink and blue chenille dress – low cut, tight round the hips, with buttons all the way down the front. We talked for a while – mostly about her – had another drink, then collected our coats from the cloakroom. It was only a few minutes walk to the dance and we walked there hand in hand. I was careful to walk on the outside of the pavement, and to change sides when we crossed the road, taking her elbow to guide her across, like Dad always did with ladies. The rest of the evening was idyllic. We danced every dance together, except when we had to change partners in the Paul Jones. She pressed her breast against my chest, and I felt very restricted and uncomfortable. I bought coffee and biscuits in the interval and at the end we stood shoulder to shoulder for God Save The King.

She lived near the dance hall. Near her house we went into a dark shop doorway to say goodnight. She moved in close, and lifted her lips invitingly. After about ten minutes I plucked up the courage to unbutton her dress. She moved back a little, and put both arms around my neck. "Won't you miss the bus?" she whispered.

"I don't care – I'd rather be with you," I answered, my voice surprising me with its huskiness. I fondled her breasts. They were full and firm. She grunted and I swallowed involuntarily. Trembling, I reached a hand down to her thigh, lifting her dress. She withdrew her lips. Softly she murmured, "Not now – not here." Reluctantly I removed my hand and she looked up at me. "I've got to go in now. I'll see you tomorrow night if you like. We'll go for a walk." Did I like? She buttoned her dress, combed her hair, and I walked her to her door. We arranged to meet the following night outside the Key Club at seven o'clock, and she stroked my cheek as we parted.

I set off on the Kimbolton road. I felt elated. My genitals felt light. I had been in the RAF just over three years and was still 'virgo intacta'. All the girls I'd been out with up to now had been nice girls, and nice girls didn't do it before they were married. But now I was on the edge of the big breakthrough, and tomorrow night couldn't come quickly enough. I was glad to get an early lift from an army lorry.

Johnny was asleep when I got in so I couldn't tell him about the girl in the Key Club. He would know the one. He'd noticed her there on our first visit. I lay awake – I couldn't go to sleep, wondering what the next night would be like. I kept remembering what she had said. "Not now – not here." That implied that it was only the time and the place that had deterred her. There would be lots of time and lots of places if we went for a walk, and it would be dark by nine o'clock. My imagination ran riot. At last, at twenty-one and a half, I was going to make it with a girl. Everything looked set fair, and nothing was going to stop me now. I would wear my raincoat – didn't want to get my greatcoat muddy. And who knows how it would progress afterwards? It might even become regular. I felt a bit guilty about Drus, but what the eye can't see the heart won't grieve. And I must call in at the station barber shop to buy a condom. I thought I'd better not trust the packet in my field dressing pocket – it was three years old. I drifted off into sleep, immersed in my fantasies.

The first thing I thought about when I woke up in the

morning was my date for the night. The anticipation had been so dominant in my mind that I hadn't thought about the possibility of my not being able to keep it. The disappointment of finding that we were on a night op was almost unbearable, even painful. I still might die before I know what it is like to have a woman. The disappointment turned into the now familiar dread when I learned the target. It was the airfield at Steenvijk in Holland – surely that could have waited for another night. I felt cheated and victimised. I wondered whether anybody had ever done a swap on ops and was astonished at my puerility. And as I reached for the tit in 'M Mother' at 2300 hours, the irony of the act struck home hard and painful. A perfect 'cope' from 30,000 feet held no compensation whatsoever for what I had missed out on.

[16 September 1944. Operation Market Garden. Bomber Command's main operations on this night were in support of the landings by British and American airborne troops at Arnhem and Nijmegen, which took place the following morning.

200 Lancasters and 23 Mosquitoes of 1 and 8 Groups bombed the airfields at Hopsten, Leeuwarden, Steenwijk and Rheine, and 54 Lancasters and 5 Mosquitoes of 3 and 8 Groups bombed a flak position at Moerdijk. The runways of all the airfields were well cratered but there were only near misses at the flak positions, although its approach road was cut. 2 Lancasters lost from the Moerdijk raid.]

It had been an early op, and I was still cursing my luck the following morning when the news of operation Market Garden broke. The airborne assault on the bridges at Eindhoven, Nijmegen and Arnhem had started at dawn, and Steenvijk had been one of four Dutch airfields heavily bombed during the night to crater the runways and stop the Luftwaffe from taking off to attack the gliders and troop-carriers. I was completely indifferent to the revelation – my thoughts centred on that girl, and how to get in touch with her.

It was going to be difficult. I didn't know where she lived, having failed to notice where we had walked to from the dance, and all the streets looked the same in the black-out. I knew she wasn't on the telephone at home, and the question of where she worked during the day hadn't been raised. She had probably fumed at having been stood up and was probably already looking for another fellow, as she had me on discarding the Flight Lieutenant at the Key Club. I had to find her again quickly. So near and yet so far again from my first coition, she was my primary objective – indeed, the only one in view. I had discarded the little WAAF, who had promised similar possibilities – not from choice, but at the 'suggestion' of a frighteningly large Flight Sergeant gunner of 582 Squadron. So I went to Bedford the next night almost straight from Boulogne. We had been woken at 0700 hours for briefing at 0830 hours, and were to mark the French port for a force of 750 Lancasters and Halifaxes. The Allied armies had by-passed the Channel ports after the capture of Cherbourg and Le Havre and struck out for Paris and Brussels, leaving a containing force to keep the remaining Germans trapped in Boulogne and the Pas de Calais. They had refused to surrender, so Eisenhower had called on Bomber Command again.

[17 September 1944. Boulogne. 762 aircraft – 370 Lancasters, 351 Halifaxes, 41 Mosquitoes – dropped more than 3,000 tons of bombs on German positions around Boulogne in preparation for an attack by Allied troops. The German garrison surrendered soon afterwards. 1 Halifax and 1 Lancaster lost.]

One raid on Boulogne proved sufficient, and the German Commander surrendered as soon as the raid was over. Nine thousand Germans were taken prisoner, and Bomber Command received a message the following day from Lieutenant Generals Crere and Simmonds of the First and Second Canadian Army Corps: "Timing and accuracy of bombs on target excellent and devastating. At least half

freedom of city owed to Bomber Command." But my second
sortie of the day was abortive. I failed to find the girl in the
Key Club or in any of the pubs in the vicinity, and my efforts
to retrace the walk from the Corn Exchange to her home
were unsuccessful.

I went again the next night. There was a dance at the Corn
Exchange and I hoped she would be there, but she wasn't.
Totally obsessed with my search, and again not listed, I went
for the third night in succession. I found her at last in the Key
Club, in the company of a Captain in the USA Army Air
Corps. She gave me a fleeting smile as they left the club for
whatever they were planning for the rest of the evening.
Perhaps she was taking him for a walk – the one she had
been going to take with me. I felt so miserable, I could have
cried in my beer. I was as far away from it as ever, and in the
depths of despair again. Was I ever going to do it? I still got
a spotty face from time to time, and somebody had told me
it was because I wasn't doing it. I finished my pint and
ordered another. I had a whisky too. Then another. I must
have looked the picture of misery, and when the barman
asked, "Are you all right, Sir?" I thought I'd better return to
base. I caught the early bus back to camp and went to the
Mess for a last pint before going to bed.

I wandered disconsolately into the ante-room, to find one
of those spontaneous and unplanned occasions rapidly
gaining momentum. As I had been told, they happened
from time to time when, quite by accident, the usual
ringleaders – not on ops, not dining out, and not
womanising – had drifted up to the Mess for a quick pint
before the bar closed, to find each other there at a similar
loose end.

There were about twenty officers there, encouraging
Ferdy to 'drink chug a lug'. He had to down a pint at one go
while they sang the ritual "Here's to Ferdy, he's true blue,
he's a drunkard through and through, he's a drunkard so
they say, he wants to go to heaven but he'll go the other way,
so drink chug a lug, chug a lug, chug a lug."

I bought myself a pint and sat watching. One of the senior

officers ordered "Extension on the bar", resulting in long faces on the part of the bar staff, who had seen it all before and knew they were going to be long out of bed.

Tiring of 'chug a lug', the obstacle course was laid out in the middle of the room – chairs and tables that had to be climbed over while balancing a pint of beer on your head. The dry-cleaners in Bedford loved this one. The spectators shouted encouragement, and, beginning to feel pleasantly relaxed after another pint, I heard one of them telling another of one of the assembled group's extraordinary ability to paralyse anyone by manipulating nerve points in their body while they lay face down on the floor. "Balls," the other replied. "He certainly can, I've seen him do it. He's done it to me. I'll get him to show you. Hey, Mike!" he shouted to one of the group. "Come and show Rawlings your paralysing trick – I'll volunteer."

"Ah no, not tonight," Mike replied from nearby. "I'm going to bed."

"Ah come on – he doesn't believe you can do it." They all joined in. "Yes – come on – show us again," they chorused, so, although seemingly reluctant to prove his know-how, he took off his tunic, rolled up his sleeves, and moved into the centre of the room. His volunteer lay face down on the floor – arms and legs extended.

I watched intrigued from the circle that quickly gathered round the participants. The paralyser stood over the prostrate volunteer, reached down with his hands, feeling for the pressure points in the shoulders, arms, back, and legs, and pressing hard on each one in turn. Seemingly satisfied with his manipulation, he stood aside and triumphantly announced his volunteer paralysed.

Grunting and grimacing, the inert volunteer twitched and trembled, striving to release himself from the disabling effect of nerves rendered quiescent by the manipulator. Unable to move, he gave up the struggle and lay motionless. Those in the circle, witnessing the act for the first time, murmured their astonishment, until the recumbent figure – still able to speak – pleaded to be released. Watched in silence, the paralyser stood astride his victim, bent down and felt again for the nerves that had been immobilised, and as he stood up, the prone figure rolled over on to his back, stretched, and scrambled to his feet, none the worse.

Instantly the silence was broken by exclamations of appreciation of the ease with which the manipulator had practised his art. "Amazing, extraordinary, unbelievable," they professed their astonishment. "And can you do it to anyone?" they asked.

"No, it's like hypnosis – some are easy, some difficult, and others impossible. The young and thin are the most difficult – like young Smithy here – he'd be able to break free easily."

Their attention moved in my direction.

"Come on then – let's see you do it on Smithy," they chorused.

"No – I'd rather not try. I know I couldn't do him." He seemed so sure that he would fail, and beginning to enjoy the centre stage, I joined in the exchanges. It would be a feather in my cap if I could resist his expertise. Something to brag about later on. "Yes, come on – try me," I piped up, encouraged by my supporters.

"Yes – come on – try Smithy – bet you can't!" they taunted.

"Oh all right – but I know I can't."

I pulled off my tunic, helped by several hands, and confidently stretched myself out on the floor – face down – arms and legs outstretched. "Good old Smithy!" they shouted, before silence again descended as the reluctant Mike bent over me. He pressed on my elbows, the back of my neck, and fumbled for his objectives in the middle of my back. I couldn't feel anything happening to me and I flexed my fingers to prove I still could. He'd been right – he couldn't do it to me.

But he tried to the last – moving down with his probing fingers to my ankles. The crowd had been quiet until then, but as he did so, a few of them gave involuntary – quickly stifled – titters. I felt one of my ankles being gripped and then my leg being lifted from the floor. He hadn't done that to the first volunteer. Faces within my view were breaking into grins and I sensed that something was about to happen to me that hadn't happened to the other person. I lifted my chin from the floor and started to turn my head round towards my feet. But too late. I gasped as the cold torrent swept down my trouser leg, engulfing my private parts in a pint of mild and bitter.

The raucous laughter, which instantly erupted, cut right through me. The disappointment at the Key Club, temporarily assuaged by the prospect of adulation from my seniors, but now exacerbated by this blatant exposure of my naiveté, released waves of conflicting emotions. I felt them surge through my body. Initially – and fortunately for me, momentarily – distress, verging on tears. But as I leapt to my feet, soaked from the waist down, a wave of anger, and the thought of my new uniform trousers swamped in sticky beer, thudded at my temples.

I flung myself fists flying at the practical joker who had found me a sitting duck – naive and gullible as a boy in short pants. The merriment around me exploded anew as many restraining hands hauled me away and sat me on a stool at the bar. Pats on the back, a pint thrust into my hands, and shouts of "Well done Smithy!" all indicated that my anger, and the desire to punch the paralyser in the teeth, was the normal reaction to the deception. And gradually, apart from the discomfort from my waist down, I began to enjoy myself. I was the centre of attraction and it felt reassuring to be patted on the back and called "Good old Smithy" by such as these. Only the walk back to the hut was unpleasant, feeling stickier and stickier with every step. But the showers were warm and relaxing and the other blokes in the billet promised me that my pants would be as good as new after they had been dry-cleaned. I wasn't so sure from the look of them, but they all seemed sure of the dry-cleaner's art from their own experiences of spilt beer.

So it had been an eventful night, and I was expected not to tell Johnny about having been paralysed in the hope that he would be the next victim. Though he wouldn't have cared much. He was too happy having Celia around again to let anything so trivial disturb his bliss.

I took my trousers to be cleaned in Bedford the next afternoon wearing a pair borrowed from Bob Palmer, one of the eight inhabitants of our hut; my spare pair hadn't fitted properly and were back with the tailor in Cambridge to be altered. Bob was a Flight Lieutenant pilot on his second tour of ops – he'd done a first tour in Wellingtons like me. He'd been in the Mess the night before, pint in hand as I always remembered him. Everybody remembered Bob Palmer for the posthumous Victoria Cross he won three months later, flying a Lancaster in daylight over Cologne on his 110th op. Oboe equipment had been installed in a 582 Lancaster that was leading a force of 25 other Lancasters in formation on a precision bombing attack on the marshalling yards in Cologne, which was a focal point for troops moving to the battle zone. The bombers formed up on Bob's leading Lancaster with instructions to drop their bombs on seeing the leader drop his. Everything hinged upon a successful run by the Oboe Lancaster. Cloud cover had been forecast at the target, but in the event the run was made in clear skies, and in the face of intense and accurate heavy flak. Bob's aircraft was hit several times and was on fire at point D, but carried on to the aiming point to release its bombs at the briefed height, speed and heading. The other Lancasters followed suit and the marshalling yards were virtually destroyed. But Bob's Lancaster was by this time a mass of flames and it crashed on the city with no survivors.

CHAPTER 20

Nine to Five

It was another three days, and six days after the raid on Boulogne, before we were on ops again, rare indeed for a 109 crew in the late summer and autumn of 1944. Not to our liking, the offensive had really switched back to Germany, and it was no surprise to find that the target on the night of 23 September was the heavily defended town of Neuss, on the other side of the Rhine from Dusseldorf. We were aiming at the oil refinery – take-off 1930 hours – and it would be dark by the time we got over the target.

We were a primary on this one, our reserves being Flying Officers Relph and Cresswell. Our signals faded early into the run, and we were spared the joyride through the flak, which we could see ahead of us above the 10/10ths cloud that covered the target. Our reserve settled on the run quickly after being called in, and we heard him reach B and C. But then his signals faded out as well. There didn't seem to be much happening over the target as we took a backward look. The flak above the clouds had subsided and there was no glow from below them to indicate that anybody else had coped. It seemed to be becoming increasingly difficult to achieve a 'cope' on German targets, but no doubt the back-room boys were working on it, and in any case it wasn't our problem. It just meant that we missed out on the flak at the aiming point, and we were back in the Mess a little earlier.

[23 September 1944. Neuss. 549 aircraft – 378 Lancasters, 154 Halifaxes, 17 Mosquitoes – of 1, 3, 4 and 8 Groups. 5 Lancasters and 2 Halifaxes lost. Bomber Command's report states that most of the bombing fell in the dock and factory areas. A short local report only says that 617 houses and 14 public buildings were destroyed or seriously damaged, and that 289 people were killed and 150 injured.]

It had been past midnight by the time we had been de-
briefed and were sitting down to our bacon and egg after the
Neuss trip. It was a bit late for our usual games of billiards
and darts before going to bed after an evening op, but we
played out the ritual. It seemed to erase whatever thoughts
still lingered about any traumas we'd had on the op, and
brought us back to normality. What could be 'more normal'
than two blokes having a quiet game of billiards late at night
before going to bed. I never once beat Johnny at billiards,
hard as I tried, but then he never beat me at darts. And by the
time we'd walked back to the billet, we'd forgotten all about
losing our signals three hours ago over a German town we'd
never heard of before.

We didn't expect to be on the list for the next day and lay
in bed until an SP arrived on his bicycle around 1100 hours
to tell us we were on again – briefing 1200 hours – obviously
a daylight op, and probably Germany. The crew room was
packed with crews when we arrived, all waiting for the
briefing in the nearby ops room.

My frown as the target was disclosed turned into a
positive beam at the sight of the red ribbon cutting itself
short at the closest possible target – Calais. With the run to
the target beginning and ending over the English Channel,
and on a pleasant autumn afternoon, I could almost taste the
proverbial piece of cake. And the aiming point was
agreeable too – German troops.

After Boulogne, it was now Calais's turn to be cleared of
the trapped Wehrmacht. And they were sitting ducks. No
danger this time of bombing our own lads who were
standing well back from the aiming point, and with the
tracking stations in close proximity, the Oboe Mosquitoes
dropped their markers relentlessly throughout the raid. We
had a thirty-yard error from 22,000 feet – almost low-level
by our norms – and saw our sky markers ignite over the
10/10ths cloud that covered the target. We might have been
on an ops exercise from Warboys, my only disappointment
being that there had not been enough time to swap seats and
back again before crossing the South Coast.

[24 September 1944. Calais. 188 aircraft – 101 Lancasters, 62 Halifaxes, 25 Mosquitoes. The German positions were completely covered by cloud at 2,000 feet and only 126 aircraft bombed. Most of these bombed Oboe-aimed sky marker., but some aircraft came below cloud to bomb visually and 7 Lancasters and 1 Halifax were shot down by light flak, which was very accurate at such a height.]

We touched down at 1805 hours, just one hour and fifty minutes after take-off. It was 2000 hours by the time we were leaving the dining room. The billiards tables were booked so I wrote my letters at a table in a corner of the ante-room: the daily one to Drus, the fortnightly one to Mother and Dad, the monthly one to Nan and Grandad, and to anybody else to whom I owed a letter. I wrote to Jack Barnes, my cousin, who was a sergeant in the REME now. I didn't know his present address so wrote to the last one I had as the only option. Letters rarely failed to find the addressee sooner or later; while at Kairouan I had received a letter addressed to me at Miami, which had crossed the Atlantic to Canada, down the eastern seaboard of America to Miami, back up again to Moncton, then back across the sea to the UK where it probably got temporarily stuck in the bottom of a mailbag. On its discovery, it was progressed via Bobbington, Chipping Warden, Croft Spa, Moreton-in-Marsh, Algiers and finally to Kairouan, arriving thirteen months after Mother had posted it in the pillar box at the bottom of King Street, Manchester, on her way to the office.

I wrote to 'Scottie' – John William Laurie, a Scot from Peebles, another navigator and, after Paddy, my closest friend. He was on a second tour in France in the Wellingtons of a night reconnaissance squadron. I wrote to Pearl in answer to a letter I'd received via Mother. She had – for the third time – confirmed her intention of visiting England after the war was over, so I told her that I had become engaged to be married and I never heard from her again.

I left the Mess at nearly 0100 hours after posting my letters in the post box by the front door. Johnny was asleep as I put the light out in the billet at 0130 hours. Unless something woke me up, I wouldn't open my eyes again for seven hours, with just enough time to make breakfast by 0900 hours.

It wasn't something, but someone, who woke me up at 0430 hours, just three hours after I'd pulled the sheets up around my neck. I didn't take kindly to being woken up in the early hours, even when gently shaken and called 'Sir' by a corporal SP. "Briefing in forty-five minutes, Sir – please sign here." I signed where his finger pointed and resumed my prone position 'for just another few minutes', which would have been curtains again but for my intrepid captain of aircraft, already half-dressed and making obscene threats if I didn't get up pronto. With five minutes to go to briefing, I was pedalling sleepy-eyed twenty yards behind him, the taste of Macleans toothpaste fresh in my mouth.

Calais again – take-off 0830 hours. Time for a couple of hours on the bed in the billet in the afternoon before a night out in Bedford.

[25 September 1944. Calais. 872 aircraft – 430 Lancasters, 397 Halifaxes, 45 Mosquitoes – were again sent to bomb German defensive positions but encountered low cloud. Only 287 aircraft were able to bomb, through breaks in the cloud. No aircraft lost.]

Couldn't be better. A good 'cope', back in dispersal by 1030 hours, two hours sleep after lunch and dressed ready for dinner by 1900 hours couldn't have been more civilised. But I didn't get to Bedford. I joined the drinking session in the Mess instead and went to bed drunk. My head thumped sickeningly when the same corporal SP woke me up at 0600 hours and left with my indecipherable signature. Take-off was 1000 hours, and the aiming point had been moved a few miles to Cap Gris Nez, where Hitler had stood to gloat at the sight of the white cliffs of Dover after the fall of France.

It was a big raid with over 700 heavies aiming at four sites marked by the Mosquitoes. The flak around the main force was intense, and one Lancaster crashed in the middle of the red TIs. As we watched, a line of yellow markers went down across the bombing run dropped by the 'long stop'. He was a recent addition to the Pathfinder Force, designed to stop 'creep back'. The tendency of bomb-aimers to drop their bombs at first sight of a red at the cross-wire of their bomb-sight inevitably resulted in hits creeping back from the aiming point. The yellow markers dropped by the 'long stop' on the instructions of the Master Bomber indicated 'no bombs this side of the line', and woe betide any bomb-aimer whose aiming point photograph showed him short of the line.

[26 September 1944. Calais area. 722 aircraft – 388 Lancasters, 289 Halifaxes, 45 Mosquitoes – carried out 2 separate raids. 531 aircraft were dispatched to 4 targets at Cap Gris Nez and 191 aircraft to 3 targets near Calais. Accurate and concentrated bombing was observed at all targets. 2 Lancasters were lost.]

The one raid on Boulogne had been enough to induce its garrison commander to surrender, but obviously the one at Calais didn't anguish over the needless loss of his troops in a hopeless cause, as the torch shining in my eyes the next morning at 0430 hours confirmed. But in fact I had hoped for another early-morning raid on Calais. We were going on a week's leave the next morning – we got leave every six weeks while on ops – and an op in the morning would hopefully ensure that we wouldn't be on ops the night before our leave started. So we were in good heart after our fourth successive daylight raid on Calais as we made for the Mess and our bacon and egg.

[27 September 1944. Calais area. 341 aircraft – 222 Lancasters, 84 Halifaxes, 35 Mosquitoes – of 1, 3, 4 and 8 Groups. The target areas were covered by cloud but the Master Bomber brought the force below this to bomb visually. The attacks on the various German positions were accurate and only 1 Lancaster was lost.]

We were packed and in bed by 2000 hours ready for a flying start out of camp at 0800 hours the next morning. I was going first to Pontefract where Drus was doing her initial training with the ATS, and as it wasn't far from Middlesbrough, I reluctantly accepted a lift on the Manxman, thankfully knowing that it would be for the last time. Johnny was swapping it for a second-hand car his father had bought for him.

I was looking forward even more than usual to this leave – my first in my new uniform, and with the unique Pathfinder Force badge to boot. But it was 1230 hours the next day before we left the perimeter fence behind us after having been to Calais yet again in 'K King'. We had marked the target first from 22,000 feet with four green TIs and came back downhill all the way.

[28 September 1944. Calais area. 494 aircraft – 230 Lancasters, 214 Halifaxes, 50 Mosquitoes – of 1, 3, 6 and 8 Groups to attack 4 German positions at Calais and 6 battery positions at Cap Gris Nez; approximately 50 aircraft were allocated to each position. Only 68 aircraft bombed at Calais before the Master Bomber cancelled the raid because of worsening cloud conditions and only 198 (from 301) aircraft bombed at Cap Gris Nez. No aircraft were lost.]

We were halfway through de-briefing before the next crew had started their rum and coffee. Still in battledress, we pedalled our way up to the Mess, had our meal, changed into full uniform, and were setting course due north on the Manxman exactly 105 minutes after we had landed. This was just about the same time as the Germans at Calais were surrendering to the Canadians. I hadn't even stopped to write up the op in the log book, which I usually did right away; it had been my sixty-eighth. But ops were the last things on our minds as we sped along the Great North Road, singing 'She'll be Wearing Tartan Bloomers when She Comes'.

Johnny dropped me off at a seedy-looking hotel in

Pontefract with a 'Vacancies' sign in the window. We weren't sorry to see the back of each other. We had lived in each other's pockets for the last six weeks and had experienced together every emotion from great elation to abject fear. "Have a good leave," I said as I lifted myself thankfully off the pillion seat. "And you," he grunted as he sped off without a backward glance.

 After I had booked in at the almost empty hotel, I had a tepid bath that cost me sixpence and, resplendent in my greatcoat and peaked cap, I made my way to the nearby ATS camp to wait by the guardroom at 1900 hours for Drus to appear. I was quite dismayed at first sight of her in uniform. Drus the civilian had been an exceptionally attractive young woman, but the Army had quite definitely done nothing for her at all. Her uniform had to be worn as issued, with skirt well below the knee, horrid thick stockings and even more horrid low-heeled shoes. Her ample bust had virtually disappeared beneath a tightly buttoned tunic, but I assumed it was still there somewhere. As I expected, she flung her arms round me when we met, but instead of rapturous smiles, there were floods of tears. Between her sobs, and in answer to my condolences, she said tearfully, "I've lost my irons."

 At first she was inconsolable at the loss of her 'irons' – her issued knife, fork and spoon – which had disappeared from her locker. "Do what everybody else does," I said. "Pinch somebody else's." This didn't go down at all well and the tears flowed anew as we walked back to the hotel. I tried another tack. "I'll buy you a set from Woollies tomorrow."

 "But they'll know they're from Woollies, won't they?" she protested. True – the ones at Woollies had bone handles and could hardly be mistaken for service irons. Finally, I persuaded her to report to her corporal that they had been stolen from her locker, which brought the smile back to her face.

 On arrival at the hotel, we went up to my room to spruce ourselves up for the local hop. The proprietor was waiting for us at the bottom of the stairs when we came down – a stern, reproving look on his face. He remonstrated with me for taking Drus up to my room and indignantly asserted that 'things like that' weren't allowed in his hotel. I must confess that the possibility of 'things like that' had crossed my mind, but as I knew that it would have been a non-starter, I'd quickly discarded the idea – reluctantly. His rebukes only added insult to injury, so assuming the air of an officer and a gentleman, I told him to piss off and said I wouldn't stay another night in his pathetic little dump. He stomped off to his office and we giggled our way to the dance hall.

It was a good dance too, with an RAF dance band – not the famous Squadronaires, but nearly as good. There were several RAF aircrew there, and most of them seemed to know Drus. My God, I thought, she's only been here two weeks and already knows all the aircrew for miles around. One of them remarked to her, "Might have known you'd have a fella in the Pathfinder Force," which did wonders for both our egos. She had to be back in camp by eleven o'clock, and we kissed goodnight outside the guardroom together with about two hundred other couples.

I stayed another night in Pontefract – in a different hotel – and spent the rest of my leave in Wallasey via a night in Salford. Civilians were fascinated by stories of operations over Germany and hung on every word. I told them everything, except of course about Oboe, and again I didn't tell Mother about the flak. She absolutely beamed when an Army sergeant marching a squad of soldiers gave them the 'eyes right' as they passed me on our way to Grove Road Station to catch the train to Lime Street.

I was glad to be going back to normality after the artificial existence of the past week. After more than three years in uniform, I felt awkward and out of place among civilians and the trappings of a civilian existence in unattractive wartime Britain. Eagerly looked forward to, leave inevitably dragged on to its boring close.

The second battle of the Ruhr had started on 6 October with a 500-bomber raid on Dortmund, just about the same time that I had been having a few last-night-of-leave pints in the Nelson. I was first back at Little Staughton on 7 October. Johnny arrived back at midnight and woke me up. God, he looked awful. He always did on his return from leave. God knows what he got up to. We filled each other in with our news, and just made breakfast after only a few hours' sleep. We learned about the raid on Dortmund, and the loss of one of our Mossies on the night of 4 October when F/L Russell and F/O Barker had failed to return from Heilbronn. And it wasn't long before Johnny and I were back in the action. After the usual 24 hours to recover from leave, we were on the battle order for 9 October – briefing 1400 hours.

It was to Bochum in the Ruhr, just two miles east of Essen. 109 and 105 had sole responsibility for the marking, with the four-engined Pathfinders stood down for the night. I had a telephone call from the little WAAF just before leaving the Mess to go up to 'flights'. I had been unwilling to resume contact since the warning from her 582 Squadron gunner friend; she informed me that he had gone missing during our leave, but either from deference to his memory or fear of his return, I felt it prudent to keep her at arm's length, at least for the time being.

Because the Lancaster Pathfinders were stood down, there was no Master Bomber to control the raid, no 'long stop' to cancel any wayward TIs and prevent 'creep back', no 'backers-up' to top up our TIs between runs, and no visual centres to correct any material errors on our part. So everything depended on our TIs. To compensate, we carried two flares and two TIs so that the main force could decide for themselves by the light of the flares, either to bomb the TIs or choose their own aiming point.

We were flying as reserve to Flight Lieutenant Williams and Flying Officer Cresswell, and took off at 1850 hours. Operational height at the target was 32,000 feet and we were at about 24,000 feet as we crossed the enemy coast. We continued the climb and had reached 28,000 feet about twenty miles from the turning-on point when it happened for the first time – instant excruciating toothache. It was like a hammer blow with no warning whatsoever. I was talking to Johnny on the intercom at the time, and we lost fifty feet as he jumped at hearing my shriek as the pain hit me. I had been on the point of giving him a change of course, but I lost all interest in the proceedings as a result of the agony that tore at my face. With no response to his frantic requests as to "What the fuck is the matter?" he became more agitated as I sat speechless beside him, rolling my head from side to side. After what seemed a long time I was able to mutter "Toothache," before dragging myself back to re-computing the extent of the dog-leg and the new course that would bring us to the turning-on point on time. Grimly, I gave him the new course through the pain that filled my head. Regardless of the flak that might lie ahead, my thoughts were only on the dentist's chair that I would have to face on our return.

The primary was having a good run as we followed him down – his signals clear and without sign of a dot or a dash. However, at C his signal ceased abruptly and we were called in. With one hand clutching hopelessly at my face, I switched on to find us with the slightest of dots, and within twenty seconds we were settled on the constant note. Automatically, I reached for the bomb tit as we received the D signal. Aware of nothing but the pain in my face, I waited interminably for the release, hardly aware of my instinctive reaction to hearing the signal in my ears. With no sense of satisfaction, I felt nothing but the raging toothache, my thoughts only on getting back to base and the Cephos powders that I had somewhere amongst my kit.

On course for home, I sat miserably holding my head as we descended towards the coast. Miraculously, as the altimeter needle touched 28,000 feet, the pain ceased as instantaneously as it had started, and with not a trace of an ache, we made our way home and back to the runway.

[9 October 1944. Bochum. 435 aircraft – 375 Halifaxes, 40 Lancasters, 20 Mosquitoes – of 1, 4, 6 and 8 Groups. 4 Halifaxes and 1 Lancaster lost. This raid was not successful. The target area was covered by cloud and the bombing was

scattered. The local report says that there was some damage in the southern districts of Bochum, with 140 houses destroyed or seriously damaged and approximately 150 people killed.]

"Better get to the dentist tomorrow," Johnny said as we landed. "Yes," I agreed, knowing that I wouldn't and that I would do anything rather than face an encounter with the Dental Officer. I pretended to go to the Dental Section while Johnny went up to 'flights' the next day and told him that I'd had the tooth filled when I met up with him later. Probably won't happen again, I kidded myself, though I knew that I would be waiting with great apprehension for 28,000 feet to appear on the clock on our next trip.

It was two nights later that my ailing tooth was put to the test. Briefing was a late 2200 hours, which meant a take-off in the early hours of the morning. We accepted the tablets from the MO that would keep us wide awake for six hours, at the end of which sleep would descend like a curtain. We took off at 0330 hours on an 'Overture', the code name for an Oboe Mosquito bombing op, carrying bombs instead of markers. Some of the newer Mosquitoes had been modified to carry a 4,000lb 'cookie', and we lifted off from the runway with one nestling inside the pregnant-looking belly of 'U Uncle'.

The main force wasn't operating on the night, the weather being unsuitable for the heavies, and only the Mosquitoes kept the Germans awake and their sirens wailing. Our target was Heilbronn, ten miles north of Stuttgart. Only forty miles short of Switzerland, it was our deepest penetration into Germany. The route took us through Belgium and Luxembourg into Germany, through the Saar skirting Mannheim, on to the River Neaker and finally to Heilbronn. The greatly extended range of Oboe operations had been made possible by the advance of the Allied forces through France, and the Pathfinder Force had wasted no time in equipping caravans as mobile Oboe ground stations, adding more than a hundred miles to our range.

With our heavy load it took a long time to reach 28,000 feet. The Gee signals had faded sixty or seventy miles back, and I had nothing to do but wait for our call sign. I was greatly relieved as we passed 28,000 feet over the city of Luxembourg, then to 29,000 on our way to our operational height of 32,000 feet. But my relief was short-lived. At 29,400 feet it happened again – like a sledge hammer, just as it had on the first occasion. This time I was going to have to bear it for at least thirty minutes before we would be back down to 29,400 feet. There wasn't any flak at the target as the pain raged and raged. Automatically I pressed the tit as I heard the release signal and then gave Johnny the first course for the return.

The relief came, as before, instantaneously, at the height at which it had struck, 29,400 feet. What blessed relief! But now I definitely had a problem. Johnny knew it too. I had been unusually uncommunicative on the intercom and he guessed why. I was able to placate him by suggesting that we give the 'new filling' time to settle down.

[11 October 1944. 46 Mosquitoes to Berlin. 8 to Wiesbaden and 4 to Heilbronn. 1 aircraft lost from the Berlin raid.]

I was preoccupied with my problem at interrogation and sullenly sipped at my rum and coffee. Eating my egg and bacon later in the Mess, I marvelled at the complete lack of reaction from the tooth, which only two hours before had caused me such agonising pain. I was still reliving the experience as I pulled the sheets around my neck at 0930 hours. I had been out of bed for twenty-six and a half hours, and while I felt exhausted, I couldn't get to sleep with the problem on my mind. Could I really face the sight of those dreaded forceps disappearing into my mouth? I knew without a doubt that I couldn't, not voluntarily anyway. I would just have to grin and bear it for as many ops as it would take to finish my tour.

Obviously, I reasoned, the instant pain was the result of pressure on the nerve of the tooth at high altitude. I couldn't hold my tongue over the tooth for half an hour, and in any case I didn't know exactly where to hold it. I was suddenly awake as the answer became obvious – the operational chewing gum. All I had to do was to stick it firmly around the offending molar and make sure I didn't dislodge it. That would keep the pressure from the tooth and the problem would be solved. It was so simple.

I tested it the next day. I chewed a piece of gum then stuck it around the tooth. I had to remove it at meal times, and as it was in short supply, had to stick it behind my ear until after the meal. After a bit of practice, I was able to keep it firmly in place, though my speech sounded a bit stultified. Johnny asked me about it later in the day, so I told him I'd bitten my tongue.

"Really?" he said. "Painful, isn't it?"

I was quite looking forward to trying out my remedy in practice and felt confident of success. I just hoped that it wouldn't coincide with a trip to the Ruhr, but it did of course. Duisburg was to be the venue for the confrontation between the barometric pressure and the chewing gum.

Again, it was an early hours of the morning take-off at 0135 hours in 'L London', the aircraft in which we had done our first marking operation to Andersvelk. We were flying as reserve to Flt Lt Mahood and F/O Bell. We could see the fire glow in the sky before we reached the Dutch coast. Duisburg had suffered a devastating attack only eighteen hours earlier by more than a thousand bombers carrying a large proportion of incendiary bombs. And now another thousand bombers were on their way to add another 5,000 tons of high explosives and incendiary bombs while it was still reeling from the effects of the first attack. Large areas of the city were on fire, and I didn't much fancy the chances of any aircrew unfortunate enough to have to bale out over the target.

My chewing gum was still firmly in place as we flew over the Zuider Zee, and I was being extremely careful not to do anything to dislodge it. The fires were now plainly visible as we reached 30,000 feet at the German border with my face blissfully free of toothache. My home-made remedy was proving 100% effective as we turned on to the run at 32,000 feet with the burning city now dead ahead of us.

The primary was having a good run as we followed him towards the aiming point. The sky was clear of cloud and with nothing for me to do but stand by and await our call sign should the primary fail, I sat and viewed the destruction of Duisburg. I had never seen anything like this before. We were marking late in the raid, and could see the effects of the 10,000 tons of bombs dropped by two thousand bombers in less than twenty hours. It was like Dante's Inferno down there. Fires flickered everywhere. The old fires, from the day before, were ochre-coloured, and radiated a deep, bright blackness. The new fires were yellow and wispy. I could not see the individual surges of flame, but the yellow colours pulsed with varying intensity. Everything in the city was either burnt to cinders or on fire. More red TIs were cascading down on to the burning buildings, and a few greens were falling on the edge of the conflagration. Smoke had reached almost up to our altitude where there was a total absence of flak. Not so 10,000 feet below. The Germans continued to pound away at the heavies, and the flak down there looked as intense as I'd ever seen it, except on that first raid on Essen eighteen months ago. We saw several Lancasters silhouetted against the fires, lumbering along. Two doomed ones were held in searchlight cones. At the apex of each cone was the inevitable concentration of flak bursts, white explosions that looked like spray out of an uncorked champagne bottle. One of the coned bombers turned slowly over onto its back and fell towards the flames. Within seconds another aircraft was held in the irresistible and deadly grip of German searchlights and exploding shells. The aircraft in the other cone was swaying drunkenly, desperately surviving, as it disappeared from view under the nose of our aircraft.

We heard the primary receive his release signal, and we were free to leave this horrendous scene. We didn't look back. We'd seen enough of this target. And I saw it all again as I lay awake in my bed behind the drawn curtains of the billet.

[14 October 1944. Duisburg. This raid was part of a special operation that has received little mention in the history books. On 13 October Sir Arthur Harris received the directive for operation Hurricane: "In order to demonstrate to the enemy in Germany generally the overwhelming superiority of the Allied Air Forces in this theatre ... the intention is to apply within the shortest practical period the maximum effort of the Royal Air Force Bomber Command and the VIIIth United States Bomber Command against objectives in the densely populated Ruhr." Bomber Command had probably been forewarned of the directive because it was able to mount the first part of the operation soon after first light on 14 October. No heavy bombers had flown on operations for 48 hours and 1,013 aircraft – 519 Lancasters, 474 Halifaxes and 20 Mosquitoes – were dispatched to Duisburg with RAF fighters providing an escort. 957 bombers dropped 3,574 tons of high explosive and 820 tons of incendiaries on Duisburg. 14 aircraft were lost – 13 Lancasters and 1 Halifax; it is probable that the Lancasters provided the early waves of the raid and drew the attention of the German flak before the flak positions were overwhelmed by the bombing.]

I listened to the mundane noises outside – the clanking bicycles and the voices of those residents of Little Staughton who hadn't seen Duisburg burning a few hours earlier, making their way to the messes for breakfast. For the first time I thought of what would be happening as daylight dawned on the people in the smouldering rubble, and the survivors stumbled out of their shelters and into the burning streets. Few people would be sitting down to breakfast in Duisburg that morning.

We were on our way to St Neots by 1930 hours, intent upon a heavy night's drinking. We had gone in Johnny's car, and I was really tanked up by the ten o'clock closing time.

Boisterously, we moved out to the car – Celia, Johnny, myself and two or three others. Celia got into the front seat and I clambered into the back after the others. I was nearly in, and still holding on to the door pillar with my right hand when somebody slammed the door shut. I could quite definitely feel three of my fingers trapped in the door, but I couldn't feel any pain. They all thought I was joking when I mildly complained. It was Celia – she was quite sober – who realised that I wasn't joking, and who hastily reached over to open the door, and subsequently minister to my split fingers. Blood was flowing from all three. Johnny was completely unconcerned. But then so was I. I couldn't feel much pain. I vaguely realised that my hand was hurting, but not unduly so and I joined in the singing as we weaved our way back to base. Somebody, unusually, had a handkerchief, which was used to bind the injured hand and stem the flow of blood. My fingers felt numb by the time we were dropping the girls off at the WAAFery, and, shortly afterwards, falling into bed.

I woke up two hours later – sober and with a throbbing pain in my right hand. Sleep was impossible so I sat up in bed and viewed the damage. The handkerchief was now dark red and firmly stuck to my fingers. Completely un-ambidextrous, with my left hand of little use to me, and now with the right one out of action, I paced our little room, fumbling to light a cigarette, with Johnny immersed in his alcoholic cocoon.

I didn't get much sleep after that, and reported sick immediately after breakfast. It was the first time I'd gone sick as an officer, a much more civilised procedure than as an airman, and the first time since Tunis. A male medical orderly, after soaking my hand in warm water to allow the 'dressing' to be removed, inspected the damaged fingers. I was horrified at first sight of them – gangrene had surely set in, I thought. "Mmm," said the MO, as he examined them. "How the hell did you do this?" So I told him. A slow shaking of the head. I was suitably chastised as he declared me unfit for operations for a week at least.

I was quite chuffed at first. A week off ops was marvellous but, on second thoughts, could only be enjoyed if I was fit to enjoy it. The three fingers of a person's right hand, so I found out during the next week, were very important indeed. I managed to eat my meals reasonably well, and put on my clothes with extreme difficulty. Other more basic functions proved vastly more difficult. Fortunately, I was able to drink left-handed and, being 'hors de combat' for at least a week, there was lots of time for drinking. I wondered how my bank balance was standing. I felt sure that I had written cheques for more than I should have, but having had a bank account for only six weeks, I didn't know what would happen if I had. It all seemed so easy. Just write out a cheque and sign it, and that was it. I soon received a letter from the bank, quite a nice one really. It was no doubt due to an oversight, it said, that I had allowed my account to become overdrawn by two pounds one and elevenpence, about which they would take no action. Reluctantly, however, they would be obliged to refer any further payees to me until my account was in credit again. Actually, the bank manager had mentioned it to Mother, and she had paid off the overdraft. It was about a half week's pay for her at the time.

I was dismayed to find that I had become overdrawn after only six weeks, and resolved to ensure that it didn't happen again. It did, of course, several times, and it took a little while to adapt to a monthly salary cheque instead of the money-in-the-pocket system of pre-commission days, when, if you hadn't got money in your pocket or in your wallet, you were broke.

My exceptionally good healing flesh proved itself once again, and with the X-rays showing no damage to the bones of my fingers, I was declared fit for duty eight days after they had been crushed by the clot who had slammed the car door shut. I was released for duty on the morning of Tuesday 23 October, and sure enough we were on the battle order, briefing at 1300 hours. The squadron had marked German targets only during our eight days of inactivity, and we'd lost an aircraft on the night of 18 October when Flt Lt

Kay and F/O Hynes failed to return from Happy Valley. "I bet it's Essen tonight," I said to Johnny as we went late into the smoke-filled briefing room. Essen had been notably absent from the list of German targets that the squadron had marked during our absence, and I just knew what the briefing officer was going to say. "Your target for tonight gentlemen, is Essen."

CHAPTER 21

Essen to the End

It was nineteen months since my last visit to that hated place. I'd been on its doorstep at Gelsenkirchen and Bochum, but not actually to Krupps in Essen. Johnny was unconcerned, or seemed to be. "Crews opening the attack can expect heavy opposition," said the briefing officer. As Johnny and I had had a week off, and had missed at least two of Harris's maximum efforts against German targets, it was no surprise to find that we were one of the two crews detailed to open the attack. The forecast was for 10/10ths cloud, which was slightly comforting. In such conditions the German flak batteries sometimes held off until the first sky markers had gone.

We took off in a sombre dusk in 'K King' carrying two TIs and two flares, the TIs primed to cascade below the clouds and the flares to ignite above them. If the clouds were too thick for the TIs to be seen, the bomb-aimers would aim at the sky markers. With the dubious honour of opening a maximum effort Bomber Command operation, we were very close to the turning-on point and right on time as we were called in.

The sky was clear ahead of us until just after B, when it erupted. I could feel my face grimacing at the sight of the murderous barrage in front of us. Any second I was expecting to be amongst it, but it was still being predicted ahead of us well past C. I was wishing it had been behind us where I couldn't see it, and all the time I was expecting it to close in. A few bursts were closer, but not close enough to disturb us, and it was with a feeling almost of disbelief at the ease of it all that I released our markers at the end of the run. Our error was just 18 yards, and our markers were burning on the roofs of the Krupps factories with 'K King' unmarked as she cleared the Ruhr Valley between Oberhausen and

Duisburg to make her way to the Zuider Zee and on to Little
Staughton.

*[23 October 1944. Essen. 1,055 aircraft – 561 Lancasters,
463 Halifaxes, 31 Mosquitoes. This was the heaviest raid on
Essen so far in the war and the number of aircraft dispatched
was also the greatest number to any target so far; these new
records were achieved without the Lancasters of 5 Group
being included. 5 Lancasters and 3 Halifaxes were lost.*

*4,538 tons of bombs were dropped. More than 90% of this
tonnage was high explosive (and included 509 4000-
pounders) because it was now considered that most of the
burnable buildings in Essen had been destroyed in earlier
raids. The greater proportion of high explosive, against all the
trends in earlier area-bombing raids, was now quite common
in attacks on targets that had suffered major fire damage in
1943. A report from Essen states that 607 buildings were
destroyed and 812 seriously damaged; 662 people were killed,
a figure that included 124 foreign workers, and 569 people
were injured.]*

The Mess was empty as we got up from our post-
operational meal close to midnight, and we lingered over
our games in the billiards room. All was well with us at that
moment, and we enjoyed it as long as possible, reluctant to
let it go, until fatigue finally forced us to bed. It was usually
between eight and twelve hours between the posting of the
battle order and the climb down the ladder and on to the
tarmac, and when it was an early hours of the morning take-
off, we were usually desperate for sleep. On this occasion I
just felt pleasantly tired as my senses slipped away.

But terrors aren't conquered that easily, and the familiar
depression engulfed me again when we were listed again
two days later for a daylight raid on Essen.

Eight crews attended briefing at 0930 hours – take-off
1330. We were reserve to Squadron Leaders Spedding and
Rimmer, and were the second of the four pairs detailed to

mark the target. There wasn't much cloud as we flew into Germany, and while we were safe from fighters because of our own fighter cover, we were fair game for the visually predicted flak. We saw it way ahead of us as we made the rendezvous with our primary at the turning-on point and flew with them down the run in formation. The flak ahead of us looked intense and concentrated over a small area, obviously aimed at the first pair of markers. It had stopped by the time we had reached point B, but it started exploding all around us just after point C.

Bang after bang sounded above the roar of the engines. I hardly heard the dah-di-di, dah-di-di, dah-di-di at point D, the signals interspersed by two enormous explosions that rocked the plane.

We kept in formation with our primary through it all to within less than a minute of release when the signals faded, too late for us to be called in. The primary turned to starboard across our track, but Johnny chose the shorter way out, due east, anywhere to escape the Essen flak that was still bursting around us. Two minutes later we were in virgin sky, unsullied by smoke or fire. An instant turn of ninety degrees to port, then another ninety a few minutes later, and we were crossing the run on our way to the Dutch coast. There was no hanging about to watch the heavies today. We were just too thankful to be able to retire.

[25 October 1944. Essen. 771 aircraft – 508 Lancasters, 251 Halifaxes, 12 Mosquitoes. 2 Halifaxes and 2 Lancasters lost.

The bombing was aimed at sky markers, because the target area was covered by cloud. The Bomber Command report states that the attack became scattered, but the local Essen report shows that more buildings were destroyed – 1,163 – and more people were killed – 820 – than in the heavier night attack that had taken place 36 hours previously. The foreign workers, who were now present in large numbers in German industrial cities and who usually had poorer air-raid shelters than the German people, once again suffered heavy casualties; 99 foreigners and 2 prisoners of war were killed. A photographic reconnaissance flight that took place after this raid showed severe damage to the remaining industrial concerns in Essen, particularly to the Krupps steelworks. Some of the war industry had already moved to small dispersed factories but the coal mines and steelworks of the Ruhr were still important.

The Krupps steelworks was particularly hard hit by the two raids and there are references in the firm's archives to the 'almost complete breakdown of the electrical supply network' and to 'a complete paralysis'. The Borbeck pi-iron plant ceased work completely and there is no record of any further production from this important section of Krupps.

Much of Essen's surviving industrial capacity was now dispersed and the city lost its role as one of Germany's most important centres of war production.]

We thought we must surely have been hit, as we told the groundcrew at dispersal. But 'K King' had suffered not a scratch. We had been lucky. Of the eight 109 aircraft on the raid, three had been damaged over the target. Two of them made it safely back to Little Staughton and the other just made it to Manston, where it crash-landed with the crew miraculously uninjured.

Air Marshal Harris wasn't very popular that day with the crews of 109 and 582, and he was quite definitely out of favour with me, though really I had little to complain about. Except for Gelsenkirchen, the tour so far had been far from nerve-racking, though it only needed one fatal op to finish it. But this hadn't been the one, and those long draws on the Woodbine as we sat in the truck making our way to debriefing gradually brought my ragged nerves under control. It was only when I was drinking my rum and coffee at the interrogation table that I realised that I was still subconsciously protecting the wad of chewing gum that protected my tooth, and which was still firmly in position.

We had a day off after our confrontation with the Essen flak in daylight, and we weren't on the ops list posted on the following morning. Instead, we were detailed to take the station Oxford to Manston with two Oboe technicians to collect the secret equipment from the Mosquito that had crash landed there after the Essen raid.

It was a clear day, and the Manston runway could be seen many miles away; it was more than twice as long and twice as wide as a normal runway. Situated on the Kent coast near Dover, it was the haven for shot-up aircraft trying to maintain sufficient height to pancake gratefully on its runway. Together with similar coastal airfields at Woodbridge and Carnaby, Manston saved the lives of countless aircrew.

We landed on the side of the main runway; in fact, it was wide enough for the Oxford to have landed across it. Having shown our authorisation and proved our identities, we were driven through the aircraft graveyard to the 109 Mosquito. It was a graveyard unique in the history of aviation. As far as the eye could see there were aircraft of every description, of both Allied Air Forces, and of the Luftwaffe. Some we'd heard of but never seen like the Mitchells, Heinkels, Focke-Wulfs and Messerschmitts. But mainly they were Lancasters, Fortresses, Halifaxes and Stirlings. They stood in rows, and were obviously charted and listed, for the driver of the truck took us directly to the 109 Mosquito where two Service Policeman were standing guard over her.

Again we had to produce our authority to remove the Oboe equipment and one of the Service Policemen came back with us to the control tower where he handed us over. We had to wait again until authority was given for us to take off again for Little Staughton, where we landed at 1710 hours.

Johnny was spending the evening with Celia, and I went with Ferdy to St Neots where we met two WAAFs and took them back to the billet where we forgot about Essen for a little while before escorting them on the short journey to the WAAFery.

I didn't like the torch being shone into my eyes in the pre-dawn blackness at any time, but on the next morning, with that Essen daylight flak still vividly fresh in my mind, I was very reluctant to write my signature to accept the call. Harris had all but destroyed Duisburg, and he was probably intending the same for Essen.

The island of Walcheren was nobody's guess for the target that morning, but I for one was grateful to Eisenhower for borrowing Bomber Command back again after relinquishing his control. The port of Antwerp had been captured weeks ago, but the Allies were unable to use it because the mouth of the Scheldt was guarded by the guns on the island fortress of Walcheren, which was still held by the Germans. We were marking the dykes that held back the North Sea. They had already been breached in places in earlier raids but several guns were still on dry ground. The heavies that followed us in finished the job, and the island was flooded successfully. With no opposition on the run, it had been a pleasant and successful morning's work, and we were feeling in a relaxed mood on the way back to base with the prospect of the rest of the day free to hang around the Mess with our feet up.

[28 October 1944. Walcheren. 277 aircraft – 155 Halifaxes, 86 Lancasters, 36 Mosquitoes – of 4 and 8 Groups carried out raids on gun positions at 5 places on the rim of the newly flooded island. Most of the bombing appeared to be successful. 1 Halifax and 1 Lancaster were lost.]

But just three hours after we had landed back from Walcheren we were airborne again and setting course for Cologne in 'K King'. We were quickly de-briefed after the raid on the dykes, and were back in the briefing room an hour after we had landed.

Briefing revealed that we were flying reserve to the squadron CO, Group Captain Grant, and his navigator, Squadron Leader Finlater, and were the third pair of four down the run. The raid would be ten minutes old by our time over the target, and the flak gunners would be concentrating on the heavies. In accordance with the new daylight procedure, we were to meet up with the primary at the turning-on point and fly with them down the run. And on this trip there was another innovation. The reserves would release their markers on hearing the release signal provided that they had kept in close formation with the primary.

The CO's aircraft was not in sight at the turning-on point when his call sign was transmitted, and we were almost at point B before we saw him ahead and to port. As we formed up on his starboard side the sky ahead of us was beautifully clear of flak except for some lingering smoke. We could see the Lancasters ahead and below, making their lumbering, heavily laden run in to the target. I was watching three of them who were quite close together when the leading one received a direct hit from the flak. The Lancaster just disappeared into a large pall of black smoke. Not a sign from our height of any remains of an aircraft falling to earth, just a ball of smoke. Aircraft and seven aircrew blown to pieces by two tons of high explosives. The other two Lancasters shied away from the explosion, lucky not to have been damaged themselves, though they were probably not so close to the explosion as they appeared to be from our height. And soon we lost sight of them under our port wing. Johnny had seen it too, and we exchanged grimaces and shakes of the head as we passed point C, with still no flak at our height. Just before point D the CO's signals cut out and we were called in. I switched on the transmitter, but we didn't receive any signals, and two minutes later, with no hope of a 'cope', we both turned away and made for home. We landed back at base just ahead of the CO as dusk was falling.

[28 October 1944. Cologne. 733 aircraft – 428 Lancasters, 286 Halifaxes, 19 Mosquitoes. 4 Halifaxes and 3 Lancasters lost.

The bombing took place in 2 separate waves and the local report confirms that enormous damage was caused. The districts of Mülheim and Zollstock, north-east and south-west of the entire centre respectively, became the centre of the

*2 raids and were both devastated. Classed as completely
destroyed were 2,239 blocks of flats, 15 industrial premises,
11 schools, 3 police stations and a variety of other buildings.
Much damage was also caused to power stations, railways
and harbour installations on the Rhine. 630 German people
were killed or their bodies never found and 1,200 were
injured. The number of foreign casualties is not known.]*

We soon forgot the Lancaster and the abortive run, and,
after a double ration of rum, we sat down to our third
operational meal in less than eleven hours. We weren't on
the ops list for the next day and spent the evening quietly
and sedately in a deserted and subdued Mess. 582 Squadron
had also been busy and everybody seemed to be having an
early night.

With no money to call on, we were unable to contemplate
a night out as we cycled to 'flights' the next morning. I was
feeling decidedly worse off as a Pilot Officer than I had been
as a Flight Sergeant, and Johnny as a Warrant Officer was
quite definitely so. Had we looked forward to a night out,
we would have been disappointed, for we were one of the
eight crews on the ops list that was posted shortly before
noon. We guessed that it would be Cologne again after the
previous daylight raid, and this time, at night, it should be
even easier. Our guess was right, and as 10/10ths cloud was
forecast at the target, it was a sky marking raid. We carried
two red flares to ignite above the clouds for the bombers to
aim at, and two 500lb bombs for good measure.

We were a primary on the night in 'L London', a new Mark
XVI Mosquito; these pressurised aircraft had been
gradually replacing the unpressurised Mark IXs for the past
few weeks. Operational height was 34,000 feet, our
maximum, so I was more than usually meticulous in the
fixing of my chewing gum, chewing an extra stick for good
measure. We took off at 1735 hours. It was already dark, and
we climbed through a lot of cloud before emerging into a
clear sky at about 12,000 feet, probably indicating the
predicted 10/10ths cloud over the target. In fact it was only

5/10ths at the turning-on point, 3/10ths at A, 2/10ths at C, and from then on no cloud whatsoever above or below us as we pressed on to the target.

We'd never been coned before. It was something that I didn't care to think about. When it happened, it was an eerie, skin-tingling experience. One moment we were flying anonymously under the cloak of darkness with my shaded navigation light giving grainy illumination over a page-sized area, when, with a startling flash, the cockpit was as light as day from the glare of the master searchlight. I felt bathed in a dry, intrusive and abrasive light. Other searchlights swung over to form an apex, with 'L London' firmly held in its grasp. Like frightened rabbits, we stared wide-eyed at each other, the light etching terror on Johnny's face, unable to deviate from our track down the run.

My watch face radiated light and I saw that we had three minutes to go to release. In normal times these three minutes took ages. I could not imagine that we would now be able to last that long before the flak hit us. I shuddered and tensed myself, pushing my body into the seat. A minute passed – two more to go. The flak must start arriving at any second, shooting up along the needles of light. I was shaking. I had the bomb tit in my hand at one and a half minutes to go. Still no flak. I kept my thumb clear of the nipple in case I should involuntarily press it if my shaking became uncontrollable, or if we were hit. But either the flak batteries were asleep, or we were too fast and too close to turning off to enable them to set fuses for our height and fire in time to hit us. We were still coned and unscathed as we received our five dots and a dash at the aiming point. 'L London', relieved of her load, and as if angry at her nakedness, responded instantly to Johnny's controls, and with throttles forward and nose down, we streaked free of the searchlights and into the all-enveloping refuge of darkness. We scurried out of the target area as the flak started to burst below us, and made haste back to base to tell our story at the de-briefing table. The Intelligence Officer wrote in his report: "Aircraft coned for three minutes. Still coned on release. Successful cope with no damage to aircraft." It sounded so banal and matter of fact, hardly worth reporting, with no hint whatsoever of the trauma of the three-minute breath-holding eternity.

[29 October 1944. Cologne. 30 Mosquitoes. No aircraft lost.]

Listed again the next day, and as if to give the Cologne anti-aircraft defences another chance, it was a repeat of the previous night's all-Mosquito raid on the cathedral city. We were a reserve this time and, as such, prime participants in yet another innovation. With the stepping up of Bomber Command's onslaught on the German towns and cities, two Oboe squadrons were obviously proving to be inadequate, especially with the need to provide a reserve for every primary in an attempt to reduce the number of 'technical failures'. It must have been cause for concern at the top, that so many aircraft were within minutes of the target, only to lose their signals and abort the release. It invariably happened towards the end of the run, leaving very little time for the reserve to settle down on his approach after being called in. So, the planners deduced, if the reserve hadn't been called in shortly after C, there was little point in his carrying on any further. Also, if he then turned about and scurried back up the run, he could be back in position at point A to act as reserve to the next primary.

For the third time in three days we set course for Cologne, this time in a brand new aircraft – 'O Barred' – again carrying two flares and two bombs. The first primary was crewed by Henry A'Court and Freddie Waterman, and they were in position and on time at the turning-on point. We could hear their signals as we followed them, hopefully close to the run, the reserve aircraft having no signals of its own to indicate how far it might be off track.

Everything was going well for the first primary and we duly turned back 180 degrees shortly after we heard him receive the C signal. Four minutes later, when we were nearly back up at A, we heard him receive the release. As we hadn't been called in I had had ample time to keep my

airplot going, and so far the dual role was posing no
problems whatsoever. We heard our second primary being
called in at almost the precise time of my ETA back at point
A, and after a few faint dots he settled on the run. Shortly
afterwards we did our about turn to follow him in to the
target. As we did so we saw flares ahead of us and slightly to
starboard, exactly where they should have been. Making the
small alterations of course to take in the curve of the 'beam',
they gradually came round to dead ahead. Meanwhile, our
second primary was still receiving clear signals, and with
the target just a few miles ahead of us, he got his release too.
We let our two bombs go a minute later, and brought the two
flares back for future use.

*[30 October 1944. Cologne. 59 Mosquitoes to Cologne. No
aircraft lost.]*

We felt pretty good. We hadn't been used but we'd been
ready for either primary to fail. And after four ops in three
days we were looking forward to a night off. I had a date
with a WAAF from the parachute section, and I planned to
take her to Little Staughton village for a drink.

But it was not to be. Instead, we took off at 1810 hours with
a 'cookie', destined for Saarbrucken. It was the last day of
October 1944. The target was the rail network through
which troops and armour were passing to oppose General
Patton's rapid advance through France. It was a long trip for
us, nearly three and a half hours, and I didn't particularly
care for these 'Overture' raids. I could imagine the German
radar passing us on from control to control – one solitary
aircraft making its furtive way to an unknown target. And I
could imagine the flak gunners having ages and ages to
predict our exact position in the sky. The Germans must
have known that these solitary aircraft were Oboe
Mosquitoes on their way to precision bomb a specific target.
But there was no sign of any reaction from the ground as I
pressed the tit to release our 'cookie' over Saarbrucken.

We had seen photographs of the damage they caused

when they exploded. They had a thin casing and exploded immediately on contact with the ground, causing the maximum blast over the maximum area. We knew the moment of impact without looking down at the target. Even at a height of six miles there was a momentary brightening of the sky, but we didn't see it this time through the 10/10ths strato-cumulus cloud over Saarbrucken. Untroubled, we retraced our path across Europe and back to the flare path. We had seen absolutely nothing outside the aircraft since we had left base three and a half hours previously.

[30 October 1944. Saarbrucken. 4 Mosquitoes to Saarbrucken. No aircraft lost.]

We landed bumpily at half past nine – 2130 hours – and by half past eleven I had suffered my worst defeat ever on the billiard table. I was finding it difficult to relax after seven ops in the eight days back from leave. Six of them had been to German targets, and each time I'd awaited, with knotted stomach, the arrival of the flak. And I had started thinking of what the next op might hold for us, which I'd never done before. I had done forty ops on 109, nowhere near the end of the tour, but already I was wishing it were over. And already the winter was beginning to set in.

At last we had a stand-down, and a truckload of us went over to Bourne to visit our sister squadron – 105. The airfield was about fifteen miles to the east on the other side of St Neots, a little further on than Caxton Gibbet, another RAF station; the gibbet stood on the grass at the junction with the Huntingdon road. Three miles south-west was Gransden Lodge, one of the biggest Lancaster Pathfinder stations, just a few of the thirty or more airfields that had been levelled out of the flat countryside of Cambridgeshire and Huntingdonshire. A football match had been arranged between the two squadrons, followed by dinner and a party in the Mess in the evening. I was playing inside right, and I rather fancied myself as a budding George Mutch, United's best player. I'd had a trial for Salford boys, but hadn't made the team. The game against 105 Squadron was only a few minutes old when the ball came to my feet in the centre circle. Bringing it under control, I set off on a dribble for 105's goal. Then, without warning, something hit me from behind. It felt like a five-ton van. I crashed to the ground, winded, and desperately trying to breath air into my deflated lungs. I was pained and bruised as I looked for the cause of my downfall. It hadn't been a five-ton van after all, just George Paterson. He was playing left half for 105 Squadron and, as such, was expected to take care of the opposing inside right. He had certainly taken care of me. I recognised him from newspaper photographs as he helped the trainer revive me with the magic sponge. George Paterson – Scotland's left half back!

I played on for the rest of the game, but my heart wasn't in it any more. I wasn't looking for the ball – I was looking out for George Paterson. That was the day that my footballing ambitions ended. George Mutch was welcome to his United shirt if there were such as George Paterson to contend with.

I had stiffened up by the time we sat down to dinner, but the flow of alcohol soon loosened the joints, and I was able to join in the rugger match that took place later in the Mess. I remembered the match starting, though I'd got through a lot of beer and two or three whiskies, then nothing else until I woke up in my own bed at Little Staughton – fully clothed with my tie cut off below the knot.

I couldn't move. Not so much as a finger. I thought I must be paralysed. And I ached. Oh God, how I ached. Johnny was nowhere to be seen. His bed was empty, and I was alone – and paralysed. Slowly, very slowly, and with a lot of pain, I managed to sit up on the edge of the bed. Standing upright was even more difficult. But, finally, after a great deal of effort, I was able to change into battledress and shuffle slowly out to my bike, to make my way stiffly up to 'flights'. After a little way I saw Johnny cycling towards me on his way back to the billet. "We're not on," he shouted. "I'm off with C," as he sped past. My attempt at a U-turn was disastrous, and I crash-landed on the tarmac. I pushed the bike back to the billet, and half an hour after dragging myself up and out of bed I was back in it, and fast asleep.

I slept until the evening when I had to get up to go for dinner. My toy-soldier-like movements evoked no sympathy in the Mess, only merriment. I had a few beers in the ante-room after dinner, and fell asleep in front of the fire. The Mess was deserted when I woke up – it was past midnight – and I fell over as I got up and tried to walk out of the ante-room, cursing the comedian who had tied my shoelaces together while I slept.

I was still as stiff as a poker the next morning, and the thought that we would probably be on ops gnawed at me. Briefing was late – 1700 hours. I hoped it wasn't going to be one of those early hours of the morning take-offs, and I didn't much like the target when it was revealed. Bochum again. We were starting November as we had started October. And again we were flying as reserve.

At briefing there was another innovation for the reserve aircraft on both Channels 1 and 2. We were reserve on Channel 1, not to two primaries, but three. Flying up and down the run three times filled me with dismay, and meeting one of the primaries head on didn't bear thinking about, even if a collision between two Oboe Mosquitoes did seem so remote as to be beyond the realms of probability.

We took off at 2135 hours and started badly when I found with horror, as we approached the Dutch coast, that I was chomping away at my chewing gum. To replace it, I had to take off my oxygen mask and silk gloves, before carefully re-packing it around the dud tooth. All this was watched by Johnny without comment until I had resumed the office work with gloves and oxygen mask replaced.

"What was all that in aid of?" he finally asked.

"Er – nothing," I said.

"Have you got toothache again?"

"Of course not," I said as flak suddenly burst around us at the Dutch coast, the interrogation quickly forgotten.

Nothing further untoward happened until point D on the

run down with our first primary. He was the opening marker for the raid and had gone well until D, where his signals cut out. We were on our way back up to A as we heard our second primary being called in. Minutes later I took a look back to see what was happening at the target, just as red TIs cascaded down from the Channel 2 aircraft, followed almost immediately by greens from the backers-up.

But for Channel 1, it was a night of utter failure. Both our remaining primaries lost their signals at D, and when we were finally called in we had drifted off course. We made the beam two minutes after D, and though we got a release, we were skidding way off the heading and aborted the drop.

[4 November 1944. Bochum. 749 aircraft – 384 Halifaxes, 336 Lancasters, 29 Mosquitoes – of 1, 4, 6 and 8 Groups. 23 Halifaxes and 5 Lancasters were lost; German night fighters caused most of the casualties. 346 (Free French) Squadron, based at Elvington, lost 5 of its 16 Halifaxes in the raid.

This was a particularly successful attack based upon standard Pathfinder marking techniques. Severe damage was caused to the centre of Bochum. More than 4,000 buildings were destroyed or seriously damaged; 980 Germans and 14 foreigners were killed. Bochum's industrial areas were also severely damaged, particularly the important steelworks. This was the last major raid by Bomber Command on this target.]

In the event the raid had been successful, with the Channel 2 Mossies coping one after the other, reds and greens tightly grouped and the bomb flashes from 700 Lancasters and Halifaxes erupting in their hundreds in the middle of them. But the heavies couldn't have had an easy ride on the night in the glare from the dozens of fighter flares we had seen hanging in the sky on their track. They must have been grateful for their stand-down the night after, when the weather conditions were deemed unsuitable for a main force raid. Not for the Mosquitoes, though.

The ops list was posted shortly after we arrived at 'flights' in the morning. Briefing was at 1330 hours, and November looked like continuing to be as busy for us as the last week of October had been. The raid was an all-Mosquito attack on Stuttgart with 109 doing the marking and 60 Mossies of the Light Night Striking Force providing the high explosives. We carried the usual load for an LNSF raid – two TIs and two 500-pounders – and took off in fading light at 1750 hours. It was going to be the deepest penetration into Germany to date for Johnny and me, and the flight plan broke the four-hour mark for the first time.

This was a marathon compared with those short sprints to the French coast and the 'buzz bomb' sites, and evidence of the still further advance of the mobile ground Oboe stations into Europe. The range of Gee had been extended by the capture of French territory, and the new Loran, based on Gee, had still to prove itself. Unequipped as we were with H2S, the airborne ground scanner that defined the built-up city areas on a cathode ray tube, the Mosquitoes were more than usually dependant on the forecast winds after Gee had faded.

Bright clear skies had been forecast for several miles on the run in to the target, no doubt the reason for the main force stand-down on the night. The forecast was confirmed as we flew in a moonlit cloudless sky from the Dutch coast. Visibility at 32,000 feet was quite abnormal at the turning-on point, where we were two or three miles adrift. Settled on the run by the time I got the A, we could see for miles and miles ahead.

Suddenly I saw it coming towards us – very fast and slightly to starboard. The closing speed was 600 or 700 miles an hour, but I saw it quite distinctly as it sped past us about a hundred yards away. It was an aircraft, but nothing like the shape of the normal German night fighters – it was squat and stubby with a lot more body than wings. It disappeared behind us and out of sight. Johnny had only caught a fleeting glimpse of it so I filled him in with its description. "Keep an eye open behind," he said. I knelt on my seat, peering nervously at the moonlit void behind us for sight of the aircraft that had flashed past us at our level. I was still kneeling on my seat looking backwards when I pressed the bomb tit at the release signal, at which precise moment the blue master searchlight flicked on to us, flooding the cockpit with its ghostly light. Johnny's reaction was immediate and violent. I was pressed hard against the back of the cockpit as the nose went down and we banked tightly to starboard, the manoeuvre taking us out of the searchlight beam in a matter of seconds.

Mouth dry and heart thumping, I knelt again on my seat to keep an all-round look-out as we set course 300 degrees for the Scheldte, nearly an hour and a half flying time away. It seemed like many hours before we were over the safety of the North Sea and, shortly afterwards, within sight of the station beacon.

[5 November 1944. Stuttgart. 65 Mosquitoes to Stuttgart – in 2 waves – and 6 to Aschaffenburg. No aircraft lost.]

At interrogation we learned that another crew had seen the mysterious aircraft on the run, flying in the opposite direction.

It was the main topic of conversation in the crew room on the following morning. Intelligence no doubt knew that the Germans had an operational jet aircraft, but they had kept the knowledge to themselves. The news had quickly spread amongst the crews, and those of us who had seen it were pressed for information. But we had little to tell, other than that it was smaller than a Mosquito and much faster. The fact that it was at the same height and within a hundred yards of us was, I thought, no coincidence!

Denied a date, yet again, with the WAAF from the parachute section, I was back in the briefing room at 1530 hours the next day. The target was Herford in northern Germany, destined to receive eight 'cookies' from 109 Mosquitoes. Untroubled by flak or jet fighters, we bombed from 28,000 feet at the end of a quite immaculate run on which we were credited with a nil error. On course for our exit point on the Belgian coast, and beginning our normal downhill exit from the target, we were feeling relaxed and out of danger. Preferring the shortest route home, we rarely kept to the briefed flight plan, and on this occasion our route took us a few miles north of Munster. We were down to 24,000 feet as I plotted our dead reckoning position adjacent to the town. Totally unexpectedly, the night sky around us was suddenly transformed into daylight by brilliant white flares on our starboard side.

Way off our briefed track, we had blundered into a Five Group raid on the Dortmund-Ems Canal. In the bright light we could see Lancasters just below us. This was no place for our vulnerable twin-engined aircraft. Preferring the threat of the Munster flak to the Browning guns of the Lancasters, we turned away over the town and quickly out again into undefended territory.

[6 November 1944. Herford. 8 Mosquitoes to Herford. Same day 235 Lancasters and 7 Mosquitoes bombed the Mittelland Canal at its junction with the Dortmund-Ems Canal at Gravenhorst. 10 Lancasters were lost.]

Stood down the next day, I celebrated with a night out in Bedford with the WAAF from the parachute section. We went to the pictures and I kissed her goodnight outside the WAAFery. Very obviously another 'nice girl', she was nevertheless good to be with, and with ops lately less numerous, I was back to my normal self again.

But that torch in the eyes at 0530 hours the next morning wiped the smile from my face and brought back the tight stomach and the retching with the first cigarette. It was probably going to be another Ruhr daylight, I thought gloomily, it being a beautiful autumn morning as we cycled up to 'flights' just as the sun came up.

The target was Wanne-Eickel in the middle of the Ruhr,

between Gelsenkirchen and Castrop Rauxel, and we were marking the oil refinery for a force of 250 Lancasters. We were flying as primary and marking late in the raid, so with no dashing back up and down the run we should be back at base two and a half hours after take-off, scheduled for 0900 hours.

It was like the rush hour in Piccadilly Circus over the Dutch coast at 0930 hours, with aircraft and vapour trails visible in all directions. The Spitfires came up to have a look at us, quickly peeling off and away again. There was hardly any wind to cause us any variations from the flight plan, but the cloud below us slowly built up in density near the target, and almost up to the height of the Lancasters of the main force. They crawled like laden ants along the grey carpet below us until we left them five minutes from the target, our signals gone again.

[9 November 1944. Wanne-Eickel. 256 Lancasters and 21 Mosquitoes of 1 and 8 Groups to attack the oil refinery. Cloud over the target was found to reach 21,000 feet and the sky markers dropped by the Oboe Mosquitoes disappeared as soon as they ignited so the Master Bomber ordered the force to bomb any built-up area. The town of Wanne-Eickel reported only 2 buildings destroyed, with 4 civilians and 6 foreigners killed. It must be assumed that other towns in the Ruhr were hit, but no details are available. 2 Lancasters lost.]

After the raid on Wanne-Eickel on 9 November, we began to feel unwanted when, day after day, Johnny and I were stood down at lunchtime. The other crews weren't busy either. There was a big daylight raid on 16 November, but we weren't on it. 582 Squadron didn't seem to be doing much either, and night after night the Mess was crowded. In fact, we were stood down for eight consecutive days, before being listed on 18 November for a daylight on Munster, an amenable lightly defended target for our return to the fray.

Take-off was 1325 hours and, with cloud forecast at the target, we were carrying the new sky markers – smoke puffs.

They were primed to burst above the cloud and give off a coloured smoke for the bomb-aimers to aim at. Cloud at 7/10ths or 8/10ths lay along latitude 52 degrees, our track from Orford Ness to The Hague, Arnhem and the target. Fifteen minutes from Munster we had overhauled the leading Halifaxes, on a similar track to ourselves. Settled on the run, there seemed to be no reason why the ground station should key us off halfway down, but they did. Again, we turned off the run, switched off and back on to intercom, shortly to be exiting the Dutch coast.

There had been no opposition and no sign of the new German jet aircraft. Had they turned up, they would have had their hands full with the several RAF fighters along the route.

Throttled back, and in no hurry, we approached the English Channel at about 8,000 feet. The cloud had dispersed and the lowlands of Norfolk and Cambridgeshire looked beautiful in the autumn sunshine. We were down to 5,000 feet, nearing Cambridge, when there was a loud bang from what appeared to be the bomb bay, and a blast of pressure in the cockpit. The aeroplane reared.

"What was that?" we both shouted at each other. For me, it could mean only one thing – the flares in the bomb bay must have ignited from the barometric pressure at 5,000 feet. I had only one thought – get rid of them before they set the aircraft ablaze.

"It's the flares!" I screamed at Johnny. "Jettison!"

Immediately the four flares were on their way towards the Cambridge countryside, but better that than an aircraft on fire. I sat waiting for the flames to burst through the floor of the aircraft, and Johnny urgently advised base to watch out for a burning Mosquito. We arrived over base with a priority pancake, other aircraft on the circuit being told to orbit the field. A fire tender and an ambulance raced across the grass, following behind us, as we turned off at the first intersection and braked to a halt, ground and fire crews surrounding us.

The Mosquito was quite obviously intact. Not a sign of

smoke or fire damage. In fact, it looked almost just about out of the showroom, as in fact it almost was. It was the new 'O Barred'.

At de-briefing we had to explain, to the Wingco no less, why we had dropped our flares on friendly Cambridgeshire. After we had explained, our decision to jettison was confirmed, if a little reluctantly, as correct, as, after all, if it *had* been the flares the squadron would have been minus its new Mark XVI.

> [*18 November 1944. Munster. 479 aircraft – 367 Halifaxes, 94 Lancasters, 18 Mosquitoes – of 4, 6 and 8 Groups. 1 Halifax crashed in Holland.*
>
> *The raid was not concentrated and bombs fell in all parts of Munster. The only item of interest mentioned in the local report was a direct hit on a concrete shelter, which killed 68 people. The total number of deaths in the town was 138.*]

Fortunately, the flares had done no damage, and the bang was diagnosed as a sudden release of the pressurisation inside the cockpit due to a faulty valve. It had stuck at around 10,000 feet and released itself at 5,000, letting in 5,000 feet of pressure difference in an instant, or so we were told.

Apprehensive now of the Mark XVI, it was no great hardship to be in a Mark IX on our next op four days later to Sterkrade in the Ruhr, a new target for us. The aiming point was the large synthetic oil refinery, and we were the first primary, with Flt Lt Fellowes and F/O Bowley as our reserve.

We were airborne in 'P Peter' at 1930 hours into clear night skies, which persisted all the way to the turning-on point, where, at our operational height of 30,000 feet, the southerly run down to the target was also crystal clear. Almost immediately we had a clear signal; we were only a few seconds late, and exactly on the flight plan heading. It was ominously quiet ahead, and we exchanged uneasy glances as we 'felt' the German radar plotting our path. We waited for the blue searchlight to flick on and the white ones to cone us, but they never did, and, dead on time, we coped with a twenty-six-yard error. The flak erupted behind us as the defences gave up the waiting game; every gun on the ground seemed to fire at the same time. We skidded quickly out of harm's way as the 250 heavy bombers, mostly Halifaxes, swept into the target area and into the flak. Looking back after five minutes, we saw our red markers and the greens of the backers-up clustered together. A marking 'cope' at last, after a miserable series of technical failures.

[20 November 1944. Sterkrade. 270 aircraft – 232 Halifaxes, 20 Mosquitoes, 18 Lancasters – of 4 and 8 Groups. 2 Halifaxes lost.

The target was again the synthetic oil refinery. Bomber Command's report says that the plant was not damaged, though some labour barracks nearby were hit. No local details are available.]

November continued damp and miserable, with either fog or low cloud. The heavies were unable to operate for several nights, and only the Mosquitoes were operating, either to Berlin or on 'Overture' raids. We were listed for one of the 'Overtures' three nights later with five other Oboe Mosquitoes. The target was Gottingen, a town in the middle of Germany near Kassel. We had a 'cookie' in the bomb bay, and entered cloud at 2,000 feet, emerging at 10,000 feet into a clear sky. Our bombing height was 20,100 feet – quite low for us, and made possible by the mobile Oboe caravans, now nearly at the German frontier. Soon Berlin itself would be within Oboe range, and with its defences second only to Essen, I viewed the prospect with fear.

It was another of those sinister treks along a line of latitude – 51 degrees 40 minutes this time, just north of the Ruhr. We would be easy prey for the new German jet fighters, which had been sighted several times in the past few weeks, but no attacks had been made on any 109 aircraft so far. Not tonight either – in complete darkness we coped, and released our 'cookie' over the aiming point.

The starboard engine cut for the first time just after we'd bombed, but this was no problem at all for a Mosquito at 20,000 feet with ample time to compensate with higher revs on the other engine. Hardly had Johnny made the adjustment and put the nose down than the engine picked up again, sweet as a bell.

It cut out three more times on the return journey, and each time it picked up again, the third time over the North Sea when we were approaching the English coast at Felixstowe. Shortly on the circuit at Little Staughton, both the engines were in full song. Johnny reported the cut-outs to the control tower, and we were given priority to land ahead of two aircraft already on the circuit. I packed my bag as we turned off the downwind leg and onto the approach.

We were down to 600 feet in the funnel, wheels down, full flap on, and throttled back, when the engine cut again. 'P Peter' fell like a stone. From being in the green area of the approach lights we were in the red, down almost to the deck, and slewing off the approach. I didn't know what was happening. All I *did* know was that we were suddenly dangerously close to the ground. We were still airborne, but the runway lights were level with the nose and off to port. I watched, frozen, as Johnny thrust the port engine throttle forward, then pulled up the undercarriage lever. He was going to put her down wheels up on the grass – presuming we were going to make the grass.

Down to deck level, we were clearing the hedges by inches, as gradually the nose came round towards the runway. Now, mercifully, almost at the perimeter track, Johnny pushed the undercarriage lever down again and yelled, "Pump the undercart!" I pumped frantically at the handle by my side, eyes shifting from the instrument panel to the runway creeping closer and closer to our port wing. The green 'wheels down' light came on as we made the edge of the runway halfway along. Then those marvellous

welcome back-fires as the engines were cut, followed by the
thump of two wheels hitting the runway, bouncing twice
before rolling in contact – but rolling fast, and unable to
brake hard, or we would surely ground-loop and collapse
the undercart with disastrous consequences.

I watched the end of the lighted runway pass behind us
and felt the bumpy ground of the surrounding area under
the wheels. Still travelling fast, with the blackness ahead of
us, we thudded on and on. "Hold on!" Johnny shouted. I
was holding on – like grim death. Dimly I could see the
hedge ahead of us and feel the deceleration from the brakes
and the soft ground. We hit the hedge at thirty knots, went
straight through it and arrived at the ditch by the side of the
country road. Down went the nose into the ditch, up went
the tail, and we jolted forwards, restrained by our straps.

Petrol! We could smell it immediately, and within seconds
we had the top escape hatch off and were sliding down the
nose and into the ditch. But she didn't go up, and we lay
some yards away on the grass verge of the little country
road, by the side of the airfield, speechless as the feeling of
relief flooded over us.

Neither of us saw him until he shone his torch at us. We
were startled. The torch moved on to the aircraft – its tail
hanging perilously over the road – then back on to us. Then
he spoke.

"You can't leave that there!"

It was a policeman – a civilian bobby – standing between
us and the aircraft, and holding on to his bike as he shone his
torch to the aircraft, then back again to us. For seconds we
were struck dumb. Still in a state of shock, I stared
unbelievingly at this preposterous figure in front of me,
talking to me as if I was a naughty schoolboy. Behind him the
Mosquito looked absurd, ridiculous and impotent – her
nose in the ditch and her tail in the air. I felt the hysteria
welling up inside me. I shook uncontrollably, unable to
absorb with any coherence the transition from abject fear to
farcical pantomime.

Johnny, at first unbelieving too, exploded in anger,

hurling threatening abuse at the dark figure standing over us. I didn't know whether I wanted to laugh or cry – to join in the altercation or get up and run away. Just a few minutes earlier I had been packing away my instruments and looking forward to bacon and egg. Now here I was, sitting on a grass verge, listening to Johnny and a policeman shouting at each other. I felt cold and sick, and suddenly weary of events.

Then there were other voices around us, headlights, and the sound of wagons arriving. First the blood wagon, then a fire tender and two vans. Figures surrounded us, one kneeling down beside me enquiringly, an arm around my shoulders. Familiar voices brought me out of my confusion and back to sensibility. The shouting had subsided, with there was now no sign of the policeman and his bicycle.

A young medical orderly picked me up, and after assuring himself of my well-being, moved over to Johnny to be similarly convinced, before wandering back, seemingly frustrated at the lack of customers, to his ambulance. And soon we were in the Wingco's van and on our way round the perimeter track with Johnny recounting the details of his struggle to stay airborne and make the runway. My composure was regained by the time we were sitting down at the de-briefing table. I gratefully accepted the neat rum and the cigarettes proffered by the Wingco, the details of the night's raid almost forgotten, obliterated by the events of the few minutes from funnel to grass verge.

[24 November 1944. Minor operations. 58 Mosquitoes to Berlin and 6 to Gottingen.]

The interrogation over, and our senses back to normal, even a little elevated after the rum on an empty stomach, we didn't linger in the Mess after the meal. We cycled to the billet, pulled on our pyjamas, and lay on our beds with the light on, staring at the ceiling. The experience and the alcohol had left me very tired, but I couldn't go to sleep. Johnny couldn't either.

"Did you know that we went under the high-tension wires?" he said. I didn't and I didn't really want to know. It had all been a bit too much for me, and fatigue finally shut my eyes until daylight.

At 'flights' the next morning we learned that we had been credited with a nil marking error and had been exonerated from pranging the aircraft. We were the third aircraft that month to prang on the airfield. On the 11th, W/O Reid had crashed on the runway and blocked it for a time, and on the 23rd, Flt Lt Shaw had crashed on take-off. Everybody had got out unharmed. But the luck ran out on the 27th when Flt Lt Williamson and F/O Kitchen failed to return from a raid on Neuss, three nights after our escape in 'O Barred'.

We had also been flying on the same night as the missing crew. We were in 'O Oboe' on a precision bombing raid to Hallendorf, a small town deep inside Germany. We were carrying a 'cookie', and were fitted with wing tanks, with little more than enough fuel for the round trip. In cloud by the time we had reached 3,000 feet, we were quickly out of it and in clear skies most of the way to the target. We had another good 'cope', and bombed from 32,000 feet. Everything had gone exactly the same as on the trip to Gottingen, except that both engines were singing sweetly.

But our run of bad luck hadn't finished yet. One of the wing tanks refused to empty into the fuel system, leaving us with not enough fuel to get back to base, and barely enough to make the English coast. Throttled back, we made for Woodbridge, the emergency landing field on the coast of East Anglia.

We flew on in silence and as soon as we were over the North Sea, made our 'Darkie' call.

"Mayday, mayday, mayday." Johnny's voice was firm and insistent. There was an instant response from Woodbridge, listening out on the emergency channel. Johnny informed them that we were 'short of gravy' and requested immediate landing facilities. Did we want a QDM, they asked.

"No thanks, we're heading straight for you."

But they gave us one nevertheless, just to be sure, as we coasted downhill. "Runway cleared," they reported reassuringly. That was the good news. Then the bad. The coast was enveloped in fog and our hearts sank. Then once again, that calm reassuring voice: "Fido landing procedure." The Fog Intensive Dispersal Operation consisted of a pipeline on each side of the runway through which petrol was pumped and set alight, dispersing the fog along the landing strip.

We saw it a long way ahead of us, visible through the fog. They called us every two or three minutes, "How's your gravy?" and repeated the QDM. As we approached we could see the fog being dispersed and, as we got closer, the cleared passage along the runway, an illuminated strip surrounded on all sides by a grey blanket of fog. Turning into the funnel, we ran into the fog, with the two strips of burning petrol clearly discernible ahead.

It was violently turbulent from the heat of the flaming petrol and the aircraft was tossed about frighteningly. It was like flying into the jaws of hell, with great sheets of flame on either side of us as Johnny fought to put her down against the up-currents from the hot air. If we didn't get down first time we would have just about enough fuel to go round once again.

Even if we did get down, to slew off the runway would plunge us into the flames. But Johnny, erect in his seat, concentration etched on his face, dropped her on to the runway, plumb in the middle, halfway along. And as we came to a halt, still in the middle, a van swept in front of us with lights to guide us to dispersal. The moment we were off the runway, the Fido was turned off and the fog swirled in again over the runway. We had become one of the 2,694 aircraft to be rescued by Fido during the war.

[27 November 1944. Hallendorf. 7 Mosquitoes to Hallendorf.]

We had to stay overnight at Woodbridge and were debriefed by a very attractive WAAF officer. We slept in the Officers' Mess, warm and comfortable in the luxury of the sheeted beds provided for visiting aircrew. The fog was slow to disperse on the next day, and it was three o'clock in the afternoon before we were airborne again for the fifteen-minute flight to base.

Back at Little Staughton we learned that it was a compulsory dining-in night. We had to change into best blue and behave ourselves throughout the evening in front of the senior officers and their ladies. It was all very formal, nobody dared put a foot wrong, and we left as soon as possible, promising ourselves a pub crawl in Bedford the next night.

In the event we did have our pub crawl in Bedford on the following night, but only after returning from Dortmund round about teatime. It had been a knockout of a trip and we celebrated accordingly. We had taken off at 1305 hours as reserve to F/L Skitch and Sergeant Pritchard and flew with them in formation down to C, where they abruptly lost their signals and we were called in. We were on the run immediately and marked the steelworks in Dortmund with an error of eighteen yards. It had been another day of torment for the German cities with Allied aircraft filling the skies over the Ruhr.

[29 November 1944. Dortmund. 294 Lancasters and 17 Mosquitoes of 1 and 8 Groups. 6 Lancasters lost.
    Bad weather caused the marking and resultant bombing to be scattered, but fresh damage was caused in Dortmund.]

As we had been marking Dortmund, other Mosquitoes of 109 and 105 Squadrons had been leading three squadrons of Mosquitoes of the Light Night Striking Force to Duisburg, all carrying 'cookies' and in close formation on one of the new 'Oboe leader' raids, another innovation, which looked like becoming increasingly used by Bomber Command.

Designed for use on small but important targets, twelve 'cookies' landed simultaneously on an area the size of a football field, ensuring obliteration. However, they weren't popular with the crews – a direct hit by flak on any one of the twelve aircraft involved would have brought the lot down.

So it was with a little trepidation that I went to briefing on the following day. I'd missed breakfast in exchange for an extra hour in bed in deference to my hangover. It was a relief to find that we were on a normal night raid to Duisburg, evidence of the changed times in late November 1944. Feeling relief at a night raid to the Ruhr was new indeed.

The oil plant in Duisburg had been bombed earlier in the day by a force of Pathfinder Mosquitoes, and they had started fires that were still burning under the clouds as I prepared to drop our sky markers over the unfortunate city. We had been called in at C after the primary had lost his signals, and I lost mine too with only seconds to go to release. We brought our markers back, but there was no shortage of red TIs burning over the city of Duisburg that night.

[30 November 1944. Duisburg. 576 aircraft – 425 Halifaxes, 126 Lancasters, 25 Mosquitoes – of 1, 4, 6 and 8 Groups. 3 Halifaxes lost.

The target area was completely cloud-covered and the attack was not concentrated, but much fresh damage was still caused. Duisburg reported 528 houses destroyed and 805 seriously damaged, but no industrial buildings were mentioned in the report. 246 people were killed, including 55 foreign workers and 12 prisoners of war.]

And so ended November. We had flown just ten ops during the month, all to Germany, and we'd had six 'copes' and four failures.

It was Mother's birthday on 2 December, and I managed to 'come by' a duck on the previous day, to send as a present. It was already a freezing December, and the duck would be safe from putrefaction for a few days. I carefully parcelled it up and cycled to the camp post office to post it off to Wallasey. It arrived there four days later, just after the telegram from the Air Ministry.

I'd cycled through snow and ice to the post office on 1 December, and it was no surprise to find that there was no battle order that day, or on the following day as the wintry weather continued, with snow-filled clouds and the temperature below zero. It was like Moncton in January 1942. I tried to ring Mother at Wilsons several times during the day, but every time all trunk lines were engaged, and I finally gave up.

I was going to try again the next morning, but by 0810 hours we were airborne with four red TIs bound for the small town of Heimbach in support of the US Army. The early morning call had been quite one of the worst. We'd been woken up at five o'clock. It was freezing in the billet with the only warmth a mile away in the Mess where we lingered until the last possible moment over our operational meal.

We were one of four Oboe Mosquitoes detailed to mark the bridge in the town. The Met forecast over the target was 3/10ths cloud, but as we progressed into Germany the cloud thickened up and on the run it was 5/10ths or 6/10ths. The first Mosquito on the run failed. We heard him lose his signal and we were called in immediately. The Lancasters, nearly two hundred of them, approached the target from our starboard side, moving in and out of sight under the scattered cloud. Twelve thousand feet below us they looked to be unopposed, and were no doubt scanning the scene ahead of them for sight of our markers. They would see them soon. We were halfway between D and release, with the 'cat' signal consistently devoid of merging dots or dashes, the bomb doors open, and my thumb hovering over the bomb tit. Conscious of the Lancasters moving in expectantly, and of the failure of the Mosquito ahead of us, I was willing the signals to continue for just another ninety seconds. I watched the seconds finger on my astro watch, jerking its way round towards our time on target, then pass through it with no sign of the release. Twenty seconds later I received the first of the five dots in my headphones, and triumphantly flourishing my free hand towards Johnny's face. I felt the elation of the 'cope' as I plunged my thumb down on the bomb tit.

We both looked over at each other simultaneously. Something was wrong. We hadn't felt the familiar lurch that even target indicators gave to the aircraft when relieving it of their weight. Swinging round towards the selector panel, I checked for hang-ups, knowing before I did that the check would confirm my fears. Four hung-up TIs nestled in the bomb bay.

"The fucking things are still there – must have been an electrical failure," I grumbled to Johnny, disappointed at our failure to mark. I could imagine the heavies having to go round again, ever hopeful of the sight of burning TIs, and the Master Bomber seething at the delay.

"Bloody gremlins," growled Johnny, philosophical as ever, as we settled on our course for the Zuider Zee and back to base. And at interrogation, unaware of our TIs on their way back to the bomb dump, the Intelligence Officer's congratulations on our being the only ones to cope turned to dismay as we recounted our story of the hang-ups. We left him writing up his report, our own disappointment shortly to be forgotten in the comfort of the ante-room armchairs.

[3 December 1944. Heimbach. 183 Lancasters and 4 Mosquitoes of 1 and 8 Groups to bomb this small town in the Eifel region, probably in support of an American ground attack in this area. The Master Bomber and the Pathfinders could not identify the target and the Lancasters were ordered to abandon the raid. No aircraft lost.]

The next day was Tuesday 4 December 1944, the day that I took off on my ninetieth operation. It was cold in the hut that morning. The two blankets on my bed had been inadequate during the night, and I'd got up to put my greatcoat on top of them. Outside it was bleak. The snow that had fallen a few days earlier had been trampled under foot and had now turned to ice. It lay slippery and unyielding, and I hoped that we wouldn't be on ops that night as I peered out of the window at 0700 hours and started to dress.

We cycled up to the Mess for breakfast, my hands numb on the handlebars, then up to 'flights' to hang about for hours. 1030 hours was the usual time for signs of activity from the Wingco's office, but no orders had arrived by twelve noon and I started to look forward to the evening dozing in front of the fire in the Mess. But just as we were preparing to drift off to lunch, the unmistakable signs of night ops made themselves evident. "Shit," I thought. "I bet we're on again." We were. Briefing 1400 hours, with not a lot of time to have lunch and a quick kip before cycling off to the briefing room.

[4 December 1944. Karlsruhe. 535 aircraft – 369 Lancasters, 154 Halifaxes, 12 Mosquitoes – of 1, 6 and 8 Groups. 1 Lancaster and 1 Mosquito lost.]

The target was Karlsruhe, which lay ten miles north of Stuttgart in the south of Germany. It was a long trip for us, and on a night far from ideal for flying. There was going to be a lot of cloud to climb through, with icing on the leading edges to contend with. We were marking from our maximum height of 34,000 feet, but we were flying in 'O Oboe', which had been warm and faultless on the two previous ops we had done in her. We were marking as primary, with Flt Lt Smith and F/O Jones as our reserve on Channel 2. Marking on Channel 1 at the same time as us were F/O Relph and his navigator, F/O Davis.

As we were flying in a warm aircraft, there was no need to take our fur-lined Irvin jackets or silk gloves, though without them we felt cold on the way out to dispersal, and were glad to get the engines going and the heating on in the aircraft. We were airborne at 1803 hours. All being well, we would be back in the Mess by half past ten, and on the billiard table by eleven.

We were in cloud by 3,000 feet, still in it as we neared the English coast, and out of it over the North Sea, where I selected the bomb switches. We were at 30,000 feet at the Dutch coast, on track and on time with Gee still just about workable. Still climbing, we changed course for the target, and I busied myself with plotting the last of the Gee fixes. Approaching Aachen, we had been airborne for nearly an hour and were still on track when we collided with Relph's Mosquito.

CHAPTER 22

The Return to Base

Slowly waking up, I became aware of the cold. I
reached down for the bed clothes to pull them
tighter round my neck, but I couldn't feel them. I
rolled over on to my back and opened my eyes. It
was so dark, and the cold was intense. I felt confused and
unable to think straight. "Where am I, and why am I so
cold?" I lifted my head, tried to sit up, wincing at the pain
in my ankle. Then memory flooded back, tightening my
chest and gripping my stomach. Fully conscious again, I sat
up, leaned back on my hands and looked around me. "I *am*
alive, aren't I? I am, yes – I am, I am." I covered my face with
my hands and lay down again on my back, the cold
forgotten. I lay motionless, living again the terror of those
last few minutes in 'O Oboe' up to the moment when I had
felt the pain, then nothing more until I had regained
consciousness.

For several moments I lay there, before sitting up again
and looking around me. I was surrounded by frozen snow.
My knee-caps and my face hurt, as well as my ankle. Unable
to see the ground as I had landed, my legs must have
buckled and my knees thrust into my face, knocking me out.
I reached into my battledress pocket for a cigarette, and
pulled out a crumpled packet of Woodbines. Dammit, only
two in it. Worse, only one match in my matchbox. Please
God, don't let it blow out before my cigarette lights.
Cupping the naked flame in both hands, I sucked at the
cigarette in my mouth, gratefully feeling the smoke filling
my lungs. And there I sat, in a frozen field somewhere in
Europe, smoking a Woodbine.

What next? It had to be to light the second Woodbine from
the stub of the first. The slight tugging at my shoulders
reminded me that I was still attached to my parachute. I

twisted the clasp, punched it, felt the harness fall. I heard it slither away, pulled by the billowing parachute.

I smoked the second cigarette until it burned my fingers, then, getting to my feet, I started to make my way towards 'O Oboe'. She was still burning a few hundred yards away. My left ankle hurt as I walked on it, and I wondered whether it was broken. It was quite obviously swollen – my flying boot felt tight around it. Mustn't take the boot off or I'd never get it on again. The glow from the burning aircraft silhouetted the obstacles in my path and I was able to make reasonable progress towards it. As I came within sight of the flames, I reached a tarmacadam road that ran beside the field in which 'O Oboe' had landed. As I started to cross the road, I saw the lights of a vehicle approaching along it, so I scampered away and lay down in the ditch at the side of the road.

The vehicle stopped within twenty yards of where I lay. Two men got out, and before making their way over to 'O Oboe' talked in guttural German-like voices. Germans! I must have landed in Germany. So, as they walked over to the burning aircraft, I got up out of the ditch, and limped away from the scene. I fell several times until finally, safely away from 'O Oboe', I fell heavily over a tree trunk lying in a ditch. Dismayed at the early set-backs, I lay motionless and miserable over the fallen tree.

I began to feel cold after a little while and decided to move on, conscious of the German voices I'd heard, and that I was probably on the wrong side of the border. As I began to move my hands along the tree trunk to push myself back on to my feet, I became more aware of its shape and fabric. It didn't feel much like a tree trunk now, and it smelt horribly. As I moved my hand along it I felt, at its extremity, the smooth roundness of a steel helmet. I was lying on a dead soldier in a ditch. Panic gripped my throat and, picking myself up, I ran blindly into the blackness, through bracken and hedges, falling and stumbling, but with only one thought – to put as much distance between me and the corpse as I possibly could, until finally, exhausted and breathless, I slumped down against a tree to recover my composure.

I was wearing battledress, my white submariner's sweater and flying boots – hardly sufficient to keep out the bitter cold. I had my escape kit tucked away in my battledress blouse. It contained Horlicks tablets, glucose sweets, water-purifying tablets, fishing line, razor, penknife, soap, chewing gum, chocolate, maps and two tiny compasses. I also had a compass hidden in one of my battledress buttons, and another in my front collar stud. Each compass had a small fluorescent dot to indicate magnetic north, and I started to walk due west using the collar stud compass, with the dot lying ninety degrees to the right of my heading.

Walking across open countryside on a night as black as this was difficult and hazardous. I couldn't see what lay a yard in front of me, but the ground felt solid and level, and after the first few faltering steps I gained in confidence and walked a little faster. I wasn't sure where the battle lines lay. There were gun flashes in the sky all around me, but they were all far away, and I didn't know whether they were from field guns or flak batteries. I wasn't sure that I was in Allied territory, though the dead soldier pointed to the battle having passed through the area. I had no alternative but to trudge on westward, and hope to locate my position in daylight. I munched the Horlicks tablets as I moved on.

Maintaining direction in the dark without sight of the stars proved impossible. I looked at my little compass every few minutes, and every time had to correct my heading. I had baled out at around seven o'clock, and it would be another twelve hours to the light of dawn. Gradually the even ground gave way to more uneven territory, and I stumbled and fell countless times. Occasionally I turned my ankle over, the pain excruciating, stopping my progress until it had eased. After what seemed to be hours later, I fell down a bank and came to rest in foliage. I felt bruised, grazed, desperately tired and reluctant to get up from where I had fallen. In need of rest, I gathered up the ferns into which I had fallen, piling them on top of me as I lay down and tried to sleep.

Within minutes of lying down under the blanket of ferns, I began to shiver, and with the thought that if I *did* go to sleep in the bitter cold, I would be unlikely to wake up again, I dragged myself back to my feet and resumed my westward trek.

As I progressed I convinced myself that I was in friendly Belgian territory, but as I became more and more cold and tired, I didn't really care whether I was or wasn't. I envied the aircrew in the aircraft that I could hear above me returning to their egg and bacon and the warmth of the Mess, and, Germany or Belgium, I must be in Allied territory, so decided to get help at the first house I found.

Shortly afterwards I walked into a low brick wall, my right knee striking it painfully. As I bent down to rub the knee, I could make out the dark outline of a building. I climbed the wall and crept furtively over to it, feeling my way around until I found a door. I felt up it for a knocker, found one, and knocked three or four times. There was a ferocious barking of a dog from inside. It sounded like an Alsatian or something as big, so I turned and ran – straight into the wall, with the same knee. I was so terrified at the thought of being savaged by the dog that it was only after I had clambered over the wall and limped off into the night that I felt the pain of the impact. I could hardly walk, with my left ankle and now my right knee injured.

But at least I was now on firm tarmacadam, and I could just make out the direction of the narrow little road on which I was walking. After a few more minutes, I could discern the outline of another building to my right, lying a few yards off the road. I decided to try again.

I felt my way around the building to a door, and knocked on it several times. No barking dog this time, and shortly a bedroom window opened directly above the door. A male voice enquired in French, something like, "Qu'est-ce que c'est? Qui est la?" French – then I must be in Belgium.

Haltingly, in my best school French, I replied, "Je suis un aviateur RAF. J'ai parachuté. Je me suis blessé. Voulez vous m'aidez?"

The response was instant and totally unexpected. "Yes, certainly, I will come down and let you in." English! The voice had answered in English.

I could hardly believe my ears as lights went on inside the house. Then the door opened, and a youth of about 16, with a welcoming smile on his face, beckoned me. "Come in, please, come in." The relief I felt was overwhelming. I was alive and in friendly hands, and as the youth and his father on either side of me put their arms around my waist to help me along the hall and into the living room, I felt tears of gratitude welling up in my eyes. I hastily blinked them away as I was gently lowered on to a couch and instantly offered a cigarette, which I gratefully accepted.

I was with the Munnix family – father, mother and five children. Joseph, he who had opened the door, was sixteen and the oldest of the five. The youngest was six. They all came downstairs to stare and listen to the conversation between Joseph and me. He kept them informed all the time, by translating the exchanges. And all the time they stared – except Joseph's mother, who had gone to make coffee.

Joseph spoke English very well, and the answers he gave to my questions were good too. Yes, he assured me, the fighting in the area had ended weeks ago, and I was in liberated territory. There was an American command post about three kilometres away in Gemenich, the nearby village. When I asked for directions he wouldn't hear of my leaving. The family obviously didn't intend parting with me, and I was becoming increasingly embarrassed by the warmth of their welcome and their obvious adulation. Their eyes never left my face, nor their smiles their own.

"It is a great honour to help the RAF," announced Joseph, and after a few words with his father, who instantly left the room, he told me that his father would go on his autocycle to the Americans in the village, and bring them back with him.

So, as I sipped the ersatz coffee, made from acorns, I wrote a note to the American commander while Joseph's father prepared himself for the short journey to the village. When he was ready, scarfed and gloved against the cold, he took the note, carefully depositing it like a despatch rider in the pocket of his leather jacket, and, beaming delightedly, left on his mission.

Joseph and I talked about the German occupation of his country, by which in fact they had been little affected. His father being a farmer, they had been left to get on with their farming, though with scant compensation for the produce compulsorily taken by the Germans. I recounted my narrow escape, and gave Joseph one of the escape compasses, waving away his profuse and genuine thanks. And still they stared and smiled, except for the youngest, who had fallen asleep in his sister's arms. Mme Munnix had boiled me an egg, and after I'd eaten it she bandaged my ankle, which was by now almost balloon-like.

About an hour after M Munnix had left the house, there was the sound of a vehicle outside, then silence for several minutes. I thought it must have been a passing motor car, until suddenly the door of the room was flung open and M Munnix was prodded slowly into the room by two American soldiers at the point of their guns. As they entered the room two more GIs quickly followed them in, and instantly covered me with their rifles. I froze. With two loaded guns pointing directly at me, this was no time for any sudden movements. I had a feeling that they would shoot first and ask questions afterwards. Forcing a weak smile, every other muscle in my body rigid, I croaked huskily, "Hello – thanks for coming to help me." Taking in the scene, and reassured that this was no booby trap, the four Americans relaxed. Out came the cigarettes and soon the room resounded with laughter as they played with the kids and joked with Joseph and me.

I briefly told the sergeant my story, and after about half an hour I said goodbye to the Munnix family, exchanging addresses and promising to write to each other.

The Americans helped me into their jeep and we moved off around four o'clock. It was still dark and freezing cold and I was glad when we arrived at the warm village school that served as US Headquarters. I was interrogated by an amiable major from Arkansas who plied me with cognac, and I fell asleep while he was writing up his notes. I was woken up very gently at eight o'clock. My transport had arrived to take me to the field hospital close to the airfield, which was being used to ferry American battle casualties back to the UK.

It was daylight by now and as we drove through the Belgian countryside I was staggered by the amount of 'window', the thin metal strips dropped by the heavies to confuse the German radar. It hung like tinsel from every tree and covered the hedges. Otherwise the countryside looked flat and unblemished by the passage of war, its scars hidden under the blanket of snow.

Before long the transport arrived at the field hospital, consisting of a huge marquee, or several marquees joined together. Inside there were rows and rows of hospital beds, each one numbered. The ground was covered with matting and there were several heaters giving out a quite agreeable amount of warmth. I was taken on a stretcher to a bed deep inside the marquee, and a label was pinned to my battledress blouse giving my name, rank and number. Almost every bed was occupied, and the place was a hive of activity. Some of the patients were being tended by medics, with others lying prone on their beds, alone and unattended. Some were sitting up in their beds, and others sitting on the edge of them. The relatively uninjured like me wandered enquiringly in their immediate vicinity.

As I explored my section of the marquee, I saw for the first time men wounded in battle. Some had minor flesh wounds, and there were others with horrific injuries and close to death. At sight of these I retreated to my bed, humbled and subdued. I suspected that with only a badly swollen ankle, I was probably the most minor casualty in the whole of the field hospital.

During the day there was a constant turnover of occupants, with ambulances arriving and departing all the time, and after I had been there for twenty-four hours, all those who had been around me had gone and been replaced by others. I was beginning to think I had been forgotten, until late on the morning of the next day two German soldiers arrived at my bedside carrying a stretcher. They helped me on to it, then carried me out to a waiting ambulance. I was intrigued at my first sight of the enemy. They weren't at all like the sub-human brutes who had been depicted on the propaganda posters. They were both of poor physique, mild mannered, polite, and utterly subservient. But being prisoners of war, no doubt they would be.

They lifted me on the stretcher into the ambulance, and after about half an hour's drive we arrived at the airfield, where I and my fellow patients were lifted out of the ambulance and into a waiting Dakota.

I was strapped on to my stretcher and we were loaded in tiers of three on each side of the aircraft. Almost immediately we taxied out and took off, and at 1400 hours on 7 December I was once again airborne and on my belated way back to the UK. We were heading for the RAF airfield near Bournemouth, and flew at 5,000 feet in constant cloud for a very bumpy two and a half hours. I was the only one of the passengers not to be sick during the flight, and for some of the badly wounded it was obviously a painful experience. It was so turbulent that even I was glad to feel the bump and screech of the tyres on the runway at RAF Bournemouth.

While I had no complaints about my treatment by the Americans, I was looking forward to getting back as soon as I could to the familiar surroundings of Little Staughton. I could see out of one of the windows of the aircraft that we were parked near the control tower, and as there were no ambulances in sight, I left the aircraft and walked over to control in the hope of getting a lift back to the squadron. The Flight Lieutenant Control Officer, however, wasn't at all enthusiastic about the idea, and considered that I should stay with the travelling hospital until I was discharged. On reflection, I agreed with his logic, and shortly after I had returned to the Dakota, ambulances began to make their way round the perimeter track towards it. We were quickly transhipped into the ambulances and, after a short drive, were soon arriving at the American military hospital at Blandford Forum.

The hospital catered for all the American battle casualties from Europe. It was a busy place and covered many acres. On arrival we were quickly lifted out of the ambulances and loaded on to individual trolleys, then wheeled away to our respective wards where we were met by the duty ward doctor. In my ward this proved to be a not unattractive female, who ticked my name off on her list. "How d'yer feel, soldier?" she enquired, obviously her standard greeting.

I didn't feel inclined to go into any lengthy explanation of why I wasn't a soldier, and instead protested that they shouldn't really be wasting their time on my paltry injuries. "There's not much wrong with me actually, and I'd like to return to my squadron if you don't mind." She was distinctly unimpressed, and after informing me that she would see me later, gave instructions to the stretcher bearers to take me to my allotted bed where a medic told me to undress and get into bed. There was nobody available to whom I could register any further protest, so I donned the regulation pyjamas, climbed into my bed and looked around at my ward mates.

On the opposite side, in the bed in the corner by the door, was an American soldier, obviously of native Indian origin. He was propped up with his bedclothes rolled down. He had no legs. Below his trunk were just two stumps wrapped in bloodstained bandages. Next to him, also propped up, was a swarthy Italian American, the bottom half of his face held together with wire. The occupant of the bed next to him lay prone with his eyes shut, and with cages under his bedclothes. Two stands by his bedside held bottles out of which tubes disappeared under the bedclothes.

Next to him was a fellow sitting on the edge of his bed, nonchalantly swinging his legs to and fro and sucking an orange. The next two beds were occupied by pale sleeping figures who obviously were very ill.

On my side of the ward only one bed besides mine was occupied, the four empty ones obviously being those of the four soldiers who had been playing cards at a table in the middle of the ward. They had viewed my entrance with curiosity, not immediately recognising my RAF battledress. Within minutes the mobile patient from the other side had made his way over to my bed. He was very outgoing, and curious to know the background to my arrival at Blandford.

The card players forgot their game and joined him as I started to recount my adventures, all of them sitting or lying on my bed, leaving me little room to rest my throbbing ankle. Three of them were smoking, and I was longing for a cigarette. I hadn't had one all day. I had no money on me to buy any, and I had been able to scrounge only the occasional one at the transit hospital where they appeared to be not very plentiful.

Apologetically, I asked if anyone could spare me a cigarette, and within seconds of asking I had a thousand of them. Every one of the five GIs had instantly gone to his locker and returned with a two hundred carton, which they threw on to my bed. I was completely taken aback, and protested, rather weakly, that I had no money to pay for them. "Aw, forget it," they each shrugged. So I lay back in my bed talking to these instant friends and chain-smoking Lucky Strikes until the dinner wagon arrived. They left me to go to the Mess hall for their meal, and I leaned back and enjoyed a very palatable three-course lunch, washed down with the inevitable delicious coffee.

Later I limped my way to the ablutions, passing the lady doctor on the way. "I thought there was nothing wrong with you," she said, pointing at my ankle. "Oh, it's nothing," I bravely countered. And it wasn't compared with the misfortune that had befallen the boy in the corner bed who had lost his legs. He had stepped on a mine and was lucky to have survived. I soon made friends with him too, as I had with the other GIs.

It wasn't difficult to make friends with Americans, as I found out for the second time. They seemed to have an extraordinary capacity for being able to break through the

English reserve, and by lights out I knew all of them by their first names.

I got up during the night to go to the lavatory, and as I passed the boy in the corner by the door I thought I could hear sobbing noises from his bed. When I came back from the lavatory, I stood by the door for a moment and, sure enough, hc was sobbing quietly in his bed. So I went to his bedside and asked if he was all right, instantly regretting my insensitivity. I sat down on the chair by his bed, and in a heart-rending voice he whispered, "I've lost my legs." He'd been so cheerful during the day, but now, in the dead of night, he was despairing. So I sat and cried with him, until he went to sleep, and I went back to my bed.

I was taken for an X-ray the next morning, and tried unsuccessfully to telephone Little Staughton and my parents. There weren't any public telephones in the hospital and I was becoming frantic to let somebody know that I was alive and safe in England. The problem was solved on the following afternoon when an American padre walked into the ward and asked if anybody wished to send a telegram. We were only allowed one each and couldn't disclose where we were, so I asked him to send it to my parents. "Safe in England. Letter follows."

On the same day, the injury to my ankle was classified as severely torn ligaments with no fractures. It was by now multi-coloured – black, brown and yellow – but becoming less painful all the time, and I was pronounced fit to eat in the Mess hall with the other five walking patients from the ward.

I was out of harm's way and being well cared for at Blandford, and though I felt out of place, I wasn't pressing for my return to more normal surroundings. And there was no intent on the part of the hospital authorities to allow me to leave until my ankle was sufficiently improved to allow them to pronounce me fit for duty. So I settled into the routine of the hospital and awaited developments.

There was a film show in the hospital cinema on my fourth evening of residence, and I went along with my five new mates. We arrived at the cinema about a quarter of an hour before the film was due to show, and a few minutes later the tannoy requested, "Pilot Officer Smith of the British Royal Air Force to report back to his ward immediately."

The Americans advised me to disregard the request absolutely. Apparently there was a principle involved. I was 'off duty' and 'off limits' and entitled to call my time my own.

"I'd better go," I protested lamely. But it was five to one.

"It's probably for an injection," one of them said. Well, now it was six to none, so I accepted my friends' advice.

The film started on time – a musical starring Mitzi Gaynor. Neither attracted me. I'd only gone to the cinema to relieve the monotony and to be with the others. So, five minutes after the film had started, I quietly left my seat on the end of the row and made my way back to the ward. Injections were only given during working hours, so I was probably safe from the needle.

Hesitantly, I walked along the corridor of the ward block, past the ward and opened the door of the sister's office. In addition to the duty sister and a US Army doctor, there were three other people sitting in the room. Knowing it to be so unlikely as to be virtually impossible, it took me several seconds to take in what I was seeing. The three others were Drus, Mother and Dad.

The sister and the Major left us, and after I had convinced my visitors that I was comparatively uninjured, I told them my story and they told me theirs. They had received the Air Ministry telegram informing them that I was missing, presumed dead, early on the afternoon of 5 December. The duck arrived two hours later. They couldn't eat it and gave it away.

Four days later, early in the evening, their despondency had been relieved by the telegraph boy, his red Post Office bicycle propped up against the wall of 37 Cliff Road, Wallasey, proffering the telegram that the American padre had sent from Blandford. After the initial euphoria, the next day found them impatient for further news. Drus and Mother, neither of them inclined to let the grass grow under their feet, and both war-trained telephone switchboard operators, contrived to use their expertise – and the nation's priority telephone lines – to trace the source of the telegram. After several unsuccessful calls they rang an unlisted number in Liverpool and the Wing Commander who answered took down details of every letter of the telegram. He rang back within an hour with the information they had been seeking all day.

"Pilot Officer Smith is in an American Army hospital in Blandford. I've spoken to the ward doctor. Smith's all right, but suffering from shock. (So that's what the injections had been for.) He'd like you to go and see him if you can."

They caught the midnight train from Liverpool, and arrived at the ward sister's office eighteen hours later. True to form, the Americans made them welcome and gave us a private room where we sat and talked until midnight. Reassured, they left the next day with Drus's forty-eight-hour pass rapidly running out. The Americans provided accommodation for them at the GIs' canteen in Blandford – the Doughnut Dugout – and gave Drus an escort to discourage advances from over-ambitious GIs.

I had to stay at the hospital for a few more days to await my clearance, during which time I managed to get through to Little Staughton to confirm my survival. Finally, I received the news that I was 'free to leave', and was taken by ambulance to Blandford railway station to catch the train to London, complete with a railway warrant to St Neots, my cigarettes, and a bag of chocolate bars donated by my fellow patients. I had to change main-line stations in London via the Tube and, dressed as I was, capless, in battledress, flying boots and white sweater, clutching a bag full of cigarettes and chocolate, must have presented a highly suspicious spectacle. I envisaged several tiresome confrontations with service and civilian policemen. But nobody took the slightest notice of me as I made my way between stations, and three or four SPs passed me without asking for an explanation of my being improperly dressed. Bit disappointing really. I wouldn't have been averse to a little admiration as a parachutist from a doomed aircraft, and further frustration was forthcoming when I enquired at the ticket office for the next train to St Neots. The old bloke at the ticket window explained that St Neots was difficult to get to from London and suggested that I might like to consider a more easily accessible destination. Having convinced him that it was St Neots or nothing, he began to delve through his timetable, while a queue started to form behind me. In retrospect, I should have plumped for Bedford – it was also on a main line and only slightly further from Little Staughton than was St Neots. Finally, he beckoned me into the ticket office. It was warmer in there, and I was given a mug of tea. The train wasn't due out until the early hours, change at Huntingdon at about 4.00am and catch the milk train to surrounding stations. There was a long wait for the train, so I was invited to settle down in the ticket office where, with the friendly warmth from the coke fire, I fell asleep.

I was awakened in good time to catch the train and wandered out into the biting cold after another mug of tea. The train was unheated, and clanked its miserable way towards the Fen country. This was not at all like the homecoming that I had envisaged, and there was more deflation when I rang the squadron MT section from St Neots at around 6.00am on that icy December morning. The duty MT officer was anxious to help, but all his available vehicles were booked for duty and he could offer little more advice than that I wait in the town square for the daily morning truck to pick me up at 10.00am.

So I sat in the cold station waiting room until 9.30am, before trudging into St Neots and taking a seat on a bench in the town square, there to await the transport. It was after 11 o'clock before it arrived, and I was dropped off outside the 109 crew room just as everyone was leaving for lunch. From the Wingco I heard of Johnny's return, his report that I had probably not got out, and that he had gone on survivor's leave. "You'll be interested in this no doubt," he said, showing me a new back-type parachute for the use of Mosquito navigators. It was to be introduced immediately, and had I been wearing one it would have made my exit from 'O Oboe' no problem at all.

I was also told about events back at base on the night of 4 December. The ground stations, having received no response from 'O Oboe' when they called us up, had then called up our reserve, who marked the target successfully from 28,000 feet. F/O Relph and his navigator, F/O Davis, had also marked the target and returned to base to report that they had been involved in a mid-air 'brush' with another aircraft near Aachen. Their own aircraft had been only slightly damaged and had continued on its way. When we failed to return, it was assumed that we had been the aircraft involved in the collision. The squadron records read: "O Oboe failed to return having probably collided with aircraft piloted by F/O A C Relph."

The navigator of the other aircraft, F/O J R Davis, had trained in Miami on the course after mine. We had been trained by the same Pam-Am instructors and against all possible odds we had, on that fateful night, somehow contrived to navigate our respective aircraft to exactly the same position in the sky at exactly the same moment.

The Wingco stayed behind while I wrote out my report and, after a fruitless search for my bicycle, which had disappeared from where I'd left it, he drove me to the Mess for my long-overdue post-operational meal of bacon and egg.

After lunch I made my way to the billet. Having been 'unaccounted for' for more than three days, all my clothing and possessions had been removed, parcelled up, and posted off to my next of kin. Not so much as a collar stud remained in my chest of drawers. Even the sheets had gone from my bed. Johnny's half of the room was as normal. He'd got back before the three days were up.

I had a sleep before going back up to 'flights' to get a travel warrant from the adjutant. All my records had gone off to the Air Ministry in London, so I was off strength as far as the squadron was concerned. This didn't disturb me unduly, nor was I against having some time off, as I told the Wingco. So, still in battledress, but this time with a 1st Class travel warrant and RAF leave pass in my pocket, I left Little Staughton the following morning on survivor's leave. It was just before Christmas, and I was due to be married in less than two months, on 17 February 1945.

Survivor's leave was officially two weeks, but it was five weeks before I received orders to report to the Air Ministry at Adastral House in Kingsway, where I duly presented myself. A guide took me along the maze of corridors to the examination section for yet another aircrew medical.

I sailed through it – even my old problems with the mercury seemed to have been overcome – and at sixty seconds I could have held it for another sixty. At the end of it, I dressed and sat in the lounge drinking tea and reading *TEE EM*. After only a few minutes, I was shown into the SMO's office and took the proffered chair on the other side of the desk.

He offered me a cigarette, and we smoked and chatted for a while about ops in general and the last one in particular. "How do you feel about going back on ops with the squadron?" he enquired, more or less as an afterthought, as he opened my file. "Well...," I started to answer, to be interrupted, "Because you're unfit for aircrew duties at present. I'm sending you on sick leave for a few weeks then we'll see you back here again."

Two hours later I was sitting in a packed 1st Class railway compartment between a Wren Officer and an Army Colonel, pondering my new status. 'Unfit aircrew duties'. I hadn't been told why – just that I was, for the present at least. But with the wedding only a little more than two weeks away, I was happy to accept what the doctor ordered.

So Drus and I were married on 17 February 1945 – she was 18, I was 21. As convention dictated, we left the reception in New Brighton for our honeymoon, just as the party was warming up with the barrel of beer still half full, arriving

late at night at the boarding house at Pensarn where I'd
spent the annual summer holidays. Nervous and with
juvenile shyness, we sat down for supper with the landlady
and a boisterous Army Major, billeted in her house,
blushing at his obvious enjoyment at our embarrassment.
We were even more embarrassed when he called up the
stairs to us on the following morning, "Come on Smithy,
time's up." Two days later, orders arrived from the Air
Ministry to report to Adastral House for another medical, so
I cabled back "On honeymoon – request seven days
extension." A reply came back within hours: "Extension
granted – report Adastral House on 1 March."

Two days later we were back in Wallasey to hear the
dreadful news that Scottie, who had put back his leave to
attend the wedding but hadn't arrived for it, had been killed
when his night reconnaissance Wellington had crashed in
Holland. First Jim, then Paddy and now Scottie – my three
closest friends – all dead. And me, off ops, and now with a
lovely wife, on leave and with the war in Europe coming to
an end, the immediate future lay pleasurably ahead. It
didn't seem right, but then, there but for the grace of God…

At Adastral House on 1 March, the same Wingco MO
greeted me at the end of the medical. "Enjoy your
extension?" he said with a smile. Sheepishly, I confirmed
that I had, very much. "How do you feel now?"

"Pretty good, Sir," I replied.

He closed my file and leaned on his desk. "You failed the
medical again, and it is the decision of the Board that you are
to be remustered for ground duties. How do you feel about
that?"

"Is that a final decision?" I asked, not really knowing
what I thought about it, not being unduly worried at the
prospect of an op-free existence, but reluctant to relinquish
my operational status.

"I'm afraid so," he said. "After all, you've done ninety.
That's enough for anyone, don't you think?"

I didn't feel inclined to argue, and, after he'd wished me

good luck, I was soon walking along Kingsway hearing his words over and over, and beginning to relish the thought of being 'tour expired' for the second time.

They were delighted at my news when I got back to Wallasey for yet another spell of leave to await my next posting, and even more delighted to read in the *Liverpool Echo* several days later of my DFC awarded for "the young Wallasey officer's courage and resourcefulness under exceptional and trying circumstances", which sounded a bit over the top after reading it innumerable times. Hardly in keeping with my attempted show of modesty, I was in Liverpool early the next morning, buying the purple and white medal ribbon, and sporting it under my brevet in the Boot Inn shortly after opening time.

It was three more weeks before the official buff envelope came via the postman with a railway warrant for Nairn, up near Inverness in the highlands of Scotland. It was snowing when the train steamed out of Lime Street, and still snowing several hours later as it struggled on, with the barren Highlands rising awesomely on either side. Gradually losing momentum, it ground to a halt, with the blizzard still raging outside. Alone in the compartment, I opened the window, hastily closing it again in the face of the icy blast. Held tight in the grip of the snow drifts, it was more than two hours before the train, after a shuddering shock, moved slowly on its way, coupled to the snow plough engine that had rescued us. Two days later I was southbound again on the local train to Inverness, to find the town with torrents of water flowing through it from the melted snow. The two days had been spent with other 'tour expired' aircrew, being interviewed and assessed for ground duties. With two others, it had been decided that I should be trained to be a station adjutant, with an immediate posting to join the course commencing at RAF Credenhill, Hereford, in three days time. I arrived there the day before the course commenced, with a new peaked cap complete with interior wire, my operational cap – lovingly moulded into operational shapelessness – being deemed unsuitable for my future role as enforcer of King's Rules and Regulations.

The transition from operational aircrew to trainee administrator was from one extreme to the other. Day after day we sat in the lecture room, KRRs, one on every desk, notebook after notebook scribbled in, every note referenced to its paragraph and section in the military testament. Mock situations ranging from requests for compassionate leave to court martials were enacted daily, any jesting or exuberance lost on the lecturers, discouraged, and after the first week, non-existent. Bored, disinterested and frustrated, I occasionally fell asleep during lectures.

CHAPTER 23

Another Crash

I woke up lying in bed in a strange room, the door closed, the sun struggling to break through the curtained windows. A white-coated figure hovered over me. I tried to speak, to ask where I was, but couldn't find the words.

"Ah, you're awake," he said, and as I frowned enquiringly, he continued, "You're in the RAF Officers' Hospital at Cleveleys. You've been here since yesterday." He seemed to melt away as I felt the prick of the needle in my arm.

I spent nearly two weeks in the bedroom, in a world of sleeping and drowsy waking, hypodermic syringes, pentathol and 'Quiet please' notices hung on door handles outside in the corridor, at the end of which I was allowed by the neurologist – an Australian Squadron Leader – to join the other recovering patients downstairs in the hotel lounges. They were mostly Bomber Command aircrew for whom, like me, it had all been – as he put it – "just a bit too much".

Over the course of many listless, blurry days, I learned that I had suffered a stroke. A stroke at the age of 22. But I was also suffering from what would later be called 'shell-shock'. I was given very early doses of electric shock treatment. Drugged and drowsy, I would be wheeled into a room, fitted with electrodes, then torn by flashes of pain that seemed to cut deep into my body.

The war in Europe came to an end while I was still a patient at the Hydro. Winston Churchill gave us the news of Germany's unconditional surrender, and the next day was declared a national holiday. The publicans, anticipating the event, had conserved their supplies, and were allowed to stay open from ten in the morning until midnight. Those of us who were able to, spent the day in the pubs of Cleveleys, with the carnival atmosphere spilling out into the main street. Everybody was laughing, singing, dancing and joining the conga processions in and out of the pubs, with everyone in uniform hugged and kissed – our faces smeared with lipstick. It was the first time I'd been drunk in more than three months.

A few days later the demobilisation plans were published. The war continued in the Far East, but those of us in Europe who had been in the services prior to 1942 were to be progressively demobbed over several months under a points system. For most of us in the hospital, the points were of academic interest. Unfit for aircrew duties, and untrained for anything else, we were medically discharged and sent on demob leave, at the end of which we relinquished our commissions.

Four years to the day – from the splendour of Lord's Cricket Ground to the luxury of the Cleveleys Hydro – I became, once again, a civilian.

I Find the Crashed Mosquito

For many years after the war I was more interested in recovering my health than in reliving the battle. Post-war Britain wanted to look forward, not back, and that was my attitude also. I wrote every couple of years to the Munnix family who had taken me in at Gemenich. Over time, as my two sons, Stephen and Ian, grew up, they became interested in the history of the Second World War, and in my war service. But at the start of their questioning I was reluctant to answer. The war had, at one and the same time, been both the most intense and uplifting period of my life, and the most terrifying and depressing.

But as the events became more distant, I was able to talk more and more about them. Eventually, I began to cherish the memories. But these memories were often about dead friends. As I thought more about it, so I felt I needed to make some gesture to the friends I had lost. My three best friends in the RAF had all been killed. I went to Roermond to see the grave of Scottie Laurie, who died in a Wellington on a special low reconnaissance flight. I went to Lorient to see the grave of Paddy Veal, who died in a Wellington bombing the U-boat yards. I went to Kiel to see the grave of Jim Eckton, who died in a Wellington bombing the Kiel Canal.

In response to my sons' urgings, I wrote the manuscript that eventually became this book.

After I finished the manuscript, I began to wonder about the aeroplane that I had crashed in, and about the stumbled journey to rescue that I made through the Belgian countryside. And so, in early 1995, I wrote to the Mayors of Aachen, Vaals and Gemenich and asked if they had any records of a crashed Mosquito from the night of 4 December 1944. They had not.

However, in August 1995 I received a letter from an

471

archival organisation, Heemkuunderkring Sankt Tolbert, in Vaals. They had been passed my letter by the Mayor of Vaals, and they had also searched the records and found nothing. So they made enquiries in the area. Eventually they met an old forester who remembered going to a crashed aeroplane in December 1944. He had scrambled to the site of the crash and had tried to douse the flames, but made no impact. He knew that if the aircrew were inside, they must be dead.

The site, he recalled, was about 750 yards south of the Drielandenpunt, the place where the borders of Germany, Holland and Belgium meet.

They found the site and dug. As they recovered pieces of the aircraft, they realised that this was not the Mosquito, but a Flying Fortress. The remains of the American crew were still in the aircraft, and they reported its whereabouts to the authorities so that it could be recorded.

But they resumed their search for the Mosquito, and discovered reports of an unrecorded crash site a few kilometres south of Vaalsberquartur, a German village between Aachen and Vaals. They started knocking on doors in the region asking the old people if they remembered any planes crashing in the area.

Eventually an 83-year-old man said, "It was early December. It was very, very dark outside. From my kitchen window, I suddenly saw a burning object falling from the sky. It hit the ground with a great crash."

He said it must have crashed at the forest border. He also remembered a jeep driving off in the direction of the crash, no doubt containing two of the inhabitants of Vaals who had been recruited by the Americans to guard the border. Another inhabitant, Mme Wolken, said that her brother, who was staying with her in December 1944, had heard a crash nearby. The next morning he had gone to the scene and had found two badly burnt engines, some tangled pieces of metal, and some pieces of charred wood.

Another person, Mme Kankenberg, vividly remembered a crash one evening in December 1944. "You know," she said, "in those days I had just started courting my husband. He lived about five minutes from my home. Since the Americans had arrived some weeks before, we were not allowed out between seven in the evening and seven in the morning. My future husband and I always stayed together until the very last moment of the curfew. I arrived home at exactly seven in the evening, and just as I came through the door, I heard an enormous crash. I looked behind me and could see a blaze at the edge of the forest."

Mme. Kankenberg took Dolf Baltus and Peter Sparla, the Secretary and the Director of the Heemkuunderkring Sankt Tolbert, to the crash site on the next day. On the way she pointed to the place where she had found, the day after the crash, a tailplane. But they could not find the main site.

However, they persisted. They tracked down a M Zimmerman of Aachen who knew of a crash site on the edge of the forest. He had found it in December 1944, had returned there in 1974, and had taken some pieces of the aircraft. M Zimmerman had an aerial photograph of the area, and he offered to take Dolf and Peter to the site. An acknowledged expert in wartime crashes, he added that he knew the aircraft was a Mosquito because he had found tell-tale brass wood-screws amongst the wreckage.

So Dolf and Peter began to dig. They were joined by Dolf's grandson, Glenn. They got a metal detector, and soon began to dig up pieces of metal and Perspex. They found a very rusted Very pistol.

They took these pieces to M Ploes, another acknowledged expert on crashed Second World War aeroplanes. He confirmed that the brass wood-screws were from a Mosquito.

By now Dolf and Peter were sure that they had found the site. They wrote to me enclosing an aerial photograph of the site, and a map of the area.

I arranged to visit Dolf and Peter and see the crash site. My two sons would, of course, come with me. One of my sons' colleagues, Mark Fuller, came too. He was American, and I was pleased to have an American on the trip, grateful as I was for the help and kindness and generosity they had shown me in 1944.

We met Peter and Dolf at Vaals, and had breakfast at a restaurant at Drielandenpunt. Dolf and Peter had arranged for the proprietor to give us this free of charge. Also the press was there, and they took pictures.

We walked to the crash site. It was a very touching moment for me, to stand at the site of the destroyed 'O Oboe'. Around me were my sons and these kind young people who had given up their time to find my aeroplane. And Dolf's grandson made me feel that yet another generation would not forget what had happened in the war. I felt immense gratitude to these people for completing an important connection in my life.

We scrambled up the steep side of the gully, and crossed a small tarmacadam road and went into the adjoining field. I took my bearings and sat at the spot where I must have sat on that terrible evening. I lit up a cigarette, just as I had fifty-one years ago. I looked over my shoulder to the dirt road where I heard the jeep and the German-sounding voices on 4 December 1944.

Dolf and Peter wrote a full description of their researches. The postscript to the letter that Dolf and Peter wrote to me read: "Our report ends here, but there is something we want you to know. Our inquiry has caused a lot of anxiety, and it was a lot of work. But we did it with great pleasure. You owe us nothing at all, we are very grateful to you, because you are one of the many who fought for the freedom that we still enjoy now."

It is now July 1998. Perhaps because of the emotions that the return to Gemenich triggered, I had a bad stroke a few weeks after my return to England, and I am now very frail, but still alive. Ironically, it was about the same period of time after my crash in 1944 that the strain of war caused me to have a stroke aged 22.

I have been lucky.

Epilogue

Following his stroke my father became weaker and increasingly disorientated. Just after New Year, in January 2000, my brother and I were with him. We went for a short walk in Cambridge, where my brother lives. Dad had to rest every hundred yards or so. At one point we sat on a garden wall. Dad talked about the friends he had lost in the war, and about the soft but persistent guilt he felt at surviving them.

"I've had a good life – especially through you boys. But I feel I am getting close to the time when I will join my wartime friends."

Two weeks later he did.

Index

Stackpole Military History Series

Real battles. Real soldiers. Real stories.

Stackpole Military History Series

Real battles. Real soldiers. Real stories.

Stackpole Military History Series